LLOYD'S

STEAMBOAT DIRECTORY,

AND

DISASTERS ON THE WESTERN WATERS,

CONTAINING THE HISTORY OF THE

FIRST APPLICATION OF STEAM,

AS A MOTIVE POWER;

THE LIVES OF

JOHN FITCH AND ROBERT FULTON,

LIKENESSES & ENGRAVINGS OF THEIR FIRST STEAMBOATS.

EARLY SCENES ON THE WESTERN WATERS, FROM 1798 TO 1812---HISTORY OF THE EARLY STEAMBOAT NAVIGATION ON WESTERN WATERS--ENGRAVINGS OF THE BOATS.

FULL ACCOUNTS OF ALL THE STEAMBOAT DISASTERS SINCE THE FIRST APPLICATION OF STEAM DOWN TO THE PRESENT DATE, WITH LISTS OF THE KILLED AND WOUNDED—A COMPLETE LIST OF STEAMBOATS AND ALL OTHER VESSELS NOW AFLOAT ON THE WESTERN RIVERS AND LAKES—WHEN AND WHERE BUILT, AND THEIR TONNAGE:

Maps of the Ohio and Mississippi Rivers,

Towns, Cities, Landings, Population and Distances correctly laid down on the Ohio, Mississippi, Missouri, Tennessee, Cumberland, Kentucky, Green, Illinois, Arkansas, White, Red and Yazoo Rivers.

LIST OF

PLANTATIONS ON THE MISSISSIPPI RIVER;

Daguerrean Views and Sketches of

Pittsburgh, Wheeling, Cincinnati, Louisville, Falls of Ohio, Nashville, Cairo, Falls of St. Anthony, Gates of the Rocky Mountains, St. Louis, New Orleans, and Mobile—Sketches of the Ohio and Mississippi Rivers, and their Tributaries, Sources, Length, Area of country drained, &c. Names of all the U. S. Licensed Pilots and Engineers—Fast Time of Boats,

THE EARTHQUAKE IN 1812, &c., &c.

ONE HUNDRED FINE ENGRAVINGS, AND FORTY-SIX MAPS,

Being a Valuable Statistical Work, as well as a Guide-Book for the Travelling Public.

BY JAMES T. LLOYD.

CINCINNATI, OHIO:
JAMES T. LLOYD & CO.
1856.

Stereotyped and Printed by JESPER HARDING,
NO. 57 SOUTH THIRD ST., PHILADELPHIA.

PREFACE.

With all that profusion of literature for which the present age is remarkable, an opportunity sometimes offers to supply the public with a book which everybody acknowledges to be a desideratum. We hope it is not presumptuous on our part to believe that the present work is one of that class which the American public cannot easily dispense with, inasmuch as it presents a record of facts and events which form an interesting and important part of our country's history. In this volume, if we do not greatly deceive ourselves, the reader will find a more complete account of the beginning and progress of steam navigation in the United States, and in the Western States especially, than has ever been comprised in any previous publication. As incidental to the history of steam navigation in the West, we have introduced a copious detail of those awful and distressing accidents which have been of too frequent occurrence in that region. Our object in the presentation of these narratives is not to gratify a morbid taste for the horrific, but to suggest, in a practical way, the means of abating an evil which is acknowledged to be of immense magnitude. Whoever reads and compares the facts related in our registry of Steamboat Disasters will be able to trace those sad effects to their true cause, viz: to that gross and criminal mismanagement of steam power which has made the navigation of the Western waters so eminently perilous and destructive to human life. We have used the most diligent research, and spared no labor or expense in order to make this record of casualties complete and authentic in every particular; and we believe we have so far succeeded, that no accident of sufficient importance to deserve notice in such a publication as this, has been overlooked.

We have, likewise, embodied in this work a vast amount of valuable information respecting the history, growth, prosperity, commerce and manufactures of the Western Cities. We have furnished a comprehensive and reliable statement of the present condition of steam navigation in the great West, including ample statistical tables of Boats, Engineers, &c. In short, we have more than redeemed the promises made in our prospectus, by supplying the American public with a book which we hope will deserve a place in every public and private library. It is scarcely necessary to say anything respecting the mechanical execution and artistical embellishments of this work, as their beauty and excellence will be discoverable at a glance. We conclude these prefatory remarks, therefore, with

A WORD TO SUBSCRIBERS.

With respect to the *price* of this book, we owe some explanation to the public. It was our original purpose to charge but one dollar for the volume, but as its size has been considerably increased, and much material, and many extra engravings have been added, we have been compelled, by additional expenses, to augment the charge to *two dollars.* We hope, however, that this alteration in the price will not cause any dissatisfaction among our readers, when the laborious research and heavy expenditures which the publishers of this book have incurred, shall be duly considered. We learn with much surprise and regret, that several persons, representing themselves as our authorized agents, have been collecting money, ostensibly, on our account, in the Western States. We wish to have it distinctly understood, that no person or persons whatever have had any authority from us to make such collections, and that we cannot be responsible in any way, for the acts of the villainous imposters who have thus made an unauthorized use of our name.

J. T. LLOYD.

Cincinnati, January 1, 1856.

INDEX.

ILLUSTRATIONS.

INTRODUCTION.

STEAM.

ITS FIRST ADOPTION AS A MOTIVE POWER—GRADUAL IMPROVEMENT IN THE MODES OF APPLYING IT—AND ITS ADAPTATION TO THE PURPOSES OF NAVIGATION.

In connection with the special objects of this work, we have thought it expedient to give some historical account of that great Motor, which, more than any other human contrivance, except the art of printing, has been instrumental in improving the social, moral, and physical condition of our species. The first thing to be observed under this head, is the great uncertainty, the profound and almost impenetrable mystery, in which the origin of the steam-engine is involved. No age, no country, and no individual is permitted to enjoy the exclusive and undisputed honor which is due to the discovery. Some writers—with a good deal of fanciful license—have referred the first employment of this motive power to an early date in Egyptian history, simply because they were unable to conceive how the pyramids could have been constructed without such machinery, or some apparatus of equal force. However absurd may be this claim made in behalf of the ancient Egyptians, the modern Spaniards have set up pretensions almost equally ridiculous. It is pretended by the compatriots of Don Quixote, on the authority of certain documents, real or imaginary, preserved in the royal archives at Samancus, that a Spanish sea-captain, named Blasco de Garay, exhibited to the Emperor and King Charles V., in the year 1543, an engine, intended to propel ships and other vessels of the largest size, even in a perfect calm, without the assistance of sails or oars. The description given of this machine is amusingly accurate, being, in fact, a mere pen and ink sketch of a modern steam-engine. These particulars are given in a recently published Spanish book, purporting to be a collection of original papers relating to the voyage of Columbus.

The narrative proceeds to state that Captain De Garay brought his steam-engine to an experimental test, by applying it to the propulsion of a vessel of 209 tons, in the harbor of Barcelona. The experiment was tried in the presence of the Emperor and his son, Philip the Second; and among other distinguished spectators were Henry de Toledo, the governor; Peter Cardona, the treasurer; and Ravago, the Vice Chancellor. It is added that the experiment was entirely satisfactory to the Emperor, the Prince, and to all the high officers of state who witnessed it, and that the machine would have been brought into immediate requisition, had not some envious men of science denounced the engine as an expensive contrivance, not forgetting to hint at the probability of explosion. By these representations the opponents of Captain De Garay's project succeeded in frightening the royal family, and the consequence was that the world was deprived of the benefit of the steam-engine for several hundred years, and Spain lost the credit due to the discovery. The Emperor, however, to mollify the bitterness of De Garay's disappointment, gave him a bonus of 200,000 maravedies, and ordered all the expenses of the experiment to be paid out of the public treasury.

There is little reason to doubt that this story is purely fictitious, as the record is not regularly authenticated, and there is an obvious improbability in the circumstance that Spain should have permitted her claim to the invention of the steam-engine to lie dormant for more than three centuries.

Some faint conceptions of the utility of steam as a motive power, seems to have been entertained by ingenious and reflective men living at different periods, long before the invention was brought to any practical result. Bulwer, in his novel called "The Last of the Barons," illustrates this supposition by introducing an imaginary inventor, called Adam Warner, the type of a large class of men, "wise beyond their age," who at every period of the world's history have suffered for their temerity in attempting to bring their cotemporaries up to their own intellectual level. The first persons mentioned in veritable history, who attempted to use steam-power, seem to have satisfied themselves with making it subservient only to purposes of amusement. We have seen a pictorial representation of "the first steam-engine," in the form of a human head, the boiler being placed inside, while the steam, escaping from an aperture at the mouth, gave motion to a wheel resembling in construction the fans of a wind-mill.

There was another steam toy which, notwithstanding the priority claimed for the one just spoken of, appears to have been of a still more ancient date. This was the Æolipile, or ball of Æolus, which is described as a metallic globe, having a long neck terminating in a minute orifice. This globe being filled with water, and subjected to the action of fire, generated steam, which was seen rushing with great force through the aperture. Although the power of steam was thus exemplified, it does not appear that the ancients ever applied it to any useful purpose; indeed it was impossible for them to do so, by means of any contrivance similar to that just described; for, in order to make the force of steam available, it is necessary to preserve it from contact with the atmosphere, or any thing colder than itself, because if its temperature is lowered by such contact, it is immediately reduced to an inert mist or vapor.

One of the first writers who mentions the vast powers of steam, and suggests the possibility of making these powers useful to mankind, is the French Engineer, Solomon de Caus, who flourished about the beginning of the seventeenth century. In the year 1623, De Caus published at Paris a folio volume on Moving Forces, in which he mentions the experiment of heating water in a metallic sphere, in order to produce steam, adding that if the aperture be closed, the ball will burst with a detonation like that of a cannon. He also describes a method of raising water in a perpendicular tube by the application of heat, the agent being the steam from that portion of the water to which the heat is applied.

The next pioneer to the march of improvement in steam apparatus, was the Marquis of Worcester, author of a celebrated book called "The Century of Inventions." The Marquis was not merely a speculative inventor, but in many cases reduced his theories to practice. He appears to have made a variety of experiments with steam, and succeeded so well in some of them that he has occasionally been called the inventor of the steam-engine. The "method of raising water," which was simply proposed by De Caus, was practically illustrated by Worcester. We do not find, however, that he made any further progress in the application of steam-power than by using it to raise water in a column, on precisely the same principle which had been suggested by De Caus forty years before. If the machinery used in this operation was a "steam-engine," De Caus, and not Worcester, was the *bona fide* inventor. The Marquis, however, gives a more precise and intelligible account of the process than his French predecessor. He conducted his experiments, as he tells us, by using a cannon for his boiler; and according to his own statement, he succeeded in projecting water to a height of forty feet, merely by the force of expansion or the generation of steam in the lower part of the column. This noble gentleman has been suspected of adding a little romance to the reality of his inventions; but he was unquestionably a person of great enterprise and ingenuity. An account of his experiments with steam is given in the sixty-eighth proposition, in connection with the ninety-ninth and one hundredth of the "Century," and is entitled "An Admirable and Most Forcible Way to Drive up Water by Fire."

About twenty years later, (A. D. 1683,) Sir Samuel Morland prepared a manuscript work, (the original copy of which is still preserved in the British museum,) in which the author describes a method of employing steam as a mechanic power, seeming to claim for himself the credit of the invention. Morland's plan is merely a modification of the contrivances of De Caus and the Marquis of Worcester; and there is reason to suppose that he subsequently became ashamed of his "invention," (probably on account of the ridicule which it excited,) for when his book was afterwards published at Paris, the account of the steam-engine was suppressed. The only particular in which Morland may be allowed to claim originality in this matter, is a calculation, which approximates to the truth, respecting the vast difference in the space which water occupies in its natural state and that which it fills when expanded by heat, so as to assume the form of steam. As numerically designated by Morland, this difference is proportioned as one to two thousand. Recent experiments prove that one cubic foot of water will produce about seventeen hundred cubic feet of steam; so that the unassisted observations of Morland are measurably correct.

We will next speak of the discoveries and improvements of Monsieur Denis Papin, an ingenious Frenchman, who, during a temporary residence in England, near the end of the seventeenth century, devoted a great part of his time to pneumatic experiments. This gentleman, and several other experimenters who followed in his track, did not propose to make steam the prime agent in the production of a moving power. The force which they designed to use was that of atmospheric pressure, steam being called into requisition merely as an auxiliary power, or to produce what the scientific men of that day were pleased to call a *vacuum.* Long before this time it had been proposed to employ the pressure of the atmosphere as a counter-balance; and several simple machines, on this principle, had already been constructed. The principle, in fact, was that of the common sucking-pump, the object being to exhaust the air in a tube, beneath a block or piston exactly fitted to the cavity. The pump principle was modified by attaching the piston-rod to one end of a cross-beam, from the other extremity of which the weight to be raised was suspended. Various plans had been devised for exhausting the air in the lower part of the tube or cylinder. Otto Guericke used the air-pump for this purpose; but it occurred to Mons. Papin that the object might be attained with less labor and more expedition. In order to produce the desired "vacuum," his first idea was to explode a small quantity of gunpowder in the bottom of the cylinder, which, as he supposed, would expel the air through a valve opening upwards through the piston, while the immediate falling back of the valve would prevent the readmission of the air. It was found on trial, that a "complete vacuum" could not be effected by this method, and Mons. Papin, after revolving various expedients in his mind, concluded at last to employ steam as the exhausting agent.

The reader will observe, that in all previous attempts to use the power of steam, the sole object had been to raise water to a higher level; and that purpose was effected merely by applying the steam *directly* to the surface of the water to be raised. Papin was the first to make the force of steam more generally available, by preparing for it a separate chamber, as it were, in the hollow of the cylinder;—this he did by the introduction of the piston, and here was a long stride towards the perfecting of the steam-engine. In sober truth, Mons. Papin was the first who really made a machine which deserved that name; although, as we have previously observed, he was aiming at a different object, viz: the construction of an engine to be worked by atmospheric pressure. He is entitled to the credit due to the first application of two principles, which all his predecessors in their work of discovery had entirely overlooked. 1. Mons. Papin demonstrated the practicability of applying the moving force of steam, by means of the intermediate agency of the piston and its rod, to bodies on which it cannot act directly. 2. He recognized, as a constituent of the motive power, not the expansiveness of steam only, but its *condensibility;* without which its expansive quality would be of little service. It was the misfortune of Mons. Papin to overlook the fact, that the motive power he sought would be more readily obtained by making steam the principal agent, instead of a subordinate. To this same inventor we are indebted for another important attachment to the steam-engine, namely: the safety-valve, which was employed by him in the apparatus called "Papin's Digester," which is still used to produce a powerful heat in cooking and chemical preparations.

It had been remarked by De Caus and others, as an incidental fact, that water, when converted to steam, may be restored to its original state by the mere application of cold;—but Papin was the first who endeavored to make this circumstance useful in the operation of the machine. His method of condensation, however, was extremely awkward and dilatory; so much so, at first, that the best expedient he could devise was to remove the fire, and then permit the enclosed vapor to cool of its own accord.

Captain Savery is the next person on the record, who is supposed to have contributed to the progress of this invention. Several anecdotes are told of this gentleman, which seem to signify that his attention was accidentally directed to the subject which afterwards occupied so much of his thoughts. It is reported that he was one day refreshing himself with a bottle of wine at a tavern, and having thrown the flask into the fire, he observed that the small quantity of liquor which had been left in the vessel, became so expanded by the heat, as to fill the bottle completely. Captain Savery then took up the bottle and plunged it, mouth downwards, into a basin of cold water, which stood near him, and admiringly beheld the water rising into the receiver, in which the condensation of the steam had produced a partial vacuum. This trivial incident, it is said, first suggested to Savery the possibility of applying steam, or any other expansive and volatile fluid, to the most important uses. But it does not appear that he prosecuted his discovery far beyond that point which had already been reached by others. His greatest achievement was the adaptation of steam power to the production of a vacuum in a simple machine, which merely answered the purpose of a sucking-pump of considerable power, which was found to be of practical utility in the process of raising water from wells or mines. He did not avail himself of Papin's improvements, but reverted to the old method of applying the steam directly to the surface of the water, which had been employed by the Marquis of Worcester many years before. Captain Savery, however, possessed so much ingenuity and mechanical skill, that he was enabled to contrive many facilities and improvements in the machinery constructed on these principles; and his engines came to be in great request for supplying dwelling houses with water, and for other purposes.

After the death of Captain Savery, (A. D. 1718,) his contrivance was much improved and simplified by Dr. Desaguliers. This last-named gentleman introduced an improved method of condensing the vapor in the receiver, by injecting a small current of cold water, whereas it had been the practice of Savery to effect this object by dashing water over the outside, which occasioned a great loss of time and waste of fuel.

It has previously been remarked, that Monsieur Papin was the original contriver of the safety-valve for a special purpose, but Dr.

Desaguliers first made it a customary attachment of the steam-engine. The safety-valve is a lid or stopper which covers an aperture in the boiler, and is retained in its place by a weight sufficient to resist the expansive power of the steam up to a certain point, while it must yield before the accumulated force of the confined vapor could terminate in an explosion.

Two humble mechanics of Dartmouth, Devonshire, England, John Newcomen, a whitesmith, and John Calley a glazier, are the next to take up this chain of invention. Newcomen, with the assistance of his friend and colleague, completed the working model of an atmospheric engine in 1711. The main principle adopted by them was that of Monsieur Papin—making the weight of the atmosphere the moving power, and using steam merely to exhaust the receiver. They also used Savery's method of condensation, by pouring cold water over the external surface of the cylinder; but this method they soon abandoned for the more economical and convenient plan of Desaguliers, which, with a little modification, is still in use. Newcomen and Calley, being persons of little erudition, are said to have been totally unacquainted with the experiments of De Caus, Worcester, Papin, &c., but arrived at the same conclusions by the force of their own unassisted ingenuity. They were indebted to an accident for the discovery of the improved mode of condensing the steam by the injection of cold water into the cylinder. Newcomen's engine possessed several decided advantages over that of Savery. The latter was practically useful only so far as it could be made to do the service of a sucking-pump, and it ceased to be serviceable in raising water, when the column raised became equal in weight to a column of the atmosphere of equal base. It was almost unavailable, therefore, for the purpose of pumping water from mines—the use for which such engines were chiefly in demand at that time. The superiority of Newcomen's engine in this particular was most remarkable. Many mines which had been inundated for years were, by the help of this invention, cleared of water, and preserved in that condition until the excavations were carried to unprecedented depths. For many other important purposes, this new apparatus was found to be eminently serviceable. But how obviously defective was the construction of this engine! How unsatisfactory were its operations, when we place it in the scale of comparison with the perfect machine of our own day! As, in the process used, the cylinder was completely cooled after every stroke of the piston, the waste of fuel was so great, that Newcomen's engine could not be economically employed in circumstances which permitted the use of animal power; and besides this, its operation was slow, distressingly slow. Moreover, as the machine derived all its energy from the weight of the atmosphere, its force was necessarily limited to fifteen pounds on each square inch of the superior surface of the piston, making no allowance for friction, or the imperfection of the vacuum beneath; circumstances which must make a very considerable reduction in our estimate of its power.

It should be borne in mind, that the expansive force of steam was not used in this engine, and that all the uses which steam performed in the movements of the apparatus could have been executed by an air-pump, or any other agency capable of expelling or withdrawing the atmospheric fluid from beneath the piston. Up to this time, therefore, it may appear that the plan of a genuine steam-engine, *i. e.*, one in which steam power was indispensable, had never presented itself to any human being. And for more than fifty years afterwards no progress was made in the adaptation of steam to the purpose of giving motion to machinery. It is true that various minor improvements were made on Newcomen's apparatus, but the main principle continued the same—the power of steam being made subordinate to the weight of the atmosphere. Mr. Brighton, in 1718, so far improved on Newcomen's plan as to make the machinery itself open and shut the cocks which supplied the apparatus with steam and water, instead of having those services performed by an attendant.

The cause of steam was in this condition, when (A. D. 1736) the attention of James Watt, a native of Greenock, Scotland, was attracted to the subject. Mr. Watt was born of parents whose condition in life was respectable, though not opulent. The condition of his bodily health was so feeble as to prevent him from pursuing his early studies with regularity at the public seminaries, but such was his thirst for knowledge, that no obstacle could prevent him from obtaining such education as accorded with the direction of his genius. Even in his childhood his favorite study was mechanical science, and to this study he applied himself, at home, with the utmost assiduity. At a very early age his attention was attracted to the employment of steam as an operative power in machinery; his first thought, in connection with this subject, being turned towards the propulsion of land carriages by steam power.

In the winter of 1763 a small model of Newcomen's engine came into his possession; and by studying the operations of this machine, he first conceived the fortunate idea that the steam might be made to perform a more important duty than Newcomen and his predecessors had ever thought of. The defects of Newcomen's engine were manifestly presented to his observing genius. The disproportionate size of the boiler, and other errors in the construction of the model, were corrected by Watt, who also substituted a cylinder of cast iron for that of brass, which had been used by Newcomen; for he observed that the brazen cylinder abstracted more of the heat from the steam, and so lessened its expansion, occasioning thereby a proportionable loss of power. But his thoughts were soon turned aside from the correction of Newcomen's minor mistakes, to the rectification of the primary error which had made all the engines constructed on the atmospheric principle comparatively inefficient. In short, Mr. Watt recognized the great advantage which might be gained by advancing steam from its subservient position to that of a principal agent. This idea he followed up with the most indefatigable application, trying innumerable experiments for the purpose of ascertaining all the powers and properties of the agency which he proposed to use. The results of some of these experiments were of great consequence in his future researches. For example, he found that the rapidity with which water evaporates, depends simply on the quantity of heat which is made to enter it, and that this quantity of heat was proportioned to the extent of surface exposed to the fire. He also ascertained the amount of fuel required for the evaporation of any given quantity of water, the heat at which water boils under various pressures, and many other particulars which had never been taken into consideration by any previous observer.

Having thus made himself thoroughly acquainted with the agent, he was eminently prepared to control or direct its action to the best advantage. In the first place, he remarked that the inartificial methods adopted by his predecessors for cooling the cylinder, occasioned a waste of at least three-fourths of the fuel. If the cylinder could be kept permanently hot, this waste, and much loss of time, could be avoided. After mature reflection, during which many expedients were thought of and rejected, he began to consider the possibility of withdrawing the steam from the cylinder to be condensed in some other vessel. If this course should be practicable, the separate vessel alone, *i. e.*, the "condenser," would be cooled by the water used to cool the steam; and it appeared to him, as experiment afterwards proved, that the cooling of the condenser would quicken the process of condensation rather than retard it. The benefits of these alterations were soon made obvious to every perception. By keeping the cylinder constantly at the same temperature, one-fourth part of the fuel formerly used was found to be quite sufficient; and besides this important item, the saving of expense in the maintenance of the engine, much power was gained by the production of a more perfect vacuum in the cylinder, in which no water was now admitted to generate new steam, while it expelled the old. Watt's first expedient to cool the steam in the condenser was keeping that vessel enclosed in another of cold water; preferring this method to the admission of cold water into the condenser itself, as its accumulation there might occasion a difficulty in removing it as rapidly as was necessary. But with a view to the attainment of greater speed in the movement of the machinery, he found eventually that the best contrivance was to admit a sufficient quantity of water into the condenser, and remove it afterwards by a pump of suitable power.

Several other difficulties, some of which, at the first view, appeared quite formidable, were finally overcome by the perseverance and ingenuity of this distinguished inventor. His pecuniary resources were enlarged by a contract made with Dr. Roebuck, who advanced the funds required for prosecuting Mr. Watt's experiments, for the consideration of two-thirds of the profits, to be secured to him in case the new machine should come into successful operation. In these circumstances, Mr. Watt took out his first patent in 1769; but his colleague, Dr. Roebuck, having, as the phrase goes, "too many irons in the fire," soon became involved in pecuniary embarrassments, and was unable to fulfil his part of the contract by advancing the stipulated sums. Owing to this unfortunate state of affairs, Mr. Watt was compelled, for the term of five years, to engage in the business of a Civil Engineer; but, at length, (A. D. 1774,) having formed a business connection with an extensive hardware manufacturer at Birmingham, he was enabled once more to revert to his favorite pursuit. The first measure adopted by Mr. Watt and his partner was to erect an engine in their manufactory at Soho, which they submitted to public inspection; and soon after the firm of Boulton & Watt commenced the manufacture of steam-engines as a regular business.

Respecting the first application of steam to the propulsion of vessels, a variety of facts will be detailed in our sketches of the lives of John Fitch and Robert Fulton.

JOHN FITCH.

Before we begin our biographical sketch of this ingenious but very unfortunate man, it may not be out of place to give some account of the state of human knowledge in reference to steam navigation at the time when Fitch commenced his experiments. It was said, in the preceding article, that Mr. Watt's first intention in the employment of steam power, was the impelling of land carriages. From such a project a man's thoughts might, by a very easy transition, turn to the propulsion of vessels by the same agency. This application of steam was too obvious, we might suppose, to escape the attention of any man who had seen a steam-engine in operation. We dare say, therefore, that from the time the first engine was erected at Soho, it was very common for men of mechanical genius to imagine the probability that the new invention might become serviceable to navigation. In 1737, more than thirty years before Mr. Watt took out his first patent, a certain Jonathan Hulls, of London, claimed to be the inventor of "a machine for carrying vessels out of, or into, any harbor, port or river against wind and tide, or in a calm." A draught of this machine is still preserved, and we must aver that it looks surprisingly like an old fashioned steamboat, being furnished with chimneys, propelling wheels, and other customary appurtenances. We have no account of the mode in which Mr. Jonathan Hulls generated his moving forces, but it is evident, from the smoking chimney and other significant indications, that *fire* had something to do with the matter. Hulls obtained letters patent for this invention from George II., but it is presumed that want of funds, or some other fatal obstacle, prevented him from bringing his project to a practical result, as we have no further account either of Mr. Jonathan Hulls, or his marvellous invention. And although we find several allusions to the practicability of steam navigation, not forgetting the celebrated couplet of Dr. Darwin—

> "Soon shall thy arm, unconquered steam, afar
> Drive the swift barge or urge the rapid car"—

yet practical men were content to leave the whole subject in the dominion of poetry and romance, until an obscure native of Connecticut, with the homely name of John Fitch, undertook to realize what had hitherto been considered one of the most extravagant dreams of fancy.

JOHN FITCH.

Fitch, with a stroke of melancholy sarcasm, terms it the greatest misfortune of his life, "to have conceived the idea that a vessel might be carried through the water by the force of steam." Nevertheless, it appears from the manuscript records of his life, which he deposited in the Philadelphia Museum, that he was familiar with the aspect of misfortune from his very birth. He was born near East Windsor, Connecticut, in the year 1743, on the 21st of January, old style. His father, who was a farmer in good circumstances, appears to have been a person of a sordid and morose temper; and the best report his son can make of him is, that he always provided a sufficiency of pork, beans, codfish and potatoes for the use of his family. We should have been better pleased with him if he had furnished his son John with the usual facilities for the acquirement of useful knowledge. He appeared to think it quite sufficient for every useful purpose if the lad learned to read the Bible, and to give correct answers to all the questions in the catechism.

With such a parent as is here described, what difficulties and discouragements must have been encountered by a mind hungering and thirsting after knowledge! But, even at that early day, John's resolute spirit of inquiry was invincible. He obtained an old copy of Hodder's Arithmetic, and in the hours of relaxation from the labours of the farm, succeeded, without assistance, in mastering all the difficulties of that elementary work. At this time he had not completed his eighth year. Some time after, when his father had repeatedly refused to supply him with a copy of Salmon's Geography, he contrived to earn the money required to buy one, by devoting the little time allowed him for recreation to the cultivation of a small potato-patch on a piece of unoccupied ground. By dint of such untiring exertion, young Fitch, in spite of all the disadvantages of his situation, contrived to obtain a moderate English education before he reached the years of maturity. In devising a mode of maintenance for his future life, he made an experimental sea voyage at the age of seventeen, but his tastes and habits did not much incline that way; and, soon after his return, he applied himself to learning the trade of clock making, having always had a predilection for machinery. The master artist who undertook to instruct Fitch in this branch of manufacture, kept him employed in domestic duties, such as rocking the cradle and attending to the cookery, by which occupations his knowledge of horology was not much advanced; and at the end of two years he left his instructor, very much dissatisfied with his acquirements. But there were other wooden clock makers in Connecticut, even at that early period, and John Fitch soon found one who did not connect the operations of the business with cooking and cradle rocking. On the contrary, this new employer resolved that his apprentice should learn clock making and nothing else, although a part of the business of the shop was the repairing of watches, with which process likewise John desired to become acquainted. Matters were so conducted that he was never permitted to see a watch taken to pieces or put together. But this churlish treatment was not the only inconvenience he was doomed to suffer; for, as he tells us in his manuscript narrative, although he possessed but a moderate appetite, he was never permitted to satisfy it except on one occasion, when, by nice management, he contrived to make "a good hearty meal on potatoes."

The reader will believe that John was not tempted to remain for an unreasonable length of time under the jurisdiction of this Connecticut clock-maker; in fact, he soon thought it most expedient to set up business for himself, and within the space of two years he managed to accumulate the sum of fifty pounds, "which to me, at that time, (says John,) appeared to be an inexhaustible treasure." It was soon exhausted, however, and his patience likewise, for having injudiciously married a young lady of acid disposition, named Miss Lucy Roberts, she "led him such a life," (to borrow the phraseology of John's manuscript,) that he was obliged to withdraw precipitately from his domestic altar, and take refuge in the village of Pittsfield, Massachusetts. Not meeting with any encouragement there, he removed to Albany, N. Y., and from thence again he wandered into New Jersey, where, becoming reduced in circumstances to a very low level, he performed the services of a day-laborer on a farm. His feeble bodily condition unfitted him for this duty, and he finally established himself at Trenton in the useful and respectable, though not very lucrative business of button-making.

When the Revolution commenced, Fitch, of course, ranged himself on the side of patriotism, and rendered most acceptable service to his country by repairing arms for the continental troops. While the war was in progress, duty carried him to the West, where he was taken prisoner by the Indians, and remained in captivity for several months, enduring many hardships, but finally managed to make his escape. At the end of the war he returned to New Jersey.

It was about this time, (April, 1785,) when his thoughts were first directed to the subject of steam conveyance; and he seems to have afterwards considered it highly presumptuous for a man as poor as himself to engage in such a stupendous project. "If I had not the most convincing proofs to the contrary, (says he,) I should certainly charge myself with being *non compos mentis* at the time." He likewise assures us in his manuscript autobiography, that when he first conceived the idea of employing steam power for propelling vessels, he did not know that such a thing as a steam-engine existed, although Mr. Watt had erected one in England ten years before. Fitch believed the idea to be original with himself, until his brother-in-law one day showed him a drawing and description of the machine invented by Watt. He was "amazingly chagrined," as he tells us, to find that his grand discovery had been anticipated; but he comforted himself with the reflection, that if steam could be made to turn a wheel on the land, there was nothing to prevent it from becoming equally useful on the water. In short, he was more than ever convinced that his plan of navigation by steam was altogether practicable.

It is shown by the most irrefragable testimony that John Fitch was the first man, in America at least, and probably in the world, who ever carried this idea of applying steam power to the propulsion of vessels to any determinate result. A certificate from Dr. Thornton of the Patent Office at Washington, states that Fitch took out a patent for the application of steam to navigation, in the year 1788, before which time no similar patent had been issued in this country. The earliest ascertained experiments of Mr. Fulton in steam navigation took place about the year 1798, ten years after the date of John Fitch's patent.

Oliver Evans in 1804 propelled a mud-scow by steam on the Schuylkill river. Mr. Fulton's first experimental boat was built at Paris, in 1803. His first American steamboat was launched in the spring of 1807. Fitch brought his plan to the test of experiment on the Delaware river a short time after he took out his patent. The following description is given of the machinery as contrived by Fitch:—"The cylinder is horizontal, the steam working with equal force at both ends. The piston moves about three feet, and each vibration of it gives the axis forty revolutions. Each revolution of the axis moves twelve oars or paddles five and a half feet; they work perpendicularly and are represented by the strokes of a paddle of a canoe. As six of the paddles are raised from the water, six more are entered, and the two sets of paddles make their strokes of about eleven feet in each revolution. The crank of the axis acts upon the paddles about one-third of their length from the lower ends, to which part of the oar the whole force of the axis is applied. The engine is placed in the bottom of the boat, about one-third from the stern, and both the action and reaction turn the wheel the same way."

FITCH'S PHILADELPHIA BOAT—1786.

This description was written by the inventor himself, and was first published in the Philadelphia Columbian Magazine, vol. 1, for December, 1786.

Fitch's boat was tried, as previously stated, on the Delaware river, in front of Philadelphia. The boat was ordered under way at slack water, and, by the most accurate measurement, was found to go at the rate of eight miles per hour, or one mile in six minutes and a half. It afterwards went eighty miles in a day.

The Governor and Council of Pennsylvania expressed their satisfaction with the result of this experiment by presenting to the proprietors of the boat a superb silk flag, emblazoned with the arms of the State. But, after all this magnificent demonstration, the most glorious achievement of American ingenuity was permitted to fall into utter neglect.

Dr. Thornton states that the company which had been formed under the Fitch patents to give the plan a proper trial—now, when the trial had been made, and when all reasonable doubts respecting the practicability and utility of the invention should have vanished—refused to advance any more money. It seems that those noble spirited gentlemen, who constituted the first steamboat company ever organized, disbanded themselves because they were afraid to meet the "unceasing ridicule" which this project had excited. Not even the practical realization of the plan could prevent fools from laughing at it as an insane speculation; nor could the sight of a veritable steamboat, paddling along the Delaware, enable wise men to treat this idiotic merriment with contempt. The company was dissolved, the boat was laid up in the docks, and the whole matter was abandoned, and John Fitch was fated to descend to the tomb without seeing the great object of his life accomplished, or the importance and value of his invention duly appreciated by his countrymen.

Justice to the memory of John Fitch forbids the omission of one particular incident of his life, which establishes, beyond all cavil, his claim to the invention of the steamboat. Before the dissolution of the company just referred to, Aaron Vail, Esq., one of the members who was then the American consul at L'Orient, sent over a request for Mr. Fitch to visit France, in order to have the steamboat experiment tried in that country. Fitch went over, accordingly, but on his arrival, owing to a scarcity of shipwrights, and other causes incident to the French revolution, the enterprise failed, and Fitch returned to his own country, leaving his draughts and documents relating to his invention in the hands of Mr. Vail. These papers were exhibited by Mr. Vail to Robert Fulton, when that gentleman visited France several years afterwards, and Mr. Fulton took copies, notes and memoranda which enabled him subsequently (he being more fortunate than John Fitch in finding assistance and resources) to complete the great work of which so considerable a part had already been executed by the ill-starred Fitch.

To the very end of his life John Fitch had unwavering confidence in his neglected and despised contrivance. He struggled manfully to bring it once more into the scope of public observation, but the public,

FAC-SIMILE OF THE WRITING OF JOHN FITCH,
From his manuscript Autobiography in the Franklin Library, Philadelphia.

I know of nothing so perplexing and Vexatious to a man of feelings, as a turbulant Wife and Steam Boat building, I experienced the former and quit in season, and had I been in my right sences I should undoubtedly treated the latter in the same manner, but for one man to be teised with Both, he must be looked upon as the most unfortunate man of this World, when it had kindness enough to refrain from mockery, merely made an exclamation of sorrow and pity, like that of Ophelia—

"Oh, what a noble mind is here o'erthrown!"

Once, when he had been explaining the benefits of steam navigation to a party of gentleman, who heard his glowing descriptions with significant smiles, one of his auditors remarked, after he had retired, "What a pity that the poor fellow is crazy!"

When the experimental boat had been finally laid up, as aforesaid, Fitch, in a letter to Mr. Rittenhouse, wrote, "It would be much easier to carry a first-rate man-of-war by steam than a boat, as we would not be cramped for room, nor would the weight of the machinery be felt. This, Sir, will be the mode of crossing the Atlantic in time, (there spoke a true prophet!) whether I bring it to perfection or not."

Fitch returned from Europe to his own country, destitute and heartbroken. For two years he was obliged to depend for his daily bread on the kindness of a relation, Colonel George King, of Sharon, Connecticut. But having purchased some cheap lands in Kentucky, while he was surveying there in 1796, he now went thither to take possession of this little property in the wilderness. But even this gratification was not allowed him, for having been thrown into a fever by fatigue and exposure, he died two or three days after his arrival. According to his request, John Fitch was buried on the shores of the Ohio, where, (to use his own enthusiastic language,) "the song of the boatmen would enliven the stillness of his resting-place, and the music of the steam-engine sooth his spirit." His manuscript journal contains the following prophetic exclamation:

"The day will come when some more powerful man will get fame and riches from my invention, but nobody will believe that poor John Fitch can do any thing worthy of attention!"

The fate of this man is a melancholy exemplification of the treatment which the world often accords to its best benefactors. Further comment is not required.

"We can no more,—by rage, by shame suppress'd,
Let tears and burning blushes speak the rest."

ROBERT FULTON.

WHILE we accord to John Fitch the credit which is justly due to him as the true and original contriver of the steamboat, with equal justice we will make the acknowledgment, that the subject of the present sketch, by his firmness of purpose and energy of character, no less than by his brilliant genius and correct judgment, carried the enterprise through to a successful and glorious termination. Robert Fulton was born in the town of Little Britain, Lancaster County, Pennsylvania, (A. D. 1765). His father, a native of Kilkenny, Ireland, was in very moderate circumstances, which may explain the fact that Robert's early education was somewhat neglected. His earliest tastes inclined him to observe the operations of different mechanics, in whose shops he passed most of his leisure hours. Having a natural talent for the use of the pencil, he began, at the age of twelve years, to cultivate this gift, and before he had reached his fifteenth year, he became, in the estimation of his rural neighbors, quite an expert artist. Two years later he practised portrait and landscape painting in Philadelphia. Here he soon acquired money enough to purchase a small farm in Washington County, where he provided his widowed mother with a comfortable home, while he made preparations for a voyage to England, according to the advice of some of his friends, for the purpose of exhibiting some of his paintings to his countryman, Benjamin West. Mr. West, at this time, enjoyed the favor and patronage of the British government, and his reputation as one of the first painters of the age was already established. He received young Fulton with much kindness, gave him all possible encouragement, and offered him a home in his own house, where he remained for two years. At the end of that time Mr. Fulton travelled through different parts of England, and became acquainted with several distinguished men of science.

It is supposed that, at this period of his life, he began to devote his attention exclusively to mechanical inventions. In his 25th year, (A. D. 1793,) he was actively engaged in a project to improve inland

ROBERT FULTON.

navigation, and one year later he obtained from the British government a patent for a double inclined plane, to be used for transportation. We have no particular account of his transactions during several years following, though in 1794 he submitted to the British Society for the promotion of Arts and Commerce, an improvement in his invention of mills for sawing marble. His patents for two machines, one for spinning flax, and the other for making ropes, are dated 1795. In the next year he published at London his treatise on the Improvement of Canal Navigation. In this work he expresses his preference for small canals, and boats of light burden, and contends for the use of inclined planes instead of locks. His plans were highly approved by the British Board of Agriculture.

Mr. Fulton was now engaged in the profession of a civil engineer, and employed the pencil merely to execute plans and draughts of machinery in connection with his professional duties. He now visited France, for the purpose of introducing his canal improvements into that country. In the year 1797, he became acquainted with the celebrated Joel Barlow, who then resided at Paris. In the family of this distinguished American gentleman, Mr. Fulton took up his abode for several years, during which time he studied the French, Italian and German languages, and perfected himself in the high mathematics, chemistry and natural philosophy.

In 1797 Messrs. Fulton and Barlow made experiments on the river Seine with a machine which the former had constructed on the torpedo principle, the object of which was to destroy an enemy's ships by submarine explosions. These experiments proved unsuccessful. But not at all discouraged by his first failure, Mr. Fulton pursued this object until his plan for propelling and steering a boat under water was brought to perfection. When this satisfactory result was attained, he applied to the French Directory for pecuniary assistance, but that body did not appreciate the invention. He then applied to the British government, but met with similar discouragement in that quarter. In the meantime, Buonaparte had placed himself at the head of public affairs in France, and he, not being one of the "old fogy" school, promptly responded to Mr. Fulton's application by appointing a commission to examine the new warlike machine. The examining committee having made a favorable report, Mr. Fulton was supplied by Napoleon with a sufficiency of funds to bring some of his plans to the test of experiment. He first made a trial of the "plunging boat" at Brest, in 1801. Notwithstanding many imperfections in the machinery, and other disadvantages incident to a first experiment, he demonstrated that, by means of this contrivance, a sufficiency of light and air could be obtained under water; that the boat could be made to descend to any depth, or rise to the surface with perfect facility, and that she would tack or veer as rapidly as any common sailing-boat. On the 7th of August, Mr. Fulton descended with a store of air compressed in a copper globe, and was thus enabled to remain under water nearly four hours and a half. He next attempted to put this invention to its proper use by blowing up English vessels cruising near the harbor of Brest; for this purpose he provided his plunging boat with a torpedo, or submarine bomb, and approaching a small British vessel within the distance of two hundred yards, he blew her to atoms. A similar attempt was made on an English seventy-four, which saved herself at the critical moment by an accidental change of position.

The advantages of submarine warfare were not fairly estimated in Europe, and Mr. Fulton, having become disgusted with the tardy action of several European governments in relation to this subject, returned to his own country, in 1806. He found the American government very propitious to his undertakings, and a grant of sufficient funds was made to enable him to put the capabilities of his torpedo to a fair trial. By means of one of these jewels of Bellona, he blew up, and totally annihilated, a large hulk brig, which had been prepared for the purpose in the harbor of New York. In 1810 Congress granted $5000 to meet the expenses of additional experiments with Fulton's explosive apparatus, and a committee was appointed to superintend these trials. The old sloop-of-war Argus, under the direction of Commodore Rogers, was prepared for defence against the torpedoes, and that skilful Commander did his best to make them ineffective. In these circumstances, Mr. Fulton did not succeed in his main design of blowing up the vessel, but he approached in his submarine boat near enough to cut off a fourteen inch cable attached to the Argus. He himself did not consider this experiment on the Argus a failure, attributing his want of success to various defects in the explosive machinery, for which it was easy to find remedies.

But the thoughts of Fulton now reverted to the subject of steam navigation, a subject on which he had bestowed considerable study during his residence in Paris. In this enterprise he possessed one grand advantage over all who had preceded him, being enabled to avail himself of the great improvements which Watt and others had made in steam machinery. But for certain adaptations of that machinery to the object required, he was obliged to depend on his own inventive powers, in the absence of all precedent to direct his course. The paddle-wheel now used in steamboats appears to have been originally devised by Mr. Fulton. It should have been mentioned, by the way, that Messrs. Fulton and Livingston made an actual experiment with steam propulsion in France, in 1803. This experiment, however, was on a very small scale, and the result being not quite satisfactory, and as other objects demanded Mr. Fulton's attention, this project was temporarily laid aside, nor was it resumed until some time after his return to this country.

Mr. Fulton took out his first patent for improvements in steam navigation on the 11th day of February, 1809, and on the 9th of February, 1811, he obtained supplementary patents for further improvements in his boats and machinery. The pecuniary means required for carrying out these great designs were supplied by Mr. Livingston, a gentleman of great wealth and equal liberality, who had assisted Mr. Fulton in his steamboat experiments at Paris, and never at any time withheld his aid when the enterprise required it. The legislature of New York having passed an Act which secured to Messrs. Fulton and Livingston the exclusive benefits of steam navigation on the waters of that State for the term of twenty years, the last-named gentleman caused a boat of about thirty tons to be built, but her dimensions being found insufficient, she was soon abandoned. In 1807 a steam-engine was ordered from the manufactory of Watt and Bolton, of Birmington, England; it was constructed according to the specifications furnished by Mr. Fulton, who did not permit the manufacturers to know for what purpose it was intended. A suitable boat for the reception of this engine had been built at the ship-yard of Charles Brown, on the East river. The engine was put on board, and the boat was soon after moved by her machinery to the Jersey shore. This experimental trip was witnessed by a number of the principal citizens, including several men of science, whom Messrs. Fulton and Livingston had invited to be present on the occasion.

At this time it is difficult to believe that a great majority of the people of that day had no faith in this undertaking. The common belief was that the boat could not be made to move a foot from the wharf, and the crowd of spectators now assembled to behold the result very freely indulged in sarcastic remarks, aimed at what they were pleased to call the folly or insanity of the projectors. When, therefore, the boat actually left the shore, and began to plough her way through the still waters, the multitude for awhile stood gazing in mute astonishment, mingled with awe, at what they considered a miracle of art. But

CLERMONT—1807.

when the boat, having reached the centre of the river, turned her head down the stream, and began to rush forward with increased velocity, the whole concourse, as if moved by one spirit, uttered a deafening and prolonged shout of applause and congratulation. Who can imagine the feelings of Robert Fulton at that moment? The day of recompense had arrived; his toils, travels, severe studies and frequent disappointments were unrequited no longer. He knew then that he had achieved a triumph which the world would acknowledge in all time to come. Here then, for once, a public benefactor received while living the homage which his genius and his services to the cause of human progress had deserved.

This first boat, whose performance so electrified the spectators, was called the Clermont. When some errors in the construction of the machinery had been corrected, she made a trial trip to Albany, and performed that voyage of one hundred and fifty miles in about thirty hours against the wind. Soon after, the Clermont became a regular passage boat between New York and Albany. Certain Quixotic persons conceived about these times that "pendulum power" might be made to rival steam as a propelling force, and a boat was actually built on that principle. As many had foreseen, however, the momentum of the pendulum could not overcome the resistance of the water, and this boat remained as stationary as the dock itself.

The exclusive right to steam navigation on the rivers of New York, which the legislature had granted to Livingston and Fulton, was not duly respected, for several opposition boats were soon started. These were slightly varied from Fulton's mode of construction, in order to avoid an obvious infringement on his patent. Fulton and Livingston attempted to assert their rights by recourse to the law, and applied to the Circuit Court of the United States for an injunction; but this Court decided that it had no jurisdiction in the case. The application was renewed in the Chancery of the State, but after hearing the argument, the chancellor refused to grant an injunction. The Supreme Court, however, reversed the chancellor's decision, and ordered a perpetual injunction on the opposition boats.

In the year 1812, two steam ferry boats for crossing the Hudson river, and one for the East river, were built under Mr. Fulton's directions. Thenceforth steamboats began to increase and multiply, and improvements were gradually introduced by Mr. Fulton up to the time of his death. It has been remarked, in commendation of his progressive skill and judgment, that the last boat built by him was always the best, the swiftest, and most convenient.

About the beginning of the last war with England, Mr. Fulton exhibited to a committee of citizens of New York the model of a steam man-of-war, provided with a strong battery, furnaces for red hot shot, &c. Several distinguished naval commanders had already pointed out the advantages which must result from the employment of steam in propelling war vessels, and Mr. Fulton's plan was so well received, that in the spring of 1814 Congress passed a law authorizing the President to cause to be built, equipped and employed one or more floating batteries, for the defence of the ports and waters of the United States. In conformity with this law, the steam frigate Fulton the First, was built at New York, and on the 4th of July, 1815, she made her first trip to the ocean and back, a distance of fifty-three miles, in eight hours and twenty minutes. Henry Rutgers, Samuel L. Mitchell, Thomas Morris, and Oliver Walcott, Esqs., commissioners of the navy, were present. Mr. Stoudinger, successor to Robert Fulton, was the engineer.

Before this vessel was completed, Robert Fulton had ceased to exist. While superintending the works on board of the steam frigate, he exposed himself too long on deck, on a wet and stormy day; an attack of pleurisy followed, which terminated his valuable life on the 24th day of February, 1815. Mr. Fulton was married, in the year 1806, to Miss Harriet Livingston, a relative of chancellor Livingston, his friend and associate in the steam navigation enterprise. He left four children, one son, Robert Barlow Fulton, and three daughters. In another department of this work we shall have occasion to speak of the part Mr. Fulton took in the establishment of steam navigation on the western waters.

GLIMPSES OF EARLY LIFE ON THE WESTERN WATERS.

All who are infected with that prevailing taste for romantic horrors, which distinguishes the fictitious literature of our day, may employ themselves agreeably in examining the records of early life on the western rivers. The most extravagant fiction which the morbidly excited imagination of a modern novellist has produced, could scarcely furnish parallels for the veritable exploits and wild adventures of some of those daring and reckless men who navigated the Ohio and Mississippi before the era of steamboat travel had commenced. The life of these primitive navigators so abounded with labors and perils, that the occupation of an ancient knight-errant might be called safe and delightful, by way of comparison. The dangers and embarrassments encountered by Tasso's hero in the enchanted forest, will appear in description to be quite insignificant when we compare them with the daily experience of the Mississippi or Ohio boatman, who flourished some forty or fifty years ago.

Before the panting of the steam-engine was heard on these waters, the only river conveyance for freight and passengers was a species of boat called a barge, or *bargee*, according to the French nomenclature. The length of this boat was from 75 to 100 feet; breadth of beam from 15 to 20 feet; capacity, from 60 to 100 tons. The receptacle for the freight was a large covered coffer, called the cargo-box, which occupied a considerable portion of the hulk. Near the stern was an apology for a cabin; a straightened apartment six or eight feet in length, in which the aristocracy of the boat, viz: the captain and *patroon*, or steersman, were generally quartered at night. The roof of the "cabin" was slightly elevated above the level of the deck, and on this eminence the helmsman was stationed to direct the movements of the boat. The barge was commonly provided with two masts, though some carried but one. The chief reliance of the boatmen was on a large square sail forward, which, when the wind was in the right direction, accelerated the progressive motion of the boat, and relieved the hands, who at other times were obliged to propel the barge by such laborious methods as we are about to describe. But before we exhibit the process used in navigating these rivers at that period, the reader should be made acquainted with the peculiarities of the rivers themselves.

EARLY NAVIGATION ON THE WESTERN WATERS.

The Mississippi, in particular, is celebrated for its turbulence and impetuosity, and truly it deserves its reputation, for its violent demeanor is such that its own shores are unable to control it. It scorns the limitations to which other rivers are subject; and, sometimes, in its capricious fury, it sweeps away fields or forests, or any other obstacle to its headlong course. Sometimes, indeed, it succeeds in obstructing its own progress with a conglomerated mass of earth and trees carried down by its current, and then an inundation of the neighboring country is the usual result.

From this description it may appear that the navigation of such a stream by the methods formerly in use was no holiday amusement; especially when it became necessary to stem the torrent in ascending the river. "*Facilis est descensus*"—to go *down*—in this use, as on many other occasions, was comparatively light labour, but to *return*, that, as Virgil remarks, in reference to another subject, was the grand difficulty. This was a service which required men of iron frame and undaunted resolution. Several different modes of propelling the barges were used by hardy boatmen. The work required about fifty men to each boat. At times, all these "hands" were employed in rowing; which, however, against such a stream as that of the Mississippi, was generally a great waste of labor to very little purpose. When circumstances permitted, the navigators resorted to the use of the *cordelle*. This was a stout rope or hawser, one end of which was attached to the bows or foremast of the barge, and the other extremity carried along the

3

shore or beach on the shoulders of the whole boat's crew, who thus performed the same duty that a horse does when towing a boat on a modern canal. It very often happened that this mode of progression was unavailable, as when the shores offered no convenient tow-path, or were obstructed by trees. In these circumstances, the "warping" process was adopted. The yawl was sent out with a coil of rope, which was fastened to a tree on shore, or a "snag" in the river, and while the hands on board were pulling up to this point, another coil was sent out to be fastened to some object farther ahead, and so the warping process was repeated. Again, it was expedient, at times, to use the setting poles, one end of which being set in the bed of the river, a sufficient purchase was obtained to enable the men to push forward the boat with their shoulders. This latter mode of propulsion was used chiefly on the Ohio; the bottom of the Mississippi was too yielding and the current generally was too rapid and powerful to make the use of the poles eligible in that river. By these changes from towing to warping, from warping to poling, and from poling to rowing, we are informed that the crews of the boats were "rested and refreshed;" and as "variety is the spice of life," it is presumed that they found their diversified labours altogether agreeable. By the way, it may puzzle some of our indolent cotemporaries to guess how men could be found who were willing to engage in this toilsome occupation, while any other possible means of subsistence were within their reach. Well says the proverb, that "there is no accounting for tastes;" but apart from this consideration, it may be observed that the life of a western boatman was not without its pleasures and enjoyments, as well as its pains and perils. The men who entered this service were such jolly, roving blades as could not be content with the dull hum-drum occupations of every-day life—but such as required excitement and even the prospect of danger to stir up their animal spirits.

The earliest history of the Mississippi is associated with narratives of piracy and murder. Buccaneers infested the mouths of the river, as its bays and creeks afforded places of concealment for themselves and their ill-gotten wealth. These aquatic banditti flourished to some extent, even after the war of 1814, and their last leader, Lafitte, is renowned in tale, song, and history for his courage, cruelty and crimes. His vessels were usually concealed in the land-locked bay of Barataria, to the westward of the mouth of the river.

When these celebrated sea-robbers had been extirpated by the American government, and while the hunting grounds of western Virginia and Kentucky were being gradually wrested from the Shawnee Indians, the population became more dense, and the Mississippi itself became the means of communication and barter with the more northern tribes. Another race of aquatics now succeeded, who, if history and tradition do not greatly wrong them, were not much more exemplary in their conduct than the pirates and buccaneers who preceded them. We refer to the Mississippi boatmen. The reader has been made acquainted with some of the difficulties with which they had to contend, while struggling for weeks or months, without intermission, against the impetuous current, but they were obliged, in addition to all this, to "fight their way," very often with the skulking Indians on the banks, or with the scarcely half-civilized white inhabitants of various districts contiguous to the shores of the river. The boatmen who ascended the Ohio were not unfrequently assailed by the savages, who, taking up the most favorable positions, either poured down the contents of their rifles on the boat as she passed, or, taking advantage of the dense fogs, boarded them in their canoes, and exterminated the crew of the barge without mercy. The crews of different boats likewise had their feuds or rivalships, and when these hostile barges happened to meet on the river, battles and bloodshed were the usual results.

Such a course of life was well calculated to make these boatmen lawless, desperate, and ferocious; but it appears that there was one bright spot on the dusky disc of their reputation. Their "redeeming virtue," as we are told, was scrupulous fidelity to their employers, the merchants, who entrusted them with valuable cargoes, without insurance, or any other guarantee except the receipt of the steersman, who possessed no other property than his interest in the boat. Nevertheless, this scrupulous integrity may appear to have been based on policy rather than principle, for the boatman's business depended solely on the confidence of the merchant in his honesty and fair dealing. It is reported, that numbers of wealthy travellers, who had occasion to take passage in these boats, never uttered any subsequent complaints of ill-treatment, unless these complaints were made to the catfish at the bottom of the river! Mysterious disappearances were of frequent occurrence at that time, and it required a stout heart to make a voyage down the Mississippi, if the voyager carried with him any property which might tempt the cupidity of these piratical boatmen.

The model hero of this tribe was the famous Mike Fink, who, if we mistake not, has figured on the pages of more than one popular romance of our day. The veritable Mike, without any fanciful embellishment, was a ruffian of surpassing strength and courage, his rifle was unerring, and his conscience was as easy and accommodating as a man in his line of business could wish. He had not been regularly trained from youth in the vocation of a boatman, but originally belonged to a company of government spies, or scouts, whose duty it was to watch the motions of the Indians on the frontiers. This peculiar service is thus described:—At that time Pittsburgh was on the extreme verge of white population, and the spies, who were constantly employed, generally extended their *reconnoissance* forty or fifty miles to the west of this post. They went out singly, lived in the Indian style, and perfectly assimilated themselves in habits, tastes and feelings to the red men of the forest. A kind of border warfare was kept up, and the scout thought it as praiseworthy to bring in the scalp of a Shawnee as the skin of a panther. He would remain in the woods for weeks together, using parched corn for bread, while for meat he depended on his rifle. At night he slept in perfect comfort, rolled up in his blanket with nothing but a magnificent canopy of stars, or, as it might happen, with a drapery of clouds over his head.

Mike Fink, after having pursued this delicious mode of life for some time, appears to have got tired of his land service, and betook himself to the water. He now engrafted several other occupations on that of the boatman; for while he dealt liberally and honestly with his friends and mercantile patrons, he put all the rest of mankind under contribution; and, in fact, was known from Pittsburgh to New Orleans as a regular freebooter.

An anecdote illustrative of his address and presence of mind is thus related:—One day, while he was making a little excursion in the woods, creeping along, according to his Indian habits, with the stealthy tread of a cat, his eye fell upon a beautiful buck, browsing on a barren spot, about three hundred yards distant. The temptation was too strong for the old woodsman, and he resolved, although the place was right perilous on account of Indian neighbours, to have a shot at all hazards. Repriming his gun and picking his flint, he made his approaches in the usual noiseless manner. At the moment he reached the spot from which he meant to take his aim, he observed a large savage, intent upon the same object, advancing from a direction a little different from his own. Mike shrunk back behind a tree with the quickness of thought, and keeping his eye fixed on the hunter, awaited the result with patience. In a few moments the Indian halted within fifty paces, and levelled his piece at the deer. In the meanwhile Mike presented his rifle at the body of the savage, and as the smoke issued from the gun of the latter, the bullet of Fink passed through the red man's breast. He uttered a yell, and fell dead at the same instant with the deer.

Mike reloaded his rifle, and remained in his covert for some minutes, to ascertain whether there were more enemies at hand. He then stepped up to the prostrate savage, and having satisfied himself that life was extinct, he turned his attention to the buck, and took from the carcase such choice pieces as he could conveniently carry off.

Mr. Fink's skill in the use of the rifle is exemplified in the following instance. While descending the Ohio in his boat, he once made a wager with a passenger that he would, from the mid-stream, with his rifle balls, cut off the tails of five pigs which were feeding on the banks. He executed this feat with such dexterity, that the unfortunate porkers were deprived of every vestige of their ornamental appendages, not a stump being left to indicate the position which said appendages had occupied.

The death of Mike Fink was melo-dramatic at least, if it wanted the dignified characteristics of tragedy. He had a friend, one of his barge companions, named Joe Stevens, on whom he had lavished his good offices, taught him the use of the rifle, and many other accomplishments suited to his situation in life. Mike likewise had a sweetheart, the daughter of one of the early settlers, who dwelt in a cottage or shanty on the bank of the river, and performed the duties of laundress for the boatmen, among whom she had many admirers. Fink for some time appeared to be the most acceptable of this young lady's numerous lovers, but he was aroused at last from dreams of bliss, as delusive as they were delicious, by the fatal discovery that his friend Joe Stevens had fully *realized* all that felicity which he himself had enjoyed only in visionary perspective. Burning with rage and jealousy, Mike contrived to hide his resentment while he awaited a fair opportunity for vengeance. That opportunity came at last. On a certain fine autumnal afternoon, the crew of Fink's boat were recreating themselves on shore with the rifle exercise, shooting at a mark, which was a very common divertisement among gentlemen of their profession. Fink's reputation as an accurate marksman was so well established that his companions frequently allowed him to fire at a tin cup placed on the head of one of their number, and the man who supported this target, having a perfect reliance on Mike's skill, never considered the valuable contents of his knowledge-box endangered in the least by this experiment. On the occasion now referred to, a stranger was present, and Fink, apparently with a desire to show off his exquisite accomplishment, proposed to shoot at the tin cup in the manner just described. The person whom he selected to bear the target was his rival in love, and the object of his fierce but hitherto concealed resentment, Joe Stevens, who was wholly unsuspicious of the deadly malice which lurked in Mike's bosom

Joe cheerfully consented to be the cup-bearer, and having assumed the glittering but perilous diadem, he placed himself at the proper distance, and requested Mike to "blaze away." Mike *did* blaze away with a vengeance, but instead of aiming at the cup, as the spectators supposed he would, he directed the piece a few inches lower, perforated the skull of the unlucky Stevens, and laid him dead on the spot. A brother of Stevens was present, and he, suspecting that the bloody deed had been premeditated by Fink, levelled his gun at the latter, and shot him dead likewise. And thus the eventful life of this illustrious personage was brought to a sudden termination.

Another river hero of great celebrity was James Girty. Western Pennsylvania has the honor of giving him birth; and some of his family, before his time, had acquired unenviable distinction. His two uncles, Simon and George, had adopted the Indian habits and costume, and were supposed to be the principal instigators of many of the atrocities committed by the savages on the frontier settlements. James Girty, the boatman, is represented to have been a natural prodigy. He was not constructed like ordinary men, for, instead of ribs, bountiful nature had provided him with a solid, bony casing on both sides, without any interstices through which a knife, dirk, or bullet could penetrate. He possessed, likewise, amazing muscular power, and courage in proportion, and his great boast was, that he had "never been whipt."

This man had been engaged in some of the most desperate adventures, and several times subjected himself to the severest penalties of the laws, but his customary good fortune saved him in all extremities. At one time, while he commanded a barge called the Black Snake, his boat's crew were fleeced, and some of them severely beaten by a strong party of gamblers at Natchez. The men refused to get the boat under weigh until they obtained vengeance; and Girty, in order to save time, agreed to accompany them to the dance-house, where the gamblers held their head-quarters, to assist in punishing the villains as they deserved. Several of the gamblers were killed, and others badly wounded in the affray which followed; Girty and some of the other ringleaders of his party were arrested, and afterwards tried for manslaughter; but the *lady* who kept the dance-house, and who appears to have been a particular friend and admirer of Girty, so managed it that the principal witnesses were not forthcoming at the trial. One witness only refused to absent himself at this lady's request, but she secured his silence by giving him a strong dose of arsenic a day or two before the trial came on. And so, as nobody appeared against Mr. Girty, he was "honorably acquitted."

The river men were generally on the most friendly terms with the hordes of robbers who infested the neighboring country. In fact, these "land rats and water rats," as Shylock would call them, were allies and associates, assisting each other in a variety of nefarious undertakings. A beautiful and romantic spot, called Cave-in-rock, on the Ohio river, was the general place of rendezvous for freebooters and boatmen. Here they held their grand councils, divided their plunder, and formed plans for future depredations.

From the accounts here given, the reader may judge what was the state of human society on and about the western rivers fifty years ago. Travelling on those rivers, at that period, was not less dangerous than expensive and dilatory. Robberies and murders were the common incidents of westward travel, either by land or water. The barges were manned chiefly by men of desperate fortunes and characters, fugitives from justice, and other outcasts from society, who were prepared to commit any crime on the slightest provocation or inducement. We are now prepared to estimate the importance of that great change which may be called the *Steamboat Revolution*, a particular account of which will be given in the next article.

COMMENCEMENT OF STEAM NAVIGATION ON THE WESTERN WATERS.

FROM the year 1786 to 1811, the only regular mode of transportation on the western rivers was such as we have described in the preceding article. The entire commerce of those rivers was transacted by means of those clumsy contrivances called barges and flat-boats, which consumed three or four months in making the trip from New Orleans to Louisville, a trip which is now made by steam power in five or six days, and has been made in a little over four. The price of passage from New Orleans to Pittsburgh was then $160; freight $6.75 per hundred pounds. The introduction of steam has reduced the price of passage between these two cities to thirty dollars, and merchandise is carried the whole distance for a price which may be regarded as merely nominal. Besides this great saving of time and money effected by steam navigation on these waters, the comparative *safety* of steam conveyance is an item which especially deserves our notice. Before the steam dispensation began, travellers and merchants were obliged to trust their lives or property to the bargemen, many of whom were suspected, with very good reason, to be in confederacy with the land robbers who infested the shores of the Ohio, and the pirates who resorted to the islands of the Mississippi. These particulars being understood, we are prepared to estimate the value and importance of the services which the steam-engine has rendered to the commerce and prosperity of the Western States.

The earliest account we have of the navigation of the Mississippi, refers to a period more than three hundred years ago, when Ferdinand De Soto, the first discoverer of that mighty stream, was engaged in his famous and fantastic exploring expedition in search of "the fountain of youth." About one hundred years later, Father Joliet, a Jesuit ambassador and envoy from France, again disturbed these waters, by launching on their bosom a bark which had been transported by his fellow adventurers on their shoulders across the territory between the Fox and Wisconsin rivers.

The first vessel ever built on the waters of the West was the brig Dean, which derived her name from her builder and original proprietor. She was launched at the present site of Allegheny city, near Pittsburgh, in 1806. She afterwards made a voyage from Pittsburgh to the Mediterranean. When making her entry at the custom-house, at Leghorn, in 1807, the officer objected to her papers, declaring that such a port as Pittsburgh did not exist in the United States! A map was produced, and the captain guided the finger of the officer along the courses of the Mississippi and Ohio, by Cincinnati to Pittsburgh, and the astonishment of the custom-house gentleman was unspeakable when the location of this new city in the wilderness was pointed out. This incident may give the reader some idea of the ignorance and incredulity which prevail in Europe in relation to the rapid growth and prosperity of this country.

After the purchase of Louisiana from Napoleon, in 1803, some eastern capitalists sent out mechanics, and built several ships on the Ohio. In 1805, Jonas Spoir built the ship "Scott" on the Kentucky river, twenty miles above Frankfort, and near the residence of that celebrated western pioneer, General Charles Scott. This ship was the first that ever made a successful trip to the Falls of the Ohio. She remained there for several months before the occurrence of a rise in the river sufficient to float her over. In the meantime, two other vessels from Pittsburgh, built by James Berthone & Co., had arrived at the Falls, and in the attempt to get over, the longest one was sunk, and soon after torn to pieces by the violence of the current. This accident was so discouraging, that no further attempts at ship-building were made on the Ohio.

In 1811, Messrs. Fulton and Livingston, having established a ship-yard at Pittsburgh, for the purpose of introducing steam navigation on the western waters, built an experimental boat for this service; and this was the first steamboat that ever floated on the western rivers. It was furnished with a propelling wheel at the stern, and two masts; for Mr. Fulton believed, at that time, that the occasional use of sails would be indispensable. This first western steamboat was called the Orleans. Her capacity was one hundred tons. In the winter of 1812, she made her first trip from Pittsburgh to New Orleans in 14 days. She continued to make regular trips between New Orleans and Natchez, until the fourteenth day of July, 1814, when she was wrecked near Baton Rouge, on her upward-bound passage, by striking a snag.

The first appearance of this vessel on the Ohio river produced, as the reader may suppose, not a little excitement and admiration. A steamboat, at that day, was to common observers, almost as great a wonder as a flying angel would be at present. The banks of the river, in some places, were thronged with spectators, gazing in speechless

FIRST BOAT BUILT ON THE WESTERN WATERS, 1812.

astonishment at the puffing and smoking phenomenon. The average speed of this boat was only about three miles per hour. Before her ability to move through the water without the assistance of sails or oars had been fully exemplified, comparatively few persons believed that she could possibly be made to answer any purpose of real utility. In fact, she had made several voyages before the general prejudice began to subside, and for some months, many of the river merchants preferred the old mode of transportation, with all its risks, delays, and extra expense, rather than make use of such a contrivance as a steamboat, which, to their apprehensions, appeared too marvellous and miraculous for the business of every day life. How slow are the masses of mankind to adopt improvements, even when they appear to be most obvious and unquestionable!

The second steamboat of the West was a diminutive vessel called the "Comet." She was rated at twenty-five tons. Daniel D. Smith was the owner, and D. French the builder of this boat. Her machinery was on a plan for which French had obtained a patent in 1809. She went to Louisville in the summer of 1813, and descended to New Orleans in the spring of 1814. She afterwards made two voyages to Natchez, and was then sold, taken to pieces, and the engine was put up in a cotton factory.

The *Vesuvius* is the next in this record. She was built by Mr.

Fulton, at Pittsburgh, for a company, the several members of which resided at New York, Philadelphia, and New Orleans. She sailed under the command of Capt. Frank Ogden, for New Orleans, in the spring of 1814. From New Orleans she started for Louisville in July of the same year, but was grounded on a sand-bar, seven hundred miles up the Mississippi, where she remained until the 3d of December following, when, being floated off by the tide, she returned to New Orleans. In 1815, '16, she made regular trips for several months, from New Orleans to Natchez, under the command of Capt. Clement. This gentleman was soon after succeeded by Capt. John de Hart, and while approaching New Orleans with a valuable cargo on board, she took fire and burned to the water's edge. After being submerged for several months, her hulk was raised and refitted. She was afterwards in the Louisville trade, and was condemned in 1819.

The *Enterprise* was No. 4 of the Western steamboat series. She was built at Brownsville, Pa., by D. French, under his patent, and was owned by several residents of that place. The Enterprise was a small boat of seventy-five tons. She made two voyages to Louisville in the summer of 1814, under the command of Capt. J. Gregg. On the 1st of December, in the same year, she conveyed a cargo of ordnance stores from Pittsburgh to New Orleans. While at the last-named port, she was pressed into service by Gen. Jackson. Her owners were afterwards remunerated by the United States' government. When engaged in the public service, she was eminently useful in transporting troops, arms, and ammunition to the seat of war. She left New Orleans for Pittsburgh on the 6th of May, 1815, and reached Louisville after a passage of twenty-

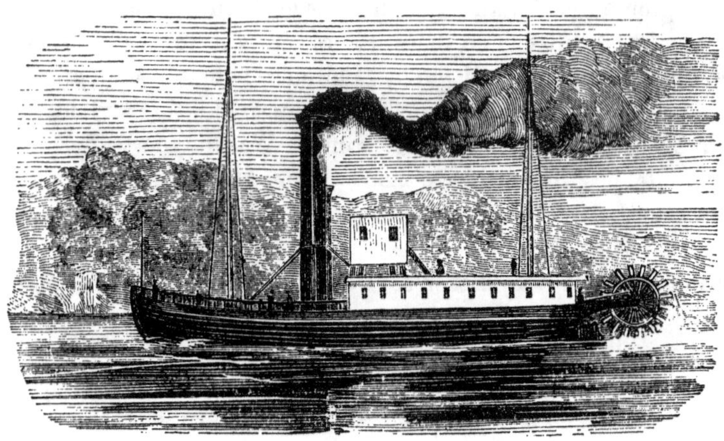

ENTERPISE ON HER FAST TRIP TO LOUISVILLE, 1815.

five days, thus completing the first steamboat voyage ever made from New Orleans to Louisville. But at the time the Enterprise made this trip, the water was so high that the banks in many places were overflowed; consequently there was no current. The Enterprise was enabled to make her way up without much difficulty, by running through the "cut-offs," and over inundated fields, in still water. In view of these favorable circumstances, the experiment was not satisfactory, the public being still in doubt whether a steamboat could ascend the Mississippi when that river was confined within its banks, and the current as rapid as it generally is.

Such was the state of public opinion when the steamboat Washington commenced her career. This vessel, the fourth in the catalogue of western steamboats, was constructed under the personal superintendence and direction of Capt. Henry M. Shreve. The hull was built at Wheeling, Va., and the engines were made at Brownsville, Pa. The entire construction of the boat comprised various innovations, which were suggested by the ingenuity and experience of Capt. Shreve. The Washington was the first "two decker" on the western waters. The cabin was placed between the decks. It had been the general practice for steamboats to carry their boilers in the hold; in this particular Capt. Shreve made a new arrangement, by placing the boilers of the Washington on deck; and this plan was such an obvious improvement, that all the steamboats on those waters retain it to the present day. The engines constructed under Fulton's patent had upright and stationary cylinders. In French's engines vibrating cylinders were used. Shreve caused the cylinders of the Washington to be placed in a horizontal position, and gave the vibrations to the pitman. Fulton and French used single low-pressure engines. Shreve employed a double high-pressure engine, with cranks at right angles; and this was the first engine of that kind ever used on the western rivers. Mr. David Prentice had previously used cam wheels for working the valves of the cylinder; Capt. Shreve added his great invention of the cam cut-off, with flues to the boilers, by which three-fifths of the fuel were saved. These improvements originated with Capt. Shreve, but although they have been in universal use for a long time, their origin is not known.

On the 24th day of September, 1816, the Washington passed over the Falls of Ohio, on her first trip to New Orleans, and returned to Louisville in November following. While at New Orleans the ingenuity of her construction excited the admiration of the most intelligent citizens of that place. Edward Livingston, after a critical examination of the boat and her machinery, remarked to Capt. Shreve, "You deserve well of your country, young man; but we (referring to Fulton and Livingston's monopoly) shall be compelled to beat you (in the courts), if we can."

An accumulation of ice in the Ohio compelled the Washington to remain at the Falls until March 12th, 1817. On that day she commenced her second voyage to New Orleans. She accomplished this trip and returned to Shippingsport, at the foot of the Falls, in forty-one days. The ascending voyage was made in twenty-five days, and from this voyage all historians date the commencement of steam navigation in the Mississippi valley. It was now practically demonstrated to the satisfaction of the public in general, that steamboats could ascend this river in less than one-fourth the time which the barges and keel-boats had required for the same purpose. This feat of the Washington produced almost as much popular excitement and exultation in that region as the battle of New Orleans. The citizens of Louisville gave a public dinner to Capt. Shreve, at which he predicted that the time would come when the trip from New Orleans to Louisville would be made in ten days. Although this may have been regarded as a boastful declaration at that time, the prediction has been more than fulfilled; for in 1853 the trip was made in *four* days and nine hours.

After that memorable voyage of the Washington, all doubts and prejudices in reference to steam navigation were removed. Ship-yards began to be established in every convenient locality, and the business of steamboat building was vigorously prosecuted. But a new obstacle now presented itself, which, for a time, threatened to give an effectual check to the spirit of enterprise and progression which had just been developed. We refer to the claims made by Messrs. Fulton and Livingston to the exclusive right of steam navigation on the rivers of the United States. This claim being resisted by Capt. Shreve, the Washington was attached at New Orleans, and taken possession of by the sheriff. When the case came for adjudication before the District Court of Louisiana, that tribunal promptly negatived the exclusive privileges claimed by Livingston and Fulton, which were decided to be unconstitutional. The monopoly claims of Livingston and Fulton were finally withdrawn in 1819, and the last restraint on the steamboat navigation of the western rivers was thus removed, leaving western enterprise and energy at full liberty to carry on the great work of improvement. This work has been so progressive that, at the present time, no less than *eight hundred* steamboats are in constant operation on the Ohio and Mississippi and their tributaries, and this mode of navigation has there been carried to a degree of perfection unrivalled in any other part of the world.

THE OHIO RIVER.

No man who has the least appreciation of natural beauty, ever beheld this river and its diversified shores without a feeling of admiration. The Frenchman, boastful of his refined tastes, and the uncultivated savage of the wilderness, agreed in giving it the name which, in the language of each, signified "*The beautiful river;*" and never was a complimentary title more truly deserved than in this instance. The banks on either side present a succession of tall and picturesque cliffs, with alternate valleys, meadows, and woodlands, which nature seems to have arranged with more than her customary regularity; while numerous islands, decorated with superb trees and luxurious verdure, complete a natural panorama which nothing of artificial production can ever equal.

The Ohio river is formed by the junction of the Alleghany and Monongahela rivers at Pittsburgh. Flowing generally in a south-westerly direction, it separates the States of Ohio, Illinois, and Indiana on the right, from Virginia and Kentucky on the left. The Ohio river unites with the Mississippi ten hundred and sixteen miles from the mouth of the latter, in lat. 37° N., long. 89° 10′ W. The whole length of the Ohio is nine hundred and sixty-four miles. In breadth, it varies from four hundred to six hundred yards. At Cincinnati it is about six hundred yards wide, which may be considered as the mean breadth of the river.

The Alleghany river, whose confluence with the Monongahela forms the Ohio, rises in Potter county, in the northern part of Pennsylvania, and after a circuitous course through a part of New York, it again enters Pennsylvania, and unites, as previously stated, with the Monongahela at Pittsburgh. For nearly two hundred miles from that city the Alleghany is navigable for boats. Steamboats of a small size have occasionally ascended to Olean, two hundred and fifty miles from the mouth of this river.

The Monongahela is formed by the union of the West-Fork and Tygart's Valley rivers, which rise in Randolph and Lewis counties, Virginia, and meet one mile from Fairmont, in Marion county of the same State. The Monongahela is navigable for large steamboats as far as Brownsville, Pennsylvania, thirty-five miles from the mouth of this river; and for boats of a medium size, as far as Fairmont, Virginia. The whole length of the river, exclusive of its branches, is one hundred and fifty miles. The obstructions to navigation which formerly existed in the lower part of this river have been removed, or obviated by various artificial contrivances.

The principal tributaries of the Ohio are the Muskingum, Great Kanawha, Big Sandy, Sciota, Miama, Green, Kentucky, Wabash, Cumberland, and Tennessee rivers. Of these tributary streams, the three last named are the most important.

The Tennessee river is the largest stream which pours its waters into the Ohio. It is formed by the union of two branches, called the Clinch and Holston rivers, which have their sources among the Alleghany mountains, in the north-west part of Virginia. These branches unite at Kingston, North Carolina, and from thence the river Tennessee flows westerly into the State of the same name, then makes an extensive circuit through the northern part of Alabama, and then, changing its course again, runs nearly northward, through the States of Tennessee and Kentucky, and falls into the Ohio at Paducah, in lat. 37° N., and long. 88° 35′ W. The length of the Tennessee, from the junction of its branches, is eight hundred miles, but in connection with Holston river, its longest branch, it is computed to be eleven hundred miles long. For six hundred miles the Tennessee is navigable for large boats, and for boats of a smaller size, four hundred miles more. Steamboats of the first class ascend this river as far as Florence, Alabama, which is situated on the north bank at the foot of the rapids called Muscle shoals, which are between Lauderdale and Lawrence counties, Alabama. The river here has a descent of about one hundred feet in the course of twenty miles, and no boats can pass over the shoals except in the highest stages of water. The channel at this place varies from one to two miles in width, but at the lower termination of the shoals it is contracted to half a mile. The bluffs on each side are composed of an upper stratum of flint, and a lower stratum of fine limestone. In 1840, a canal twelve miles long was built around the shoals, but unfortunately the locks were made too short to admit even the smallest steamboats that navigate that river; it was soon abandoned, and the channel has been filling up for the last fifteen years. Thousands of wild geese and ducks resort to this locality to feed on the species of shell-fish from which the name of Muscle Shoals is derived. Above the rapids, boats run at all seasons to Knoxville, Tennessee, on the Holston, a distance of five hundred miles.

Cumberland river, one of the largest affluents of the Ohio, rises among the Cumberland mountains, near the south-east boundary of Kentucky. After flowing westwardly about two hundred miles through the State of Kentucky, it takes a meandering course through a part of the State of Tennessee, until it reaches Nashville. From this point it flows N. W., and again enters the State of Kentucky about ten miles east of the Tennessee river. Its course afterwards is nearly parallel with that of the Tennessee, until it enters the Ohio river at Smithland. During the time of high water, large boats ascend to Nashville, about two hundred miles from the mouth of this river, and small boats go three hundred miles further. The area drained by the Cumberland river is estimated at twenty thousand square miles.

The beautiful river of Kentucky is formed by the north, middle, and south fords, which unite in Proctor and Owsley counties. It flows N. W., forming the boundary between Fayette, Jessemine, and Woodford counties on the right, and Madison, Garrard, Mercer, and Anderson on the left; then passing through Franklin county and Frankfort city, and separating Owen from Henry county, it falls into the Ohio at Carrollton, ninety miles below Cincinnati, and sixty above the Falls of Ohio. The length of the main stream is about two hundred miles, which is navigable by means of dams and locks to Frankfort at all times; and flat boats ascend one hundred miles further. In many parts of its course it flows through a deep channel, formed by perpendicular walls of limestone, and is remarkable for its picturesque scenery.

The Muskingum river has been made navigable, by means of artificial improvements, as far as Zanesville, seventy miles from its mouth; but at times of high water boats may ascend to Coshocton, thirty miles further. Sciota river admits of steamboat navigation for a distance of fifty miles. The State of Ohio contributes to the river from which it derives its name, the waters of the Muskingum, Sciota, Miami, and several minor streams, whose courses vary in length from one hundred and twenty to two hundred and fifty miles.

Green river rises in the centre of Kentucky, and flows westerly, until, having completed more than half its course, it receives the waters of the Big Barren river. In this part of its route it traverses the cavernous limestone formation, and passes over that stupendous natural curiosity, the Mammoth Cave. From its confluence with Big Barren river, it takes a north westerly course, and falls into the Ohio in Henderson county, Kentucky, nine miles above Evansville, Indiana, on the opposite shore. The whole length of Green river is estimated at three hundred and fifty miles. It is made navigable by locks and dams, at all seasons, as far as Bowling Green on the Big Barren river, twenty miles below the Mammoth Cave, and during a part of the year the navigation extends to the Cave itself. At times of high water, boats have reached Greensbury, two hundred miles from the mouth of the river.

The Ohio begins its course at Pittsburgh with graceful tranquillity. Its breadth for some distance after the conjunction of its two parent streams, is about six hundred yards. At this point the elevation of the Ohio above the level of the sea is six hundred and ninety feet; at the entrance of the Muskingum river, it is five hundred and forty-eight feet; at the mouth of the Sciota, four hundred and sixty-six feet; opposite Cincinnati, four hundred and eighteen feet; and at its confluence with the Mississippi, three hundred and twenty-five feet; making the average descent a little less than six inches to the mile.

The peculiarity of the Ohio river which distinguishes it from the Mississippi, and some others, is its extraordinary gentleness and serenity. The ordinary motion of the current is about three and a half miles per hour; its velocity gradually increases to the time of high water, when it is nearly doubled. But for nearly three-quarters of the year, the stream moves with so much gentleness, that an object floating on its bosom would be carried scarcely more than two and a half miles in an hour.

But the case is very different during one of the periodical floods, or "freshets," of the Monongahela and Alleghany, which are sometimes of such sudden occurrence that the waters of that river rise twenty feet in the same number of hours. Then, indeed, the impulse given by the swollen river to the head-waters of the Ohio, changes the usual placidity of that stream to a torrent-like violence and impetuosity. The "rush of the waters," at such times, is tremendous, and the force of the current irresistible. This rise of the river affords an opportunity for the canal boats at Pittsburgh to cast off their moorings, and commit themselves to the rapid stream, which carries them, by the mere force of the tide, to the various landing-places on the Ohio, from whence the south and west obtain their annual supplies of mineral fuel.

The falls of the Ohio, at Louisville, Kentucky, about six hundred miles below Pittsburgh, may be considered as a remarkable deviation from the usually quiet deportment of the river. The descent, at this point, is 22½ feet within two miles, which produces a current so rapid and dangerous, that this part of the river is considered often unnavigable; boats of the largest size, however, sometimes pass these rapids, by taking advantage of an unusual depth of water. In order to obviate this natural obstruction to the navigation of the Ohio, a canal of suitable dimensions and capacity has been constructed on the Kentucky side of the river, which extends the whole length of the rapids, (about two miles,) and affords a smooth and safe passage for boats one hundred and eighty-five feet in length, when the falls, for want of a sufficiency of water, are impassible. In descending the falls, the channel is near the Indiana shore ; but, in ascending, the boats are compelled to take the "middle schute," near Corn island, the situation of which is in the centre of the river. In the navigation of these falls, up or down, it is always necessary to have a "fall's pilot," and those gentlemen skilled and experienced in the art of conducting a vessel through these "troublesome waters," are to be found only at Louisville, Kentucky.

One notable circumstance connected with the topography of the Ohio river, is the vast number of beautiful islands which are enclosed by its waters. More than one hundred of these are of considerable size; some of them are exceedingly fertile, and in a high state of cultivation, and many of them are covered with trees of the largest size. There is an equal or greater number of islets of alluvial formation, whose vegetation is more scanty, and some are mere sand-banks, entirely barren, or covered in spots with a growth of willows, or other trees or shrubs, which can find nourishment in such a meagre soil. The navigation of the Ohio above the falls is obstructed, more or less, during the summer months, by a deficiency of water, and by numerous sand-bars, which sometimes extend from shore to shore, or project to a considerable distance across the bed of the stream. Steamboats which have the misfortune to be grounded on these bars are often compelled to remain in that situation until relieved by the periodical rise of the river. At those seasons, when the depth of water is insufficient for the larger class of boats, they are generally withdrawn, and their place is supplied by small "stern-wheel boats," which, even when not laden, have a draught of water not exceeding sixteen or twenty inches. These delicately constructed vessels do an exceedingly lucrative business, until the rise of the water forces them from the field of competition.

In the winter season the Ohio is commonly frozen over for six or eight weeks, during which time the business of the river is entirely suspended. At this season of inactivity the boats seek a secure harbor to avoid the running ice, and embrace the opportunity to refit and make preparations for the re-commencement of active duty in the spring. The breaking up of the ice, which usually takes place in the month of February, is caused by a sudden rise in the river, which forces the ice in huge fragments down the stream. This is a time of some peril, when boats, by any chance, are exposed to the fury of the icy torrent, which pours down with prodigious force and rapidity. Not unfrequently as many as a dozen boats are overwhelmed and submerged at "one fell swoop."

The Ohio, like a majority of rivers, is subject to great elevations and depressions. The average difference between high and low water, at ordinary times is about fifty-three feet; but in the years 1810, '32, and '47, the rise was sixty-two feet six inches. At this elevation the water reaches the second story of the houses on Water street, Cincinnati, and almost inundates Cairo, at the mouth of the river. At its lowest stages, the Ohio is fordable at several places between Cincinnati and Pittsburgh, though boats constructed for the purpose may navigate the river at all seasons.

The navigable waters of the Ohio and its tributaries is estimated at more than six thousand miles in extent; and the regions drained by these streams comprise an area of two hundred and thirty thousand square miles. Between Pittsburgh and Cincinnati, the river scenery is especially magnificent, picturesque or beautiful, as the view varies at different points. The banks, or cliffs, in some places are from one hundred to two hundred feet in height, and are often covered with dense forests, which extend down the embankment to the very margin of the stream.

The Ohio, when open for navigation, as it is for nearly the whole year, is covered with boats, and the commerce of the river amounts annually to many millions of dollars.

VIEW OF PITTSBURGH.

SKETCH OF PITTSBURGH.

PITTSBURGH is one of the largest and most important cities west of the Alleghany mountains. It is situated at the confluence of the Alleghany and Monongahela rivers, which here form the Ohio river; 357 miles West of Philadelphia; 477 N. E. by E. of Cincinnati; 1174 E. N. E. of St. Louis; and 223 N. W. of Washington. Lat. 40° 32′ N.; lon. 80° 2′ W. The site comprises the triangular plain enclosed by the Alleghany and Monongahela rivers, Grant's Hill, and several other elevations which terminate the plain on E. Fort Duquesne, a French trading post erected in 1754, formerly occupied the site where Pittsburgh now stands. In 1758, an English expedition marched against this post, which was then regarded by the youthful Washington as the key of the West. An advanced detachment, under Capt. Grant, having encamped on what is still called Grant's Hill, was attacked and defeated by a party of French and Indians from fort Duquesne; but on the approach of Gen. Forbes, with a force of 6200 men, the disheartened garrison set fire to the fort and descended the Ohio river. The victorious troops on entering, November 25th, by general acclamation called the place Pittsburgh, in honor of Wm. Pitt, then Prime Minister of England. The town of Pittsburgh began to be settled in 1765; it became a county town in 1791, was incorporated a borough in 1804, and chartered as a city in 1816. In 1845 a great fire consumed a large part of Pittsburgh, causing a destruction of property to the amount of $10,000,000. Notwithstanding this terrible calamity the city has continued to increase in wealth and population almost beyond parallel. The manufactures of Pittsburgh and its vicinity employ above six hundred steam-engines. There are about forty-five iron foundries with machine-shops, of which nine make on an average one hundred and fifty steam-engines annually; a mammoth rail manufactory, the largest perhaps in the world, is in operation there. It is capable of turning out one hundred and twenty tons of rails every twenty-four hours. Capital of the company, $1,000,000. There are twenty-three heavy blacksmithing forges, with a capital of $500,000, producing railroad axles, steamboat shafts, sugar mills, &c. Pittsburgh contains about sixty schools, and nearly an equal number in the suburbs, annually attended by eighteen thousand pupils. There are about twenty-five printing-offices, issuing newspapers and other publications, fifteen of which are dailies. A Chamber of Commerce has been organized since 1850. The manufactures of Pittsburgh are immense, and capable of being extended almost indefinitely. Indeed, there are no known limits to the elements necessary to their augmentation. Wood, coal, ores, and agricultural resources, all abound in the utmost profusion, and may be obtained with scarcely any expenditure of labor or of capital. In England it requires an immense outlay of capital to mine coal, which there lies from 500 to 2500 feet below the surface; but in Western Pennsylvania, enough coal to turn all the machinery ever constructed, may be found in rich beds underlying the hills, at an elevation above the ordinary level of the country. Millions of bushels of coal are annually shipped from Pittsburgh to the West and South.

Boats are built here in great numbers. Some of the fastest boats afloat on the Western waters were built at Pittsburgh. Machinery is here made cheap and durable, and many of the St. Louis and New Orleans commanders get their boats built and equipped here. One of the largest and best engine builders is A. Irwin, Esq., firm of A. Erwin & David Holmes. It was at this establishment that the heavy engines of the John Simonds, Buckeye State, and other large steamers were built.

Pittsburgh is rapidly improving. Population in 1810, 5000; in 1820, 7500; in 1830, 13,000; in 1840, 22,000; in 1850, 80,000; in 1856, 159,000.

MAPS OF THE OHIO RIVER.

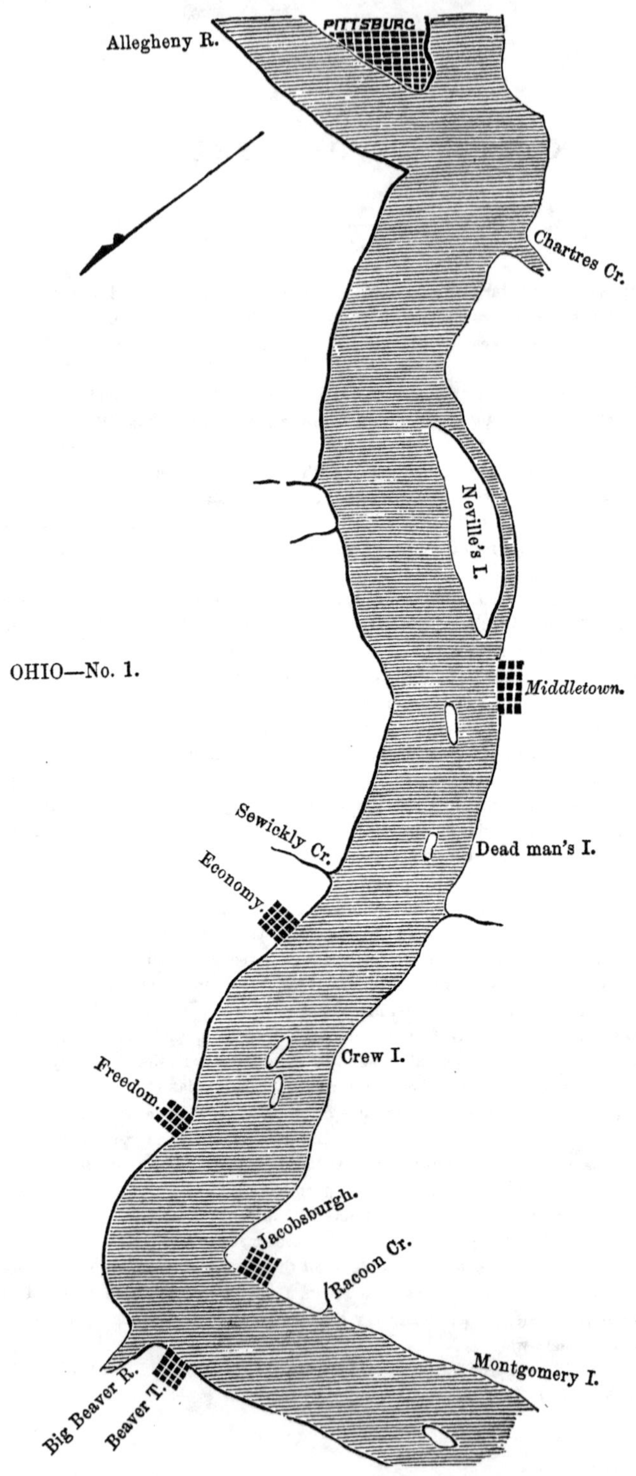

OHIO—No. 1.

LLOYD'S STEAMBOAT DISASTERS

ON

The Western Waters.

TERRIFIC EXPLOSION AND LOSS OF LIFE ON BOARD THE STEAMBOAT WASHINGTON.

THIS deplorable accident took place on the Ohio river on the 9th day of June, 1816. The Washington was the largest and finest boat which had hitherto floated on any western stream. Her commander, Captain Shreve, was skilled and experienced in all the duties of his calling; her machinery was all presumed to be in the best possible order, and no human foresight could have anticipated the fatal event. The boat left Marietta, Ohio, on Monday, June 7, and on the afternoon of the following day came safely to anchor off Point Harmar, where she remained until Wednesday morning. The fires were now kindled, and other preparations made for continuing the voyage down the Ohio; but a difficulty occurred in getting the boat into a proper position to start the machinery. While laboring to effect this object—the boat having, in the mean time, been carried by the force of the current near the Virginia shore—it became necessary to throw out a kedge anchor at the stern. Soon after, all hands were summoned aft to haul in the kedge, and while they were collected on the quarter for that purpose, by a singular and most unfortunate chance, the end of the cylinder nearest the stern was blown off, and a column of scalding water was thrown among the crowd, inflicting the most frightful injuries on nearly all of the boat's crew, and killing a number on the spot. The cry of consternation and anguish which then arose might have been heard for miles. The captain, mate, and several others were blown overboard; but all of these, with the exception of one man, were afterwards rescued from the water, but were found to be more or less injured, either by the fragments of the cylinder or the scalding water.

The inhabitants of the neighboring town, now called Harmar, were universally alarmed by the sound of the explosion, which appeared to

EXPLOSION OF THE WASHINGTON, 1816.

shake the solid earth to a considerable distance. A number of physicians and many other citizens crowded into the boat to ascertain the extent of the calamity; but no language can describe the scene of misery and torture which then presented itself to the view of the spectators. The deck was strewn with mangled and writhing human beings, uttering screams and groans of intense suffering. Some, more fortunate than their companions, lay still in the embrace of death. Among the wounded, six or eight, under the influence of their maddening torments, had torn off their clothes, to which the entire skin of their limbs or bodies adhered; the eyes of others had been put out, and their faces were changed to an undistinguishable mass of flesh by the scalding water. But the greatest sufferers, apparently, were those who had been internally injured by inhaling the scalding steam, the effect of which on the lungs is agonizing beyond all the powers of imagination to conceive. The whole scene was too horrible for description, and it made an impression on the minds of those who witnessed it which could never be obliterated.

The cause of the explosion was a disarrangement of the safety-valve, which had become immovable in consequence of the accidental slipping of the weight to the extremity of the lever. The following is a list of the killed and wounded by this calamitous explosion:

KILLED:—Peter Lanfer, B. Harvey, Anna C. Jones, Thomas Brown, James Nulta, —— Jones, passengers; Samuel Wait, carpenter, Jacob ——, colored cook.

WOUNDED:—Captain Shreve, commander, Mr. Clark, engineer, James Blair, George White, Enoch H. McFeeley, Joseph Walsh, John C. Williams, (mortally,) passengers.

Mr. Williams of Kentucky, the unhappy gentleman last mentioned in the preceding list, while lying in the cabin of the Washington, in his last moments, offered one of the cabin-boys all his money if he would knock him on the head to put a speedy end to his misery. The boy who received this offer, and who relates the incident, is now Captain Hiram Burch, of Marietta, Ohio,

Joseph ———, one of the hands, was missing; he is supposed to have been blown overboard, and carried down by the current. Several of the wounded died a short time afterwards in consequence of their injuries. At a meeting of the citizens of Marietta, a committee was appointed to provide for the sufferers, and to make arrangements for the burial of the dead.

This first steamboat accident in the West produced a great excitement among the inhabitants of that region, and occasioned for some time a strong prejudice against steamboat travel, the people being oblivious of the fact, that when the water conveyance was confined to barges and keel-boats, there was more real danger and more actual loss of life than may be classed among the incidents of steamboat navigation.

EXPLOSION OF THE STEAMBOAT CONSTITUTION.

On the 4th day of May, 1817, while the steamer Constitution was ascending the Mississippi river, and when she was off Point Coupee, the boiler exploded, making the whole front part of the cabin a perfect wreck, and killing or wounding thirty persons, eleven of whom perished instantly. As soon as the terrific report of the explosion was heard on board, numbers of the excited passengers threw themselves into the rapid current, and many were drowned or wafted down the stream before assistance could reach them. The shrieks of the wounded and dying were reverberated from the distant shores, and many a ghastly and heart-sickening spectacle presented itself on the deck of the ill-fated vessel. One man had been completely submerged in the boiling liquid which inundated the cabin, and in his removal to the deck, the skin

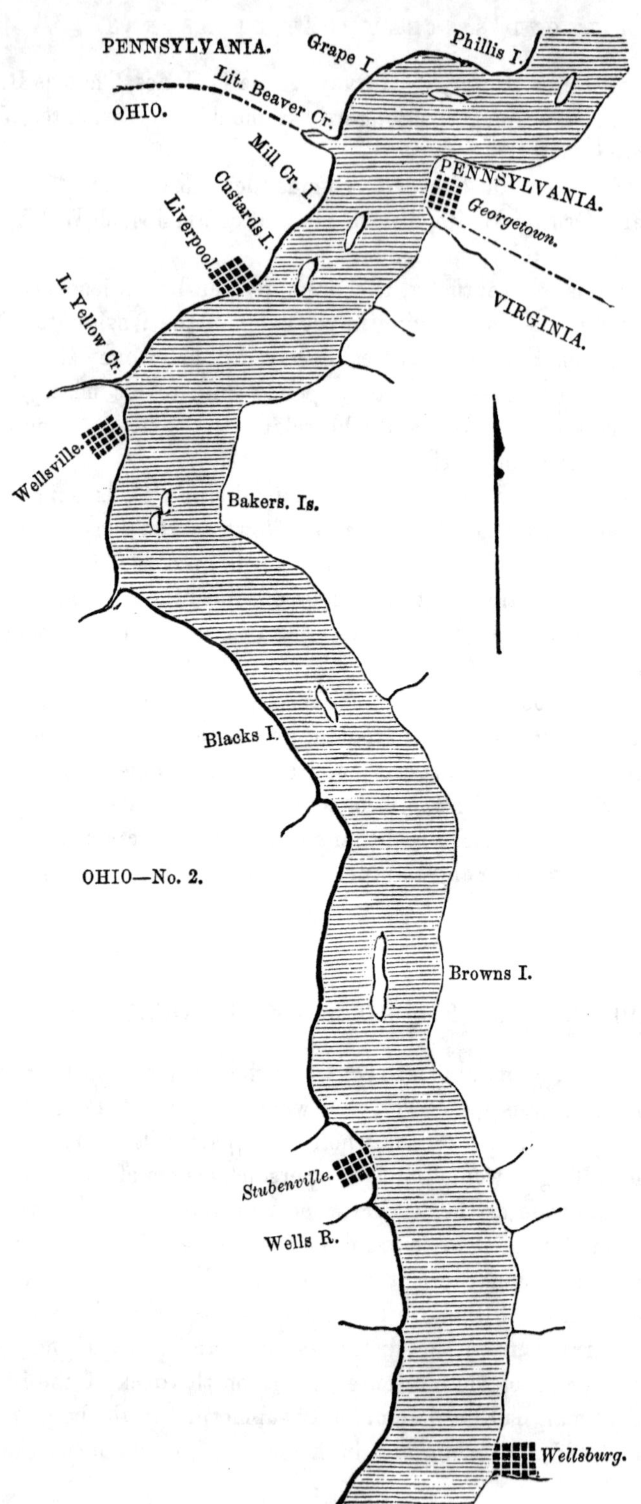

PENNSYLVANIA.
Grape I.
Phillis I.
Lit. Beaver Cr.
OHIO.
Mill Cr. I.
Custards I.
Liverpool.
PENNSYLVANIA.
Georgetown.
VIRGINIA.
L. Yellow Cr.
Wellsville.
Bakers. Is.
Blacks I.
OHIO—No. 2.
Browns I.
Stubenville.
Wells R.
Wellsburg.

had separated from the entire surface of his body. The unfortunate wretch was literally boiled alive, yet although his flesh parted from his bones, and his agonies were most intense, he survived and retained all his consciousness for several hours. Another passenger was found lying aft of the wheel with an arm and a leg blown off, and as no surgi-

EXPLOSION OF THE CONSTITUTION, 1817.

cal aid could be rendered him, death from loss of blood soon ended his sufferings. Miss C. Butler, of Massachusetts, was so badly scalded, that, after lingering in unspeakable agony for three hours, death came to her relief. Many were drowned whose names do not appear in the subjoined list of those who perished by this disaster. Besides, many of the victims were so mutilated and disfigured, that their bodies could not be identified; and owing to these causes the list may be considered as very incomplete.

Capt. Bezeau and lady, with some others, were fortunate enough to escape unhurt, being forward when the explosion took place. The following are the names of those who were killed:

William Yarnall, Va.; E. Frazier, Gibson Port, M. T.; Thomas Brown, Scotland; Wm. McFarland, Washington Co., Ky.; Joseph D. Wilson, James Carpenter, Md.; Alexander Philpot, Henry Co., Va.; William Steel, Warrenton, M. T.; Peter Huber, N. O. and Baltimore; Robert Robertson, 18 years old; William Larkin, silversmith Natchez; Amos Shorter, Wm. Albright, David Young, Theodore Wright, Mrs. Yancey, of Pittsburgh; Mrs. Amy Farmer, Patrick Dougherty, Waldo Green, W. Wheeler, John Durrick, Augustus Baer, and Dennis Fryer.

The Constitution, formerly called the Oliver Evans, was built at Pittsburgh only a short time before this fatal explosion. At that period she was one of the finest boats on the river.

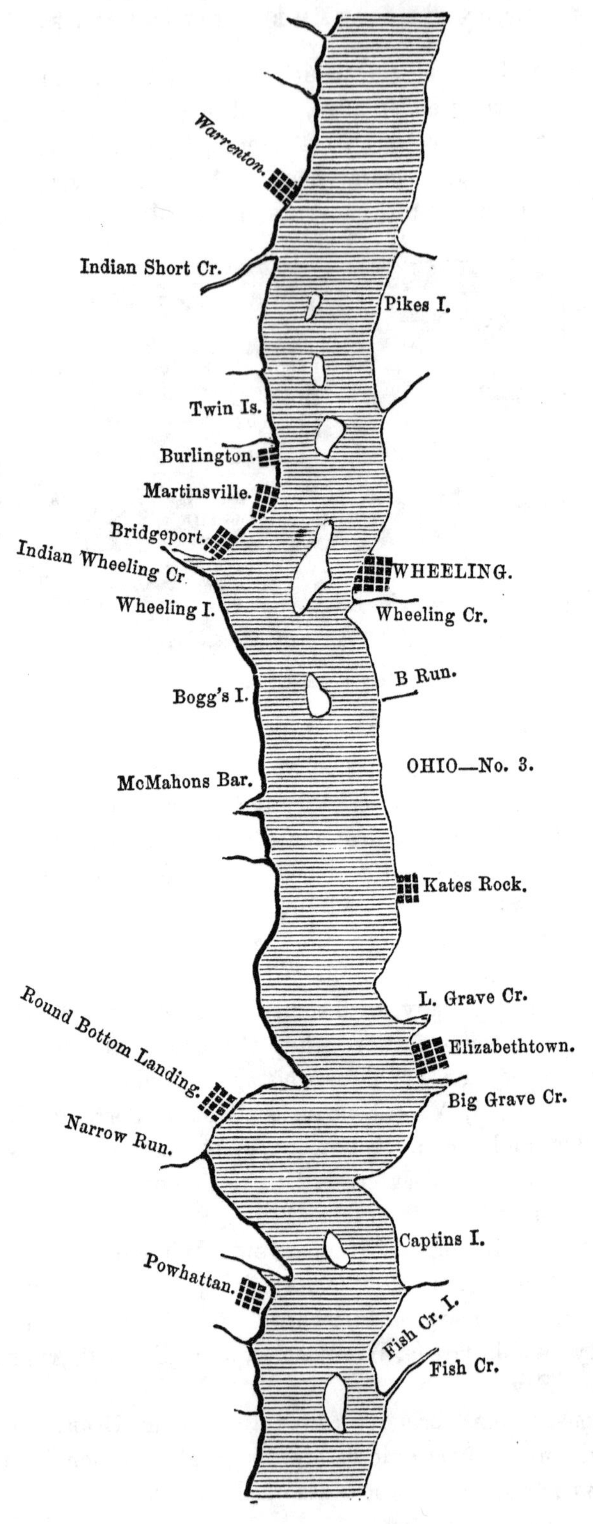
Warrenton.
Indian Short Cr.
Pikes I.
Twin Is.
Burlington.
Martinsville.
Bridgeport.
Indian Wheeling Cr.
WHEELING.
Wheeling I.
Wheeling Cr.
B Run.
Bogg's I.
OHIO—No. 3.
McMahons Bar.
Kates Rock.
L. Grave Cr.
Round Bottom Landing.
Elizabethtown.
Big Grave Cr.
Narrow Run.
Captins I.
Powhattan.
Fish Cr. I.
Fish Cr.

SINKING OF THE STEAMER TENNESSEE.

About ten o'clock, on a dark night, in the midst of a tremendous snow storm, on the 8th of February, 1823, when the steamer Tennessee, under a full press of steam, was ploughing her way up the turbulent Mississippi river, near Natchez, she struck a snag, and immediately commenced filling with water. The Tennessee was crowded with passengers, and the confusion and excitement were great among them all. The deck passengers had retired to bed. Most of those in the cabin were spending a cheerful evening together, in the enjoyment of social intercourse. The shock was great, and called every one instantly to the deck. Some supposed the boat had run into the bank, and would bound off again without injury. But the fatal truth was

SINKING OF THE TENNESSEE—1823.

soon known, and in the confusion many leaped overboard and perished. Capt. Campbell gave orders instantly to stop the leak; but the pilot, who had been down to examine the damage, with difficulty escaped from the hold, in consequence of the water so rapidly rushing in. A hole as large as a common door was torn in the hull, and the truth was soon told—the Tennessee was going down. The shrieks of the women were heart-rending at this awful news. The night was dark, and the wind howling around in its fury made the scene doubly terrible. Every one inquired of his neighbor what was to be done, and every one was anxious to provide for his own safety. The yawl and long boat were lowered, and into it the passengers, nearly two hundred in number, crowded, till it was on the eve of sinking. Those in the boat shoved off, and with one oar could not reach the shore in time to return to assist those left behind. Some, finding there was no chance in the long boat, jumped into the river and swam ashore; others pulled off the cabin doors and floated on them; some got among the fire wood, and were lost by slipping through and being covered by it; some clung to parts of the boat, which floated off with them. Mr. Keiser got upon the carpenter's bench, and Mr. A. Logan, who had fallen into the water and sunk nearly to the bottom, on coming up, fortunately caught hold of the way-plank, which formed a raft, and on which he floated down stream. Mr. Keiser soon came up with him, and leaving the work-bench joined him on his raft. They floated in company about eight miles, when, seeing a light on shore, they called for aid, and were taken up by a young man named Gibson, who conveyed them to the house of Mr. Randolph, where they were kindly treated. One man swam with his hat and cloak on, until he reached the willows, when he deliberately relieved himself from the burthen of those outside garments, leaving them on the tree till next morning, and swimming safely to shore. Another passenger swam out with a small bag in his mouth, containing $3000 in gold, which proved of essential service to him; for on getting hold of a plank, and throwing his arms over it, he found the weight of his specie, which he then carried in his hand, admirably calculated to preserve his equilibrium. One man was sick in his berth, and being told of the danger, observed that he was too weak to save himself from drowning, and appeared reluctant to get up; but on being reminded that his father was on board, and required his assistance, he sprang from his bed, and not only saved his own life, but was instrumental in saving others. A young married lady, when her husband was about recklessly to throw himself into the Mississippi, caught hold of him, and by her presence of mind took off some shutters and made a raft, upon which they both floated down the river, and were picked up by a skiff.

The boat floated down the river a short distance and lodged near some willows, upon which many of the deck passengers clung till daylight, when they were relieved from their perilous situation.

Scarcely any property was saved from the wreck; a few trunks and other light things floated off, and were picked up. Some were pilfered by a mean wretch living in the neighborhood, named Charles Goodwin, others were preserved and afterwards reclaimed by the owners. The survivors speak in the highest praise of Mrs. Blanton, formerly of Kentucky, who, in the absence of her husband, Mr. William Blanton, made every exertion for the comfort of the sufferers. By this disaster there were no less than sixty lives lost; the names of many will never be known. The following is a list as far as could be ascertained:

Cabin Passengers Lost.—M. J. Nouvel, Lexington, Kentucky; M. C. Pool, Baltimore; Mr. Maylin, Philadelphia; Mr. Caruthers, Tennessee; Dr. Young, F. A. Boulton, Andrew Stone, Maryland; Alexander Parkhurst, Mobile; Daniel Ebert, P. Striker, A. Booker, John Roberts, Kentucky; A. Perin, Alabama; W. Ashwood, Pennsylvania; A. Harmer, New York; —— Phillips, Mrs. Jenkins, Arthur Wendell, Massachusetts; Thomas Rodgers, D. Hicks, C. Conley, —— Martin, —— Anshultz, A. Derrin, P. Watson, J. Williams, Andrew Hempstead, Texas; and a lady, name unknown.

Deck Passengers Lost.—George Saunders, Lexington, Kentucky; Samuel Cooper, David Knaw, John Curby, S. Hencely, John Stewart, John Kipler, Mrs. Mausker and child, Mr. Terley, James Bradford, and three negroes, Mrs. Smith, Mrs. Walters, Miss Williams, Mr. and Miss Armstrong, Mobile, and three servants; D. Fox, Mrs. Hooper, —— Andrews, and fifteen passengers, no names reported.

This was one of the early disasters, and was the theme of conversation for months after the fatal calamity. Indeed, people, for a long time after this accident, were almost afraid to go on a steamboat; but it was soon forgotten in the narratives of the more heart-rending disasters that followed after, in rapid succession.

EXPLOSION AND BURNING OF THE STEAMBOAT TECHE ON THE MISSISSIPPI RIVER, MAY 5TH, 1825.

The S. B. Teche left Natchez on the evening of May 4th, 1825, heavily laden with cotton, and carrying about seventy passengers, many of whom came on board at the moment of departure, and were unknown to each other. Her course was down the river, and she proceeded about ten miles, when the night became so excessively dark and hazy that her commander, Captain Campbell, deemed it unsafe to proceed further, and concluded to come to anchor. At two o'clock on the following morning, May 5th, the anchor was weighed, and the steam having previously been raised, the boat had just begun to pursue her voyage, when the passengers, many of whom had been sleeping in their berths, were startled by a shock which seemed sufficient to separate every plank and timber in the vessel, accompanied by a report which sounded like the discharge of a whole broadside of the heaviest artillery.

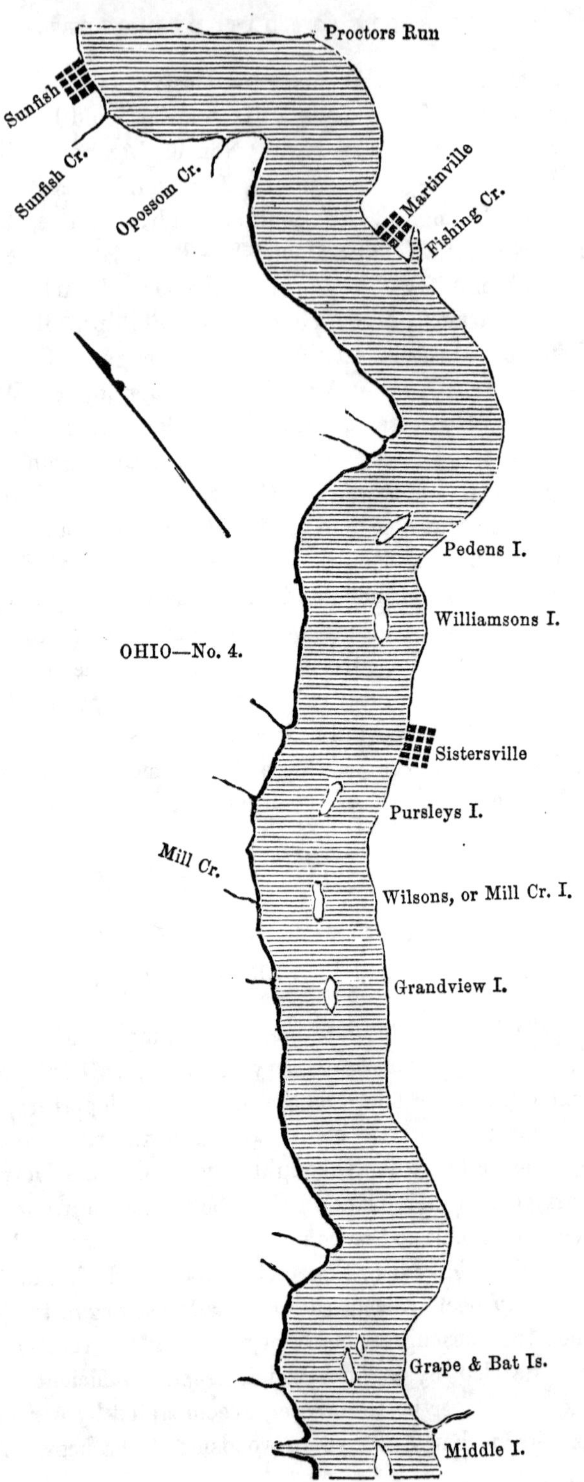
Proctors Run
Sunfish
Sunfish Cr.
Opossom Cr.
Martinville
Fishing Cr.
Pedens I.
Williamsons I.
OHIO—No. 4.
Sistersville
Pursleys I.
Mill Cr.
Wilsons, or Mill Cr. I.
Grandview I.
Grape & Bat Is.
Middle I.

Every light on board was immediately extinguished, either by the escape of steam or the concussion of the air. As the day had not yet dawned, an impenetrable darkness now hung over the scene of the disaster, the extent of which could only be imagined by the affrighted and horrified crowd collected on the deck; but at that moment of appalling danger, and still more dreadful uncertainty, was heard a cry that the boat was on fire! Then followed a scene of indescribable confusion; the passengers, in the very insanity of terror, were rushing hither and thither, through the dense and ominous gloom, and many anticipated their doom in their erring endeavor to avoid it.

EXPLOSION AND BURNING OF THE TECHE.

Mr. Miller, of Kentucky, one of the surviving passengers, who afterwards published in a New Orleans paper a narrative of the events of this fearful night, states that when the alarm of fire was given, he attempted to go towards the bow, from whence the cry proceeded, but before he had advanced ten paces, he was precipitated down the hatchway, (the hatches had been blown off by the explosion,) and after falling, fortunately on his feet, to the bottom of the hold, he found himself knee-deep in scalding water, which had been discharged from the fractured boiler. He would soon have perished in the suffocating vapor which filled the place, had not his cries for assistance been heard by some humane person on deck, who threw him the end of a rope, and thus enabled him to escape from his agonizing and perilous situation.

By this time the flames began to ascend, illuminating the deck with a lurid glare which enabled the passengers to discern the means of escape which offered, though these means were made less available by the terror and confusion which prevailed. The yawl made several trips to the nearest shore, carrying off a load of passengers at each

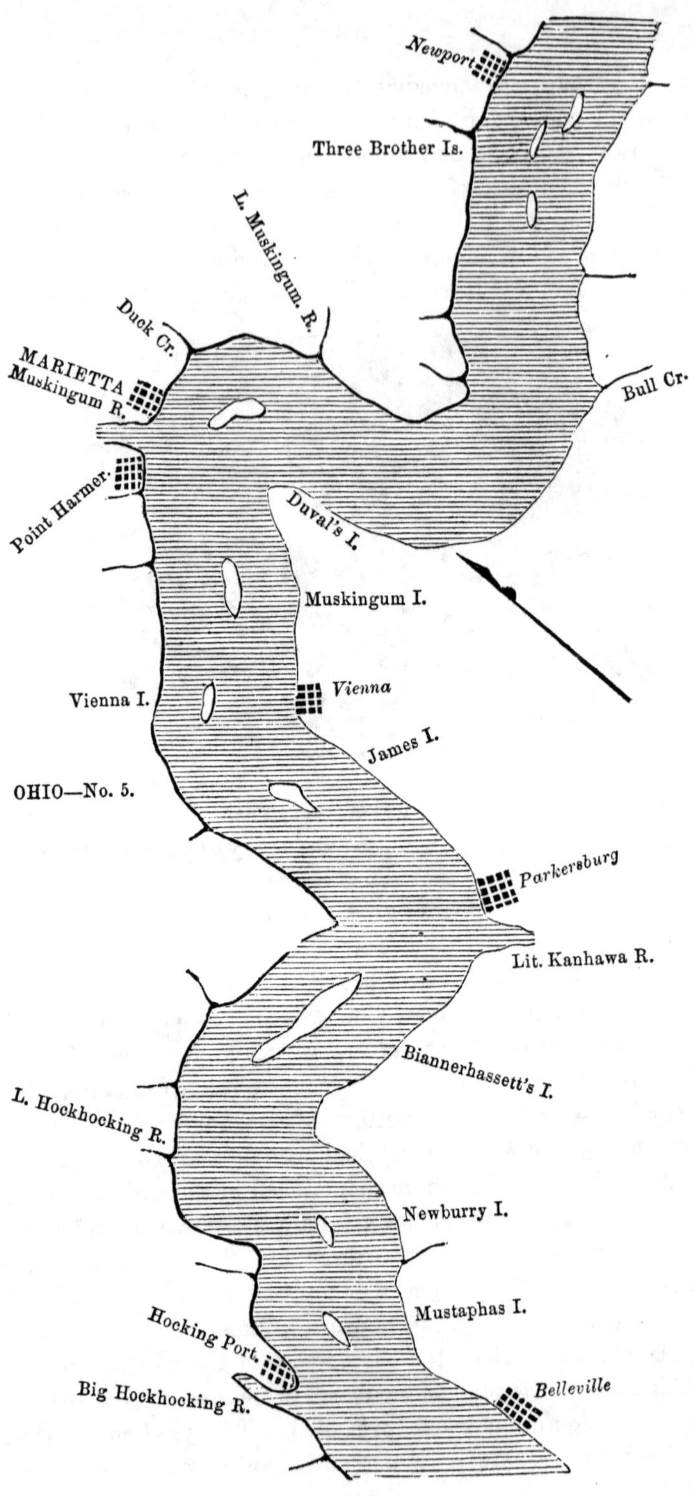
Newport
Three Brother Is.
L. Muskingum. R.
Duck Cr.
MARIETTA
Muskingum R.
Bull Cr.
Point Harmer.
Duval's I.
Muskingum I.
Vienna I.
Vienna
James I.
OHIO—No. 5.
Parkersburg
Lit. Kanhawa R.
Biannerhassett's I.
L. Hockhocking R.
Newburry I.
Mustaphas I.
Hocking Port.
Big Hockhocking R.
Belleville

trip; but as the flames began to extend rapidly over the deck, it was evident that all the people on board could not be saved in this way. In these circumstances, the Captain gave orders that bales of cotton should be thrown overboard, and on these many passengers were kept afloat until the boats finally took them off.

But the last incident of this tragic narrative is one of the most distressing. About three o'clock, A. M., the steamboat Washington, while passing up the river, was hailed by the survivors on board of the burning vessel. The Washington promptly sent a boat to their assistance, and waited to receive them. All who remained on the Teche, (about twelve in number,) embarked in the Washington's boat; and now, assuring themselves of safety, they had reached the side of the steamer, when, by some unlucky accident, the small boat was upset, and every person on board, man, woman, and child, was drowned. It would seem that their inexorable fate had doomed them to destruction.

The number of lives lost by this accident could never be ascertained. Several persons were instantly killed by the explosion, and others were so badly injured, by scalding, or otherwise, that they died soon afterwards. It is thought that not less than twenty or thirty were drowned.

EXPLOSION OF THE STEAMBOAT GRAMPUS, ON THE MISSISSIPPI, AUGUST 12, 1828.

The Grampus was engaged in towing three brigs and a sloop up to New Orleans, and was about nine miles from that city, when the explosion took place. This accident was one of the most remarkable in the whole catalogue of steamboat disasters, on account of the extensive wreck which was made of the machinery. The boat had six boilers, all of which were blown to minute fragments. The same complete destruction was made of the flues, and various other parts of the steam apparatus; and the boat itself was, (as an eye witness reports,) "torn to pieces."

The Captain, (Morrison,) and Mr. Wederstrand, a passenger, were sitting by the wheel at the time of the explosion; both were blown to a part of the forward deck fifty feet distant, where they were afterwards found, very much bruised, among a mass of ruins. The pilot at the wheel was precipitated into the water and drowned. Another pilot, who was walking the deck aft of the wheel, had a leg broken, and received other injuries, which caused his death. The brig in tow on the

Belleville I.
Murrays Ville.
Hocking port.
Shade R.
Buffingtons I.
Ravenswood
B. Sandy Cr.
Graham's Station
Old Town I.
Can's Run
Nyesville
Pomroy's Landing
Letartsville
Georges I.
Sheffield
Leading Cr.
West Columbia.
Letarts Is.
Eight mile I.
Six mile I.
Point Pleasant
Gr. Kanhawa R.
Galliopolis I.
OHIO—No. 6.

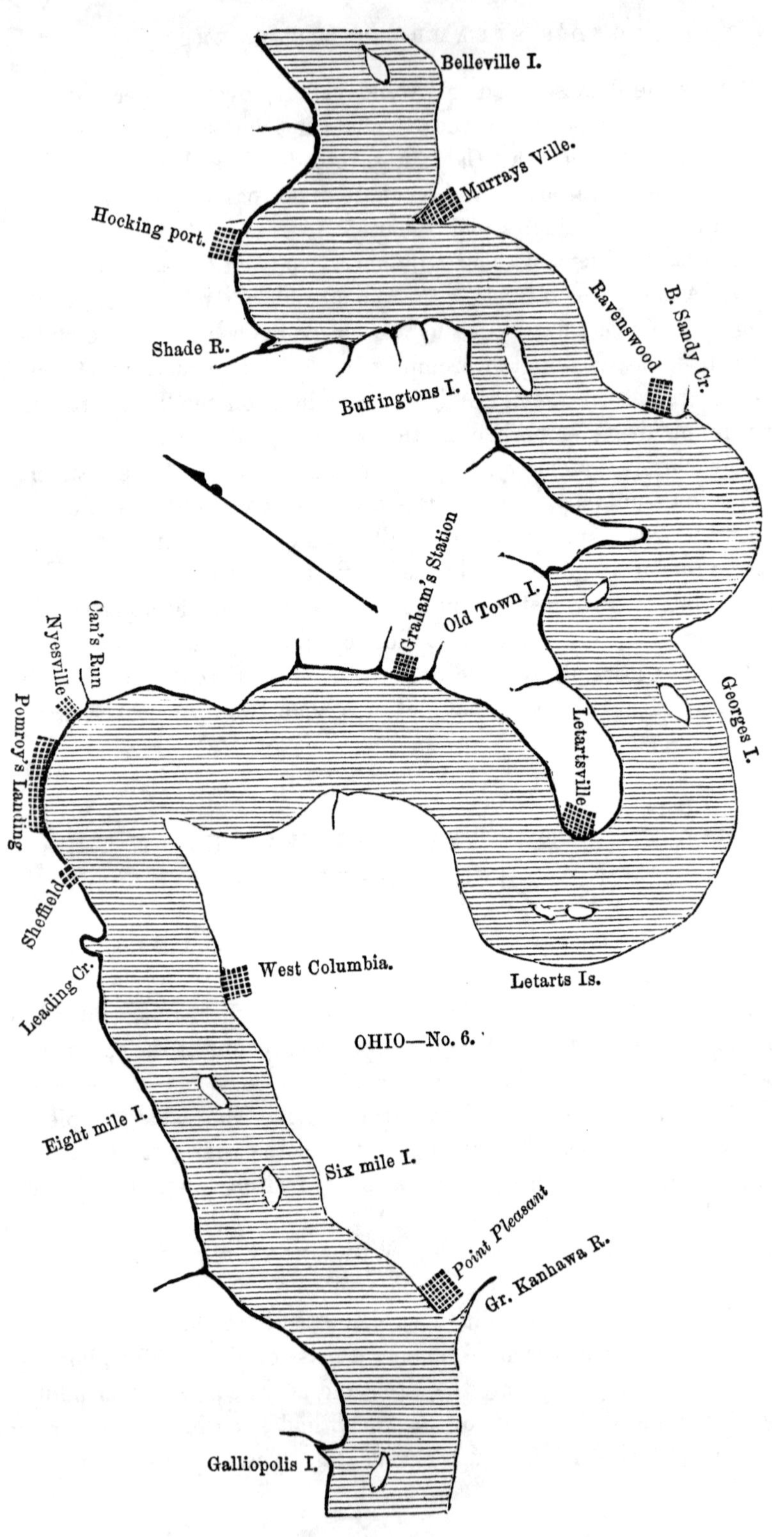

larboard side of the Grampus had both topmasts cut away by the fragments of the machinery, and her standing rigging was much damaged. A piece of the pipe fell across this brig's tiller, carried it away, and slightly injured the man at the helm. The brig on the other side of the steamer had her bottom perforated by a piece of the boiler. The other vessels, being astern, escaped without any damage.

The *cause* of this accident requires particular notice. It appears, from the statement of a passenger, that the chief engineer had "turned in," leaving his assistant in charge of the engine. This assistant, as it is supposed, went to sleep at his post, after partially shutting off the water. The consequence was a deficiency of water in the boilers; and the assistant engineer, on waking, when he discovered that the boilers were nearly exhausted, ignorantly, or imprudently, put the force-pumps in operation to furnish a supply. At this time the iron must have acquired a white heat, and the contact of the water produced such an excess of steam, that the explosion naturally followed.

KILLED, WOUNDED AND MISSING.—John Smith, a fireman, killed. George Brown, a Balize pilot, mortally wounded. One of the crew of the brig Anastasia, (name unknown,) killed. Another seaman, belonging to the same brig, badly wounded. William Taylor and John Harden, much injured. Joseph Dryden, second engineer of the Grampus, missing (so reported, but undoubtedly killed). Thomas Dodd, steersman, missing. Harry, Frank, Layden and George Mooney, all blacks, missing. Charles Craig, badly wounded. Nine were killed on the spot, or died soon afterwards, in consequence of their injuries. Four others were wounded.

EXPLOSION OF THE HELEN McGREGOR, AT MEMPHIS, TENNESSEE, FEBRUARY 24, 1830.

The steamboat Helen McGregor, Capt. Tyson, on her way from New Orleans to Louisville, stopped at Memphis, on Wednesday morning, February 24, 1830. She had been lying at the wharf about thirty minutes, when one or more of her boilers exploded, with the usual destructive and melancholy effects. The loss of life by this accident was, at that time, unprecedented in the records of steam navigation. In the bustle incident to the landing and receiving of passengers, a part of the deck near the boilers was crowded with people, all of whom were either killed instantaneously, or more or less injured. No person in the cabins was hurt. The number of those who perished at the moment

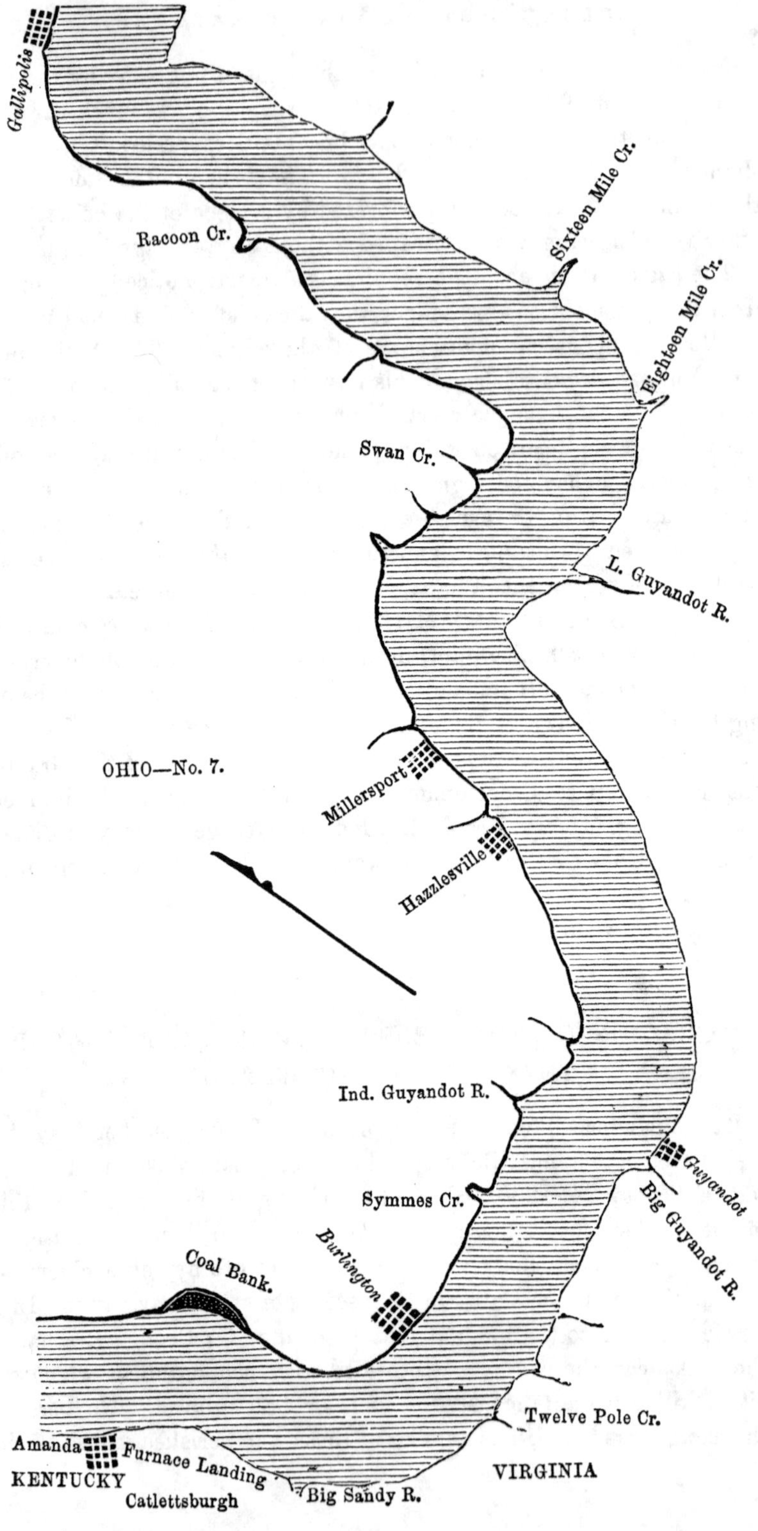
Gallipolis
Racoon Cr.
Sixteen Mile Cr.
Eighteen Mile Cr.
Swan Cr.
L. Guyandot R.
OHIO—No. 7.
Millersport
Hazzlesville
Ind. Guyandot R.
Guyandot
Big Guyandot R.
Symmes Cr.
Burlington
Coal Bank.
Twelve Pole Cr.
Amanda
Furnace Landing
KENTUCKY
Catlettsburgh
Big Sandy R.
VIRGINIA

EXPLOSION OF THE HELEN McGREGOR, 1830.

of the explosion is variously estimated at from thirty to sixty. As many of them were strangers whose homes were far distant, and whose bodies were never recovered from the water, into which they were projected, it is very plain that an accurate account of the number of the victims is not to be expected.

The following report of the killed and wounded is the most complete and reliable that could be obtained:—

KILLED.—Richard Hancock, of Louisville, Kentucky; A. Van Meeter, Hardin County, Tennessee; Mr. Talbot, of Long Beach, Ohio; James Bledso, Kentucky; Mr. Carrol, Cincinnati, Ohio; Edward P. Beadles, Clark County, Indiana; J. Dunn, Tennessee; G. B. Giles, Cincinnati; Ephraim Goble, Brookville, Indiana; John Delaney, colored; William Ewing, Clark County, Indiana; William Stockwell, Salem, Indiana; Solomon Jones, Maysville, Kentucky; J. Reaves, Harrison County, Indiana; Lewis Young, colored; Jack, a colored boy, twelve years old.

BADLY WOUNDED.—George Trey, Tipton County, Tennessee; John Cameron, Clark County, Indiana; Joshua Richardson, Indiana; John Valentine, Massachusetts; Mr. De Haven, Philadelphia; John Leland, a pilot; J. Sugg, Union County, Kentucky; John Felchen, New York; R. Bailey, firm of Bell, Hardin & Co., Tennessee; H. Heldrith, Madison County, Indiana; John Addisson, one of the crew; Thomas Drenard, Wilson County, Tennessee; J. Swan, Orange County, Indiana; J. Tenyck, Shippingsport, Kentucky; William Case, New York.

SLIGHTLY WOUNDED.—Capt. Tyson, commander of the Helen McGregor; —— Turner, engineer; P. O'Daniel, Indiana; T. L. Know-

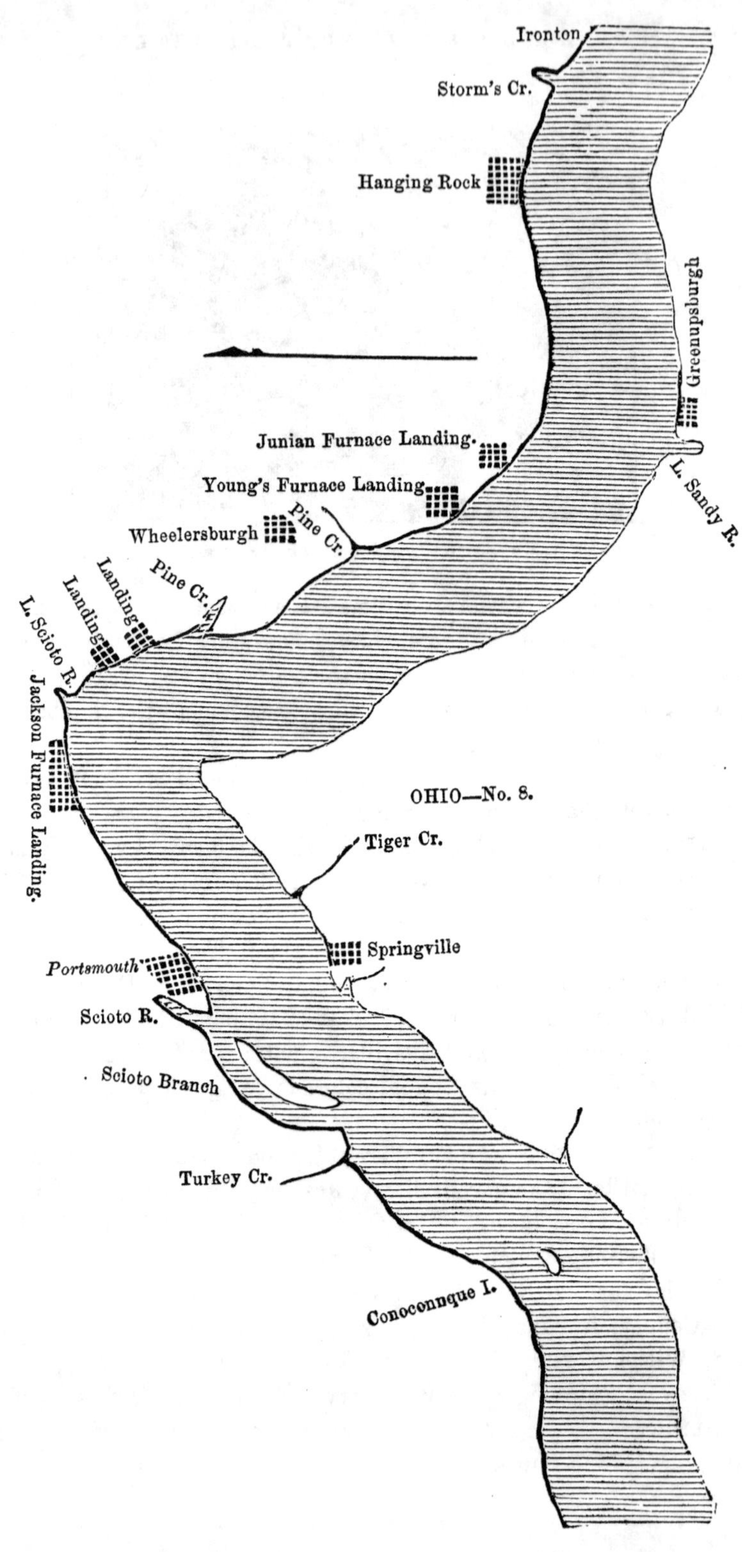

Ironton
Storm's Cr.
Hanging Rock
Greenupsburgh
Junian Furnace Landing.
Young's Furnace Landing
L. Sandy R.
Pine Cr.
Wheelersburgh
Pine Cr.
Landing
Landing
L. Scioto R.
Jackson Furnace Landing.
OHIO—No. 8.
Tiger Cr.
Springville
Portsmouth
Scioto R.
Scioto Branch
Turkey Cr.
Conoconnque I.

land, Ohio; J. Monaco, Tipton County, Tennessee; John Coons, Clark County, Indiana; William Pottorff, Clark County, Indiana; John Dougherty, Overton County, Tennessee; Thomas Bank, Lawrence County, Indiana; Green Williams, colored fireman.

EXPLOSION OF THE STEAMBOAT ROB ROY ON THE MISSISSIPPI, JUNE 9TH, 1836.

The Rob Roy was on her route from New Orleans to Louisville, and was under way, at 8 o'clock P. M, June 9th, 1836, near the town of Columbia, Arkansas, when the fatal catastrophe we are about to record took place. The engine was stopped for the purpose of oiling some part of the machinery; and although this necessary operation did not occupy more than two minutes, the accumulation of steam was sufficient to cause an explosion. As soon as the accident occurred, preparations were made to run the boat ashore, which was happily reached within a few minutes. By this judicious measure many lives were undoubtedly saved. None were lost by drowning, and the only victims and sufferers were those who were killed or wounded at the moment of the explosion. The clerk of the boat, a few days after the accident, furnished the following account of the killed and wounded, which he certified to be correct, adding, that some of those reported among the wounded had since died, and others were not expected to recover.

Killed:—John O'Brian, Michael Bregan, John Cavenaugh, (Irish,) Wm. Lynd, of Cincinnati, P. W. Banton, Madison, Indiana, Jane Vincent, Highland Creek, four men, names unknown, passengers; Levi Jackson, Jeffersonville, J. Shane, Louisville, Felix Davis, Jeffersonville, George Williams, Cincinnati, two colored men, names not mentioned. Total of killed, 17.

Scalded:—Wm. Spear, Pittsburgh, badly, John Gebhard Irishman, do., Henry Snodgrass, Parke county, Indiana, Levi Hamblin, Deboyne, Mr. Hentry, Louisville, W. Southworth, New York, E. Ford, Boston, Richard Fulton, Indiana, Wm. Reagan, Scott county, Missouri, R. A. Braden, Lawrence county, Tennessee, Mrs. Barade and two children of ditto, W. W. Creary, Scott county Missouri, Tilden Hogg, Randolph.

TERRIFIC EXPLOSION OF THE STEAMBOAT BEN FRANKLIN, AT MOBILE, ALABAMA, MARCH 13, 1836.

The steamboat Ben Franklin, on the day of this awful occurrence, was backing out from her wharf at Mobile, in order to make her regular trip to Montgomery. Scarcely had she disengaged herself from the wharf, when the explosion took place, producing a concussion which seemed to shake the whole city to its foundations. The entire population of Mobile, alarmed by the terrific detonation, was drawn to the spot to witness a spectacle which must have harrowed every soul with astonishment and horror. This fine boat, which had on that very morning floated so gallantly on the bosom

EXPLOSION OF THE BEN FRANKLIN, 1836.

of the lake, was now a shattered wreck, while numbers of her passengers and crew were lying on the decks, either motionless and mutilated corpses, or agonized sufferers panting and struggling in the grasp of death. Many others had been hurled overboard at the moment of the explosion, and such were the numbers of drowning people who called for assistance, that the crowd of sympathising spectators were distracted and irresolute, not knowing where or how to begin the work of rescue. Many—how many, it is impossible to say—perished in the turbid waters before any human succor could reach them.

Apart from the loss of life, which at that time was unexampled, the destruction produced by this accident was very extensive. The boiler-deck, the boilers, the chimneys, and other parts of the machinery, besides much of the lading, were blown overboard and scattered into fragments over the wharf and the surface of the river. Mr. Isaac Williams, a passenger, was blown at least one hundred feet high in the air, and his dead body fell into the water, about one hundred and fifty yards from the boat.

The cause of the accident is believed to have been a deficiency of water in the boiler. The boat was injured to that degree that repairs were out of the question, and she was never afterwards brought into service.

The usual uncertainty attends the estimated number of lives lost by this calamity. Many of those who perished, had just entered the boat, and had not registered their names; and, among the mangled corpses, not a few retained scarcely any vestige of the human form, so that the identification of particular persons was impossible. We have, after much research, obtained the following list of the sufferers, which we believe to be the most complete account ever published.

KILLED.—Robert Brinkley, pilot; Isaac Williams, of Wilcox County, Kentucky; James Purnell, William Jones, Jacob Patty, firemen; James Hulson, Isaac Flannegin, deck hands; Mr. Martin, of North Carolina; S. G. Simpson, carpenter; Thomas Cravin, cabin-boy; three colored men, names unknown; two slaves of Mr. S. B. Heade, and one of Mrs. Terry.

BADLY WOUNDED.—Captain H. A. Leade; R. G. Gordon, of Mobile; Colonel R. Singleton, of Baldwin County, Alabama; Capt. Scuddy, James Flommen, Clark County, Indiana; E. H. Dickerson, Montgomery; Mr. Godfrey, Washington; Joseph Thompson, William Jacobson, first and second engineers; Mr. Thompson, of Columbus, Ohio; Miss Norris and slave, of Mobile.

SLIGHTLY WOUNDED.—Samuel Murphy, bar-keeper; Dr. Tunstall, Mount Vernon; Thomas Tony, deck hand; William Hyde, Baldwin County, Alabama; J. A. Wiggins, Claiborne.

The citizens of Mobile, with their customary humanity and generosity, took the wounded in charge, and did every thing in their power to mitigate their sufferings.

Twin Crs.
Rockville
Stouts Run
Vanubury
Quicks Run.
Brush Cr.
Cycamore Cr.
Concord
Manchester Is.
Cabin Cr.
Manchester
Brook's R.
Limestone Cr.
Abberdeen
Maysville
Eagle Cr.
Red-oak Cr.
Ripley
Charleston Landing
Lavana
Straight Cr.
Dover
White-oak Cr.
OHIO—No. 9.

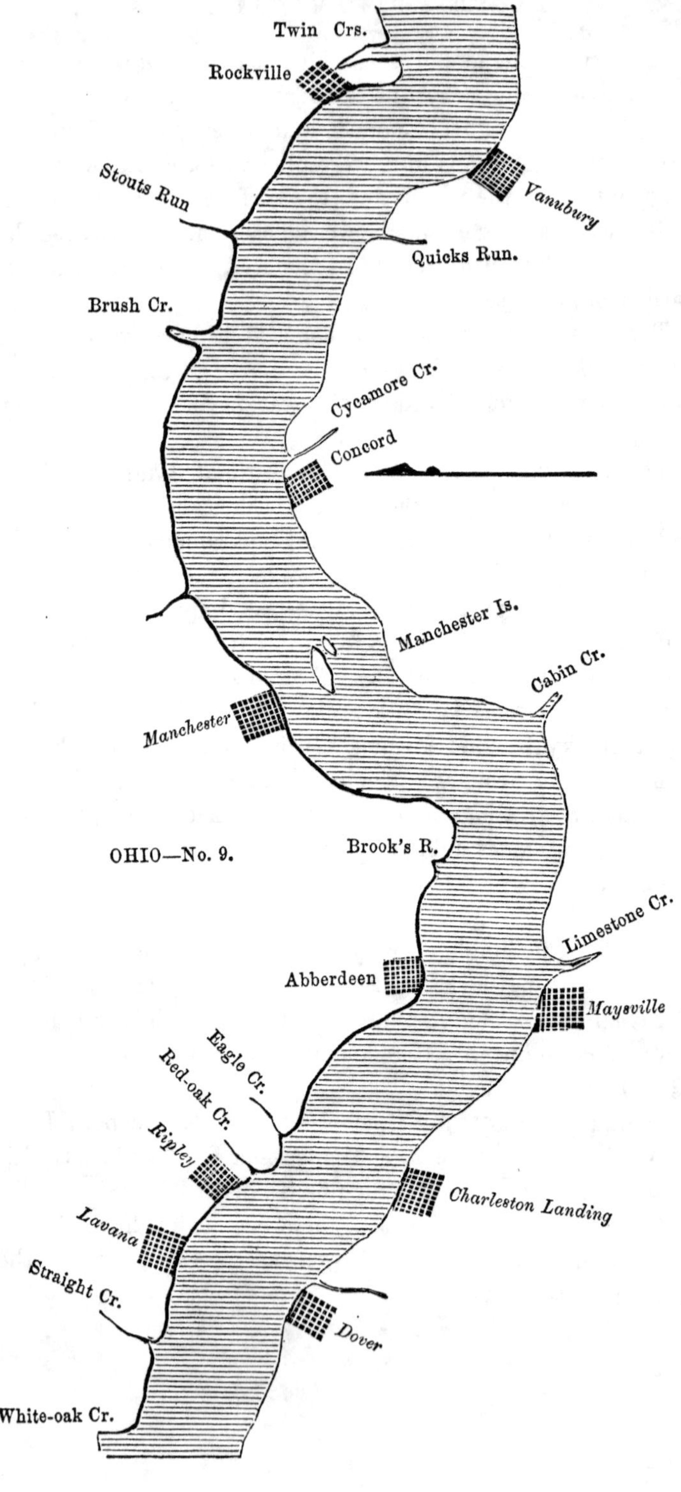

EXPLOSION OF THE DUBUQUE, AUGUST 15, 1837.

This distressing accident, by which sixteen persons were instantly killed, and several others were badly scalded, took place on the Mississippi, while the boat was on her voyage from St. Louis to Galena. The locality of the dreadful event was off Muscatine Bar, eight miles below Bloomington. The Dubuque was running under a moderate pressure of steam at the time, when the flue of the larboard boiler, probably on account of some defect in the material or workmanship, collapsed, throwing a torrent of scalding water over the deck. The pilot immediately steered for the shore and effected a landing.

When the consternation and dismay occasioned by the explosion had in some measure subsided, Captain Smoker, the commander of the Dubuque, and such of his crew as were not disabled by this accident, made their way, with considerable difficulty, through the ruins to the after-part of the boiler-deck, when it was found that the whole of the freight, and every other article which had been there deposited, was cleared off and wafted far away into the water. The unfortunate deck passengers, together with the cooks and several of the crew, were severely scalded, either by the hot water or escaped steam. Many of these wretched people, in their agony, fled to the shore, uttering the most appalling shrieks, and tearing off their clothes, which in some cases brought away the skin, and even the flesh, with them. Humanity shudders at the recollection of the scene. It was several hours before any of them died; nor could medical relief be obtained until a boat, which had been despatched to Bloomington, returned with several physicians who resided at that place. At 10 o'clock, P. M., eight hours after the explosion, the steamboat Adventure, Captain Van Housen, came up with the wreck, and took it in tow as far as Bloomington.

The following is a list of the sufferers as far as ascertained:

Killed:—John Littleton, second engineer; he was badly wounded in the head by a piece of iron, a part of the flue, and survived about three hours; Isaac Deal, of Pittsburgh, fireman; Felix Pope, Kaskaskia; Charles Kelly, deck hand, from Ohio; Noah Owen, Quincy; Jesse Johnson, colored cook, thrown overboard and drowned; Benjamin Muser, another colored cook. The rest of the killed were deck passengers, viz: James C. Carr, St. Clair county, Illinois; George McMurtry, Francis Pleasant, colored, Henry A. Carr, John C. Hamilton, Joseph Brady, and John Boland, of Dubuque; Joseph L. Sams,

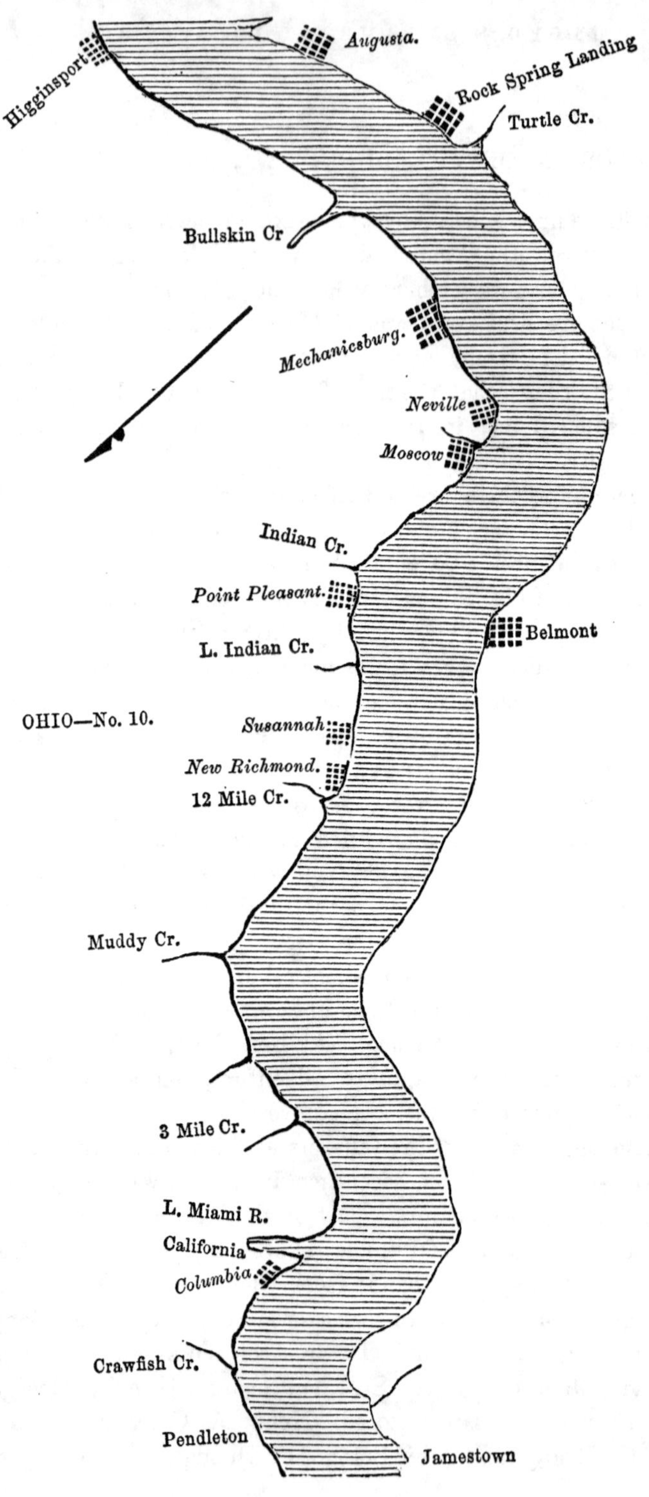
Higginsport
Augusta.
Rock Spring Landing
Turtle Cr.
Bullskin Cr
Mechanicsburg.
Neville
Moscow
Indian Cr.
Point Pleasant.
Belmont
L. Indian Cr.
OHIO—No. 10.
Susannah
New Richmond.
12 Mile Cr.
Muddy Cr.
3 Mile Cr.
L. Miami R.
California
Columbia
Crawfish Cr.
Pendleton
Jamestown

and L. B. Sams, of Clay county, Illinois; Martin Shoughnohoy, St. Louis; George Clix, of Galena; David Francour, Frenchman; wife and child of Michael Shanghnessy.

M. Shanghnessy, the husband and father of the two victims last mentioned, was badly scalded, but survived. Three other deck passengers, young men, names unknown, are supposed to have been thrown overboard and drowned; and it is strongly suspected that others beside these perished in the same manner.

CAPSIZE OF THE HORNET, JUNE 2, 1832.

On the night of Saturday, June 2d, 1832, the steamboat Hornet, Captain Sullivan, while ascending the Ohio river on her way to Kanawha, and when about thirty-three miles above Maysville, Kentucky, encountered a sudden and violent gale blowing from the southwest, and immediately capsized. Exclusive of the persons belonging to the boat, there were forty-two people on board, viz: twelve cabin and thirty deck passengers, nearly half of whom were drowned. The Hornet righted soon after the disaster, and was towed to the nearest port, Concord, by the steamboat Guyandotte, Captain Davis Embree.

Of the twenty persons drowned by this accident, all the names which have been preserved are comprised in the following list:

Thomas Duvall, of Muskingum, Ohio; Messrs. Le Clerc and Perot, two French gentlemen of New Orleans; Mrs. Garrett, of Greenupsburgh, Kentucky; Mr. Blackstone, of Guyandotte; Wm. H. Colbert, of Kingston; and two colored women, slaves belonging to passengers.

Of the boats crew, Captain Sullivan, master; John Johnston, pilot, of Gallipolis; Edward Jones, a sailor, of Cincinnati; a chambermaid and a female cook, both colored.

VIEW OF WHEELING, VA.

SKETCH OF WHEELING.

WHEELING, Virginia, is situated on the east bank of the Ohio river, in Ohio county, and on both sides of the Wheeling creek, ninety-two miles below Pittsburgh, three hundred and sixty-five miles above Cincinnati, three hundred and fifty miles northwest of Richmond, and about six hundred and thirty feet above the level of the sea; lat. 40° 7′ N., long. 80° 42′ W. The site is a narrow, alluvial tract, overlooked by precipitous hills, and extending two miles along the river. Wheeling is a port of entry, and is the most important place on the Ohio river between Pittsburgh and Cincinnati; and in respect to commerce, manufactures and population, the most considerable city of western Virginia, and next to the largest in that State. The hills that rise in the immediate vicinity contain inexhaustible beds of coal, which supply fuel at a small expense to the numerous manufactories of Wheeling. This city has eight iron foundries, seven forges, six manufactories of nails, ten of glassware, five or six of cotton goods, five of paper, three of steam-engines, three of silk goods, and several of wire. Flour, woollen goods, white lead, and many other articles are produced here. Numerous large steamboats are annually built at Wheeling, some of which are equal in speed, comfort and safety to any boats floating on the western waters; about sixty of them are owned here, with an aggregate tonnage of twenty-four thousand. It contains a fine court house, twenty churches, several excellent academies, four banks, the aggregate capital of which is two millions of dollars. Five or six newspapers are published here. The city is supplied with water raised from the river by machinery. The national road crosses the river at Zane's island, opposite the city, by the most stupendous wire suspension bridge in the world, the span of which is of unequalled length, measuring one thousand and ten feet; the height of the towers on either side are one hundred and fifty-three feet above low water mark, and sixty feet above the abutments. The bridge is supported by twelve wire cables, each one thousand three hundred and eighty feet in length, and four inches in diameter. The cost of this immense structure is estimated at two hundred and twenty-five thousand dollars. When this magnificent bridge was first thrown across the Ohio river it created a great deal of excitement among the citizens of Pennsylvania and the Pittsburgh steamboatmen. It was considered an obstruction to navigation, and various lawsuits were immediately instituted against the company to compel the removal of it. The Supreme Court of Pennsylvania decided that it must come down. At this stage of the proceedings Congress took it up, and passed an act making it a post route, which silenced all further clamor. The accompanying daguerrean view of Wheeling and the bridge is the most accurate ever taken. Wheeling became the capital of Ohio county in 1797, and is celebrated as being the site of fort Henry, which was besieged in September, 1777, by a party of nearly five hundred Indians, led on by the notorious Simon Girty. It was manfully defended by only forty-two men, of whom twenty-three were killed; and the Indians, after fighting all day, were compelled to retire, with a loss of one hundred. In 1802 it contained about seventy-five houses. Population in 1820, one thousand six hundred; in 1830, six thousand; in 1840, eight thousand; in 1850, thirteen thousand; and in 1856, twenty thousand.

EXPLOSION OF THE ENTERPRISE, NEAR CHARLESTON, S.C., SEPT. 10, 1816.

In the midst of a furious thunder-storm, accompanied by a heavy fall of rain, the steamboat Enterprise, Capt. Howard, was making her way up the river, at nine o'clock, P. M., (having but a few minutes before stopped to land some passengers on Sullivan's island,) when the boiler exploded, killing eight persons instantly, and wounding five or six others, with various degrees of severity. Fortunately, a majority of the passengers had crowded into the cabin to avoid the rain; this circumstance, no doubt, was the means of saving many persons from a horrible death; a fate to which nearly all who remained on deck were subjected. The noise of the explosion was so very slight, as to be scarcely noticed by the people collected in the cabin; and they were first made aware of the accident by hearing the hissing sound of the hot water which escaped from the boiler, and the shrieks of the persons on deck who had been scalded or otherwise burnt.

There were about seventy passengers on board the Enterprise, and providentially no women or children. Several of the persons whose deaths are reported below, were killed by pieces of the boiler and flue, some of which were blown to a great distance. Others were scalded to death, or badly burned by the ignited fuel from the furnace, which was scattered in every direction, knocking some of the people down, and overwhelming them, as it were, in a whirlpool of fire. The night was made hideous by the cries and groans of the sufferers, which rose above the din of the warring elements.

At the time of the accident, the steamer was fortunately not more than one hundred yards from the Island, from whence boats were immediately despatched to the scene of destruction, to afford that assistance which the situation of the passengers and crew required. All the survivors, including the wounded, were conveyed to the Island, where they were provided with such accommodations as their condition demanded and circumstances would admit of.

Some difference of opinion existed with respect to the cause of this accident. Captain Howard, master of the boat, and some of the passengers, held the opinion that the flue was struck by lightning, which being conducted by the metallic tube down to the boiler, shivered the latter to fragments. In opposition to this opinion, it is alleged that salt water was used for the purpose of raising steam, and as the boiler was composed of cast iron and not of copper, an explosion, according to the theory of skilful engineers, was inevitable.

As stated above, eight persons lost their lives by this accident. Their names, with one exception, Mr. Robbs, were never published. Three of those killed were colored men. Four of the crew, not included in the above statement, were so severely burned that their lives were despaired of, and it is probable that they died soon after.

COLLISION OF THE POLANDER AND HORNET, APRIL 19, 1832.

The Polander, Captain Menaugh, had just left the wharf at Cincinnati, about eight o'clock, P. M., the night being dark and foggy, when she encountered the Hornet, which was coming into port. Both vessels were considerably injured, and the Captain of the Hornet was crushed to death. One of the crew of the same vessel was severely wounded. No further particulars have been published.

EXPLOSION AND BURNING OF THE LIONESS, ON RED RIVER, MAY 19, 1833.

The destruction of the Lioness was caused by the explosion of several barrels of gunpowder, which were stowed, among other freight, in the hold. The accident, therefore, cannot be attributed to any defect in the steam apparatus, or to any mismanagement thereof. The catastrophe took place at an early hour, on a calm and beautiful Sabbath morning in spring. Many of the passengers had not left their berths. Among those that had embarked in the Lioness at New Orleans, were the Hon. Josiah S. Johnston, of the United States Senate, and several other distinguished citizens of Louisiana. The boat was commanded by Capt. William L. Cockerell; her place of destination was Nachitoches, on Red river. She had accomplished a considerable part of the voyage, and reached the north of a small stream called *Ragolet Bon Dieu*, when, on the morning referred to above, the mate and several of the crew were arranging some part of the cargo in the hold; and as the place was dark, they found it necessary to use a lighted candle. It is conjectured that a spark from the candle, in some way, found access to one of the kegs of powder; but as every person who had been at work in the hold was killed by the explosion, the mode in which the powder became ignited could never be ascertained. It is reported that

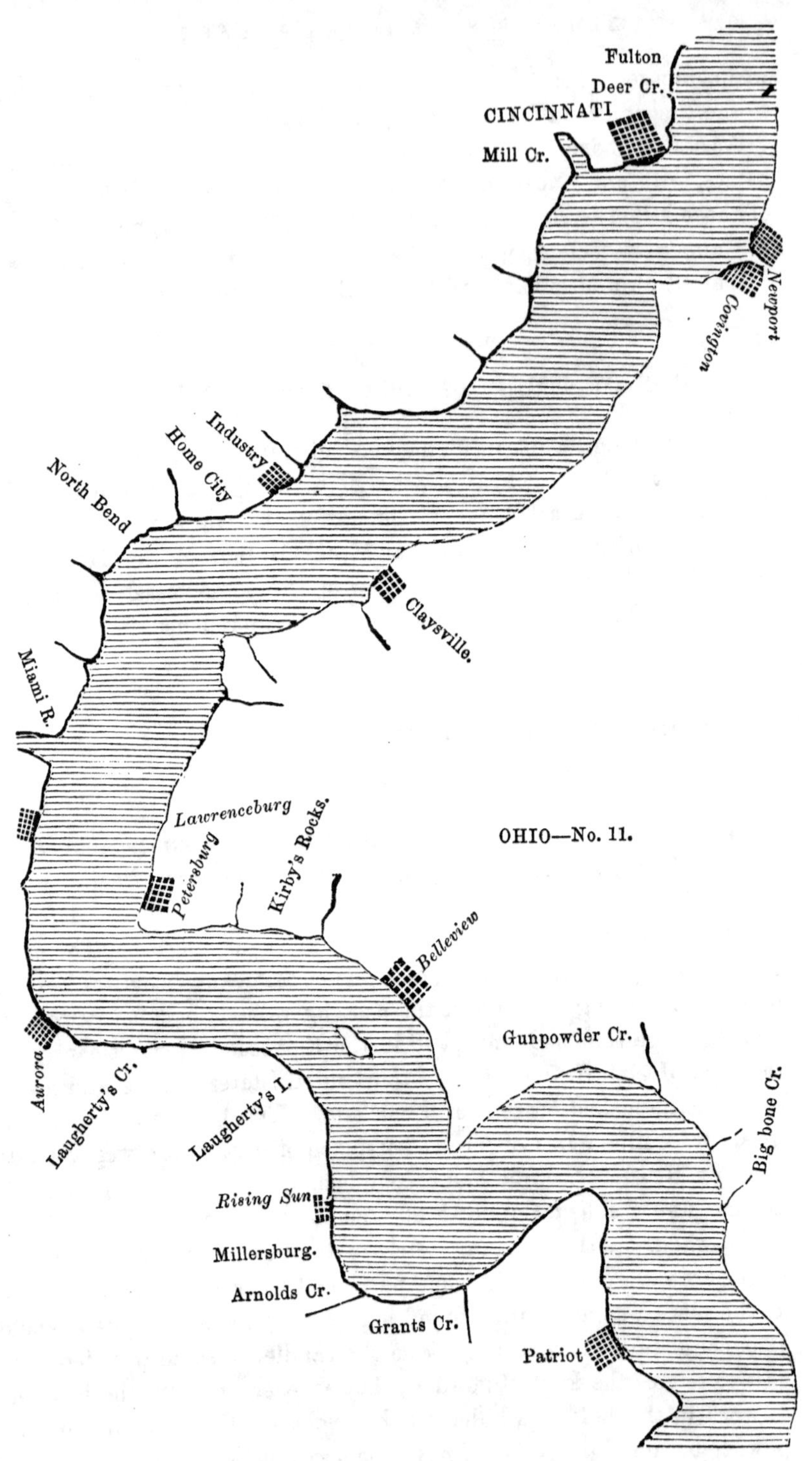
Fulton
Deer Cr.
CINCINNATI
Mill Cr.
Newport
Covington
Industry
Home City
North Bend
Claysville.
Miami R.
Lawrenceburg
Kirby's Rocks.
Petersburg
OHIO—No. 11.
Belleview
Aurora
Laugherty's Cr.
Laugherty's I.
Gunpowder Cr.
Big bone Cr.
Rising Sun
Millersburg.
Arnolds Cr.
Grants Cr.
Patriot

EXPLOSION AND BURNING OF THE LIONESS.

some articles of a very combustible nature, such as crates containing a quantity of dry straw and several casks of oil, were stowed in dangerous proximity to the powder. It was stated by some of the passengers that three distinct explosions were heard. The fore-cabin, the boiler deck, and the hold immediately under them, were literally torn to pieces, and the fragments were scatteted over the surrounding waters to a surprising distance. A part of the hurricane deck and a portion of the lady's cabin were likewise detached; and this proved to be a favourable circumstance, as the hull almost immediately sunk, and, in all likelihood, every female on board, and many other persons, would have been drowned, had they not been sustained on the detached pieces of the wreck just spoken of. As it was, all the women were saved; and the loss of life, though terrible enough indeed, was less than might have been expected, in view of all the circumstances of the disaster. The hull of the vessel was on fire almost from stem to stern, at the time she went down. All of the crew and passengers who survived, saved themselves by swimming, or were floated to the shore on fragments of the wreck. The names of the sufferers, as far as they could be ascertained, are given below.

Drowned, or Killed by the Explosion.—Hon. Josiah S. Johnston, Member of Congress, of Louisiana; B. Riggs, Esq., Michael Boyce, Esq., of Alexandria, Louisiana; Michael Clifford, New Orleans; H. Hertz and Thomas Irwin, a deck passenger, of Texas; John Coley, mate of the Lioness, Louisville; John Clarke, Englishman, steward of the same; Samuel Landis, William Kant, James Folsome, sailors; another sailor, name unknown; Mary Anderson, chambermaid; Alexander, colored cook; and a colored servant belonging to one of the passengers.

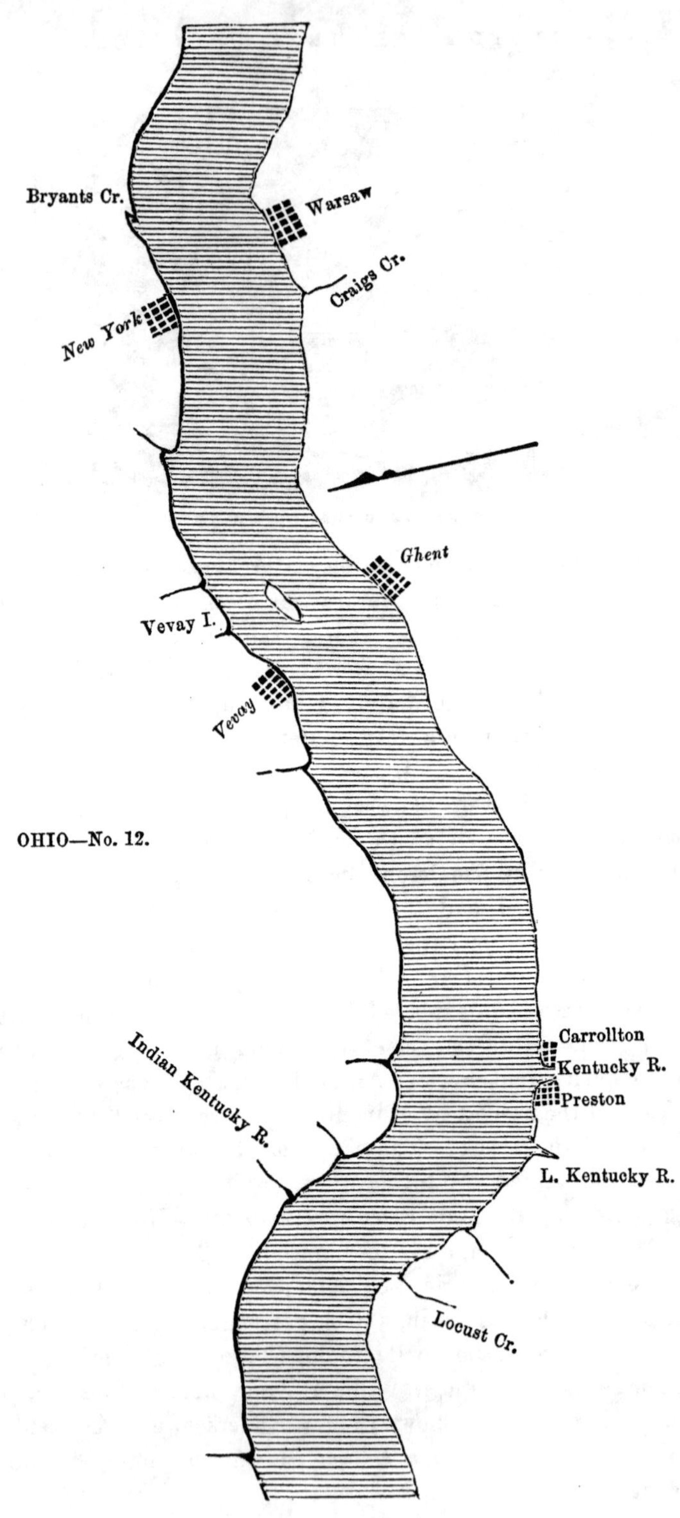
Bryants Cr.
Warsaw
Craigs Cr.
New York
Ghent
Vevay I.
Vevay
OHIO—No. 12.
Indian Kentucky R.
Carrollton
Kentucky R.
Preston
L. Kentucky R.
Locust Cr.

WOUNDED.—Josiah Johnston, Jr., son of the Hon. J. S. Johnston, mentioned in the list of killed; Hon. Edward D. White, of Louisiana; Henry Boyce, Esq., Mr. Dunbar (badly hurt), of Alexandria, Louisiana; J. H. Graham, New Orleans; Michael Colgen, J. V. Bossier, M. Rupen, of Natchitoches; Isaac Wright, Pilot; John Roberts, engineer; John Rogers, sailor; and two firemen, names unknown.

EXPLOSION OF THE BLACK HAWK, DECEMBER 27, 1837.

This awful calamity, which hurried more than fifty human beings into eternity, occurred on a cold wintry night, while the Black Hawk was about to ascend the Red river, on her passage from Natchez to Natchitoches. The boat had a full load of passengers and freight, including ninety thousand dollars in specie belonging to the United States government. She had just reached the mouth of Red river, when the boiler exploded, blowing off all the upper works forward of the wheels. The pilot and engineer were instantly killed.

The number of passengers on board is stated to have been about one hundred, nearly half of whom were women and children. No estimate of the number killed was ever published, but it appears from the best accounts we have that a *majority* of the passengers and crew perished. A large proportion of the passengers on western steamboats are persons from distant parts of the country, or emigrants, perhaps, from the old world, whose journeyings are unknown to their friends, and whose fate often excites no inquiry. When such persons are the victims of a steamboat calamity, their names, and frequently their numbers, are beyond all powers of research. So it appears to have been in the case now under consideration. Instead of a list of the slain, we are furnished only with a catalogue of the *survivors*, and these, alas, appear to have been merely a forlorn remnant. The only cabin passenger whose name is mentioned in the list of killed furnished by the clerk, was Mr. Delisle, of Natchez. Among the deck passengers, fifteen were known to be lost, three others died soon after the explosion, one was observed to sink while attempting to swim ashore, and twelve more were scalded severely, and fifteen slightly. A subsequent account added to the above list of killed Mrs. Delancey and her three children, of Boston; Dr. Van Bantz, drowned, and Wm. Tolling, who was mortally wounded and died within a few hours. The latest and most authentic account stated that not less than fifty persons must have perished by

Madison
Hanover Landing
Milton
N. London
Bethlehem
Westport
18 Mile Cr.
18 Mile I.
Charleston Landing
Grass-flats
12 Mile I.
Utica
Harrods Cr.

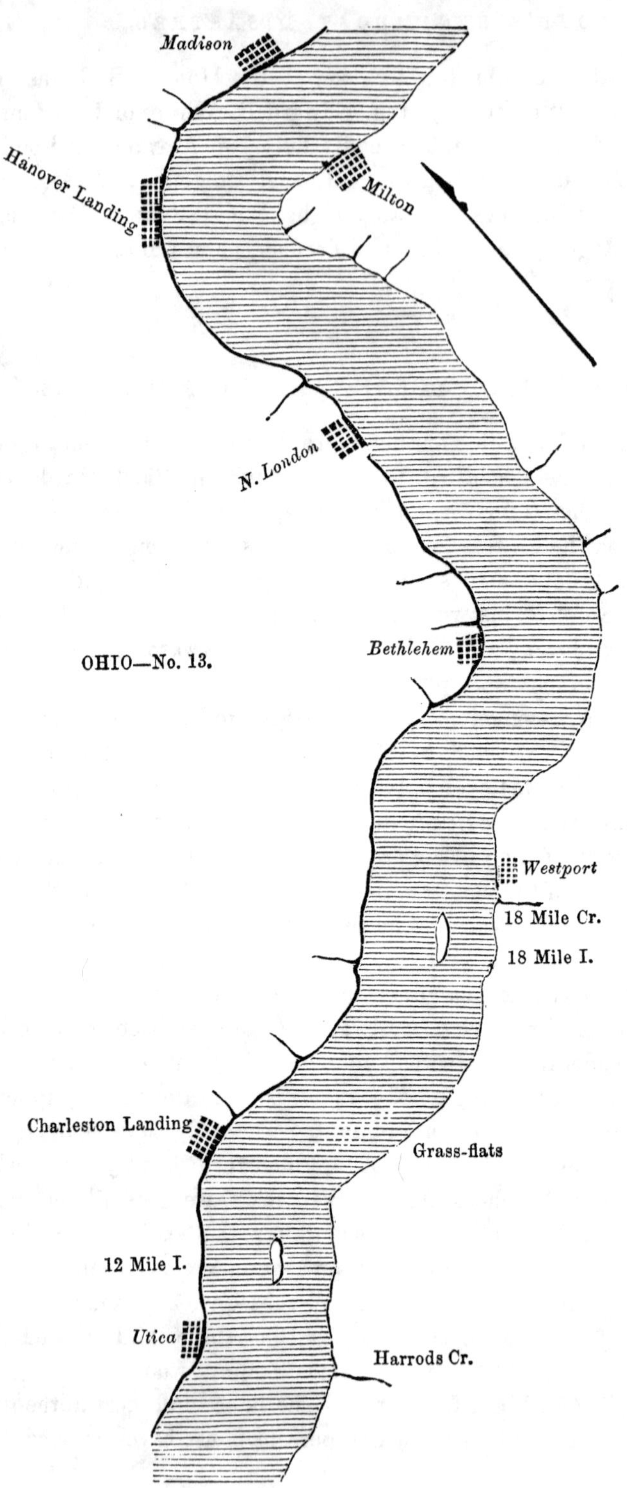

OHIO—No. 13.

the explosion of the Black Hawk. The crew of the boat suffered to a considerable extent. The pilot was blown overboard and lost. Henry Sligh, colored engineer, was killed. George Johnson, another engineer, was dangerously wounded. Felix Ray, barkeeper, was very badly scalded. Four firemen were killed, and one was wounded. Two deck hands were killed. The cook, steward, and cabin boy were all dangerously wounded. Two slaves belonging to Mr. Duffield were drowned.

After the explosion, the wreck, being all in flames, floated fifteen miles down the stream, and then sunk. Some of the passengers were taken off the burning wreck by a flat-boat. It is mentioned that the females on board of the Black Hawk rendered essential service by baling and assisting to extinguish the flames. A part of the cargo and seventy-five thousand dollars of the specie were saved. Several valuable horses, which had been shipped at Natchez, were drowned.

EXPLOSION OF THE MOSELLE, NEAR CINCINNATI, OHIO, APRIL 25, 1838.

We are now about to relate the particulars of an event which seemed for a time to shroud the whole country in mourning; an event which is still believed to be almost without a parallel in the annals of steamboat calamities. The Moselle was regarded as the very paragon of western steamboats; she was perfect in form and construction, elegant and superb in all her equipments, and enjoyed a reputation for speed which admitted of no rivalship. Her commander and proprietor, Capt. Perrin, was a young gentleman of great ambition and enterprise, who prided himself, above all things, in that celebrity which his boat had acquired, and who resolved to maintain, at all hazards, the character of the Moselle as "the swiftest steamboat in America." This character she unquestionably deserved; for her "quick trips" were without competition at that time, and are rarely equalled at the present day. To give two examples:—her first voyage from Portsmouth to Cincinnati, a distance of one hundred and ten miles, was made in seven hours and fifty-five minutes; and her *last* trip, from St. Louis to Cincinnati, seven hundred and fifty-miles, was performed in two days and sixteen hours; the quickest trip, by several hours, that had ever been made between the two places.

On the afternoon of April 25, 1838, between four and five o'clock, the Moselle left the landing at Cincinnati, bound for St. Louis, with an unusually large number of passengers, supposed to be not less than two hundred and eighty, or, according to some accounts, three hundred. It was a pleasant afternoon, and all on board probably anticipated a delightful voyage. Passengers continued to crowd in up to the moment of departure, for the superior accommodations of this steamer, and her renown as the finest and swiftest boat on the river, were great attractions for the travelling public, with whom *safety* is too often but a secondary consideration. The Moselle proceeded about a mile up the river to take on some German emigrants. At this time, it was observed by an experienced engineer on board that the steam had been raised to an unusual height; and when the boat stopped for the purpose just mentioned, it was reported that one man, who was apprehensive of danger, went ashore, after protesting against the injudicious management of the steam apparatus. When the object for which the Moselle had landed was accomplished, the bow of the boat was shoved

EXPLOSION OF THE MOSELLE.

from the shore, and at that instant the explosion took place. The whole of the vessel forward of the wheels was blown to splinters; every timber, (as an eye witness declares,) "appeared to be twisted, as trees sometimes are when struck by lightning." As soon as the accident occurred, the boat floated down the stream for about one hundred yards, where she sunk, leaving the upper part of the cabin out of the water, and the baggage, together with many struggling human beings, floating on the surface of the river.

It was remarked that the force of the explosion was unprecedented in the history of steam; its effect was like that of a mine of gunpowder. All the boilers, four in number, burst simultaneously; the deck was blown into the air, and the human beings who crowded it were doomed to instant destruction. Fragments of the boiler and of human bodies were thrown both to the Kentucky and Ohio shores, although the distance to the former was a quarter of a mile. Captain Perrin, master of the Moselle, at the time of the accident was standing on the deck, above the boiler, in conversation with another person. He was thrown to a considerable height on the steep embankment of the river and killed, while his companion was merely prostrated on the deck, and escaped without injury. Another person was blown to the distance of a hundred yards, with such force, according to the report of a reliable witness, that his head and a part of his body penetrated the roof of a house. Some of the passengers who were in the after part of the boat, and who were uninjured by the explosion, jumped overboard. An eye-witness says that he saw sixty or seventy in the water at one time, of whom not a dozen reached the shore.

It happened, unfortunately, that the larger number of the passengers were collected on the upper deck, to which the balmy air and delicious weather seemed to invite them in order to expose them to more certain destruction. It was understood, too, that the captain of this ill-fated steamer had expressed his determination to outstrip an opposition boat which had just started; the people on shore were cheering the Moselle in anticipation of her success in the race, and the passengers and crew on the upper deck responded to these acclamations, which were soon changed to sounds of mourning and distress.

Intelligence of the awful calamity spread rapidly through the city; thousands rushed to the spot, and the most benevolent aid was promptly extended to the sufferers, or, as we should rather say, to such as were within the reach of human assistance, for the majority had perished. A gentleman who was among those who hastened to the wreck, declares that he witnessed a scene so sad and distressing that no language can depict it with fidelity. On the shore lay twenty or thirty mangled and still bleeding corpses; while many persons were engaged in dragging others of the dead or wounded from the wreck or the water. But, says the same witness, the survivors presented the most touching objects of distress, as their mental anguish seemed more insupportable than the most intense bodily suffering. Death had torn asunder the most tender ties; but the rupture had been so sudden and violent that none knew certainly who had been taken or who had been spared. Fathers were distractedly inquiring for children, children for parents, husbands and wives for each other. One man had saved a son, but lost a wife and five children. A father, partially demented by grief, lay with a wounded child on one side, his dead daughter on the other, and his expiring wife at his feet. One gentleman sought his wife and children, who were as eagerly seeking him in the same crowd. They met, and were re-united!

A female deck passenger who had been saved, seemed inconsolable for the loss of her relatives. Her constant exclamations were, "Oh, my father! my mother! my sisters!" A little boy, about five years old, whose head was much bruised, appeared to be regardless of his wounds, and cried continually for a lost father; while another lad, a little older, was weeping for his whole family.

One venerable looking man wept for the loss of a wife and five children. Another was bereft of his whole family, consisting of nine persons. A touching display of maternal affection was evinced by a lady, who, on being brought to the shore, clasped her hands and exclaimed, "Thank God, I am safe!" but instantly recollecting herself, she ejaculated in a voice of piercing agony, "Where is my child?" The infant, which had also been saved, was brought to her, and she fainted at the sight of it.

Many of the passengers who entered the boat at Cincinnati had not registered their names; but the lowest estimated number of persons on board was two hundred and eighty; of these, eighty-one were known to be killed, fifty-five were missing, and thirteen badly wounded. It remains for us to give the names of the sufferers, as far as they could be ascertained; but this list, although we have searched every record of the accident, for reasons which have already been explained is still far from complete.

KILLED.—Elijah North, of Alton, Illinois; Miss Mary Parker, (drowned,) and B. Furmon, merchant, Middletown, Ohio; Job Jones, of Loudon County, Virginia; B. Mitchell, barkeeper, of Cincinnati; Capt. Perrin, master of the Moselle; J. Chapman, second clerk; T. C. Powell, of Louisville, Kentucky; H. B. Casey, of Cincinnati; James Barnet, of Missouri; Calvin R. Stone, of Shrewsbury, Massachusetts; James Douglass, of Fort Madison, Wisconsin; J. Williams, colored; Henry Stokes, second steward; Holly Dillon, fireman; J. Madder, first engineer; Robert Watt, deck hand; E. Dunn, chambermaid; James B. McFarland, Knox County, Ohio; Miss Dunham; J. M. Watkins, of Virginia; M. Thomas, first mate; A. Burns, of Philadelphia, Pennsylvania; Halsey Williams, second engineer; a child of P. Troutman; G. Kramer's wife and five children; J. Fleming, pilot, (body blown to the opposite side of the river,) and J. Dillon. Many whose names are inserted under the head of "missing" may properly be added to this list. A large number of those who perished were Irish and German emigrants, whose names are unknown.

Badly Wounded.—William H. Inskeep, St. Clairsville, Ohio; Mr. Sherwood, of Cincinnati; Benjamin Bowman, first clerk; James Tyrrell, deck hand; —— De Jaune, fireman; Stephen Bailey, carpenter; Isaac Van Hook; a brother of Capt. Perrin; D. Higbee, of Cayuga County, New York; Edward Sexton; Mr. Teed, of Worcester, Massachusetts; —— Franklin, second cook; James Fry, third cook.

Missing.—Lieut. Col. Fowl, U. S. A; two children of George Kramer; Wm. Parker's wife and two children, Dr. H. Huey, U. S. A.; Joseph Swift, Buffalo, N. Y.; Joseph Fotler, Filbain Fotler Grechan Fotler, and Jacob Fotler, of Boston, Mass.; John Beaver, Joseph Beaver, Eva Beaver, Mary Beaver, Jacob Beaver and several children of Joseph and Eva Beaver; a child of Peter Trautman, aged two and a half years; Thomas Watt, a deck hand; Michael Kennedy's wife and two children; D. Higbee's wife and two children; E. Raymond, wife and child, of Baltimore, Md.; John Endig and John Leim, and the wife and child of each; John Tyree, St. Louis; Payton Bird, fireman; John Anderson; Mr. Weber and three children; J. Weaver, St. Louis; Wilson Burrows, deck hand; Mr. Fox, first clerk; J. Duncan, wife and two children; M. Manning and J. Lander, from Ireland; Wm. Dougherty, G. Weaver, D. Brackwell.

On the day after the accident a public meeting was called at Cincinnati, at which the Mayor presided, when the facts of this melancholy occurrence were discussed, and among other resolutions passed was one deprecating "the great and increasing carelessness in the navigation of steam vessels," and urging this subject upon the consideration of Congress. No one denied that this sad event, which caused so much consternation, suffering, and sorrow, was the result of a reckless and criminal inattention to their duty on the part of those who had the management of the Moselle, nor was there any attempt to palliate their conduct.

The Moselle was built at Cincinnati, and she reflected great credit on the mechanical genius of that city, as she was truly a superior boat, and, under more favorable auspices, might have been the pride of the waters for many years. She was quite a new boat, having been begun on the 1st of December, 1838, and finished on the 31st of March, less than one month before the time of her destruction.

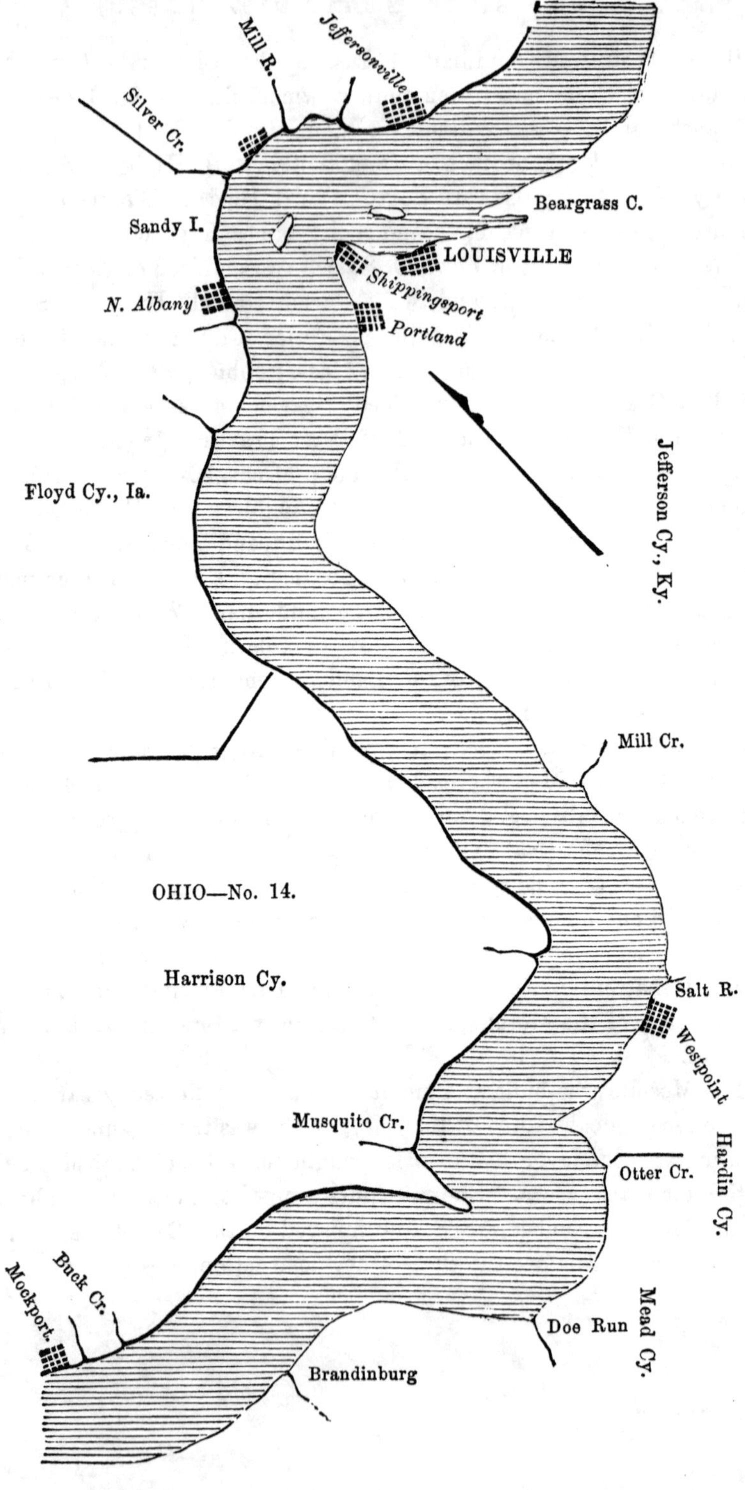

Silver Cr.
Mill R.
Jeffersonville
Beargrass C.
Sandy I.
LOUISVILLE
Shippingsport
N. Albany
Portland
Floyd Cy., Ia.
Jefferson Cy., Ky.
Mill Cr.
OHIO—No. 14.
Harrison Cy.
Salt R.
Westpoint
Musquito Cr.
Hardin Cy.
Otter Cr.
Mockport.
Buck Cr.
Mead Cy.
Doe Run
Brandinburg

EXPLOSION OF THE CHARITON, JULY 28, 1837.

Soon after nightfall, the Chariton put out from the wharf at St. Louis, and when she had run about fifty yards up the river, one of her boilers exploded, by which accident nine persons on board were badly hurt; but, happily, no lives were lost. A gentleman, who was a resident of St. Louis at that time, states that when he heard the noise of the explosion, he hastened down to the wharf, when the first object which attracted his attention was a colored man, who had just been brought to the shore in a boat. He had been taken out of the river, into which he and several other persons had been thrown at the time of the accident. He was badly scalded, and also much cut and bruised, and bled profusely. Soon another boat arrived, with two white men in a similar condition, who had also been rescued from the water. The appearance of one of these was especially frightful. Every visible part of his body, (to use the language of the narrator,) "was scorched and burned to a crisp; his eyes were put out, and his head was literally roasted!" Though it was stated that no lives were lost by the accident, it is scarcely possible that this man, so dreadfully injured, could have long survived. On the boiler-deck of the Chariton, two other wounded men were extended; one of them, the chief engineer, had been completely overwhelmed by the torrent of scalding water which the boiler had disgorged. He continually uttered the most affecting entreaties to the bystanders "to kill him at once, and put him out of his misery!" The usual applications of oil, &c., seemed to afford no relief.

The person who gives this account seems to ascribe the accident to some neglect or mismanagement; but the grounds on which he makes this accusation are not specified.

BURNING OF THE BEN SHERROD, MAY 8, 1837.

On the 8th of May, 1837, the large Louisville and New Orleans packet, the Ben Sherrod, caught fire on her upward trip, while she was engaged in an exciting race with the steamer Prairie. It was one o'clock at night, and the boat was about fourteen miles above Fort Adams, ploughing her way up the Mississippi with great velocity. The Prairie was just ahead of her, in sight, and the crew of the Ben Sherrod were determined, if possible, to go by her. The firemen were

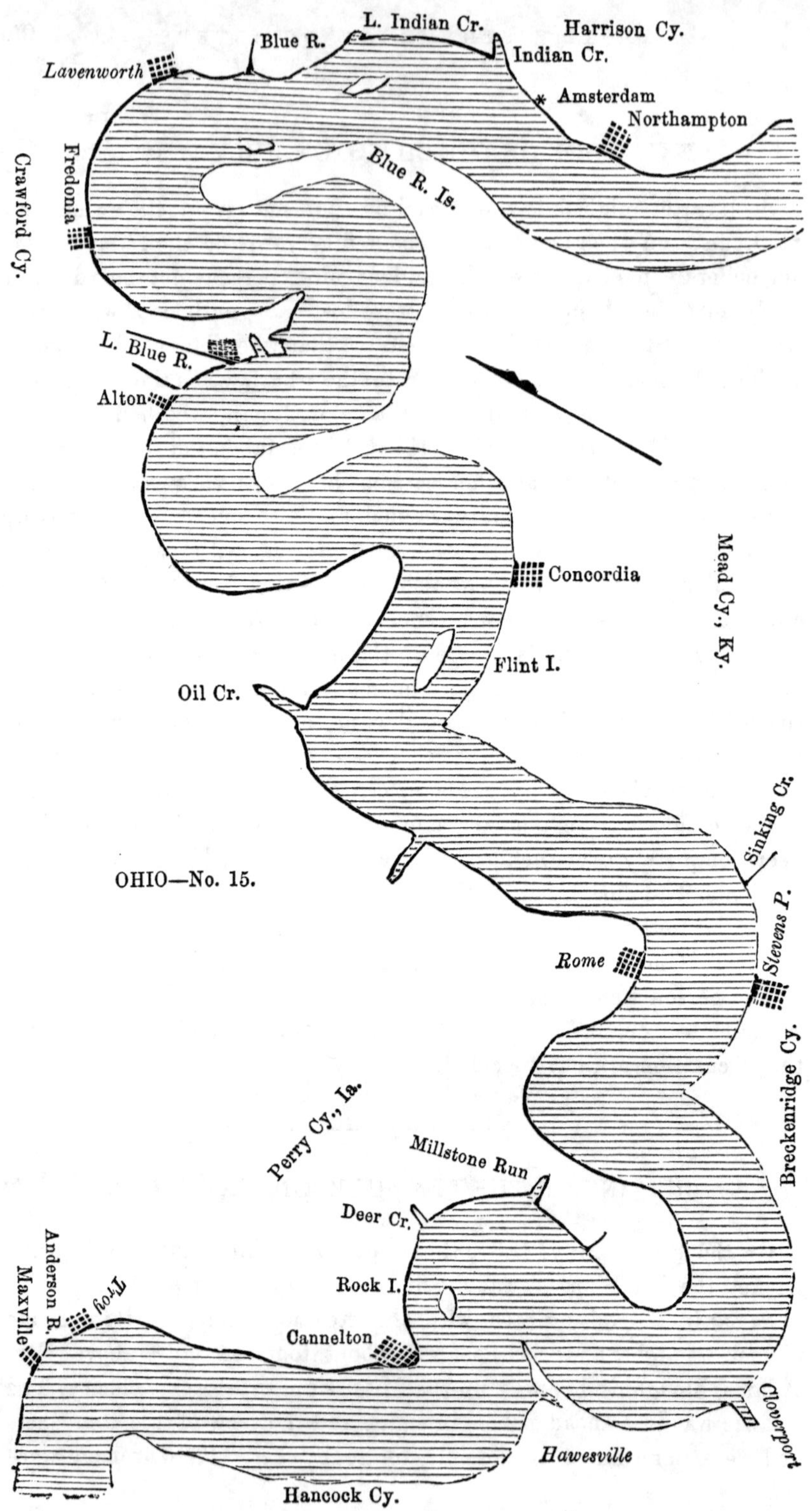

L. Indian Cr.
Harrison Cy.
Blue R.
Indian Cr.
Lavenworth
Amsterdam
Northampton
Blue R. Is.
Fredonia
Crawford Cy.
L. Blue R.
Alton
Concordia
Mead Cy., Ky.
Flint I.
Oil Cr.
Sinking Cr.
OHIO—No. 15.
Stevens P.
Rome
Breckenridge Cy.
Perry Cy., Ia.
Millstone Run
Deer Cr.
Anderson R.
Maxville
Troy
Rock I.
Cannelton
Cloverport
Hawesville
Hancock Cy.

shoving in the pine knots, and sprinkling rosin over the coal, and doing their best to raise more steam. They had a barrel of whisky before them, from which they drank often and freely until they were beastly drunk. The boilers became so hot that they set fire to sixty cords of wood on board, and the Ben Sherrod was soon completely enveloped in

BURNING OF THE BEN SHERROD.

flames. The passengers, three hundred in number, were sound asleep, not thinking of the awful doom that awaited them. When the deck hands discovered the fire, they basely left their posts and ran for the yawl, without giving the alarm to the passengers. Capt. Castleman attempted for a time to allay the excitement and confusion, by telling them the fire was extinguished. Twice he forbade the lowering of the yawl, which was attempted. The shrieks of nearly three hundred and fifty persons now on board, rose wild and dreadful, which might have been heard at a distance of several miles. The cry was, "To the shore! to the shore!" and the boat made for the starboard shore, but did not gain it, as the wheel ropes soon burnt. The steam was not let off, and the boat kept on up the river. The scene of horror now beggared all description. The yawl, which had been filled with the crew, had sunk, drowning nearly all who were in it; and the passengers had no other alternative than to jump overboard, without even taking time to dress. There were ten ladies who all went overboard without uttering a single scream; some drowned instantly, and others clung to planks; two of the number were all that were saved. Several passengers were burnt alive. One man by the name of Ray, from Louisville, Kentucky, jumped overboard, and hung to a rope at the bow of the boat, until rescued by the yawl of the steamer Columbus, which arrived at the scene half an hour after the boat took fire. Mr. Ray's face and arms were much burnt while clinging to the boat. He lost twenty thousand dollars in specie. The steamboat Alton arrived half an hour after the Columbus, but from the carelessness or indiscretion of those on her, was the means of drowning many persons who were floating in the water. She came down under full headway among the exhausted sufferers, who were too weak to make any further exertion, and by the commotion occasioned by her wheels drowned a large number. A gentleman by the name of Hamilton, from Limestone county, Alabama, was floating on a barrel, and sustaining also a lady, when the Alton came up, washing them both under. The lady was drowned, but Mr. Hamilton came up and floated down the river fifteen miles, when he was rescued by the steamer Statesman. Mr. McDowell sustained himself some time against the current, so that he floated only two miles down the river, and then swam ashore. His wife, who was floating on a plank, was drowned by the steamer Alton. Mr. Rundell floated down the river ten miles, and was taken up by a flat-boat at the mouth of Buffalo creek; he saved his money in his pantaloons' pocket. Mr. McDowell lost his wife, son, and a lady named Miss Frances Few, who was under his protection; also a negro servant. Of those who escaped, we have seen and conversed with James P. Wilkinson, Esq., Mr. Stanfield, of Richmond, Virginia, and Daniel Marshall, Esq., of Moscow, Indiana. The scene, as described by them, was truly heart-rending; while some were confined to their berths, and consumed by the flames, others plunged into the river to find watery graves. One lady, who attached herself to Mr. Marshall, and had clung to him while they floated four or five miles, was at length drowned by the waves of the Alton, after imploring the boat's crew for assistance and mercy. Mr. Marshall was supported by a flour barrel. Only two ladies out of ten who were on board were saved; one of these was Mrs. Castleman, the Captain's wife; the other was Mrs. Smith, of New Orleans.

It was said by some of the passengers, that the captain of the Alton did not hear the cries of those who implored him for assistance as he passed, it being midnight; but there can be no excuse for the monster who commanded the Prairie, for leaving a boat in flames without turning around and affording the sufferers relief. He reported her on fire at Natchez and Vicksburg.

A man in a canoe near the scene of the disaster refused to save any who were floating in the water, unless they promised to pay him handsomely for his services. So rapid were the flames that not even the register of the boat was saved; hence it was impossible to get a full list of the lost. One of the officers of the boat informed us, that out of seventy-eight deck passengers not more than six were saved. This was one of the most serious calamities that ever occurred on the Mississippi river, there being at least one hundred and seventy families deprived by it of some dear and beloved member, and over two hundred souls being hurried by it out of time into eternity, with scarce a moment's warning. During the burning of the Ben Sherrod eight different explosions occurred; first, barrels of whiskey, brandy, &c.; then the boilers blew up with a fearful explosion, and lastly, forty barrels of gunpowder exploded, which made a noise that was heard many miles distant, scattering fragments of the wreck in all directions, and producing the grandest sight ever seen. Immediately after, the wreck sunk out of sight just above Fort Adams. A large quantity of specie, which was on its way to the Tennessee Banks, was lost. One gentleman placed his pocket-book, containing thirty-eight thousand dollars, under his pillow, and though he managed to escape, he lost all his money. One scene was distressing in the extreme; a young and beautiful lady, whose name was Mary Ann Walker, on hearing the cry of fire, rushed out of the ladies' cabin in her loose night-clothes in search of her husband, at the same time holding her infant to her bosom; in her endeavors to get forward her dress caught fire, and was torn from her back to save her life. After witnessing her husband fall into the flames in the forward part of the boat, and unable to reach him, she leaped with her child into the water, seized a plank, and was carried by the current within forty yards of the Columbus, but just as she seized a rope thrown to her, both mother and child sank to rise no more. One young man, who had reached the hurricane deck in safety, hearing the cries of his sister, rushed back to the cabin, clasped her in his arms, and both were burnt to death. One of the clerks, one of the pilots, and the mate were burnt to death. All the chambermaids and women employed in the boat perished; only two negroes escaped out of thirty-five that were on the boat.

LOST—Three children and father of Captain Castleman; Mrs. McDowell, of Belfont, Ala.; Mrs. Gamble and three children, of New Orleans; Miss Frances Few, of Belfont, South Alabama; Mr. Frances, burnt to death.

PASSENGERS SAVED—James Smith, lady and son; Thomas Cook, W. H. Cloud, Wm. Beattie, Amos Brundell, Thomas Larmer, Samuel Ray, Lister Sexton.

Great praise is due to Captain Austin of the Statesman, and Captain Littlejohn of the Columbus, for their humane efforts to save the passengers of the Ben Sherrod, for had they acted as the Captain of

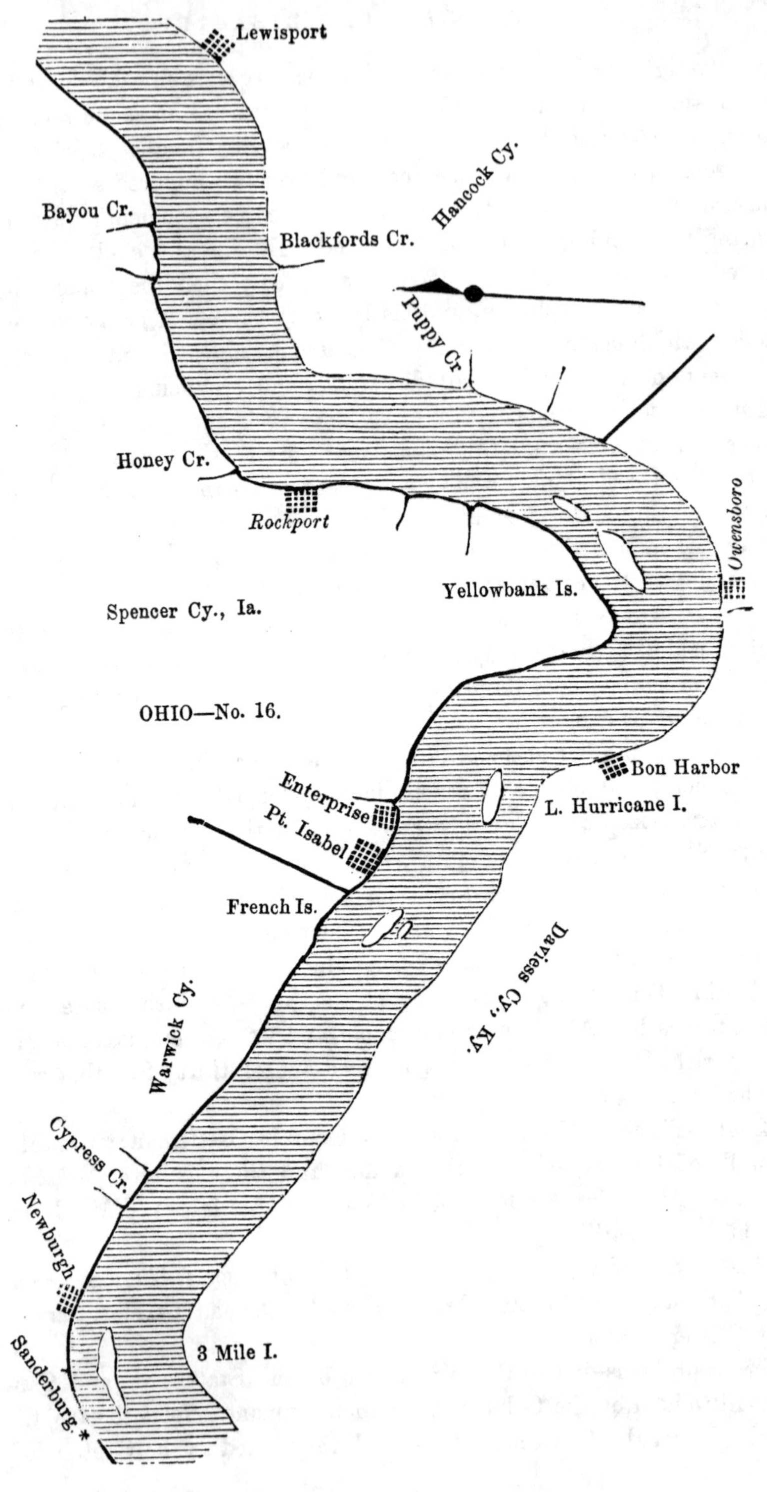
Lewisport
Hancock Cy.
Bayou Cr.
Blackfords Cr.
Puppy Cr
Honey Cr.
Rockport
Owensboro
Yellowbank Is.
Spencer Cy., Ia.
OHIO—No. 16.
Bon Harbor
Enterprise
L. Hurricane I.
Pt. Isabel
French Is.
Daviess Cy., Ky.
Warwick Cy.
Cypress Cr.
Newburgh
Sanderburg.
3 Mile I.

the Alton, not a soul would have been saved to tell the tale of that calamity. Mr. Wm. Stamp's family did everything in their power to relieve the wants of the sufferers, and they will long be remembered for their kindness to the strangers in that trying time.

LIST OF SAVED—G. Stanfield; Mr. Gamble and his son, of New Orleans; Ephraim Stanfield, Richmond, Virginia; Rosamond P. Andrews, A. H. Hartley, Arkansas; John Lowney, Indiana; Hugh Simpson, and Constantine Mahan, Tennessee; P. H. Watkins, Bedford county, Virginia; Thompson Duvall, Shelby county, Indiana; Matthew M. Orme, Natchez; Thomas W. Blagg, Alabama; J. S. Lowe, Tennessee; Charles W. Andrews, Yates county, New York; John Montgomery and James O. Phillips, Indiana; J. W. Brent, Pecan Point; John Dasua, E. Bushman, E. H. Burnes and J. M. Williams, Indiana; John Blanc, New Orleans; John A. Davis, Florence, Alabama; Erastus Griggs, Marietta, Ohio; A. Randall, Rocky Springs, Mississippi; James P. Wilkinson, Richmond, Virginia; Canton Macon, Cincinnati; Wm. Wallace, New York; Mrs. Smith, of Mobile.

LIST OF OFFICERS PICKED UP BY THE COLUMBUS—Captain C. G. Castleman and lady; George Stiles, clerk; Wm. Bell, first engineer; Stephen Hooks, second engineer; Charles Greenlee, pilot; Samuel Big, second mate; John Hill, carpenter; P. Rice, Jacob Lightstroff, John Eggman, A. Goddin, Amos Burby, Brilly John, M. P. Hard, Charles Simms, Fred. Cowen, Willis Caldwell, John Caldwell, John Johnson, Jacob Rose, Edward Fleece, B. McDaniel, Moses Caldwell, Charles Anderson, Peter Sevier, Andrew Moore, Joseph Cooper, Joseph Fisher, and John Clark.

A gentleman, Mr. Cook, floated down the river several miles before he was picked up. He hailed the wretched and despicable character who had put off in a yawl from the shore, and begged his assistance. The scoundrel, who was intent in picking up baggage, boxes, &c., asked with the utmost *sang froid*, "How much will you give me?" To the entreaties of others for help, he replied, "Oh, you are very well off there; keep cool, and you'll come out comfortable."

Poor Davis, the pilot at the wheel, was consumed; he was one in a thousand, preferring to die rather than leave his post in the hour of danger. Just before he left New Orleans, he was conversing with another pilot about the burning of the St. Martinsville; said he, "If ever I should be on a boat that takes fire, and don't save the passengers, it will be because the tiller ropes burn, or I perish in the flames." And just such men as Davis are to be found among the western boatmen; many have stood by their posts in the hour of danger, and perished rather than flinch from their duty.

BURNING OF THE BRANDYWINE, APRIL 9, 1832.

The steamboat Brandywine, Capt. Hamilton, left New Orleans on the evening of April 3d, 1832. Her place of destination was Louisville, Kentucky. Her voyage was prosperous until the evening of the 9th, at seven o'clock. When the boat was about thirty miles above Memphis, she was discovered to be on fire. Among the lading, it appears there were a number of carriage wheels wrapped in straw, as articles of that kind are usually put up for transportation on the river. These wheels were piled on the boiler-deck, near the officers' rooms, and under the hurricane roof. It is supposed that the fire was communicated from the furnaces to the highly combustible envelope of these wheels; the wind blew hard at the time, and the sparks were ascending very rapidly through the apertures in the boiler-deck, which were occupied by the chimneys, these not being closely fitted to the woodwork. It appears, too, that the Brandywine was racing with the steamboat Hudson at the time the fire broke out; and that, for the purpose of producing more intense heat, and thus accelerating the boat's speed, a large quantity of rosin had been thrown into the furnaces. This fatal *ruse* was resorted to because the Brandywine had been compelled to stop and make some repairs, and the Hudson, in the meantime, had gained considerable headway. Soon after the Brandywine had resumed her course, the pilot who was steering discovered that the straw covering of the carriage wheels was on fire. Strenuous efforts were made to extinguish the flames and to throw the burning articles overboard, but it was found that their removal allowed the wind to have free access to the ignited mass; from which cause, as Capt. Hamilton reports, the fire began to spread with almost incredible rapidity; and in less than *five minutes* from the time the alarm was first given, the whole boat was wrapped in a bright sheet of flame.

The state of affairs on board may be imagined, when it is understood that the Brandywine was crowded with passengers, and the only means of escape from a death of fiery torture which presented itself was the yawl, in which scarcely a tenth part of the affrighted people could be conveyed to the shore at a single trip. But even the faint hope of deliverance which this single mode of escape offered them, soon terminated in disappointment and despair. In the attempt to launch the yawl, it was upset and sunk. The heat and smoke had now become so insupportable, that not less than a hundred persons, made desperate by fear and suffering, threw themselves into the river.

The number of passengers on board, according to some reports, was not less than two hundred and thirty; of these only about seventy-five were saved; the rest were either drowned or burned to death. Among those who perished were nine women, and about an equal number of children.

As soon as all hope of extinguishing the flames was abandoned, an attempt was made to run the boat on shore, but she struck on a sand-bar, in nine feet water, and about a quarter of a mile from the nearest bank of the river, where she remained immovable, until she was burnt to the water's edge. Those passengers, and other persons belonging to the boat, who had the good fortune to escape, saved themselves by swimming, or floating on detached pieces of timber to the nearest island. It is reported to the honor of Capt. Hamilton and his crew, that they remained on the burning boat to the last possible moment, exerting themselves to the utmost to save the lives which had been entrusted to their charge.

In this case, as in several others which we have noticed, the number of victims cannot be ascertained with any degree of precision. The following list of the killed, although it is the most complete account that we could obtain, does not, in all probability, comprise more than *one-third* of the real number.

Cabin Passengers.—H. Hilyard, H. H. Davenport, —— Fowler, and Robert Stothart, Nashville; Mrs. Walker and child; Mrs. Sparks; three colored women, and several children.

Deck Passengers.—L. Hamilton, Joseph Ford, Abner Osborne, Byce Jackson, B. Williams, Joseph Leonard, L. Flourney, —— Ralls, B. Murell, Martin Cozine, John Myers, H. McMillan, Edward Bebee, John Mortimer, E. Wright, —— Marell, John Adams and brother, and W. Downes, Cincinnati; James Saunders, A. Stansbury, J. Knock, and Adam Abrams, New Orleans; Mrs. Johnson, Philadelphia; Miss Thompson, Baltimore; Miss Hettie Jones, Cincinnati; William Peters, St Louis; W. Williams, Chicago; Henry Hull, Detroit; James Ott, Hartford, Connecticut; D. French, New York; S. Michael, Missouri; E. Blanks, Kentucky; J. Carter, Natchez; Z. Shires, Boston; B. Colt, Memphis; Miss Blanton, Mississippi; Mrs. Williams; three children of Mr. Thompson, and Ethan Johnstone, Louisiana; and three slaves belonging to the boat.

The number of wounded could not have been less than seventy, some of whom were severely injured, and died, in consequence, soon after. Of those who escaped to the island, some were so badly burned, or otherwise injured, that they survived only for a few hours.

Green R.
Green R. Is.
Evansville
Hendersonville
Henderson I.
Is. Dam built of spiles.
West Franklin
Diamond I.
Henderson Cy., Ky.
Posey Cy., Ia.
Mt. Vernon
Slim I.
Highland Cr.
Uniontown
Union Cy.
Wabash I.
Wabash R.

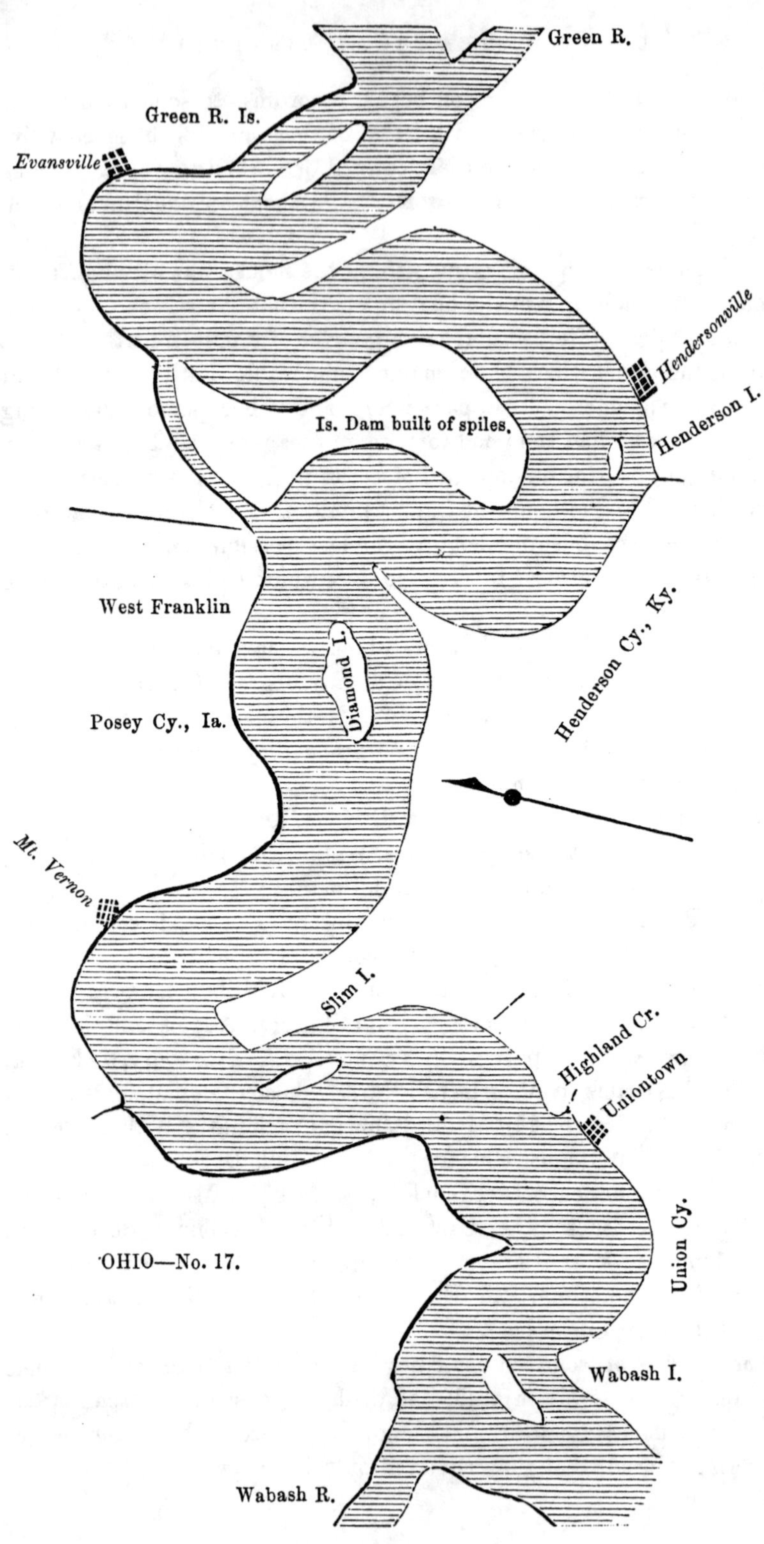

OHIO—No. 17.

EXPLOSION OF THE ORONOKO, APRIL 21, 1838.

On Saturday morning, at six o'clock, April 21st, 1838, the steamboat Oronoko, Capt. John Crawford, came to anchor in the Mississippi, opposite Princeton, one hundred miles above Vicksburg, where she stopped for the purpose of sending her yawl ashore to receive some passengers. In less than five minutes after the machinery ceased moving, a flue collapsed, spreading death and devastation throughout the boat. This accident occurred before the people on board were aroused from their slumbers. The deck passengers were lodged on the lower deck, abaft the engine, where, as is customary in western steamboats, berths were provided for their accommodation. On this occasion the number of berths was insufficient, as the boat was thronged with emigrants, and mattresses had been spread over the floor for the use of those who could not be lodged in the berths. This apartment

EXPLOSION OF THE ORONOKO.

between decks was densely crowded with sleeping passengers, when the flue collapsed, as aforesaid, and the steam swept through the whole length of the boat with the force of a tornado, carrying everything before it. Many of the crew, whom duty had called on deck at that early hour, were blown overboard; and as the scalding vapor penetrated every part and recess of the cabin and space between decks, the slumbering population of the boat, with scarcely an individual exception, were either killed on the spot, or injured in a manner more terrible than death itself. Some of these unfortunates were completely excoriated, some shockingly mangled and torn, while others were cast among masses of ruins, fragments of wood and iron, piled up in inextricable confusion.

The deck was strewn with more than fifty helpless sufferers; the

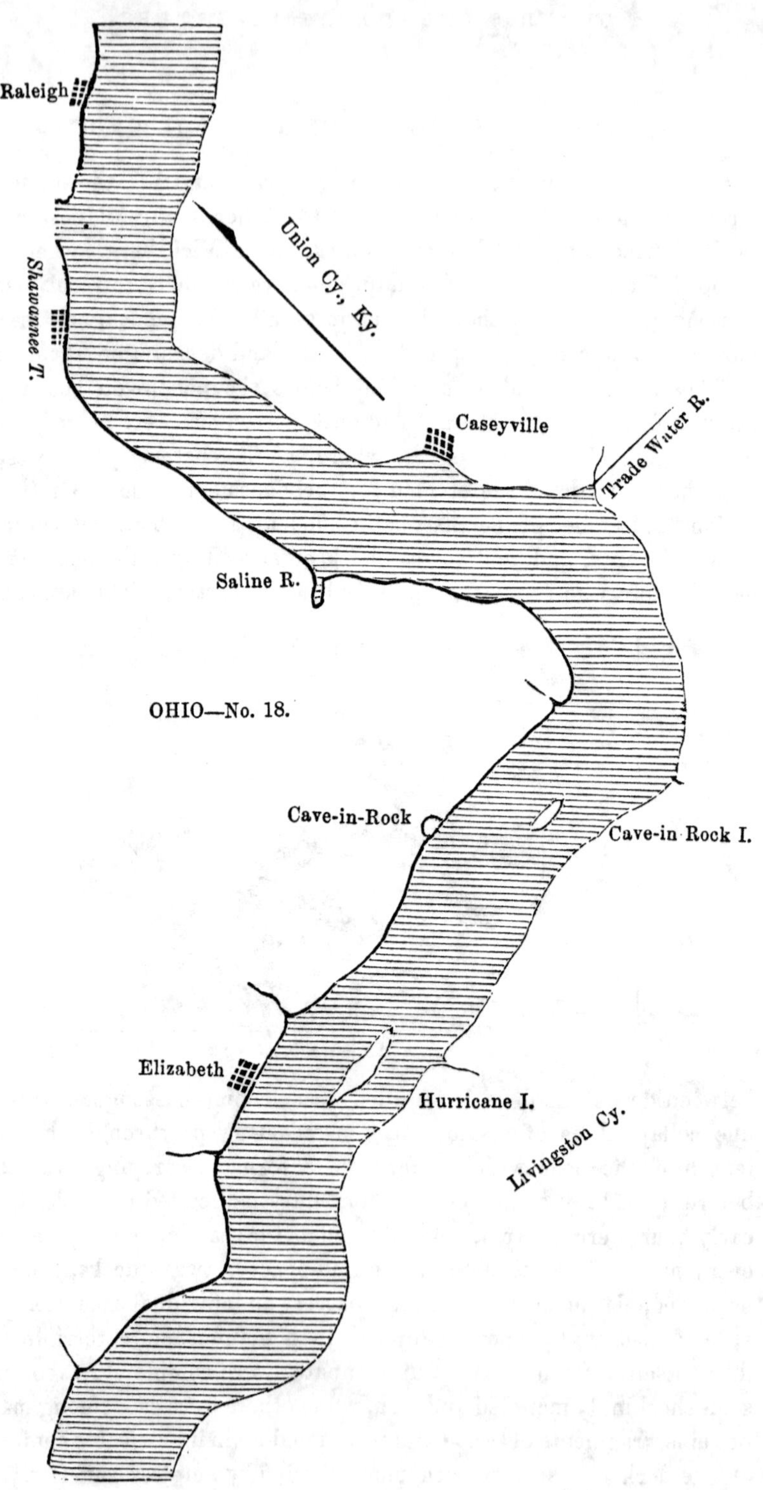
Raleigh
Union Cy., Ky.
Shawannee T.
Caseyville
Trade Water R.
Saline R.
OHIO—No. 18.
Cave-in-Rock
Cave-in Rock I.
Elizabeth
Hurricane I.
Livingston Cy.

river was all alive with those that had been hurled overboard by the force of the explosion, and those who, frantic with pain and terror, had cast themselves into the water. Some of those who had been scalded swam to the bank, and then in the wildest phrenzy, occasioned by intolerable agony, leaped back into the water and were drowned. Those persons who occupied the cabin generally escaped before the steam reached that apartment; but one gentleman, Mr. Myers, of Wheeling, while making his way forward with his child in his arms, became alarmed at the scene of confusion and distress which presented itself, and rushing back to the cabin, which by this time was filled with steam, he and the child were both badly burned, and died soon afterwards.

Nearly one hundred deck passengers are supposed to have been sacrificed, the names of a great majority of whom were unknown, and are therefore not inserted in the subjoined list.

PERSONS KNOWN TO HAVE BEEN KILLED—John Porter, second engineer, of Shippingsport, Kentucky; Owen Owens, Welshman, (blown overboard and drowned;) Mr. Myers, of Wheeling, and his child, eight months old; John Walker, fireman; E. Webb, Trumbull county, Ohio; P. McGallagher, brother and child, Mr. and Mrs. Flanegan, and two children, of Ireland; R. Hardenbroch, and Joseph Gilman, firemen, of Pittsburgh; Martha Mulligan, of Ireland; Wm. Jackson, Dr. Young, Georgia; Samuel Smith, New York; V. Armstrong, Virginia; Walter Dillon, Boston; E. D. Murray, Syracuse, New York; Dr. Williams, J. B. Clawson, M. D. Perry, Bath, Maine; Jethro Jacks, Mass.; O. Arbinger, Louisville; S. Winters, Indiana; David Few, Lexington, Kentucky; John Bloodgood, B. Hunter, New Hampshire; D. Atkinson and U. Terrebonne, Louisiana; M. Dorsey, Kentucky; Miss Wilhoite, Rhode Island; C. Torrence, Missouri; Mary Ann Bostick, Cincinnati; A. Hemfield, —— Delancy, New Orleans; Charles Olmstead, South Carolina; A. Dinwiddie, Maine; and three others, not named.

THE WOUNDED:—George Pettibone, of New York; Joseph Tunis, Baton Rouge, Louisiana; Enoch Heritage, Cincinnati, Ohio; William Clayton, Galloway county, Kentucky; George Henry, Wheeling, Virginia; Wm. Haynes, Frederick county, Maryland; S. Smith, Onondago county, New York; James Lloyd Harrington, Roxbury, Massachusetts; wife and child of P. Gallagher; George Snodgrass, Cooper county, Mo.

Several of those mentioned in the list of wounded died of their injuries. Some of those blown overboard were picked up by the yawl, and two or three were saved by a skiff from the shore. The inhabitants of Princeton did all in their power to assist the distressed crew and passengers, and to alleviate their sufferings.

Distances, Towns and their Population

ON

THE OHIO RIVER.

FROM PITTSBURGH, PENNSYLVANIA, TO

	Miles.		Pop.
Sewickleyville, Pa.,		13	1400
Shousetown, Pa.,	2	15	1600
Economy, Pa.,	3	18	1700
Freedom, Pa.,	8	26	1000
Beaver, Pa.,	2	28	3000
Shippersport, Pa.,	6	34	300
Georgetown, Pa.,	6	40	400
Glasgow, opposite, in Ohio,			200
Liverpool, Ohio,	5	45	1000
Wellsville, Ohio,	5	50	2500
Port Homer, Ohio,	5	55	100
New Cumberland, Va.,	4	59	100
Steubenville, Ohio,	12	71	8000
Wellsburgh, Va.,	7	78	4000
Warrenton, Ohio,	7	85	600
Tiltonsville, Ohio,	2	87	150
Burlington, Ohio,	3	90	100
Martinsville, "	3	93	700
WHEELING, Va.,	2	95	20,000
Bridgeport, Ohio, op.,			800
Richetown & W.Wheeling, O.	1	96	600
Benwood, Va.,	3	99	100
Belle Air, opposite,			50
Weegee, Ohio,	5	104	56
Elizabethtown, Va.,	3	107	2000
Powhaton, Ohio,	8	115	100
Sunfish, Ohio,	8	123	120
Baresville, Ohio,	9	132	140
New Martinsville, Va.,	3	135	400
Clarington, Ohio,	4	139	450
Sisterville, Va.,	6	145	460
Cochrenville,	2	147	160
Matamoras,	3	150	40
St. Mary's	13	163	80
Newport, Ohio,	1	164	1000
Marietta, Ohio,	16	180	6000
Williamsport, op., in Va.,			400
Parkersburgh, Va.,	12	192	600
Little Hockingport, Ohio,	8	200	400
Hockingport, Ohio,	8	208	400
Bellville, Va.,	5	213	180
Murraysville, Va.,	3	216	300
Ravenswood, Va.,	11	227	400
Letartville, Ohio,	13	240	300
Racine, Ohio,	6	246	190
Saracruse, Ohio,	5	251	200
Hartford city, Va.,	1	252	300
Minersville, Ohio,	1	253	220
Nyesville, Ohio,	1	254	300
Pomeroy, Ohio,	1	255	3000
Mason city, op., in Va.,			200
Coalport, Ohio,	1	256	300

	Miles.		Pop.
Middleport, Ohio,	1	257	320
Sheffield, Ohio,	1	258	400
West Columbia, Va.,	1	259	300
Cheshire, Ohio,	4	263	200
Addisonville, Ohio,	4	267	100
Point Pleasant, Va.,	4	271	300
Gallipolis, Ohio,	4	275	3000
Sample's Landing, Ohio,	12	287	100
Little Gugar, Va.,	6	293	200
Millersport, Ohio,	6	299	160
Haskilville, Ohio,	2	301	200
Guyandotte, Va.,	10	311	2000
Indian Guyandotte, Ohio,	1	312	400
Burlington, Ohio,	7	319	600
Catlettsburgh, Ky.,	4	323	600
Ashland, Ky.,	5	328	360
Ironton, Ohio,	5	333	2500
Hanging Rock, Ohio,	3	336	600
Greenupsburgh, Ky.,	6	342	500
Wheelersburgh, Ohio,	11	353	480
Sciotoville, Ohio,	2	355	380
Portsmouth, Ohio,	7	362	6900
New Hampshire, Ky.,	11	373	180
Buena Vista, Ohio,	4	377	300
Rockville, Ohio,	1	378	200
Vanceburgh, Ky.,	4	382	280
Rome, Ohio,	5	387	180
Concord, Ky.,	7	394	300
Wrightsville, Ohio,	2	396	160
Manchester, Ohio,	4	400	390
Maysville, Ky.,	12	412	8000
Ripley, Ohio,	9	421	3000
Lavana, Ohio,	2	423	200
Dover, Ky.,	2	425	880
Higginsport, Ohio,	5	430	700
Augusta, Ky.,	3	433	1600
Smith's Landing, Ohio,	7	440	100
Chilo, Ohio,	3	443	185
Neville, Ohio,	5	448	400
Foster's Landing, opposite,			200
Moscow, Ohio,	3	451	400
Point Pleasant, Ohio,	3	454	400
Bellmont, Ky., opposite,			300
California, Ky.,	4	458	180
New Richmond, Ohio,	2	460	4000
Palestine, Ohio,	5	465	500
California, Ohio,	6	471	100
Columbia, Ohio,	3	474	200
Pendelton,	2	476	200
Jamestown, Ky., opposite,			300
CINCINNATI, Ohio,	4	480	210,000

FROM CINCINNATI, OHIO, TO

	Miles.		Pop.
Industry, Ohio,		11	200
Taylorsport, op., in Ky.,			100
North Bend, Ohio,	5	16	100
Lawrenceburgh, Ind.,	7	23	5000
Petersburgh, Ky.,	2	25	200
Aurora, Ind.,	2	27	4000
Bellview, Ky.,	8	35	100
Rising Sun, Ind.,	4	39	3000
Millersburgh, Ind.,	3	42	180
Hamilton, Ky.,	5	47	440
Patriot, Ind.,	4	51	1000
Sugar Creek Landing, Ky.,	4	55	20
Warsaw, Ky.,	5	60	1400
Florence, Ind.,	1	61	130
Vevay, Ind.,	8	69	3000
Ghent, opposite, in Ky.,			500
Carrolton, Ky.,	9	78	2800
Madison, Ind.,	12	90	10,000
Hanover, Ind.,	5	95	600
London, Ind.,	5	100	216
Marble Hill, or Dean's Landing, Ind.,	5	105	80
Bethlehem, Ind.,	5	110	600
Garret's Land., op., in Ky.,			200
Westport, Ky.,	6	116	500
Herculaneum, Ind.	4	120	110
Charleston Landing, Ind.,	7	127	180
Utica, Ind.,	6	133	490
Jeffersonville, Ind.,	7	140	4900
LOUISVILLE, Ky.,	1	141	80,000

FROM LOUISVILLE, KENTUCKY, TO

	Miles.		Pop.
New Albany, Ind.,		3	16,000
West Point, or Salt River, Ky.,	20	23	600
Rock Haven,	10	33	400
Tobacco Landing,	6	39	100
Brandenburg, Ky.,	5	44	1400
Mockport, Ind.,	2	46	150
Amsterdam, Ind.,	8	54	100
Leavenworth, Ind.,	10	64	1300
Concordia, Ky.,	25	89	180
Rome, Ind.,	23	112	1000
Stephenson, Ky., opposite,			250
Cloverport, Ky.,	10	122	800
Hawesville, Ky.,	14	136	1000
Cannelton, Ind., opposite,			600
Troy, Ind.,	8	144	450
Lewisport, Ky.,	9	153	400
Grand View, Ky.,	5	158	120
Rock Port, Ind.,	5	163	800
Owensboro, Ky.,	10	173	1400
Bon Harbor, Ky.,	7	180	450
Newburg, Ind.,	23	203	1000
Evansville, Ind.,	15	218	12,000
Henderson, Ky.,	12	230	4000
West Franklin,	13	243	150
Mount Vernon, Ind.,	15	258	2000
Uniontown, Ky.,	18	276	500
Raleigh, Ky.,	12	288	200
Shawneetown, Ill.,	5	293	3000
Caseyville, Ky.,	15	308	180
California, or Cave in Rock, Ill.,	10	318	50
Elizabethtown, Ill.,	10	328	130
Roso Clair,	2	330	50
Golconda, Ill.,	8	338	400
Smithland, Ky.,	15	353	2500
Paducah, Ky.,	12	365	4000
Brooklyn,	3	368	80
Metropolis, Ill.,	7	375	800
Hillaman, Ill.,	10	385	100
Caledonia, Ill.,	15	400	500
CAIRO, Ill.,	15	415	1000

Distances on Tennessee River.

FROM PADUCAH, KENTUCKY, TO

	Miles.		Pop.
Paris Landing,		79	100
Sandy "	1	80	60
Winns' "	8	88	30
Point Mason,	12	100	40
Reynoldsburgh,	10	110	100
Mills Point,	4	114	80
Perryville,	36	150	200
Brownsport,	6	156	180
Patriot,	7	163	300
Decatur Furnace,	3	166	180
Carrollsville,	4	170	300
Clifton,	1	171	90
Swallow Bluff,	12	183	40
Saltillo,	10	193	100
Coffee Landing,	16	209	100
Savannah,	5	214	180
Crumps Landing,	4	218	49
Pittsburgh,	4	222	100
Hamburg,	4	226	120
Eastport,	30	256	1000
Chickasaw,	2	258	185
Tuscumbia,	26	284	2000
Florence, Foot of Muscle Shoals,	5	289	3000

Distances on Cumberland River.

FROM SMITHLAND, KENTUCKY, TO

	Miles.		Pop.		Miles.		Pop.
Pinkneyville, - - -		15	180	Clarksville, - - -	1	133	4500
Dyensburgh, - -	5	20	80	Davis Riffle, - -	15	148	
Eddyville, - - -	25	45	1300	Betseystown - - -	5	153	100
Tennessee R. Mill, -	10	55	600	Raworth's Landing, -	1	154	60
Canton, - - - -	10	65	200	Newton's Warehouse, -	1	155	40
Lime Port, - - -	12	77	100	Mouth of Harbor, - -	3	158	20
Tobacco Port, - - -	2	79	180	Sycamore Landing, - -	6	164	40
Dover, - - - -	12	91	100	Mouth of Marrowbone, -	3	167	80
Cumberland R. Mill, -	7	98	200	Dozier's Landing, - -	6	173	60
Bowlingreen, - -	8	106	80	Davidson's " - -	5	178	45
New York, - - -	10	116	60	Watkin's " - - -	1	179	30
Palmyra, - - -	5	121	100	Watson's " - -	7	186	80
Prices' Landing, - -	11	132	100	NASHVILLE, - - -	7	193	25,000

EXPLOSION OF THE TRI-COLOR

This sad event took place on the first day of April, 1830, at Wheeling, Va., on the Ohio river. The Captain, second engineer, and thirteen passengers, were killed. Four persons were wounded. The first engineer, who escaped unhurt, gives the following account. When the boat stopped at Wheeling to land passengers, he had the fires damped down, and was sure that there was a good supply of water in the boilers. He then went to his breakfast, but before he had finished this meal, the Captain came to the door and informed him that the steam was up, and he wished to start. The engineer arose from the table, went out, and found that the steam was very high, and the fire burning briskly.

The men were then employed in pushing out the boat from the wharf, but before the bell gave the signal to go ahead, the boilers bursted with the usual horrid effects. The engineer, who gives this account, ascribes the accident to the imprudent conduct of the captain; who ordered the men to supply the fires with fuel, without notifying the engineer that this had been done. It appears that captains of steamboats were, at that time, too apt to interfere with the engineer's duties, affecting to be more familiar with the operation of the steam-engine than the men who were presumed to have the exclusive management thereof. The names of the killed and wounded are not given. Six persons were killed.

EXPLOSION OF THE PILOT.

On the tenth of March, 1844, while the steamboat Pilot, Capt. Gow, was leaving the woodyard of Mr. Felix, opposite New Orleans, the starboard boiler burst with a terrific report. Capt. Gow and Mr. Felix were standing on the boiler-deck; both were blown overboard, and each had a leg broken, and they were otherwise severely injured, yet they succeeded in reaching the shore. William Gow, a son of the captain, was standing on the forecastle, and was frightfully mangled. His spine and both his legs were broken. He was removed to the hospital at New Orleans, where he expired on the following morning. One of the deck-hands jumped overboard and was drowned. John Nixon, first engineer, and Henry Fox, second engineer, were badly scalded. One of the steersmen was slightly scalded, and had both his legs broken. Capt. Gow himself had his legs broken, his skull fractured, and was internally injured, and it was supposed that he could not possibly recover. Several others who were on board were more or less hurt. One of the crew died of his injuries at the hospital, about a week after the accident took place.

Captain Gow and Mr. Felix were blown to the height of fifty feet in the air, and their escape from instant death is certainly one of the most extraordinary circumstances which we find in the records of steamboat calamities.

EXPLOSION OF THE GEORGE COLLIER, MAY 6, 1839.

This steamer was on her way from New Orleans to St. Louis. On the fatal day, at one o'clock, A. M., when the boat was eighty miles below Natchez, the piston-rod gave way, by which accident the forward cylinder-head was broken, and a part of the boiler stand was carried away. The steam which escaped scalded forty-five persons, twenty of whom died on the same day. A list of the dead and wounded was furnished by the clerk. We copy it, with the usual doubts respecting its accuracy, as many names must have been unavoidably omitted.

KILLED.—T. J. Spalding, fireman, of St. Charles, Mo.; Charles Brooks, *deck passenger*, residence unknown; William Blake, Boston, Mass.; Christian Herring, Germany; Mrs. E. Welch and two children, and J. O'Brian and wife, New Orleans; Seldon J. Broqua, Po-

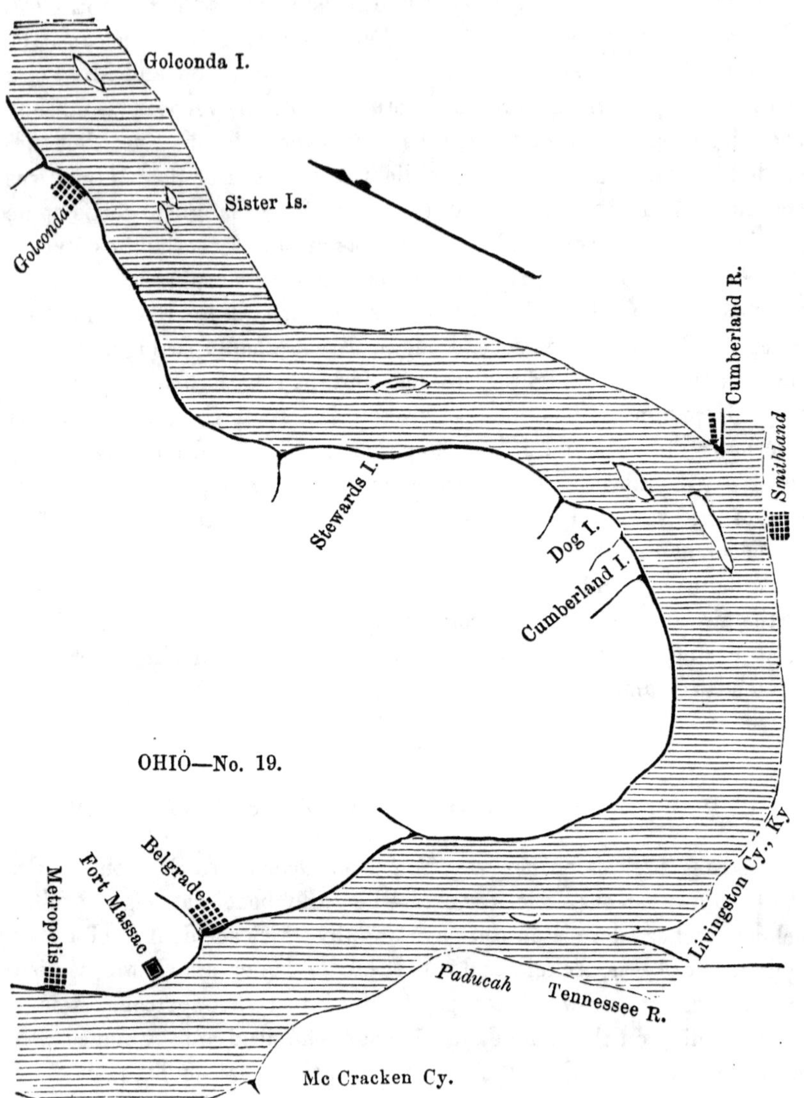
Golconda I.
Golconda
Sister Is.
Cumberland R.
Smithland
Stewards I.
Dog I.
Cumberland I.
OHIO—No. 19.
Belgrade
Fort Massac
Metropolis
Livingston Cy., Ky
Paducah
Tennessee R.
Mc Cracken Cy.

land, Ky.; John Idida, France; David J. Rose, New Orleans; Dederick Groe, Germany; Frederick Gross, and Joseph B. Bossuet, Boston, Mass.; Peter Smith, New Orleans; Joseph Lawrence, Parke co., Ind.; Charlotte Fletcher and brother, England; —— Bilch, fireman; and six others whose names are unknown.

WOUNDED.—*Passengers.*—D. Husselnanger, and Mrs Christian Herring, Germany, (both badly scalded); Thomas Fletcher and wife, England, (badly burnt); Francis Bryan and wife, and Francis Sernelly, St. Louis; Thomas Butler; Isaac Raney; Alfred Davis, deck hand; John Brown, and James McDonald, firemen; five children of Adam Woolbridge, some of them badly scalded; a slave of Thomas Johnston; Isadore Idida, deck passenger, badly scalded.

The cause of the disaster was probably a flaw or imperfection in the machinery.

BURNING OF THE TANGIPAHO, MARCH 2, 1838.

The Tangipaho, N. Sharpe, master, was on her way from the lake terminus of the railroad to the Balize, and when about forty miles from her place of destination, she was discovered to be on fire. After some time spent in the vain effort to extinguish the flames, Captain Sharpe, Mr. Wilson, the pilot, and Mr. Smith, a passenger, left the boat (being obliged to use the hatches for a raft, as there was no small boat on board), with the intention of reaching the nearest land. Mr. Phillip Grennell, the mate, and six colored men employed as deck hands, remained in the steamer. About night-fall the chimneys fell in, and then the mate and his assistants succeeded in extinguishing the fire. Mr. Grennell then constructed several sails by joining blankets together, and put the boat before the wind, hoping to reach South Pass, or some other place of security. After drifting about all the succeeding day, Saturday, March 3d, they cast anchor near the beach, and went on shore for water, but were unable to obtain any. They weighed anchor, and ran the boat on shore in the marshes on Sunday afternoon. From thence they travelled to Johnson's store on the Mississippi, where they procured a skiff, crossed to the opposite side, and were taken on board by the tow-boat Farmer, Captain Morrison.

The gentlemen who betook themselves to the hatches, viz: Captain Sharpe and Messrs. Wilson and Smith, were doubtless lost, as nothing was heard of them afterwards. All might have been saved, had the steamer been provided with a small boat!

8

EXPLOSION OF THE GEN. BROWN, NOV. 25, 1838.

For the particulars of this disaster we are indebted to Capt. Robert McConnell, now of Paducah, Ky., who was clerk on board the General Brown, and an eye-witness of the explosion and its dreadful results. This steamer, under the command of Captain Samuel Clark, left Louisville, Ky., for New Orleans on the 19th of November, 1838. This was her first trip of the season, and the water was quite low in both rivers, being only five feet in the Ohio and seven feet in the Mississippi. Circumstances seemed to threaten misfortune from the very beginning of the voyage; for in passing over a sand-bar at no great distance from Louisville, the General Brown came in collision with the steamer Washington, bound up the river, by which accident the larboard wheel of the Gen. Brown was damaged to that degree that repairs were necessary before the boat could proceed. The carpenter succeeded in fitting up a temporary wheel, which answered the purpose very imperfectly; however, the boat was enabled to continue her trip, working along slowly until the morning of Sunday, November 25th, when she reached Helena, Ark., where she stopped to land a passenger. This being done, the captain, who stood on the hurricane roof, took the bell-rope in his hand to give the usual signal of departure; but at the first tap of

EXPLOSION OF THE GENERAL BROWN.

the bell, the boilers exploded with a deafening crash, and that single stroke of the bell was to many a signal of departure to that eternal world from whence no traveller returns. Capt. Clark himself, while still grasping the bell rope convulsively in his hand, was blown overboard, together with a portion of the wood-work on which he stood. He had been holding a lively conversation with Dr. Price, of Lexington, a few moments before. Dr. P. stood on the same platform, and shared the same melancholy fate, both gentlemen being afterwards found among the dead. Captain McConnell, who gives this account, was thrown from the railing on which he stood after notifying the captain that the boat was ready to start. He fell on the deck and received but little injury. He supposes that the persons killed numbered about fifty-five, and the wounded fifteen or twenty. The names which follow are all that he could call to remembrance.

KILLED.—Capt. Samuel Clark, master of the boat; Joseph Underwood, and Hamilton McRay, pilots; James Wilson, first engineer; Basil Boons, mate; Ely Johns, second clerk; carpenter, name not recollected; Patrick Dunn, bar-keeper; eight or ten firemen and deck-hands. *Passengers*—C. Libley, D. L. Davis, N. A. Miller, and Dr. Price, of Lexington, Ky.; H. M. Blanchard, E. Hubbard, George Johnson, J. K. Gutherite, T. D. Sims, C. Keane, T. D. Levey, A. Dugan, Dr. Johnson and wife, B. Walker, C. Stansbury, O. Perry, and several others, making a total of fifty-five.

The names of the wounded are not given. Capt. McConnell exonerates the commander of the General Brown from all blame, declaring that he frequently urged the firemen and engineers to use the utmost caution, and to carry as little steam as possible, on account of the crippled condition of the boat.

EXPLOSION OF THE ELIZABETH.

The steamboat Elizabeth, Capt. Gordon, was ascending the Mississippi on Tuesday, April 3d, 1845, having left New Orleans on the preceding Sunday. About three o'clock, P. M., just as she entered the Courtauban, her boiler collapsed, making a complete wreck of her upper works. The numerous pieces of the deck, &c., blown overboard, afforded the means of escape to a number of persons who had been projected into the water.

The names of the persons who were killed or injured by this accident were given by the clerk of the boat, whose statement we copy:

J. H. Gordon, the captain, was very badly scalded and bruised. Daniel Yorke, mate, killed. Freeman B. Lamb, first pilot, leg fractured. James Marquite, first engineer, very badly injured. Nelson Hill, second engineer, missing. —— Rhodes, deck hand, missing. One colored fireman slightly scalded, and another missing.

The passengers were uninjured, except a few who were slightly bruised.

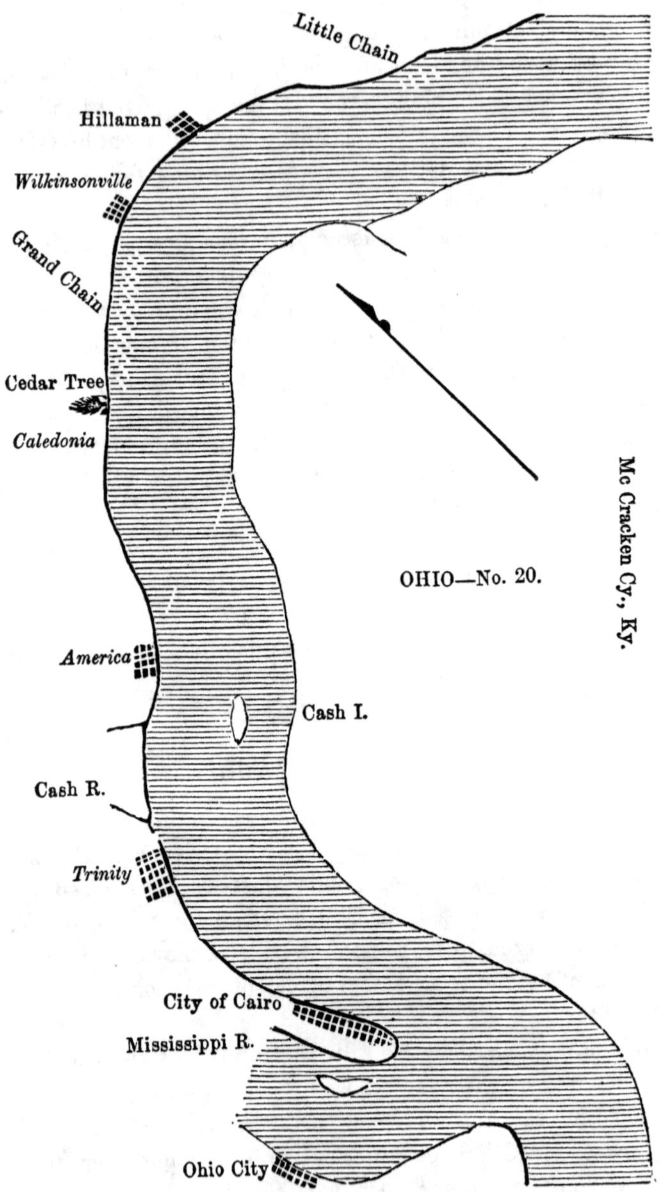
Little Chain
Hillaman
Wilkinsonville
Grand Chain
Cedar Tree
Caledonia
OHIO—No. 20.
Mc Cracken Cy., Ky.
America
Cash I.
Cash R.
Trinity
City of Cairo
Mississippi R.
Ohio City

EXPLOSION OF THE ENTERPRISE, ON THE RIO GRANDE.

On the 21st day of August, 1846, the Enterprise was about casting off from a landing-place on the river, forty-five miles above Renoza, where she had been moored during the night; and scarcely had the paddle-wheels made three revolutions, when the boiler exploded, making a fearful havoc among the passengers (U. S. volunteers) and crew, who numbered altogether about one hundred and fifty persons. The hull, and those parts of the boat adjacent to the stern, were but little damaged, but the forward works, with everything in the neighborhood of the boilers, were torn to pieces or blown overboard. There were sixteen men sleeping between the chimneys, all of whom experienced, more or less, the sad effects of the accident.

Many were shot into the air, and falling into the water, were drowned, being too much disabled to swim, or to make any other effort for their own preservation. Others fell on different parts of the boat, and were horribly mutilated. The boilers were very much shattered, the pieces flying about in every direction, and falling in a shower of iron fragments on the deck. In such circumstances, the escape of so many of the crew and passengers from death or severe injury was almost miraculous. No satisfactory account of the cause of the disaster has been given, but it was conjectured that some leakage in the boilers caused a deficiency of water therein, which is a frequent cause of steamboat explosions.

THE KILLED—Enoch Tucker, Texas; Thomas Gaufney, N. Y.; A. Boswell, Tenn.; Mr. Seaps, second cook; a passenger, name unknown.

BADLY WOUNDED—Lieutenant Dearing, of the Louisville Legion; William A. Crook, and C. B. Crook, of Tenn.; Capt. Woods, William Grey, Jacob Bowringe, and Thomas Eagle, Texas; J. C. Howard, sutler, of Baltimore, Md.; Joseph Grigsby and William Hickey, sutlers of Louisville Legion; Mr. Tabor, pilot; Thomas Kennepee, Samuel Martin, Patrick Kelley, Frank Tallant, deck hand; J. F. Clark, mate.

SLIGHTLY WOUNDED—Milton Cunningham and James Wilson, Tenn.; J. Wheeler, J. Humerick, Matthew Sampson, and Christian Coleman, Texas; J. Downing and Mr. Adams, sutlers of Louisville Legion; Edmund Newell, clerk; Capt. Kelsey, of Conn.; W. Arthines, fireman; Henry A. Emmons, second mate; Dr. H. S. Tudor.

Patrick Kelley, one of the wounded, was maddened by his sufferings, and died in a few days after the accident. The bodies of some of the passengers who were drowned, were recovered from the water and buried some miles below Renoza.

VIEW OF CINCINNATI.

SKETCH OF CINCINNATI.

CINCINNATI is situated on the right bank of the Ohio river, four hundred and ninety miles west south-west of Pittsburgh, one hundred and forty miles north-east of the falls of Ohio, seven hundred and forty east of St. Louis, Mo., and five hundred and forty miles from the mouth of the Ohio river; lat. 39° 6′ 30″ N., long. 84° 26′ W., and is five hundred and forty-nine feet above the level of the sea. Cincinnati is the capital of Hamilton county, and is the largest city on the western waters, and fourth in size and importance among all the cities of the Union. It is remarkable for its rapid growth, extensive commerce and productive industry. From its central position between Pittsburgh and the mouth of the Ohio, it has become the principal gathering and distributing point in the valley of this great river. The city is beautifully situated in a valley four miles in diameter, intersected from east to west by the Ohio, and environed by a beautiful and romantic range of hills, gradually rising to the height of five hundred feet, presenting a grand and picturesque sight to the traveller in ascending or descending the river. From the summits of these hills the most beautiful views of Cincinnati and the surrounding country for miles are obtained. The city extends four miles along the river, the central portions of it are compactly and handsomely built with wide, well-paved streets, bordered with elegant dwellings, lined with numerous shade trees and lighted with gas. Perhaps no city in the United States has grown more rapidly than Cincinnati. A few years ago it was but a small town, and now it ranks the very first city west of the mountains. At the foot of Main street is the public landing for steamboats; it is an open area of ten or twelve acres, with twelve hundred feet front. The wharf is paved with stone from low water mark to the sidewalk, affording a dry and substantial landing to the large fleet of boats plying to and from this great metropolis. In the busy seasons, this wharf is lined with boats, freights are piled up in endless quantities, waiting for shipment or storage, presenting quite a novel scene to the uninitiated western traveller.

Among the most prominent and interesting public buildings may be mentioned that edifice called College Building, on Walnut street, occupied by the Chamber of Commerce and Young Men's Mercantile Library. It is one hundred and forty feet long by one hundred feet wide, with a marble front. The Mercantile Library Association numbers about four thousand five hundred members, and has a rare collection of twenty thousand volumes of literary, scientific and other works, besides about one thousand volumes of bound newspapers; the receipts and expenditures annually amount to about twenty thousand dollars. Books are continually being added to the library, and it is justly considered one of the best arranged and conducted libraries in the country. Papers from all parts of the United States and Europe are filed here, and strangers are allowed free use of the books and papers without charge. No one visits Cincinnati without going to the Young Men's Mercantile Library.

Cincinnati is no less remarkable for the variety and importance of its manufactures than for its commerce. Perhaps there is no place in the whole country where fuel, food and the raw materials of cotton, wool and iron can be procured so cheaply. More than four hundred steam-engines are employed in the manufactories of this city. The total value of manufactured productions in 1855 was seventy-one million dollars. There are sixty iron foundries, with machine shops, which annually produce six million four hundred and thirty-one thousand six hundred dollars; ten rolling mills, which produce three million dollars; forty lard oil and stearin manufactories, which produce four million six hundred thousand dollars; twenty-six flouring mills, which produce three million one hundred and ninety thousand dollars; two hundred and forty-eight manufactories of clothing which produce two million nine hundred and forty-seven thousand five hundred and sixty dollars; two hundred and thirteen of furniture, which produce three million nine hundred and forty-eight thousand dollars, supplying almost the entire west with furniture; sixteen publishing establishments, which produce two million four hundred and ten thousand dollars; sixty wine factories, eleven paper mills, seventy-nine tobacco factories, ten cotton factories, three type foundries, eighteen bell and brass foundries, sixty manufactories of hats, thirty of edge tools, sixty of soap and candles, thirty of trunks, and ten boat yards, besides many other manufacturing establishments. Cincinnati is supplied with water raised from the Ohio river by steam power into a large limestone reservoir which holds five million gallons.

The climate of Cincinnati is favourable to the cultivation of the grape. In this vicinity the vineyards occupy about two thousand acres; wine of good quality is made here from the native Catawba grape. The annual product of the vines in the neighborhood of the city is above two hundred and fifty thousand gallons. There are constantly employed in the commerce of Cincinnati three hundred and fifty steamboats, the total tonnage of which is over one hundred thousand; and the annual number of steamboat arrivals amount to four thousand. Cincinnati is the greatest pork market in the Union. There were received here in 1855 four hundred and sixty thousand hogs, eighteen millions five hundred and thirty-two thousand eight hundred and eighty-four pounds of pork in the rough, besides thirty thousand barrels and fourteen thousand hogsheads of bacon. The assessed value of property in Cincinnati in 1846 was twenty-seven million one hundred and thirty-six thousand five hundred and twenty dollars; in 1853 fifty-six million two hundred and seventy-five thousand four hundred and thirty dollars; in 1855 sixty-four million three hundred and forty-one thousand seven hundred and twenty dollars. About twelve daily and above twenty weekly papers are published in Cincinnati, besides numerous monthly periodicals. In addition to the above, the offices of the daily journals each issue weekly and tri-weekly publications, four of the daily and four of the weekly are in the German language. The city has seven or eight chartered banks, besides numerous private banking companies, the most prominent of which is the Citizens' Bank, Wesley Smead, Esq., president, which employs over one million dollars, in discounting, &c.,

Cincinnati was first settled on December 26th, 1788, and was originally called Losantiville. It was incorporated as a city in 1819. In 1800 it contained only seven hundred inhabitants; in 1820, nine thousand six hundred and two; in 1830, twenty-four thousand eight hundred and forty; in 1840, forty-six thousand three hundred and forty-eight; in 1850, one hundred and sixteen thousand four hundred and thirty-six; in 1853, one hundred and sixty thousand one hundred and eighty-six; and in 1856, two hundred and ten thousand.

EXPLOSION OF THE CAR OF COMMERCE.

The accident to which we now refer, took place on the Mississippi river, at a place called the Canadian Reach, on the 14th day of May, 1828. We are informed that the force-pump was out of order, and did not supply the boilers with water. The engineer stopped the machinery, and made an effort to put the pump in good working order. The machinery was again put in motion, but scarcely had the wheels made three revolutions when the cast-iron head of one of the boilers was blown out. Such was the jar or concussion produced by this accident, that all the boilers, four in number, were dislodged and thrown with great violence on the deck. More than thirty persons were killed, and ten or twelve others were scalded or otherwise badly injured. In the report of this accident, made by the officers of the boat, the names of the persons killed or wounded are not given.

BURNING OF THE ERIE.

This magnificent steamer, Capt. Titus, commander, was destroyed by fire, on Lake Erie, on the 16th day of August, 1841, by which calamity more than one hundred and seventy-five persons lost their lives. The following account is given of the origin of this disaster. Among the passengers on board were six painters, who were going to Erie, to paint the steamboat Madison. They had with them several large demijohns filled with spirits of turpentine and varnish, which, unknown to Capt. Titus, they had placed on the boiler-deck, directly over the boilers. One of the firemen who survived the accident, asserts that he discovered the dangerous position of these demijohns, a short time after the boat left the wharf, and removed them to a safer locality; but some person must have replaced them, without being aware of the inflammable nature of the contents. Immediately before the fire broke out, a slight explosion was heard; the sound is said to have resembled that which is made by a single puff of a high-pressure steam-engine. The supposition is that one of the demijohns bursted, in consequence of its exposure to the heat. The liquid poured out on the boiler-deck instantly took fire, and within a few minutes all that part of the boat was in flames. The steamer had recently been painted and varnished, and owing to this circumstance, the whole of the wood-work was very soon in a blaze. There were two hundred persons on board the Erie, and of that number only twenty-seven were saved.

Mr. Mann, of Pittsford, N. Y., who was one of the passengers, gives the following narrative, which comprises a history of this memorable and most horrifying event. Mr. Mann was walking on the promenade deck, in company with a young lady, Miss Sherman, and had just reached the point above the boiler-deck where the demijohns were placed, when the singular sound spoken of above arrested his attention. This report was followed by the ascent of a volume of black smoke, which, as Mr. Mann describes it, "resembled a cloud of coal dust." Without any apprehension of danger, he stopped for a few moments—when the smoke subsided, and was instantly succeeded by a red, lurid flame, which spread with fearful rapidity, and soon enveloped every thing combustible that was within its reach, cracking the sky-lights with intense heat, and filling up the space between decks with what appeared to be a dense red flame. While Mr. Mann was looking around for some means of escape, the young lady rushed from him and disappeared; but in a short time she returned, calling on her father, who, being indisposed, had retired a few minutes before to his berth. Frantic with alarm for her parent's safety, she was again about to rush below, where certain destruction would have met her, when Mr. Mann detained her almost by force, promising to render all possible assistance to her father as soon as he had provided for her own security. A prospect of deliverance now presented itself. Mr. Mann saw a passenger force up a board which formed a part of the seats that surrounded the promenade deck, and throwing it overboard he leaped after it, and was enabled by grasping the plank to keep himself afloat. Mr. Mann followed this person's example, and succeeded in detaching another board, which he hoped to make the means of preserving the life of the affrighted girl who clung to his arm. But new difficulties presented themselves; no persuasions could induce Miss Sherman to descend to the water. In these embarrassing circumstances, he placed one end of the board over the railing at the stern; Miss Sherman was seated on the projecting extremity, and Mr. Mann earnestly entreated some men who were clustered around the rudder post, to assist him in lowering the plank and the young lady to the water, but no attention was paid to his entreaties. Miss Sherman in the meanwhile, being made dizzy by her fearful position, fell from the plank, sunk in the river, and was seen no more.

BURNING OF THE ERIE.

Having failed in his noble attempt to save this young lady, Mr. Mann now began to make some effort for his own preservation. Glancing around him, he saw Capt. Titus endeavoring to reach the ladies' cabin, and heard him give the order to stop the engine. It was a moment of overwhelming terror. From bulk-head to rudder, the flames were raging with an impetuosity which seemed to mock at all hope of deliverance. The shrieks of many human beings expiring in fiery torment within the vessel, and the cries for assistance of many others who were struggling in the water, almost deprived the listener of sense and reflection. The engine seemed to work with a double power, as if it were maddened by the appaling character of the scene. The flames, as they rushed aft, sounded like the roaring of a hurricane, threatening every moment to engulf the boat and every affrighted soul on board. Forward of the wheel-house several persons were struggling to wrench partially loosened timber from the vessel, for the purpose of sustaining themselves in the water. Below and in rear of the ladies' cabin, some thirty or forty people were clustered, each frantically endeavoring to descend by the rudder chains for safety. In this, some had partly succeeded, but were forced off by others struggling for the same object. Several persons were hanging from the sides of the boat, husbands vainly endeavoring to sustain their wives in that position, and mothers their children. But not one of all the females whom Mr. Mann saw gathered there, and not one of the children, was saved. Wives, mothers, helpless infants, all sunk "with bubbling groan" into the deep tomb of waters.

After making this survey, and abandoning every other hope of escape, Mr. Mann, who still grasped the board from which the unfortunate young lady had fallen, threw it into the lake, and immediately followed it. He sunk for a moment, but arose to the surface, fortunately by the side of the plank, to which he now clung with desperate energy, as his last resource. He had companions in the terrible struggle for life, but they were few; the greater number had already yielded to the mighty conqueror. Here was one buffeting the waves, unsustained by any thing but his own strength, but that was doubled by the energy of a last hope. There was another shrieking for aid, in a voice which became fainter every moment, and was interrupted by a gurgling sound which foretold a speedy termination of the struggle. From another direction came the voice of supplication, the last prayer of a dying man, not for deliverance from earthly peril, (for all hope of that had been abandoned,) but for pardon for himself and protection for a wife and children far distant. Then was heard the shriek of the mother, bewailing the child which she had vainly endeavoured to withhold from the distended jaws of death. Turning his agonized gaze to the deck above him, Mr. Mann saw many passengers, one after another, throw themselves into the water; the greater number, after a few feeble efforts to save themselves from the fate which threatened them, disappeared with wild exclamations of terror and despair.

When Mr. Mann left the deck of the burning steamer, she was driving ahead with a rapid motion; but having left him on his plank about two miles astern, she suddenly veered around, and again approached him; so near did she come, indeed, that he was in danger of being engulfed, but contrived, with some difficulty, to get out of her way. As the boat passed him, he saw five or six persons hanging to the anchor, and about as many more holding on to the pole which supported the liberty cap at the bow. All of them appeared to be suffering greatly from the heat. Near the bulkhead, a person stood almost surrounded by fire; he held in his hand a piece of white cloth, with which he appeared to be bathing his face, which must have been severely scorched. When he saw Mr Mann, he begged him, for God's sake, to allow him to get on the plank, as he could not swim, and therefore dare not leap into the water. Mr. Mann replied that the plank would not support two persons, but the suppliant made such piteous entreaties, that Mr. Mann was about to yield, when a heavy swell bore the blazing wreck to a distance, and carried the unhappy sufferer beyond the reach of all human aid.

When Mr. Mann had been in the water about two hours, he was taken up by the steamboat De Witt Clinton, which rescued several others of the drowning passengers.

Among others who embarked at Buffalo in this ill-fated boat, were two brothers, Charles J. Lynde and Walter Lynde, sons of the Hon. Tully Lynde, of Homer, Cortland Co., N. Y. These brothers resided at Chicago, and were returning from a visit to their parents. The wife of one of these young gentlemen, a lady of superior intellect, was the only female passenger saved. She conducted herself throughout the whole trying scene with exemplary fortitude and intrepidity. Her husband had provided two life preservers, one for her and one for himself. As soon as it became evident that the boat could not be saved, Mrs. Lynde fastened her life-preserver around her waist, and fearlessly committed herself to the water, expecting that her husband would follow immediately. But in this she was disappointed; her anxious gaze searched in vain among the floating objects on the water, for the dearest object of her affection. Yet, although she saw him not, she had no fears for his safety, as she had seen him put on his life-preserver before she left the boat. He was much excited at the time, and she exhorted him to be more calm and self-possessed. When the De Witt Clinton had taken up all the persons that could be found floating on the water, and Mrs. Lynde among the rest, she eagerly sought her husband among those who had been rescued. He was not there; but she saw the life-preserver, which she knew to be his, in the possession of a German, who was one of the deck passengers. The man declared that he had found it in the water, and made it instrumental in saving his own life. It was believed by some persons that the German, in order to save himself, had wrenched the preserver from Mr. Lynde ; but the more charitable supposition is, that Mr. Lynde, in his excitement and agitation, had failed to fasten it securely to his person, so that it came off at the moment he leaped into the water.

There was a musical band, consisting of ten persons, on board the Erie, all of whom, except two, perished in the conflagration, or in the water.

The following list of the killed, wounded and missing is the most complete that could be obtained.

KILLED.—W. M. Camp, Harrisburg, Pa. ; Willet Weeks, Brooklyn, N. Y. ; John C. Pool, New York city ; E. S. Cobb, Ann Arbor, Mich. ; Otto Fox, wife and three children, N. Y. ; Lloyd Gelston, of Erie, clerk; Mr. Joles, steward ; Mrs. Giles Williams, Chicago ; Charles J. Lynde, Milwaukie ; Watts S. Lynde, Homer, N. Y. ; Mrs. William H. Smith and child, Schenectady, N. Y. ; A. Sears, Philip Barker, Henry Weaver, William Thomas, John Evarts and Peter Finney, painters, of Buffalo ; (these six persons last named brought the fatal demijohns on board, and are supposed to have placed them in their unsafe position ; all six paid with their lives the penalty of their indiscretion ;) Miss A. Miller, of Buffalo ; (the brother of this young lady, Mr. W. G. Miller, was the master painter who employed the six journeymen named above, and sent them to paint the steamer Madison, as mentioned in the preceding narrative ;) J. D. Woodward, N. Y. ; William Gisfin, Miss. ; D. S. Sloan, Geneva ; F. Stowe, Canada ; William Sacket, Mich. ; Mrs. Spencer and two children, Mrs. Dow, Mrs. and Miss Robinson, and Miss King, Balston Spa., N. Y. ; Mr. Moore, lady and two children, moving to Mich. ; Roome Button, Fort Plain ; Orin Green, Rushville, Yates co., N. Y. ; Charles S. Mather, Mount Clemens, Mich. ; Mr. Miltmore, dentist, and wife, of Chicago ; Von Ockerman, a German, tinsmith, Buffalo ; Mr. Sherman and daughter, and John Harrington, Harrisburg, Erie Co. N., Y. ; Luther Tuller, wheelsman ; Frederick Parmalee, bar-keeper ; William Cheats, William Winters, and James Reed, colored waiters ; Robert Smith, first cook ; Henry Vosburg, second cook ; David Mills, third cook ; Israel Vosburg and William Sparks, colored porters ; Dr. Hackett, Thompsonian physician, of Lockport, N. Y. The following names are those of Swiss emigrants, who were either burned to death or drowned :—

Z. Zuggler and family, six persons; John Hang, wife and child; Martin Zulgen and wife; George Rettenger, wife and child; George Christian and family, five persons; George Neigold and family, eight persons; M. Reibold, wife and child; George Steinman and wife; Peter Kling and sister; L. Gillig, wife and child; Peter Schmidt; John Netzel; Peter Schneider and family, five persons; J. Newminger and family, four persons; S. Schapler, wife and three children; R. Tilling and wife; C. Obens; J. Korter; C. Durbur; M. Lithold, wife, sister-in-law and two children; C. Deitcherich and wife; C. Wilbur, wife and four children; C. Palmer, wife and three children; J. Garghum, wife and three children; G. Mulliman, wife and two children; C. Kellenman.; C. Mintch, and his companion, name unknown.

WOUNDED.—Jerome McBride, wheelsman, badly burned; three Swiss passengers, much injured; Capt. Titus, master of the Erie; Mr. Rice, of Buffalo, badly burned.

Among those who perished were a number of infants, not included in the preceding list, as no charge was made for their passage, and they were therefore not mentioned on the boat's books.

COLLISION OF THE STEAMBOAT MONMOUTH AND THE SHIP TREMONT.

With strict propriety of language, we might call the awful catastrophe about to be particularized, a massacre, a wholesale assassination, or anything else but an *accident*. In some instances, and this is one of them, a reckless disregard of human life, when it leads to a fatal result, can claim no distinction, on any correct principle of law or justice, from wilful and premeditated murder.

The steamer Monmouth left New Orleans, October 23d, 1837, for Arkansas river, having been chartered by the U. S. government to convey about seven hundred Indians, a portion of the emigrant Creek tribe, to the region which had been selected for their future abode. On the night of the 30th, the Monmouth, on her upward trip, had reached that point of the Mississippi called Prophet Island Bend, where she encountered the ship Tremont, which the steamer Warren was then towing down the river. Owing partly to the dense obscurity of the night, but much more to the mismanagement of the officers of the Monmouth, a collision took place between that vessel and the Tremont, and such was the violence of the concussion, that the Monmouth immediately sunk. The unhappy red men, with their wives and children, were precipitated into the water; and such was the confusion which prevailed at the time, such was the number of the drowning people, who probably clung to each other in their struggles for life, that, notwithstanding the Indians, men, women and children, are generally expert swimmers, more than half of the unfortunate Creeks perished. The captains and crews of the steamers Warren and Yazoo, by dint of great exertion, succeeded in saving about three hundred of the poor Indians, the remaining four hundred had become accusing spirits before the tribunal of a just God, where they, whose criminal negligence was the cause of this calamity, will certainly be held accountable.

The cabin of the Monmouth parted from the hull, and drifted some distance down the stream, when it broke in two parts, and emptied its living contents into the river. The stem of the ship came in contact with the side of the steamer, therefore the former received but little damage, while the latter was broken up, to that degree that the hull, as previously stated, almost instantly went to the bottom. The ship merely lost her cut-water.

The mishap, as we have hinted before, may be ascribed to the mismanagement of the officers of the Monmouth. This boat was running in a part of the river where, by the usages of the river and the rules adopted for the better regulation of steam navigation on the Mississippi, she had no right to go, and where, of course, the descending vessels did not expect to meet with any boat coming in an opposite direction. The only persons attached to the Monmouth who lost their lives, were the bar-keeper and a fireman.

It is not without some feeling of indignation, that we mention the circumstance that the drowning of four hundred Indians, the largest number of human beings ever sacrificed in a steamboat disaster, attracted but little attention, (comparatively speaking,) in any part of the country. Even the journalists and news-collectors of that region, on the waters of which this horrible affair took place, appear to have regarded the event as of too little importance to deserve any particular detail; and accordingly the best accounts we have of the matter merely state the outlines of the story, with scarcely a word of commiseration for the sufferers, or a single expression of rebuke for the heartless villains who wantonly exposed the lives of so many artless and confiding people to imminent peril, or almost certain destruction.

A MODEL WESTERN BOAT.

THE OLDEST STEAMBOAT COMPANY IN EXISTENCE.

THE United States' mail line between Cincinnati, Louisville, and St. Louis, is the oldest steamboat line on the Western waters. This company own some of the finest and fleetest boats in the world. The company was organized in 1818, and have continued together ever since, adding finer and better boats to the line every year. In 1818 this company built the steamer "Gen. Pike," which was the first boat ever constructed *exclusively* for passengers. She run between Louisville and Cincinnati, making her trips in *one day and seven hours*, a feat which is now performed in nine or ten hours by this company's boats. The Gen. Pike was first commanded by Capt. Bliss; afterwards by Capt. Penewitt and Capt. John M. Rowan. In the clerk's office of this pioneer boat was Jacob Strader, Esq., now president of the Little Miami Rail Road Company, and lately president of the Commercial Bank, Cincinnati. She was a very prosperous boat and did an immense business. In a few years afterwards the trade between Louisville and Cincinnati so rapidly increased that it became necessary for the company to build larger and better boats, and then commenced the long list of steamers, Gen. Pikes, Pikes, and Ben. Franklins, the names of which at the present time are as familiar to the Western public as household words. In 1847 the wants of the travelling public demanded a daily line from Cincinnati to St. Louis, and this enterprising company immediately built ten large and elegant steamers and placed them in that trade, and the line has been in operation ever since with marked success. Before this line of fleet steamers went into operation, the time between the two ports was seldom made in less than four or five days. Now the time is made from the Falls of Ohio to St. Louis in from thirty-nine to forty-four hours, almost rivalling the iron horse in speed, and far surpassing it in accommodations.

The company frequently add finer and larger boats to their lines, as may become necessary to the welfare and safety of the public. Possessing almost unlimited capital, they have recently constructed two of the fleetest and most gorgeously furnished boats now afloat, viz: the low-pressure steamer Jacob Strader and Telegraph No. 3; costing, in the aggregate, nearly four hundred thousand dollars. The cabins of the boats rival in grandeur the finest palaces, while their speed is equal to eighteen miles per hour. In short, we owe to this company, in a great measure, that reputation for superior architecture and equipments, which the western steamboats have acquired; a reputation which is conceded to them by all travellers, and which places them beyond all rivalship, either in this country or Europe.

The boats named in the following list compose the present line:

From Cincinnati to Louisville, the low-pressure steamers Jacob Strader, Capt. Summons, and Telegraph No. 3, Capt. Hildreth, connecting at Louisville for St. Louis with the elegant low-pressure steamers Southerner, Capt. Catterlin, Northerner, Capt. Erwin, Ben Franklin, Capt. Dollis, Moses McLellon, Capt. Barker, High Flyer, Capt. Wright, Fashion No. 2, Capt. Reed, and Alvin Adams, Capt. Boiess. This line connects at Cincinnati, Louisville and St. Louis with the railroads and steamboats, north, east, west and south. An extraordinary and most gratifying circumstance, in connection with the history of this steamboat company, should not escape our notice. Not a single explosion, nor any other frightful disaster, has occurred on any of the boats since the company was first organized, comprising a period of almost fifty years. Thus we have it demonstrated that the greatest speed in steamboat travel may, under proper management, be consistent with the most perfect security.

BURNING OF THE WASHINGTON.

A new and elegant steamboat called the Washington, was burned on Lake Erie, opposite Silver creek, June 16th, 1838. In the early part of the preceding night, the Washington passed the steamer North America, while the latter lay at the town of Erie. On the following morning, about three o'clock, when the North America was within three miles of Buffalo, the helmsman discovered a brilliant light, which appeared to rise from the bosom of the lake in the direction of Silver creek. The North America was immediately put about, and steered for the scene of the apprehended disaster. On approaching the spot, about six o'clock, the burning hull of the Washington was found driving before the wind, about four miles from land, and not a living object could be discovered on board. The surface of the lake was literally covered with hats, bonnets, trunks, baggage and blackened fragments of the wreck.

The intense anxiety of those who beheld this fearful scene for the fate of the passengers and crew of the Washington, was partially relieved by the discovery of several small boats near the shore, in which it was supposed that some who had embarked in the Washington were probably saved. In fact, the alarm had been given at the town of Silver Creek as soon as the flames were perceived from the shore, and all the boats that could be found were sent to rescue the sufferers. There were only three skiffs, however, which could be employed in this service; but these, together with the yawl of the Washington, were the means of saving all who could be found on the steamer, and all who were still floating on the water when the skiffs arrived. But, in the meanwhile, a number, variously estimated from thirty to sixty, had perished. Six dead bodies, those of two women and four children, were picked up by the boats near the burning wreck. One man died of his injuries soon after he reached the shore, and a child was found dead in its mother's arms when taken out of the lake. The mother survived, though she was insensible when found in the water, clasping her dead infant to her bosom.

The origin of the fire is not well explained, but it appears that the flames broke out in the immediate neighbourhood of the boiler. The helm was immediately put about, and the head of the boat directed to the shore, but within a few minutes, the wheel ropes were severed by the fire, and the boat became an unmanageable wreck. Had iron rods, instead of ropes, been used in the construction of the steering apparatus, it is highly probable that every individual on board would have been saved, for in that case the boat could have reached the shore without difficulty. The surviving passengers unanimously testified that no blame could be attached to Capt. Brown, the commander of the Washington. The names of the victims, with the usual allowance for defective reports, are subjoined.

PERSONS DROWNED OR BURNT TO DEATH.—Capt. Clemens, of Dudley, Mass.; Conrad Shurtz, and William Shurtz, wife and three children, Clinton, N. Y.; Wm. Sheld, St. Lawrence; Mr. Baker, wife and three children (one child of Mr. Baker was saved.) A Scotchman, name unknown, lost three children, together with his mother and sister. Several of the survivors, whose names are not given, were badly burned before they left the boat.

The Washington was built at Ashtabula; she was not more than six months old, and had made but one trip before the one which was interrupted by this deplorable accident.

EXPLOSION OF THE WALKER.

This explosion took place on Lake Ponchartrain, on the 2d day of December, 1840. The particulars were never published before. The following list of the killed and wounded was furnished by D. H. Ryder, who was clerk of the Walker at the time of the explosion:

KILLED—J. S. Harper; John Pierson, steersman; G. E. Sedenberg, of Baltimore; A. Budd, J. Cloon, Z. Ferrell, —— Smith.

BADLY SCALDED—J. H. White, of Tennessee; J. Bellow, of New Orleans; Mr. Lanier, Mr. Nelson, pilot, and R. Roach, deck hand.

SLIGHTLY SCALDED—Capt. J. A. Otway, J. H. Caldwell, Esq., and four stevedores from Mobile Bay, names unknown.

MISSING—John Dean and Wm. Powell, stevedores.

The accident is ascribed to the "weakness of the boiler," and not to any omission of duty on the part of those who had charge of the engines.

VIEW OF LOUISVILLE.

SKETCH OF LOUISVILLE.

LOUISVILLE, situated on the south bank of the Ohio river, in Jefferson county, Kentucky, is the largest town of the State, and one of the most flourishing and important places in the Western country. Its location is at the head of the Falls of the Ohio, one hundred and forty-three miles below Cincinnati, and four hundred and eighteen miles from the mouth of the Ohio, in lat 38° 3′ N., long. 85° 30′ W. The appearance of the city from every point of view is striking and elegant, and the surrounding scenery is picturesque and beautiful. A delightful view of the Falls of the Ohio, and other interesting objects, may be obtained from the city wharf. Louisville stands on a plain or plateau, elevated about seventy-six feet above low-water mark. The city is regularly laid out, the streets are spacious and well paved, and the buildings, public and private, are well constructed, with a view to permanence as well as beauty. Twelve handsome streets, parallel with the river, extend to a length of about two miles each. The direction of these streets is East and West, and their breadth varies from sixty to one hundred feet, and are intersected at right angles by more than forty others, having an uniform breadth of sixty feet; they are kept in the cleanest order, and are lighted with gas and bordered by ornamental shade trees. In short, the streets of Louisville are, for beauty and convenience, unrivaled in any of the Atlantic cities.

The most remarkable public buildings are the City Hall and Court House, the First Presbyterian Church, St. Paul's Church, the Medical Institute, and the University of Louisville, which is now in successful operation. The Medical Institute, which holds a high rank among similar institutions in the United States, was founded by an ordinance of the City Council, which appropriated $50,000 for the building and library. The number of students in 1855 was more than one thousand. The Asylum for the Blind, established by the State, is a large and beautiful building. The Mercantile Library Association has a library containing between nine and ten thousand volumes. The Historical Society of Louisville has collected many valuable documents relating to the early history of the City and State. Louisville contains a Marine Asylum, founded by the State of Kentucky. Another extensive Marine Asylum for indigent boatmen has recently been erected here, by the United States' government. Besides these public establishments, there are three orphan asylums, about fifty churches, two handsome Jewish synagogues, ten banks, and six large buildings for public schools. A new Custom House is being erected at a cost of $200,000. Seven daily newspapers, eight weeklies, and one monthly medical Journal, are published in this city.

Louisville may be said to owe its existence, in a measure, to the Falls, which interrupt the navigation of the river at this point. In 1833, a canal, two and a half miles long, was opened around these rapids; it was cut through the solid limestone rock, at a cost of nearly one million dollars. Boats exceeding one hundred and eighty-five feet in length cannot pass through the locks of this canal, a circumstance which greatly impedes navigation, and is likewise a serious disadvantage to Louisville, as all the freights for the large New Orleans and St. Louis steamers must be conveyed on drays to Portland, which is three miles below Louisville.

The canal was originally the joint-property of the United States and individual stockholders. The rates of tonnage for vessels passing through were formerly exorbitant, and the stockholders have all become rich at the expense of the boatmen. However, through the untiring exertions of the Hon. Wm. Preston, late member of Congress from that district, the United States government was induced, in the year 1854, to buy out the interest of the private stockholders. The canal is now under the charge of a superintendent, appointed by government, and the rates of tonnage are no more than is required to keep the canal in repair. The canal could easily be made passable for boats of the largest class; this great improvement is now under consideration, and will probably be carried into effect.

In 1850 the entire trade of Louisville was estimated at $55,000,000. The commerce of the city is now believed to reach a much larger amount. There are one hundred and one houses, which do an exclusively wholesale business, to the amount of $26,341,400 per annum. The number of boat arrivals at Louisville in 1854 was 3,500. The principal articles of export are flour, hemp, and tobacco. The very best steamboats now afloat were built at this city. Some of these boats have made the voyage from New Orleans, against the current, to Louisville, a distance of 1486 miles, in little more than four days, a performance which appears to be almost miraculous.

The manufactures of Louisville amount to about $10,000,000. There are twenty-one iron foundries, employing 1900 workmen; one hundred and eight tobacco factories, giving employment to 1800 persons; forty-five clothing manufactories, employing 1260 persons; thirty-six furniture manufactories, employing 612 persons; fourteen rope-walks, with 290 workmen; eleven soap and candle factories; eleven flour and feed mills; twelve tanneries; four cotton and woollen factories; four oil factories; three of white lead, and numerous other manufacturing establishments.

The population of Louisville in 1830, was 10,341; in 1840, 21,210; in 1850, 46,180; in 1852, 60,000; and in 1856, 80,000.

EXPLOSION OF THE MOHICAN.

The steam tow-boat Mohican, on the 19th day of February, 1842, while engaged, together with the tow-boat Star, in towing the British ship Edward Thorn across a bar near New Orleans, burst all her boilers, causing the death of ten or twelve persons. The Mohican took fire immediately after the explosion, and was entirely consumed. One of the boilers of the exploded vessel was found on the forecastle of the ship in tow. The accident is ascribed to a deficiency of water in the boilers.

Lieutenant Bukup, one of the revenue officers stationed at the Balize, was blown from the deck of the Mohican to the deck of the Star, and was killed instantly. The mate of the English ship was killed, and the Captain was dangerously wounded. Capt. Heaton, of the Mohican, was much injured, and two engineers, two firemen, and three deck hands, belonging to the same boat, were killed.

COLLISION OF THE BELLE OF CLARKSVILLE AND LOUISIANA.

On the night of December 14, 1844, a disastrous collision took place on the Mississipi river, between the steamers Belle of Clarksville and Louisiana, the former from New Orleans, bound to Nashville; the latter, from Memphis to New Orleans. Both vessels were heavily laden. The Belle of Clarksville was completely demolished. The hull parted from the cabin and sunk immediately, the cabin floating off with a number of passengers inside, all of whom were saved. None were drowned but deck passengers, and some of the crew of the boat. The Louisiana was immediately brought around, and every exertion was made by the captain and crew to save those persons who were floating on small pieces of the wreck. The detached cabin grounded about half a mile below the place where the boats came in contact. All the cargo and the baggage of the passengers was lost. The boat was laden with sugar, salt, coffee, and molasses. Mr. J. H. French, one of the passengers, had with him three negro slaves, and three valuable horses, among them the celebrated Ann Hayes; these slaves and horses were all drowned. The iron safe containing $12,000 was saved. The cargo was insured at New Orleans for $23,000; the boat for $8,000.

The following are the names of the persons drowned:

DECK PASSENGERS—W. Tabb, P. Linn, W. Linn, J. Ryan, A. Malisle, N. Sills, Wm. Jones, T. Whitley, N. T. Allen, A. Kirland, J. Askew, G. Hyer, a son of J. W. Hall, J. Peay, and four colored men.

BOAT'S CREW—John Holliday, assistant engineer, and twelve colored firemen, names not given.

COLLISION OF THE FORREST AND PULASKI.

On Friday night, May 5th, 1843, at 11 o'clock, as the steamer Forrest was lying to, to put off a passenger, about twenty miles above the mouth of the Alleghany river, with her head down stream, she was run into by the steamboat Pulaski, which was coming up the river with about one hundred and fifty passengers. The bow of the Forrest struck the side of the Pulaski opposite the boilers. The boilers were thrown down, the steam-pipes separated, and the steam rushed out among the passengers, scalding many of them in a terrible manner. The side of

FALLS OF THE OHIO.

the Pulaski being broken up by the collision, the boat almost immediately sunk, leaving the boiler-deck above water. Five or six persons, names unknown, were thrown overboard and drowned. One of these floated past the Forrest, calling piteously for assistance, but before it could be afforded him the current had swept him away. Another was drawn in under the wheel and drowned. One young man swam ashore after throwing himself from the cabin window of the Pulaski.

The following list of the sufferers was furnished by the officers of the wrecked steamer:

BADLY SCALDED—Wm. Coon, Erie co., N. Y.; Michael Hawkins, steward of the Pulaski; Sheridan McCullough, of Red Bank, Pa.; James Gibson, Crawford co., Pa.; Joseph Hughes, Jefferson co., Pa.; and —— Wing.

We have not been able to learn the names of the persons who were drowned.

SINKING OF THE SHEPHERDESS.

On the 3d of January, 1844, the whole city of St. Louis was thrown into consternation and feverish excitement by the intelligence that the steamboat Shepherdess had been wrecked in Cahokia Bend, only three miles from the centre of that city, and that many lives had been lost. Several boats were immediately despatched to the scene of the reported disaster, and the worst rumors were unhappily verified. The particulars of the sad event are given below:

The Shepherdess, while ascending the Mississippi river on her way from Cincinnati to St. Louis, at 11 o'clock, in a dark and stormy night, struck a snag just above the mouth of Cahokia creek. The concussion was very severe, and it is believed that several planks must have been torn from the bottom of the boat. According to the report of the officers, the number of passengers was between sixty and seventy. Most of those who were in the gentlemen's cabin had retired to their berths; four or five gentlemen in this cabin were sitting up by the stove, as it was cold winter weather. The ladies were generally undressed for the night. In less than two minutes after the boat struck, the water rose to the lower deck, where most of the passengers in that part of the boat were asleep. The Captain, who was on duty, ran to the cabin occupied by the ladies, and assured them that there was no danger: he then returned to the forecastle, and is supposed to have been washed overboard, as nothing was seen or heard of him afterwards. As soon as the shock was felt on board, one of the pilots attempted to descend into the hold for the purpose of examining the leak, but he had scarcely entered when the rush of water drove him back.

About this time shrieks and exclamations of affright and distress arose from the deck below, and several ladies, who hastened to the stern-railing, reported that they saw a number of persons struggling in the river. Certain it is that the water rushed in with tremendous rapidity, and before three minutes had elapsed it had risen to the floor of the upper cabin. Some of those persons who were on deck saved

SINKING OF THE SHEPHERDESS.

themselves by getting into the yawl, which was cut loose and rowed to the shore with a broom. The water rose so rapidly that it soon became necessary for all to seek safety on the hurricane deck. This position was not attained without great difficulty, for the bow had sunk so deep in the water that the only access was the stern. However, it is believed that all the people from the cabin succeeded in reaching the hurricane roof. In the meanwhile the boat was drifting down the stream, and a few hundred yards below, she struck another snag, which rose above the surface. This threw the steamer nearly on her beam ends on the larboard side. Drifting from this snag, she again lurched to starboard. At each lurch several persons were washed off; some of them reached the shore, but many were drowned. A short distance below, just above the first shot-tower, the hull struck a bluff-bank, which again careened the boat nearly on her side. Here the hull and cabin parted; the former sunk and lodged on a bar above Carondelet, while the cabin floated down to the point of the bar below that place, where it lodged and became stationary.

The steamer Henry Bry was lying at the shot-tower above Carondelet, and as the cabin passed, the captain of that vessel, being aroused by the cries of the passengers, took his yawl to their rescue. This little boat could only take off a few at a time, but by the strenuous exertions of the captain of the Bry many were saved. This humane gentleman almost sacrificed himself in the work of benevolence, and did not desist until he was covered with a mass of ice, and benumbed to that degree that further effort was impossible. About three o'clock the ferry-boat Icelander came down, and took off all who remained in the detached cabin.

We have thus given a general history of this calamity, but some particular incidents deserve the reader's attention. A young man, Robert Bullock, of Maysville, Ky., was one of the passengers. With heroic devotion to the cause of humanity, he took no measures for his own safety, but directed all his efforts to the preservation of the women and children. When every other male person of mature age had deserted the cabin, he went from state-room to state-room, and wherever he heard a child cry took it out and passed it to the hurricane deck. In this way he saved a number of women and children. His last effort was to rescue Col. Wood's "Ohio Fat Girl," who happened to be on board. Her weight was four hundred and forty pounds, but with the assistance of several persons on the hurricane deck, he succeeded in raising her to that place of security. A short time after, the boat made a lurch, and Bullock was thrown into the water. He swam to the Illinois shore, having previously given his coat to a lady on the wreck who was suffering excessively from cold. On reaching the land this young hero found two young ladies, who had been put ashore in a skiff, and who were nearly frozen. They were about falling asleep, which would have been fatal in such circumstances, when Bullock aroused them, and with great exertions succeeded in getting them to Cohokia, where they met with the attention which their half-frozen condition required.

An English family, from the neighborhood of Manchester, ten in number, were all saved. Five of them succeeded in getting to the Illinois shore, four to the Missouri side of the river, and one was taken off the wreck by the ferry-boat. They were all re-united on this boat at Cohokia, at a moment when each party supposed the other to be dead. A spectator of that re-union avers that he never witnessed a more affecting scene.

Mr. Muir, of Virginia, and his brother, were on board, with their mother and nine of their slaves. With the exception of seven of the slaves, all of these persons were saved. Levi Craddock, from Davidson Co., Tenn., lost three children; himself, his wife, and two children were saved. Mr. Green, of the same county and state, lost his wife and three children, and was left with two helpless infants, the youngest only three months old. Mr. Snell, formerly of Louisville, Ky., lost a son and daughter. Mr. Wright, of Mecklenburg Co., Va., and two of his children, were drowned. His wife, who survived, was in a state of distraction. The Captain, A. Howell, of Covington, Ky., was undoubtedly lost. He was in the act of ringing the bell, when the boat made a lurch, by which the boilers, part of the engine, and the chimneys, were carried overboard, Capt. H. being overwhelmed among the ruins, and he sunk with them. He left a wife and eleven children, the eldest of whom, a son, was with him on the wreck.

The bodies of two children, who had perished with cold, were brought up to St. Louis. Considering how many children were on board, it is surprising that more of these helpless beings were not lost. The Mayor of St. Louis, who personally assisted in relieving the sufferers, caused all who were saved alive to be taken to the Virginia hotel, where they were amply provided for. Forty persons are believed to have perished in this wreck. The Rev. Mr. Peck, of Illinois, who was on board at the time, makes the estimate much larger. One of the St. Louis papers averred that the number of persons lost was not less than seventy.

Capt. Howell had lately bought the Shepherdess, and this was her first trip after she became his property.

DESTRUCTIVE AND FATAL TORNADO AT NATCHEZ.

On the 7th day of May, 1840, the city of Natchez, Miss., was visited by a tornado, which occasioned an immense destruction of property and great loss of life. Several steamboats were destroyed at the wharves of Natchez, and many persons who had embarked in them as passengers were drowned. A large number of flat boats, likewise, were wrecked by the tremendous gale, and a number of boatmen, supposed to be two hundred or more, in the aggregate, perished. A tax had recently been laid on flat-boats at Vicksburg, on which account many of them had dropped down to Natchez, so that there was an unusually large number of these boats collected at the last-named city at the time of the tornado.

The steamboat Hinds was blown out into the stream and sunk, and all the passengers and crew, except four men, were lost. It is not known how many passengers were on this boat. The captain was supposed to have been saved, as he was seen on shore a short time before the gale commenced, but as nothing was heard of him afterwards, it

TORNADO AT NATCHEZ.

is conjectured that he must have returned to the boat, and shared the fate of his crew and passengers. The wreck of the Hinds was afterwards found at Baton Rouge, with fifty-one dead bodies on board, forty-eight of whom were males, and three females; among the latter was one little girl about three years old.

The steamboat Prairie had just arrived from St. Louis, freighted with lead. Her upper works, down to the deck, were swept off, and the whole of the crew and passengers are supposed to have been drowned. The number of the passengers is not known, but four ladies, at least, were seen on board a short time before the disaster. The steamboat H. Lawrence and a sloop were in a somewhat sheltered position at the Cotton Press. They were severely damaged, but not sunk. The steam ferry-boat was sunk, and also the wharf-boat "Mississippian," which was used as a hotel, grocery, &c. Of one hundred and twenty flat-boats, which lay at the landing, all were lost except four, and very few of the men employed on board were saved.

We give the names of some of the victims, but a great majority of the persons drowned could never be identified.

DROWNED.—William Stubbs and John Ervin, Louisville; David McGowan, C. Butler, Andrew Filer, Absalom Wilson, A Terry, D. Garsford, M. Dunn, E. Booker, B. Floney, and C. Carter and two children, of New York; W. Williams and wife, of St. Louis; E. McFaul, of Boston; James Orr, of Natchez; Y. Budhim, of Ind.; Thomas Rodgers, of Cairo, Ill.; D. Ewing, M. Dinwiddie, and W. Johnston, wife and two children, of Pittsburgh, Pa.; C. Phelps, G. Phillips, and Dr. Brady, of Ind.; Marcus Austin, of New Amsterdam, Ind.; M. Tooley, Philadelphia, Pa.; B. Shreve and Miss Margaret Haskell, Ky.; Mrs.

Watkins, Ohio; Mrs. Jones, Louisiana; Mrs. Dwight and daughter, Wis.; Miss Hardy, Ill.; Mrs. Walters and infant, Vicksburg; Duncan Sherman, John Root, and C. Y. Bunner, Ala.

Besides these, about two hundred flat boatmen, (names unknown,) were ascertained to have been lost. The total loss of life is estimated at four hundred. For its violence and destructive effects, this tornado was without precedent in the recollection of the oldest inhabitant of that region. The water in the river was agitated to that degree that the best swimmers could not sustain themselves on the surface. The waves rose to the height of ten or fifteen feet. Many houses in the vicinity of Natchez were blown down, and many buildings in the city were unroofed; the roofs, in some instances, being carried half-way across the river. People found it impossible to stand on the shore. One man was blown from the top of the hill, (sixty feet high,) and fell into the river forty yards from the bank. Heavy beams of timber and other ponderous objects were blown about like straws. Great was the consternation of the inhabitants of Natchez and its neighborhood, and owing to this cause, perhaps, many persons were drowned for want of prompt assistance. When the first alarm had somewhat subsided, the citizens hastened to the river, rescued some who were still living from the water, and recovered hundreds of dead bodies before they were swept away by the rapid current.

EXPLOSION OF THE LUCY WALKER, OCT. 25, 1844.

This event is especially remarkable on account of the unusual complication of calamities, (if we may so speak,) which attended it; the explosion, the burning and the sinking of the vessel, all occurring within a few minutes. The Lucy Walker, Capt. Vann, was descending the river, and when about four miles below New Albany, Indiana, some part of the machinery got out of order, and the boat was stopped to make repairs. During this pause, the water in the boilers was measurably exhausted, and about five minutes after the engine ceased working, three of the boilers exploded with tremendous violence and terrible effect.

The principal force of the explosion took an upward direction; and the consequence was that all that part of the boat situated above the boilers was blown into thousands of pieces. The U. S. snag-boat Gophar, Capt. L. B. Dunham, was about two hundred yards distant at the time of the explosion. Capt. Dunham was immediately on the spot, rescuing those who had been thrown into the water, and affording all other assistance in his power. Having been a spectator of the scene, with all its horrors, this gentleman has furnished a narrative, to which we are indebted for many of the facts related in this article. He states that such was the force of the explosion, that, although the Lucy Walker was in the middle of the river, many fragments of wood and iron were thrown on shore. At the moment of the accident, the air appeared to be filled with human beings, with dissevered limbs and other fragments of human bodies. One man was blown to the height of fifty yards, as the narrator judges, and fell with such force as to pass entirely through the deck. Another was cut in two by a piece of the boiler Many other incidents, equally distressing and horrifying, are related. Before Capt. Dunham could reach the spot where the wreck lay, he saw many persons who had been blown overboard perish in the water. But it was his good fortune to save the lives of a large number, by throwing them boards and ropes, and pulling them on board with boat-hooks. Immediately after the explosion, the ladies' cabin took fire and burned with great rapidity, but before it was consumed, the steamer sunk in twelve feet water. Thus the whole tragedy was completed within a few minutes.

EXPLOSION OF THE LUCY WALKER.

The screams and exclamations of the ladies and the other survivors are represented as awful and distressing in the extreme. However, most of the females escaped; a very few of them are supposed to have been drowned, but none of those who survived were injured. The books of the boat were destroyed; of course it will ever be impossible to ascertain all the names or the number of those who perished. There were at least fifty or sixty persons killed or missing, and fifteen or twenty wounded, some of them very seriously. Capt. Dunham took off the wounded and left them at New Albany, where they were suitably provided for by the hospitable and benevolent citizens of the place.

The following are the names of the killed, wounded and missing, as far as we have been able to learn:

Killed or Missing.—Gen. J. W. Pegram, of Richmond, Va.; Samuel M. Brown, Post-Office agent, of Lexington, Ky.; J. R. Cormick, of Virginia; Charles Dunn, pilot, of Louisville, Ky.; Philip Wallis, formerly of Baltimore, Md.; Rebecca, daughter of A. J. Foster, of Greenville, Va.; James Vanderburg, of Louisville, Ky.; Mr. Hughes, formerly of Lexington, Ky.; Mr. Matlock, of New Albany, Ind.; engineer of the steamboat Mazeppa; Nicholas Ford, formerly of Baltimore, Md.; David Vann, master of the Lucy Walker; Moses Kirby, pilot of the same; second mate, second clerk, second engineer, and bar-keeper of the boat, names not mentioned.

Wounded.—Four negro firemen; W. H. Peebler, Mr. Rainer, of Virginia, and the first engineer, all badly hurt; Capt. Thomson, pilot, both arms fractured; Mr. Roberts, of Philadelphia, slightly hurt.

Two persons, John W. Johnson and Richard Phillips, are supposed to have been in the boat. They were not seen after the explosion, and it was generally believed that they were lost. Another account says, "We understand that the bodies of Nicholas Ford, Philip Wallis, S. M. Brown, and a little girl, killed by the explosion of the Lucy Walker, have been taken from the river, and decently interred by the citizens of West Point."

Additional Incidents.—The Rev. Mr. Todd, of Natchez, was blown overboard, but saved himself by swimming. At New Albany, when the dead bodies and the wounded were brought to that city, the stores and other places of business were generally closed, flags were lowered, and the whole town wore the aspect of mourning.

Mr. Wren, of Yazoo, Miss., was thrown from the boiler-deck, and fell near the bow of the boat, in a state of insensibility. When he recovered his senses, he saw his little son, six or seven years old, with the flames raging around him, in the upper part of the boat. He watched the movements of the child, as every parent will believe, with intense anxiety. Soon he saw the boy leap overboard; the river was covered with planks and mattresses, and the lad went from fragment to fragment, until he succeeded in getting on a mattress which would support him in the water. The agonized father, who was unable to rise from the spot where he lay, continued to watch the progress of his little son, until he saw him taken off the mattress by the crew of

Capt. Dunham's boat. Who shall attempt to imagine, much less to describe, the feelings of the father at that moment?

A man and his wife and four daughters were saved separately, and in different ways. Their subsequent meeting must have been most joyous. A little girl was found clinging to the wreck when the flames were so near that she was constrained to dash water on one side of her face, to protect it from the intense heat. A man was on the hurricane-deck with his wife and little daughter, at the time of the explosion. He dropped the lady aft into the yawl, and saw that she was safe; he then threw the child into the stream, and although suffering severely with a sprained ankle and other hurts, he plunged in, and saved both himself and his little girl by swimming.

Pieces of the boiler were thrown on the Kentucky shore, and it is said that some of them were no thicker than a half dollar. When, where, or by whom could they have been inspected?

The Lucy Walker was built at Cincinnati, and finished only about nine months before the fatal termination of her career.

TERRIFIC EXPLOSION OF THE WILMINGTON.

The steamer Wilmington, bound from New Orleans to St. Louis, burst a boiler at daylight, on the morning of the 18th of November, 1839, when near the mouth of Arkansas river. The boilers, engines, and upper works were entirely demolished. In fact, there never was a more terrific explosion, although the loss of life was small, owing to there being few passengers on board

List of the Killed.—One of the pilots, Mr. Andrew Helms, who was standing near the stern of the boat, was blown overboard and drowned; Julius Fisk, the first engineer; Paul Johnson, second engineer, mortally wounded; William Hasker, John Freeman, C. Smith, John Rhoades and Dr. Brant, New Orleans; William Wills, South Carolina; C. Ebert, and nine wounded.

The Wilmington had just started from a wood-yard, and was under full headway when the explosion took place. The boat was completely riddled with pieces of iron flying through the cabin. The dead were buried at the mouth of the Arkansas river.

VIEW OF CAIRO.

SKETCH OF CAIRO.

CAIRO is advantageously situated in Alexandria County, Illinois, at the southern extremity of the State, on a point of land formed by the confluence of the Ohio and Mississippi rivers, one hundred and eighty-four miles below St. Louis, and one thousand miles above New Orleans. The situation of this town at the junction of these two great rivers, affords one of the finest positions for a commercial city that can be found in the Western States; but owing to some natural defects in the locality, the growth of the place has been less rapid than it would have been in more favorable circumstances. The banks of the Ohio at this point are low, and the surrounding country is still lower; the whole tract of land, therefore, is liable to inundation at the periodical rising of the river. These occasional overflows, and the marshy nature of the soil, are supposed to affect the health of the neighborhood; but by the industry and ingenuity of man these natural disadvantages have already been removed, to some extent, and there is no reason to doubt that all such obstacles to the improvement of the place will, in the course of time, be entirely removed. A levee or embankment, twenty-six feet high, has been erected, at a cost of $1,000,000, to protect the town and adjacent country from overflows. Since this great work was completed, Cairo has improved very rapidly. It is the southern terminus of the Illinois Central Railroad, (the largest railroad in the United States,) which extends to Chicago and Rock Island. A line of first class steamers will soon be in operation between Cairo and New Orleans, leaving each place daily, and conveying the United States mail.

The largest wharf-boat in the world, two hundred and thirty-six feet in length, is stationed at this place, under the superintendence of Messrs. Fowler & Norton, Freight and United States Mail Agents, and dealers in groceries and produce. This aquatic establishment affords great facilities to the boats in obtaining supplies, and in the shipment of freight. Messrs. Fowler & Norton are also freight agents for the Illinois Central Railroad. These gentlemen, with some other active and enterprising residents of Cairo, have been instrumental in giving a new impulse to the business of the place, and in forwarding those improvements, which bid fair to make it, at no distant time, one of the first cities of the West.

When we consider what New Orleans has effected in order to overcome the natural disadvantages of soil and situation, we cannot question the ability of Cairo to obviate those minor inconveniencies which at one time threatened to interfere with her prosperity. Judging from what has been done already, we may safely predict that this place will soon become a flourishing emporium, and command the immense trade of the West, Northwest, and South. The tardy growth of Cairo, in earlier times, has been ascribed in a great measure to the illiberal policy of the English Company which purchased the land some years ago, and attempted to establish a monopoly of the whole ground, of which they retained the ownership, and making mere tenantry of all the settlers. A better system now prevails; another company, of a far more progressive character than the preceding one, has obtained possession of the land; men of energy and pecuniary means have been induced to settle in the place; improvements of various kinds have been carried into effect, and still greater ones are in contemplation. Two excellent newspapers have been established at Cairo. The population at present is 1000, and is rapidly increasing.

COLLISION OF THE ATLANTIC AND OGDENSBURG.

At an early hour before daylight, on the 20th day of August, 1852, the steamboat Atlantic ran afoul of the propeller Ogdensburg, about six miles above Long Point, on Lake Erie. The morning was very foggy and the darkness was extreme, and for some time the extent of the damage was not apparent, even to those who were on board of the vessel which sustained the injury. The propeller struck the Atlantic forward of the wheel, on the larboard side; the shock was so little felt on board the steamer, that she continued her course without any apprehension of danger ; and, as the propellor had reversed her engine before the collision took place, the crew of it did not suppose that any serious mischief had been done to the other. However, before the Atlantic had proceeded two miles, it was discovered that she was sinking rapidly. The passengers were all in bed at the time, and when they were aroused from their slumbers to be informed of their perilous condition, the scene of confusion and dismay which followed is beyond all the powers of language to describe. The number of persons on board, including passengers and crew, is rated at four hundred and fifty. Of these, more than two hundred were Norwegian emigrants. As soon as the startling intelligence was communicated to the passengers, all were assembled on deck, to meet or avoid the fate which threatened them. The poor Norwegians, who were generally ignorant of the English language, could scarcely be made to comprehend the cause of the alarm, but observing the consternation which prevailed among the other passengers, they became wildly excited, and threw themselves into the water in spite of every effort to restrain them. The other passengers listened to the exhortations of the captain, and became perfectly calm, assisting to throw overboard settees, chairs, mattresses, and other buoyant articles, which might be the means of supporting them in the water when the boat went down. In the meanwhile, the state of affairs in the doomed vessel was such as to produce a feeling of intense anxiety. even among the bravest. The dense obscurity of the night, the damp and chilling atmosphere, the terrific hissing of the water as it rushed through the gaping leak upon the furnaces, in which every spark of fire was soon extinguished, the shrieks and cries of the affrighted women and children who remained on board, and the still more distressing exclamations of those who were struggling in the water, all these circumstances combined to make a scene of horror which appalled even those who could have met their own fate with fortitude and intrepidity.

About half past two the steamer sunk, notwithstanding all the well-directed efforts which had been made by the crew to keep her afloat.

The propeller had stopped to make repairs after the accident, and now when her crew were apprised of the dreadful condition of those who had been in the Atlantic, by the cries, shrieks, and lamentations of the drowning people, the Ogdensburg promptly steered for the spot, and was the means, under divine Providence, of saving about two hundred and fifty of the unfortunates who still survived. Hundreds were battling with the waters, and while the sympathising crew of the propeller were dragging some aboard of that vessel with all possible despatch, many others sunk into the abyss of waters, and were seen no more. From the most authentic statements it appears that more than three hundred lives were lost. A majority of the sufferers were Norwegian emigrants, of whom previous mention has been made. The books of the boat were lost, and no record of the names of those who perished has been preserved. The following is a list of the names of those passengers who obtained tickets at Erie, but it is uncertain who of them were saved and who were lost:

Mr. Osborne, wife and child, Mr. Reed, Mr. Field, wife and two children, of New York; Mr. Frost, of Boston; Mr. Calkins, Mr. Luke, Mr. Fairbrother, Mr. Bushnell and brother, of Albany, N. Y.; Mr. Lawrence, wife and two children, of Utica; Mr. Clark and child; Mr. Russell; Mrs. Cornwall, sister of Elihu Burrett; Mr. Fisher, of Canada; Mr. Shanker, Mr. Britton, Mr. Stanley, of New York; Mr. Myers; Mr. Carley and wife; Mr. Bissal, Mr. Brown, Mr. Le Fevre, Mr. Kirby, of Troy; Mr. Johnson and wife; Mr. White and wife; Mr. Crippen; Mr. Green, Mr. Burd, of Schenectady; Mr. Montgomery and wife, Cayuga Co., N. Y.

Second class passengers ticketed at the same office:—Messrs. Stevens, Hartley and wife, Albany; Toogood and wife, Troy; Marshall, Boston; Hall, Graver, Calvin, Turner, Waits, wife and two children, Hammerman, Stuart, Bird and wife, Lucas, and Hayer.

The persons named below were also on board:

A. E. Doggett, of Chicago; Mr. Walbridge, of Erie; Mr. John W. Murphy, express agent. The names of the emigrants are not given.

Nearly all of the cabin passengers were saved; also, the officers and crew, with the exception of three waiters. Captain Petty, of the Atlantic, was seriously injured. The Norwegian emigrants, of whom the greater number perished, were on their way to Quebec. About seventy-five of these people fortunately could not obtain passage in the Atlantic, and were left on the wharf.

Mr. A. Sutton, of New York, who was provided with two life-preservers, states that while he was fastening one on his wife, a ruffian snatched the other from him. Mr. S. managed, however, to save himself and his two children.

A young woman who fell overboard was saved by the exertions of a young man who jumped in after her, and supported her on the surface until she was drawn up into the boat, and at that moment her brave deliverer disappeared under the water. He had proved himself an excellent swimmer, but most likely some drowning wretch had caught hold of him and dragged him down, clutching him with the grasp of death, from which there was no means of extrication.

The dead body of a little girl was found floating on a plank. Dr. Crippen, of Michigan, saved two ladies by breaking through the deck into the state-room, and drawing them out of the water. Three men saved themselves by clinging to the binnacle-box, which had been thrown overboard.

The first mate of the Ogdensburg, who was on watch at the time of the collision, afterwards admitted that if he had given the necessary orders a few moments sooner than he did, the accident might have been prevented. The second mate of the Atlantic, who was also on watch, made similar admissions of delinquency. The officers of both boats were much censured by the citizens of Buffalo, Erie, &c., as it was generally believed that the disaster was attributable to their culpable negligence. The surviving passengers of the Atlantic held a meeting, and passed resolutions strongly condemning the Captain and owners of that steamer for neglecting to provide a sufficient number of life preservers, and small boats. The wreck of the Atlantic was found five miles below Long Point House. She sunk four miles from the nearest shore, in one hundred and sixty feet water. Adams & Co.'s Express Messenger lost $60,000, which went down with the ill-fated boat. Several attempts have been made by submarine divers to recover this lost treasure, but without success. By this accident about three hundred persons were drowned. The names of many will never be known.

EXPLOSION OF THE A. N. JOHNSTON.

This destructive and fatal accident took place on the Ohio river, about twelve miles above Maysville, Ky., on Wednesday, the 29th day of December, 1847, at 2 o'clock, A. M. The steamer, at the time of the explosion, was in the act of rounding from the shore, having just discharged some passengers on the wharf-boat at Manchester. After the explosion, she was burned to the water's edge. No circumstantial account of the accident is given, except that a great many persons were killed and wounded, and their names, as far as they were known to the officers of the boat, will be found in the list which is here appended. It is to be observed that the gentlemen who made the report were not very exact in stating whether many persons named therein were killed, wounded, or missing; but it was understood that when not otherwise designated, the persons named in the list were missing:

Passengers.—Redman, a flat-boat hand, killed; S. S. Saunders, of Cincinnati, badly scalded; J. Kirkpatrick, Massillon, Ohio, scalded; William Everhart and son, of Pennsylvania, do.; D. Rutledge, of Ohio, do.; N. Wheat, Baltimore, Md., do.; Samuel Fisher, Warren, O., do.; Samuel Pilson, Baltimore, do.; Henry Shane, Cincinnati; Arthur Foal, Pittsburgh; A. N. Johnson, wife and child, Wheeling, Va.; G. S. Weatherby, Philadelphia; —— Conway, Graham's Station; Cyrus Rollin, Lebant Falls; Jacob Schafer, Ohio, scalded; A. Bailey, Ohio, badly scalded; Robert Russell, Ohio; John Clancy and John Hardy, Cincinnati; John Kenline, of Ohio; H. J. Bonner, Hanover, Ind.; C. Hardin, Guyandotte, Va.; John Boyd, Warren, Ohio; William Beard, St. Louis; F. Platter, Ohio; S. Cunningham, Cumberland, Md.; J. Swagert, Belle Air, Ohio; J. Barnett, Dayton, Ohio; F. McDonald, Pittsburgh; William Knight, Va.; John Fowler, Ohio; William Miller, Cincinnati; M. R. Hayden and James Wickersham, Pittsburgh; F. A. Horne, Ohio; James M. Lissorm, Ohio; R. Hickson, Cincinnati; Augustus Marsh, slightly scalded; Henry Ladd and William Ladd, Randolph, Ohio; John Borum, Clarington, Ohio; William Parker, Dilley's Bottom, Ohio; A. Davis, —— Captain, O. McTygart, Mr. McCullough, Mr. Lands, and Mr. All, Parkersburg, Va.; James Bromdon and Edmund Swaggart, Belle Air, Ohio; John Gilbreath, of Pittsburgh, badly scalded; Hamilton Barebout, John Williams, James Sprouts, and A. Bacon, Warren, Ohio; William Allen, Wheeling, Va.; Anderson Bonum and Benjamin Bonum, Cincinnati; G. Parker, Pittsburgh; C.

Weaver, Wheeling, Va.; James Henderson, Belmont Co., Ohio; E. J. Pole and J. R. Deary, Athens Co., Ohio.; P. Flesher, Doddridge Co., Va.; Jacob Shoewalter, Warren Co., Ohio.

Boat's Crew.—A. Fairchild, Wheeling, first clerk, killed; Jacob Johnson, second clerk, missing; James Bellsville, carpenter, missing; John Lyle, second engineer, killed; Matthew Wilson, first mate, of Pa., leg broken; James Fennell, bar-keeper, of Cincinnati, slightly scalded; John Fennell, first steward, do., Alfred Burrows, second steward, do., both badly scalded; William Dorsey, second pilot, of Wheeling, Va., badly bruised; Samuel P. Hardin, first cook, missing; porter and barber, both scalded badly; two men found dead, names unknown.

EXPLOSION OF THE A. N. JOHNSTON.

One of the boilers was blown into a corn-field two hundred yards distant; another boiler was blown a hundred yards further into the same field. There was supposed to be one hundred and sixty passengers on board, of whom from sixty to eighty were killed or missing. Many others were wounded. All the ladies on board, six or seven in number, and four or five children, were saved. The steamer Boone went from Maysville to the scene of the disaster, and brought away thirty-seven of the dead and wounded. Some others were taken to Cincinnati. Many were so badly wounded that there were no hopes of their recovery. The death of the first clerk was attended by singular circumstances. He was blown to the distance of one hundred yards, and fell on the shore; he then sprang up, and ran in a phrenzied manner nearly a quarter of a mile to a house, which he entered, and ran under a bed. When taken from thence life was almost extinct, and he expired within a few minutes.

The engineer, just before he died, stated that he had tried the boilers a short time before the explosion, and found a sufficiency of water; but one of the clerks reports that he heard the engineer complain several times after they left Cincinnati that the pumps did not work well.

The City Council of Maysville assembled on the afternoon of the fatal day, and made an appropriation for the relief of the sufferers.

COLLISION OF THE BOONSLICK AND MISSOURI BELLE.

The steamboat Missouri Belle left New Orleans, October 24th, 1834, bound to St. Louis, and when she had proceeded about fifteen miles up the river, she came in contact with the steamer Boonslick, which was coming in an opposite direction. The Boonslick sustained but little injury, but the Missouri Belle was so badly broken up that she sunk almost instantly. The Boonslick rounded to and steered for the wrecked vessel, nothing of which remained above water, except a piece of the hurricane deck, on which most of the passengers had taken refuge. A rope was thrown out by the crew of the Boonslick, and attached to the floating piece of the wreck, and some of the passengers were thus enabled to reach the deck of the Boonslick, while the yawls were engaged in picking up those persons who had been thrown into the water. There were about one hundred and thirty persons on board the Missouri Belle at the time she sunk; thirty of these were drowned, though every possible effort was made by the captain and crew of the Boonslick to save them.

List of Lost.—Dr. Brant, Mo.; A. C. Smithers, New Orleans; Miss C. Frazier, St. Louis; W. Walters, New York; P. Matlock, New Jersey; Mrs. De Soto, Havana; Miss Mary Trimble, Miss.; John Budd, Boston; A. During, Ill.; two infants, names not known; Ebenezer Dumbolt, Germany; wife and child of Mr. C. Glass, Wis.; three negro firemen, and seven Germans, who were from Heidelberg. This is the complete list of those drowned by this accident

VIEW OF NASHVILLE.

SKETCH OF NASHVILLE.

Nashville is a very handsome city, the largest in Tennessee, and the commercial metropolis of that State. It is situated in Davidson County, on the southern bank of Cumberland river, two hundred miles from its mouth; two hundred and thirty miles E. N. E. of Memphis, two hundred and six miles S. W. of Lexington, Ky., and six hundred and ninety miles from Washington, D. C.; lat. 36° 9′ N., long. 86° 49′ W. The whole city is built on a solid rock, covered in some places with a thin soil. The site of Nashville is on a "bluff" eighty feet in height, and four hundred and sixty feet above the level of the sea. This city is the centre of an extensive trade, the river being navigable for the largest boats up to this point; several excellent turnpikes extend to various localities in the interior of the State, and the Nashville and Chattanooga railroad, one hundred and fifty miles in length, exclusive of its branches, here has its terminus. The branches of this railroad, which was finished in the year 1852, extend from various points on the road, to Shelbyville, McMinnville, Coal Mines, and North Memphis. The Nashville and Chattanooga railroad at Stevenson, Ala., connects with the Charleston Railroad which extends from the point of connection, one hundred and thirty miles, to Tuscumbia, Ala., passing through Huntsville and Decatur. The Nashville and Chattanooga railroad crosses the Tennessee river at Bridgeport, Ala. At Chattanooga it connects with the Georgia and South Carolina system of railroads. The first branch, south, connects with Rome, at the head of navigation on Coosa river; the second branch extends to Montgomery, Ala.; the third, to Columbus, Ga., on the Chattanooga river; the fourth branch extends from Macon to Americus, Ga.; the fifth branch connects with Eatonton, Milledgeville, Savannah, Augusta, Athens, and Washington, Ga., and with all the prominent points to Charleston, S. C. The Nashville and Chattanooga railroad also communicates by the East Tennessee and Georgia railroad, with Knoxville; and by the East Tennessee and Virginia railroad, with Lynchburg, Abington, &c. The Nashville and Chattanooga railroad is constructed in the most substantial and durable manner, and is doing a large and profitable business. In a few years the Louisville and Nashville railroad will be completed, and then the city of Nashville will have the terminus of one of the most extensive and important railroads in the world. The cost of this road has been $3,000,000. The president of the Nashville and Chattanooga railroad is Col. V. K. Stevenson, James H. Grant is resident engineer. This railroad is of incalculable value to the commerce and prosperity of Nashville.

The steamboat trade of Nashville is very extensive. Many first class steamers have been built at this place, and are owned by persons residing there. The shipping of the port in the year 1854 amounted to 6,440 tons, and as the business of steamboat building is carried on extensively by enterprising citizens of the place, there is a great annual increase of tonnage.

The city of Nashville is well laid out. The streets are commodious and well paved. Some of the public buildings are magnificent, and the private dwellings will compare favorably with those of any other city in the United States. The new State House, which stands on an eminence one hundred and seventy-five feet above the level of the river, is one of the most elegant and costly structures in America. The material is a fine limestone, quarried on the spot, and bears a strong resemblance to marble. The cost of this building was $1,000,000. The University of Nashville was founded in 1806. The Medical College was opened in 1851. In 1855 it had two hundred students. There are various other literary and scientific institutions, besides a great number of private seminaries for males and females. Nashville has fourteen newspaper offices, four banks, with a capital of $6,000,000, and eighteen churches. The Mineral Cabinet of the late Dr. Troorst contains the largest collection in the United States.

Cumberland river at Nashville is crossed by a magnificent wire suspension bridge, similar to the bridge over the Ohio at Wheeling, Va. The city is lighted with gas, and supplied with water raised from the Cumberland river by machinery. Nashville has expended immense sums of money on her macadamized turnpikes, which radiate in different directions to the inland districts. The country, for several miles around Nashville, is fertile and salubrious. This city is distinguished for its enterprising spirit, literary taste, and polished society. The population in 1845 was 12,000; in 1853, 20,000; and in 1856, 25,000.

EXPLOSION OF THE TUSCALOOSA.

The steamer Tuscaloosa left the wharf at Mobile, Ala., about 8 o'clock on Thursday evening, January 29th, 1847, on her way to Tuscaloosa city, the capital of Alabama; and when she had proceeded ten miles up the river two of her boilers bursted, by which accident a number of her passengers and crew were killed and wounded. The explosion completely tore up the boiler-deck, and shattered the after-part of the boat below deck considerably. Immediately after the explosion, the steamer drifted near the shore and grounded, her stern projecting towards the centre of the river. A line was made fast on shore, and an attempt was made, by pulling in the stern, to effect a landing for the passengers, but the boat was fixed too firmly in the bed of the river to be moved in this manner. The ladies were then lowered by a rope to the lower deck, and from thence were sent ashore in the yawl. All of them escaped unhurt.

Those of the male passengers who were uninjured saved themselves, and many of the wounded likewise, by constructing a raft of loose planks, on which they reached the shore in safety; but when they arrived at the banks they found it impossible to obtain a dry footing, as the river had overflowed its customary bounds to the depth of several inches, which, as the weather was exceedingly cold, made the landing (if it might be called so) very uncomfortable. In this state of things the male passengers climbed trees, where they remained spectators of the burning wreck for about three hours, when the steamer James Hewitt hove in sight, and on coming near the wreck, sent her yawl to the assistance of the survivors, who were all taken on board and conveyed back to Mobile. The dead body of Lieut. Inge, one of the passengers of the Tuscaloosa, was also taken up by the James Hewitt.

List of Killed—Wm. Tanneyhill, C. Childs, and P. F. Beasley, of Eutaw; W. R. Hassell, of Greenborough; B. Partier, second clerk; Thomas Clark, first mate; Arthur McCoy, second engineer; Abraham Flynn, volunteer for the U. S. Army in Mexico, from Green Co., Ala., and several colored deck hands.

Badly Wounded—Capt. E. P. Oliver, not expected to recover; George Kirk, first clerk, and acting Captain of the Tuscaloosa; Col. Wm. Armistead, and Capt. Asa White, of Eutaw. The last named gentleman was very badly scalded.

ACCIDENT ON THE ELIZABETH.

The boilers of the steamer Elizabeth collapsed on the 4th day of April, 1845, on the Mississippi river, at the entrance of the Courtanbleau. All the wood-work above the boilers was swept away. None of the passengers were hurt, but several of the boat's crew were killed, and others were wounded.

Killed.—Daniel York, the mate; John Rhodes, deck hand; Wilson Hill, second engineer; and a fireman, colored.

Wounded.—J. H. Gordon, the captain, mortally; Freeman B. Lamb, pilot, leg fractured; James Marquite, first engineer, badly scalded; and a negro fireman.

EXPLOSION OF THE CHAMOIS.

The steamer Chamois, Capt. Morton, exploded near Chattahochee, Fa., at the fork of that river, on Thursday, November 3d, 1842. She was aground, and the crew were endeavoring to get her off, when the accident took place. Three of the crew were killed, and several others more or less injured. The names of the persons killed were Leander Vale, first engineer, William Cannafax, steward, and Joseph Lloyd, deck-hand.

Mr. Cannafax had recently been married, and for years had been the only stay and support of his aged parents. He was a young man of great probity and worth, and his untimely death occasioned a feeling of deep regret among all who had known him.

EXPLOSION OF THE MARQUITTE.

Between four and five o'clock, in the afternoon of July 1st, 1845, the steamer Marquitte, Capt. Turpin, was about leaving the wharf at New Orleans. Her last bell had rung, and the hands had begun to cast off the moorings, when it was ascertained that the cook was on shore. The boat waited for him about fifteen minutes, during which time no steam was blown off, or passed through the cylinders. The cook having arrived, the steamer began to back out from the wharf, and when the paddle-wheels had made three or four revolutions, all the boilers exploded simultaneously, producing a sound which was heard in the most distant parts of the city. The pilot, Mr. Frederick Ostrander, who was at the wheel, was blown to a considerable distance, and fell on the hurricane deck of the steamer Yazoo City. One of his thighs was dislocated and his hip broken by the fall. It is mentioned as a remarkable circumstance, that Mr. Ostrander's hat was blown in an opposite direction, and fell on another boat. The pilot house which this gentleman had occupied, after ascending to a great height, came down on the forecastle of the steamer James Pitcher, occasioning some damage to that vessel. The wheel, (or a part of the steering apparatus,) which Mr. Ostrander held at the time of the explosion, appears to have been *annihilated*, as not the smallest fragment of it could be found afterwards. Mr. Powell, the second pilot, who was sitting on the boiler-deck, reading a newspaper, was never seen after the explosion. The cook was cut in two by a piece of the boiler; one part of his body was blown forward near the jack-staff, and the other part remained near the machinery. Capt. Turpin himself received an injury in the thigh, but was still active in affording his assistance to the other sufferers. Capt.

B. M. Martin, of the Belle Poule, was wounded by a piece of the boiler, and died a few hours after. At least forty-five others were killed, and comparatively few of their names, (as usual in such cases,) are on record. The universal excitement and consternation which prevail on board of the vessel where an explosion takes place, renders an accurate statement of particulars almost impossible. After the explosion, the boat drifted a short distance down the stream and sunk. All the cargo was lost.

The ladies and children in the cabin escaped injury, except a small girl, who was badly scalded. One dead body was taken from the wreck; it was that of a man who had his legs literally blown away, and was otherwise mangled. Three others died in a short time. Two of the dead bodies remained all night in the watch-house yard, exposed until eleven o'clock next day, in order to be recognized by their friends, if possible. The officers of the boat were Robert Smith, first mate, slightly scalded; J. F. Lee, clerk, bruised; John Orrick, bar-keeper, badly hurt; Samuel Hays, first engineer, scalded; John Hazzard, second engineer, killed; Hannibal, a slave of the captains, killed; Theodore Ostrander, pilot, severely hurt; Mr. Powell, second pilot, lost; George W. Woodhull, clerk of the steamer Belle Poule, killed; Luther Hathaway, mate of the same boat, badly injured; John Milton, New Albany, Ind., killed; Mr. Martin, Tenn., badly scalded; Mrs. Decker and child, killed.

KILLED.—Z. Vanstover, Hermann, Mo.; Mrs. Lecrist, Louisville; O. Doughty, P. Fishback and N. Drake, Cincinnati, Ohio; B. Williamson, St. Louis; D. B. Short, South Carolina; Miss Tree, England; three firemen, names unknown; Dunn O'Flaretyand Patrick Murphy, belonging to the boat; M. Music, New York; Andrew Dearborn, New Castle, Ind.; Dennis Cochran and Samuel Felt, Maine; Thomas Farrell, Rhode Island; —— Simpson, Texas; W. E. Wilbur, New Orleans; A. Spotts, Ala.; F. Hogart, Evansville, Ind.; ——Franklin, Tenn.; Hilburn Carter and D. Epsome, Canada; besides several others whose bodies were not recognized after being taken from the water.

Cabin Passengers Saved.—Miss McCord and child, Miss Lydia Page, Miss Sarah Smith and Mrs. Harriet Cook, all of Mobile; and Miss Elmira Lacy, Cincinnati, Ohio.

EXPLOSION OF THE KNOXVILLE.

On the 17th day of December, 1850, the steamboat Knoxville exploded at New Orleans, just as she was leaving the wharf at the foot of Gravier Street. The flues of both boilers collapsed, tearing all the upper works forward of the wheel-house to pieces. One of the boilers was projected through the guards of the steamer Martha Washington, which was lying at the same wharf, passing entirely through the cabin of that vessel and entering the ladies' cabin of the Griffin Greatman. Another boiler was carried by the force of the explosion one hundred and fifty yards across the levee, knocking down two large piles of flour barrels; but, happily, no person was injured in its transit, although it passed over the heads of a crowd of people standing on the wharf. An iron chest was blown high in the air, and fell on the steamboat Buck-eye, lying at a considerable distance below. The steamboat Ne-Plus-Ultra, which lay near the Knoxville, was much shattered; and the commander, Capt. Robinson, was badly scalded. The Knoxville took fire, but by the prompt assistance of the firemen of New Orleans the flames were extinguished. There were eighteen passengers on the boat at the time

EXPLOSION OF THE KNOXVILLE.

of the accident, a majority of whom were killed or missing. The Martha Washington, which lay nearly in contact with the Knoxville, was much damaged, all her upper works being swept away. We subjoin a list of the killed and wounded among the boat's crew; the names of those passengers who suffered were never ascertained, but their number is estimated to be not less than sixteen.

KILLED.—William Dowdy, second engineer; the bar-keeper and third engineer, names not mentioned, and sixteen passengers.

WOUNDED.—Capt. Irvin; Abraham Young and Henry Turner, cooks; B. H. Franklin and William Henry, pilots; Patrick Conelly, J. Collins, John Burke, Peter Millen, John Burns and Patrick Cannon, firemen; George Stackhouse; George Oldham; James Johnston, first engineer; William Bowen, clerk; and the bar-keeper of the Martha Washington.

VIEW OF THE GATES OF THE ROCKY MOUNTAINS.

SKETCH OF THE MISSISSIPPI RIVER AND ITS TRIBUTARIES.

THE Mississippi is the most important river in North America. and with the Missouri, its principal affluent, the longest in the world. It rises on the Hauteurs de Terre. the dividing ridge between the Red River of the north, and the streams flowing into the Gulf of Mexico, three thousand one hundred and sixty miles from the Gulf and sixteen hundred and eighty feet above the level of the ocean, lat. 47° N., long. 95° 54′ W. A small pool, fed by the neighboring hills, discharges a little rivulet, scarcely a span in breadth, meandering over sand and pebbles; and blending here and there with a kindred streamlet, it ripples on, forming a number of basins, until it subsides at last into Itasca Lake. From this issues a second stream, giving promise of the strength of its maturity, first flowing northward through several small lakes, and then in various directions, forming Cass Lake, Lake Winnipeg, and a number of other bodies of water. It afterwards assumes a southerly course, receives mighty rivers as tributaries, and having rolled its vast volume through more than eighteen degrees of latitude, enters the Gulf of Mexico by several mouths, lat. 29° N., long. 89° 25′ W. Though above the junction not so large as the Missouri which flows into it from the north-west, twelve hundred and fifty three miles from the Gulf, yet having been first explored, it received the name "Mississippi," which it has since retained throughout its entire course.

If we regard the Missouri as a continuation of the Mississippi above the junction, the entire length will amount to about four thousand three hundred and fifty miles. Above the confluence of the two rivers, the waters of the Mississippi are remarkably clear; but after commingling with those of the Missouri, they become exceedingly turbid, and contain about four tenths of sedementary matter. The Missouri river, ("the Mud river,") which is the longest tributary stream in the world, has its source in the Rocky mountains, lat. 45° N., long. 110° 30′ W. The springs which give rise to this turbulent river, are not more than a mile from the head waters of the Columbia, which flows westerly to the Pacific ocean. At a distance of four hundred and eleven miles from the source of the Missouri, are what are denominated the "Gates of the Rocky mountains." For a distance of nearly six miles, the rocks here rise perpendicularly from the water's edge to a height of one thousand two hundred feet. The river here is about one hundred and fifty yards wide, and for the first three miles there is only one spot, and that of but a few yards in extent, on which a man could stand between the water and the perpendicular walls. At a distance of one hundred and ten miles below this, and two thousand five hundred and seventy-five miles above the mouth of the Missouri are the "Great Falls." Here the river descends by a succession of falls and rapids, three hundred and fifty-nine feet in sixteen and a half miles. The perpendicular falls are, the first, twenty-six feet, the second, forty-seven feet, the third, twenty feet, and the fourth, eighty-nine feet. Between and below these are continual rapids of from three to eighteen feet descent, forming the grandest view perhaps in the world, surpassing in beauty of scenery and magnitude the falls of Niagara.

The bed of the Missouri commences at the confluence of three small streams, about equal in length, and running nearly parallel to each other, called Jefferson's Madison's, and Gallatin's forks. The Yellow Stone river, which is eight hundred yards wide at its mouth, is the longest tributary of the Missouri, and enters it from the southwest, twelve hundred and sixteen miles from its navigable source. The two rivers at their junction are about equal in size. Steamboats ascend to this point, and can ascend farther, both by the main stream and its affluent. Chienne river, which is four hundred yards wide at its mouth, enters the Missouri from the southwest, thirteen hundred and ten miles from its mouth. White river, which is three hundred yards wide at its mouth, enters the Missouri from the southwest, eleven hundred and thirty miles from its mouth. The Big Sioux river is one hundred and ten yards wide, and enters the Missouri from the northeast, eight hundred and fifty-four miles from its mouth. Platte river is six hundred yards wide, and enters the Missouri from the southwest, six hundred miles from its mouth. Kansas river is two hundred and thirty-four yards wide, and enters the Missouri from the southwest, three hundred and forty-four miles from its mouth. Grand River is one hundred and eighty-nine yards wide, and joins it from the north, two hundred and forty miles from its mouth; and Osage river, which is three hundred and ninety-eight yards wide, flows into the Missouri from the southwest, one hundred and thirty-three miles from its junction with the main stream. The Missouri river is three thousand and ninety-six miles long to its confluence with the Mississippi; add to this twelve hundred and fifty-three miles, the distance its waters must flow to reach the Gulf of Mexico, and the entire length, is four thousand three hundred and forty-nine miles. Through the greater part of its course, the Missouri is a rapid, turbid, and very dangerous stream to navigate. No serious obstacle, however, is presented to navigation from its mouth to the great falls, a distance of two thousand five hundred and seventy-five miles, excepting, perhaps, its shallowness during the season of the greatest drought, and the innumerable snags which are firmly imbedded in the river, by which boats sometimes meet with the greatest difficulty in ascending or descending it. The flood from this river does not reach the Mississippi river, till the rise in the Red, the Arkansas, and the Ohio rivers has nearly subsided. Vast prairies, with narrow strips of alluvium skirting the streams, compose the Missouri basin, excepting the upper portion of the river, which flows through an arid and sterile region. The entire extent of area drained by this river and its tributaries, is estimated at six hundred thousand square miles. The first five hundred miles of its course to the great falls is nearly north, then inflecting E. N. E., it reaches its extreme northern bend, at the junction of White Earth river, lat. 48° 20′ N. After this its general course is southeast till it empties into the Mississippi river, eighteen miles above St. Louis, and twelve hundred and eighteen miles above New Orleans, lat. 38° 50′ N., long. 90° 10′ W. The other principal tributaries of the Mississippi river from the northwest and west, are the St Peters, or Minnesota, which empties into it two thousand one hundred and ninety-two miles from its mouth, and the Des Moines, White, Red, and Arkansas rivers. Those emptying into it from the northeast and east, are the Wisconsin, which enters it nineteen hundred and thirty-four miles from its mouth; the Illinois river flows into it five hundred and six miles below, and the Ohio joins it, one thousand and fifty-three miles from the Gulf of Mexico. The Arkansas river, next to the Missouri, is the largest affluent of the Mississippi; it rises in the Rocky Mountains near the boundary between Utah and the Indian Territory, and pursues an easterly course several hundred miles. Near the ninety-eighth degree of west longitude, it turns and flows south-eastward, to Fort Smith, on the western boundary of Arkansas; continuing in the same general direction, it traverses that state, dividing it into two nearly equal portions, and empties itself into the Mississippi at Helena, four hundred miles below the mouth of the Ohio, and six hundred miles above New Orleans, in lat. 33° 54′ N., long. 91° 10′ W. Its whole length exceeds two thousand miles. The current is not obstructed by falls or rapids, and is navigable by steamboats, during about nine months of the year, for a distance of eight hundred miles from its mouth. The difference between high and low water in this river is about twenty-eight feet; it is from three-eighths to half a mile wide throughout the last six hundred miles of its course. White River is the next largest tributary of the Mississippi; it is formed by three small branches which rise among the Ozark Mountains, and unite a few miles east of Fayetteville, Arkansas; it flows first north-easterly into Missouri, and after making a circuit of one hundred and ten miles, returns into Arkansas, and pursues a south-easterly course to the mouth of Black River, which is its largest affluent from this point; its direction is nearly southward until it enters the Mississippi, fifteen miles above the mouth of the Arkansas. The whole length of White river exceeds eight hundred miles, and is navigable by steamboats, in all stages of water, to the mouth of Black river, three hundred and fifty miles above its mouth; and during a large portion of the year they can run to Batesville, about fifty miles higher. In very high water, boats have gone several hundred miles further up into Missouri. The navigation is not obstructed by ice in the winter. Below Batesville the channel is about four feet deep throughout the year, and is one of the most delightful and placid streams in the world.

Red River is the southernmost of the great tributaries of the Mississippi. It rises in two branches, called the North and South Forks, which unite near lat. 34° 30′ N., and long. 100° W. The principal or southern branch has its source in lat. 34° 42′ N., long. 103° 7′ 10″ W., in New Mexico, just beyond the west boundary of Texas; and the North fork in lat. 35° 35′ 3″ N., long. 101° 55′ W., within a degree of the north boundary of Texas. After the junction of the two forks, the stream varies but little from a due east course till it reaches Fulton, in Arkansas, where it turns to the south, and pursues that direction, with a slight inclination to the east, till near Natchitoches, from whence it runs a little south of east. The main or southern branch has its sources in deep and narrow fissures in the north-east part of the Llano Estacado, an elevated and barren plain, at an altitude of two thousand four hundred and sixty-one feet above the level of the sea. For the first sixty miles the escarpments rise from five hundred to eight hundred feet, so directly from the water's edge, that, in many instances, a skiff must take the channel of the stream to proceed. After leaving the Llano Estacado the river flows through an arid prairie country, almost entirely destitute of trees, over a broad bed of light shifting sands, for a distance of five hundred miles, following its sinuosites. It then enters a country covered with gigantic forest trees, grown upon a soil of the most pre-eminent fertility. Here the borders contract, and the water, for a considerable portion of the year, washes both banks, carrying the loose alluvium from one side and depositing it on the other, in such a manner as to produce constant changes in the channel, and to render navigation difficult. This character continues throughout the remainder of its course to the Delta of the Mississippi; and in this section it is subject to heavy inundations, which often flood the bottoms to such a degree as to destroy the crops, and occasionally, on subsiding, leaving a deposit of white sand, and rendering the soil barren and worthless. The entire length of Red River, including the South Fork, is estimated at two thousand one hundred miles, the main stream being about one thousand two hundred miles long. During eight months of the year steamboats regularly navigate it from New Orleans to Shreveport, a distance of about seven hundred and fifty miles, and the navigation is good in all stages of water to Alexandria. The most serious obstacle to the navigation of the upper part of Red river is the "great raft," which consists of an immense mass of drift wood and trees, which have been brought down several hundred miles by the current, and lodged here, obstructing the channel for a distance of seventy-five miles, and inundating the adjacent country. In 1834, '35 it was removed by Capt. Henry M. Shreve (who was employed by the general government) at an expense of three hundred thousand dollars; but being left many years without snag-boats to keep it clear, another and more serious raft has been formed, the lower part of which is now about thirty miles above Shreveport, and is continually growing, so that in a few years more this important stream will be rendered entirely unnavigable, unless the general government has it removed. During high water small steamers pass round the raft by means of the lateral channels or lakes which are then formed. Red River empties into the Mississippi two hundred and sixty-eight miles above New Orleans, in lat. 31° N., and long. 91° 50′ W.

The Yazoo river is another prominent tributary to the Mississippi. It is formed by the Tallahatchee and Yallabusha rivers, which unite at Leflore, in Carroll County, Mississippi. It then pursues a very serpentine course, the general direction of which is South by West. The length of the main stream is about two hundred and ninety miles. It is a deep, narrow, and sluggish stream, traversing an alluvial plain of extreme fertility, which is mostly occupied by plantations of cotton. It is probably not surpassed in navigable qualities by any river in the world of equal size. Steamboats ascend it from its mouth to its origin in all stages of water, and at all seasons of the year. The Tallahatchee, the largest branch, is perhaps as long as the Yazoo itself, and is navigable by steamboats more than one hundred miles. The Yazoo empties into the Mississippi twelve miles above Vicksburg.

The descent of the Mississippi from its source to its embouchure averages over six inches

FALLS OF ST. ANTHONY.

to the mile. The elevation of the various points are at its extreme source sixteen hundred and eighty feet. Itasca lake, fifteen hundred and seventy-five feet; falls of St. Anthony, eight hundred and fifty-six feet; Prairie Du Chien, six hundred and forty-two feet; St. Louis, three hundred and eighty-two feet; mouth of the Ohio, three hundred and twenty-four feet; Natchez, eighty-six feet; entrance of the Red river, seventy-six feet, and opposite New Orleans, ten and a-half feet. The only falls of any considerable note in this river are those of St. Anthony, which have a perpendicular fall of eighteen feet, with rapids above and below, making in all about sixty-eight feet descent in three quarters of a mile. The scenery here is grand and picturesque, especially at the time of the spring floods. The rapids of Pecagama are six hundred and eighty-five miles above the falls of St. Anthony. The river there is compressed to a width of eighty feet, and precipitated over a rugged bed of sandstone at an angle of 40°. The entire descent at this point is about twenty feet in three hundred yards. Below the falls of St. Anthony the river is navigable for steamboats. A considerable obstruction, however, is offered when the water is low, by the rapids, about nine miles in extent, a short distance above the entrance of the Des Moines river, near Keokuk, and the upper rapids, which commence below Muscatine, Iowa. These rapids are a serious obstacle to the navigation of the Upper Mississippi, and it is to be hoped that the general government will improve them at once. The average depth of the Mississippi below the mouth of the Ohio, varies from ninety to one hundred and twenty feet, and the breadth from six hundred to twelve hundred yards. Opposite New Orleans the river is one-third of a mile wide, and one hundred feet deep. The mean velocity of the current at this place is about two feet per second, or thirty-three miles per day. Between the Gulf and the entrance of the Missouri river, it is from sixty to seventy miles per day. Above the mouth of the Missouri the current is less rapid. A peculiarity of the Lower Mississippi is its extremely winding course. Sometimes a bend of thirty miles will occur, where the distance across the neck does not exceed a mile. This circumstance, no doubt, tends to check the current, and facilitate navigation. One of the important facts in relation to this great river, is that it flows from North to South. A river that runs East or West has no variety of climate or productions from its source to its mouth. The course of this stream being from North to South, spring advances in a reverse direction, and releases in succession the waters of the lower valley, then of the middle section, and finally the remote sources of the Mississippi and its tributaries. It is a remarkable fact that the waters from this last named region do not reach the Delta until upwards of a month after the inundation there has been abating. The swell usually commences towards the end of February, and continues to rise by unequal diurnal accretions till the first of June, when the waters again begin to subside.

No experience will enable a person to anticipate, with any degree of certainty, the elevation of the flood in any given year. In some seasons, the waters do not rise above their channels; in others, the entire lower valley of the Mississippi is submerged. Embankments called levees have been raised from five to ten feet high, on both sides of the stream, extending many miles above and below New Orleans. By this means the river is restrained within its proper limits, except at the greatest freshets, when the waters sometimes break over everything, causing great destruction to property, and sometimes loss of life. The average height of the flood from the Delta to the junction of the Missouri is above sixteen feet. At the mouth of the latter river it is twenty-five feet. Below the entrance of the Ohio river the rise is often fifty-five feet. At Natchez, it seldom exceeds thirty feet; and at New Orleans, about twelve feet. What goes with the water? It is known that the difference between high and low water mark, as high up as White river, is about thirty-six feet, and the current at high water mark runs near seven miles per hour, and opposite to New Orleans the difference between high and low water mark is only twelve feet, and the current little over three miles to the hour. The width and depth of the river being the same, from which we calculate that near six times as much water passes by the mouth of White river as by New Orleans. What goes with the excess? The only solution we can offer is, that it escapes by the bayous "Plaquemine," "Lafourche" and "Iberville," but when we calculate the width, depth and current of these bayous, they fall vastly short of affording a sufficient escapement. The true explanation can, we think, be given. At low water, throughout the whole extent, we see a land structure exposed, underlying the bank, or that the alluvial structure on which the plantations are, is a structure of deposit made by the river above its low water mark, which, opposite to the mouth of White river, is thirty feet thick. As you descend, the river diminishes in volume as the difference between high and low water mark diminishes and nearly corresponds to it, and wherever the bottom is exposed it shows throughout the whole extent that the bottom is *pure coarse sand;* exhibiting at many places the *ocean shingle*, through the superimposed alluvial structure mixed with fine sand. The water percolates with such facility and rapidity that the water in a well dug at a considerable distance from the river bank rises and falls with the rise and fall of the river, not varying an inch, and through the coarse sand and shingles of the bottom, it passes as rapidly as through a common sieve.

By the accurate surveys of several scientific engineers, it is ascertained that the fall of the Mississippi river is four inches to the mile. The distance from Natchez to New Orleans of three hundred miles will give twelve hundred inches, or one hundred feet. The depth of the river is less than fifty feet at high-water mark. The river debouches into the ocean from a promontory made by itself. The surface of the ocean, by measurement, below the bottom of the river, above New Orleans, corresponds with the low-water mark below New Orleans, therefore the Mississippi river is pouring through its own bottom into the ocean, the superimposed weight giving lateral pressure to hurry the subterranean current. If the reader has ever stood upon a Mississippi sand-bar in a hard rain, or seen water poured from a bucket on the sand-bar, he has seen that neither can be done in sufficient quantity to produce any current or accumulation on the surface. The river is, therefore, from the time it comes below the lime-stone stratas of Missouri and Kentucky, wasting itself through its own bottom. If the Mississippi river had to pursue its course, like the Ohio, over rocky strata, walled in by rock and impervious clap banks, the high-water mark at New Orleans would reach one hundred feet above its present limit; but running over coarse sand, walled in by a deposit made of sand, ancient duluvial detritus, and vegetable mound, no more water reaches the ocean than the excess over the amount that permeates the surrounding structure and passes off in the process of percolation or transperation in a subterranean descent to the ocean. The river, without any restraint from rock or clay in the bottom or bank, is left free to the government of no other law than the law of hydrostatics. The washing, or wasting of the banks, cannot be prevented, though the caving or sliding of large portions at one time may be easily guarded against.

The Arkansas river, west of that state, receives several large tributaries, and is itself above their junction as large as the congregated rivers after their junction within the state. Within that state it has no more tributary before reaching the Mississippi river, which has within the said district, as a consequence, a rise of fifteen or twenty feet. Sometimes it enters the stem of the main river without producing any rise at its mouth, unless the supply is maintained for a considerable time; thus the far-famed Niger of Africa, whose mouth has never been found, may be lost and wasted in the great sand plains of the Desert of Sahara, and its subterranean flood may again be collected on the surface of a subterranean stratum of rock, and projected on the surface of the earth, sustaining the opinion of Pliny, that the Niger is a western and main tributary of the Nile. The flood of the Mississippi river often carries away large masses of earth, with trees, which frequently become imbedded in the mud at one end, while the other floats near the surface, forming snags and sawyers. So changeable are the channels of the Mississippi and Missouri rivers, that to be a competent pilot, it is necessary to make trips every few weeks on these rivers, otherwise sight is lost of the channel, so suddenly does it change from one side of the river to the other. Eight hundred and sixteen steamboats are employed on the Mississippi river and its tributaries, the total tonnage of which amounts to 326,443 tons, besides twenty-three hundred flat boats and barges which are in constant operation. The total value of the steamboats annually afloat on the western rivers, is estimated at nearly $20,000,000, and the commerce at $200,000,000. The area of country drained by the Mississippi and its tributaries, is over 2,000,000 square miles. This vast region, from its almost unexampled fertility, has obtained the title of the "Garden of the World."

EXPLOSION OF THE AUGUSTA.

The Augusta left Natchez, December 3d, 1838, for Vicksburg, with the ship Jeannette in tow. On the voyage the ship got aground, when the Augusta separated from her, and proceeded to a wood-pile, where she took in some fuel, and was making her way to another pile, when the pilot, seeing some floating timber ahead, rang the bell as a signal for the engine to be stopped. The machinery was accordingly stopped until the float had passed, when the bell was again rung as a signal for the engine to be put in motion. The engineer discovered, at this moment, that the engine was at the dead point, and he immediately ran back to turn the bar, but before he had time to return, the explosion took place, laying a great part of the boat in ruins. The boilers and all the machinery were broken to minute pieces; the social hall, with all its appurtenances, was shattered, according to the common phraseology, "into atoms," and nearly all the cabin was swept away; a small part of it adjoining the ladies' cabin was all that was left. The extent of the devastation proved that the force of the explosion was tremendous. Fortunately the Augusta had but few passengers on board, otherwise the loss of life would have been very great. The names of all the victims are not known. Five dead bodies were found on board, and doubtless others were blown into the water. A considerable number were hurt; some to that degree that the physicians were hopeless of their recovery. The pilot at the wheel, Mr. Lachapelle, with his pilot box, was blown overboard, the box being broken into two pieces during its transit. By using one of these pieces for a float, Mr. Lachapelle contrived to reach the shore.

The five persons found dead on board were, Leonard Brown, clerk; W. Henderson, first engineer; George Ward, merchant, Troy, Miss.; and John Wilson and Robert Smith, deck-hands.

The captain was never seen after the explosion, and there can be no doubt that he lost his life, being probably blown overboard and drowned.

BADLY WOUNDED.—*Deck Hands*—William Johnson, James White, James Innis, James Johnson, William McDonald, and another, name unknown. The barber was so badly hurt that he died on the following day.

SLIGHTLY WOUNDED.—William Taylor, second engineer, Henry Smith, and Lewis Lachapelle, pilot.

MAPS OF THE MISSISSIPPI RIVER.

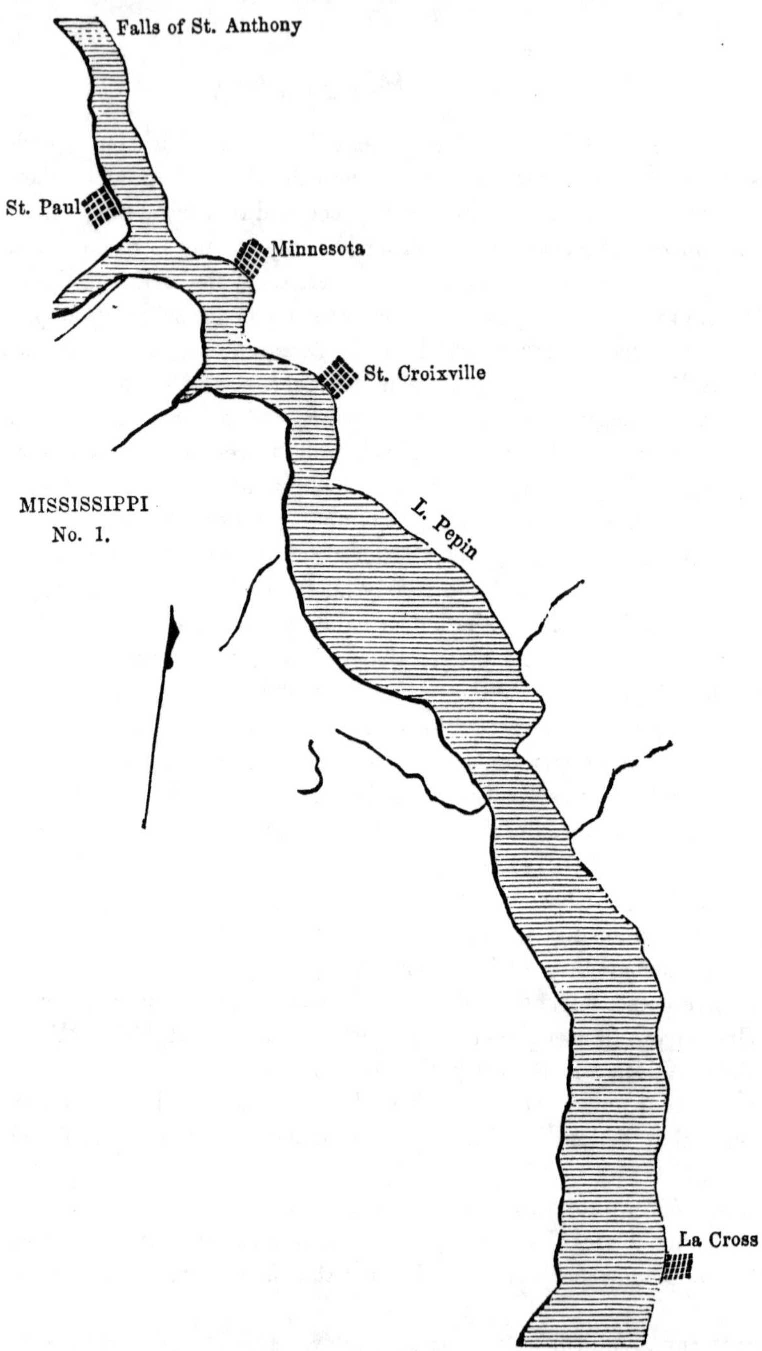

Twenty-eight deck-hands and firemen were on board; when they were called together, some time after the explosion, only *eight* could be mustered. There was but one female passenger, and she escaped unhurt. When an examination was made of the pieces of boiler found on deck, no doubt remained that this explosion was the result of culpable negligence on the part of the engineer.

EXPLOSION OF THE PERSIAN.

On the night of November 9th, 1840, the steamboat Persian collapsed her flues, on the Mississippi river, three miles below Napoleon, Ark. The Captain was asleep at the time of the accident, and, according to common rumor, the pilot was intoxicated. The boat had stopped to take in wood. Six persons were instantly killed by the explosion, seventeen died on the following day, and fifteen or sixteen others were supposed to be mortally wounded. The cabin passengers and the captain and clerk escaped uninjured.

LIST OF THE KILLED—Daniel Green, first engineer; John Williams, second mate; Oscar Brown and Washington Marks, colored firemen; six deck passengers, all of one family, named Floyd; John Cora, second cook; John O'Brien, deck passenger; Wm. S. Hanners, of Illinois; Mr. Fields, of Tennessee, and nine others, names unknown.

Thirty were scalded, with more or less severity.

BURNING OF THE CLARKSVILLE.

The popular and beautiful steamer Clarksville, a regular packet boat between New Orleans and Memphis, Tennessee, was destroyed by fire near Ozark island, on the 27th day of May, 1848; thirty deck passengers, nearly all the crew, and the commander, Capt. Holmes, lost their lives. The cabin passengers were all saved. We have obtained the following particulars of this melancholy event:

As soon as the alarm of fire was given on board, the pilot steered for the island. At the moment her head touched the shore, the flames burst into the cabin, one of the boilers burst simultaneously, and, to aggravate the calamity still more, three kegs of gunpowder, which were among the freight, exploded at the same instant. Governor Poindexter, of Tennessee, who was one of the passengers, received some injuries. Most of the passengers lost their baggage, and none of the

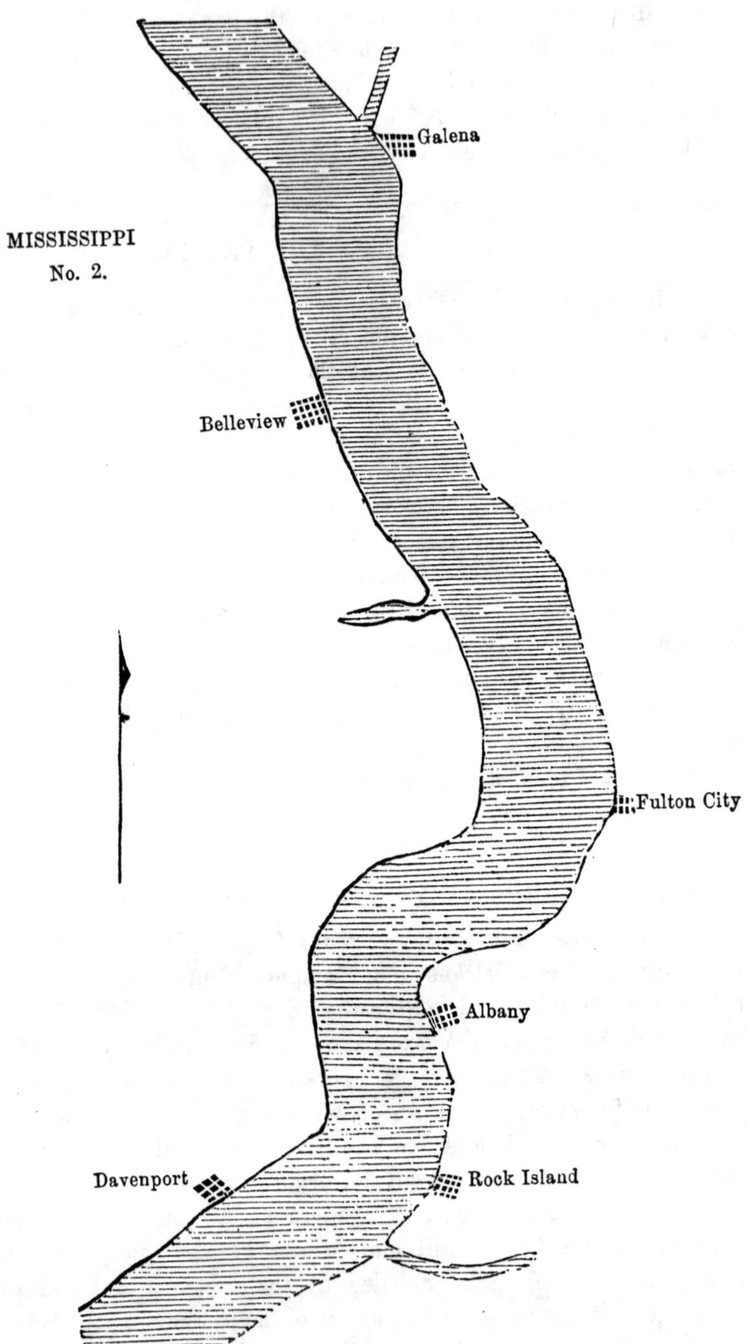
MISSISSIPPI
No. 2.
Galena
Belleview
Fulton City
Albany
Davenport
Rock Island

officers or crew saved anything. Captain Holmes acted most nobly throughout the trying scene, who, after swimming ashore with his wife, returned to the boat, and met his death in the honorable discharge of his duty. His first impulse was to save the female passengers. Rushing to the ladies' cabin, he prevailed on the affrighted occupants to take the chairs, with the life-preservers attached to them, and commit themselves to the water. He then threw the baggage, &c., overboard, to

BURNING OF THE CLARKSVILLE.

lessen the combustible material, and being now exhausted by his exertions, and half suffocated with smoke, he attempted to jump overboard, but striking against the lower guard, he fell among the burning ruins, and there perished.

The following details were furnished by a gentleman who was one of the surviving passengers of the Clarksville: The fire by which this noble boat was destroyed, was first discovered when she was about half a mile below Ozark island, at half-past 5 o'clock, P. M. Within a few minutes after the discovery of the fire, the boat reached the island to which the pilot had directed her course. The head of the steamer struck the ground, and all the passengers might easily have passed over the forecastle to the island, and many of them were saved in this way; but others, being apprehensive of an explosion, remained in the cabin until they were driven from thence by the progress of the flames, which had, by this time, cut off all retreat by the forward part

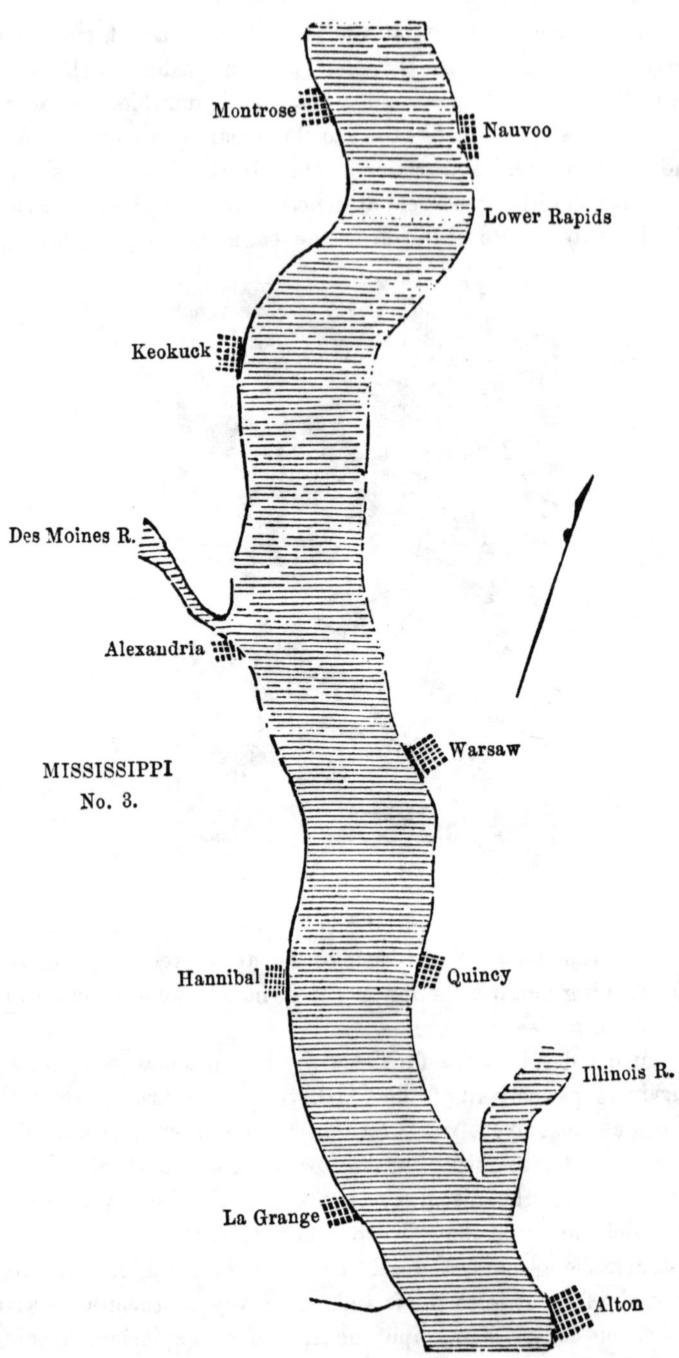
Montrose
Nauvoo
Lower Rapids
Keokuck
Des Moines R.
Alexandria
Warsaw
MISSISSIPPI
No. 3.
Hannibal
Quincy
Illinois R.
La Grange
Alton

of the boat. All that could now be done by the persons who remained aft, was to throw themselves into the river, as the stern of the boat lay out from the shore. Governor Poindexter and his lady were both injured, the former slightly, and the latter severely. The first clerk escaped without hat or coat, but saved the books of the boat and the money. The fire originated immediately over the boiler, under the social hall, and made such rapid progress fore and aft, that all efforts to extinguish the flames were unavailing. The steamer Chalmetto took off the surviving passengers.

List of the Killed.—Captain Holmes, master of the Clarksville; two ladies and a child, names unknown; Charles Quinn, a deck hand; the second steward, name not mentioned; Humphrey, Sam Johnson, Lewis, Peter Spicer, Sam Wilson, Prince, and Giles, colored firemen; a negro man, his wife and four children, slaves of a Mr. Russell; Sam, a slave of Gov. Poindexter; and a colored girl belonging to one of the passengers.

Wounded.—Governor Poindexter and lady; Mr. Barrow, and Mr. Lofton, of Memphis.

BURNING OF THE CREOLE.

The Creole was on her way from Nachitoches, on Red River, to New Orleans, with a full freight of cotton, and one hundred thousand dollars in specie, consigned to the Exchange Bank of New Orleans. She had, likewise, about one hundred passengers, including several entire families. At an early hour on Monday morning, February 22d, 1841, when the Creole had reached the mouth of Red River, she was discovered to be in flames, which spread with such rapidity as to preclude all hope of saving the vessel. The engineer and pilot remained at their posts until they were completely surrounded by the flames, and succeeded in running the boat to the nearest bank of the river, before the tiller-ropes were burned off. Unluckily, however, the bank which had been reached was steep and inaccessible; and the boat, when she struck against it, dislodged a quantity of earth, which fell on her bow, and caused her to bound off from the shore. She then became unmanageable, as the tiller-ropes by this time were consumed. Many of the passengers and crew were rescued by the steamers Baltic and Governor Pratt. The cargo, baggage and specie were all lost. The names of the killed are comprised in the following list:

Killed.—The family of A. B. Church, consisting of two grown

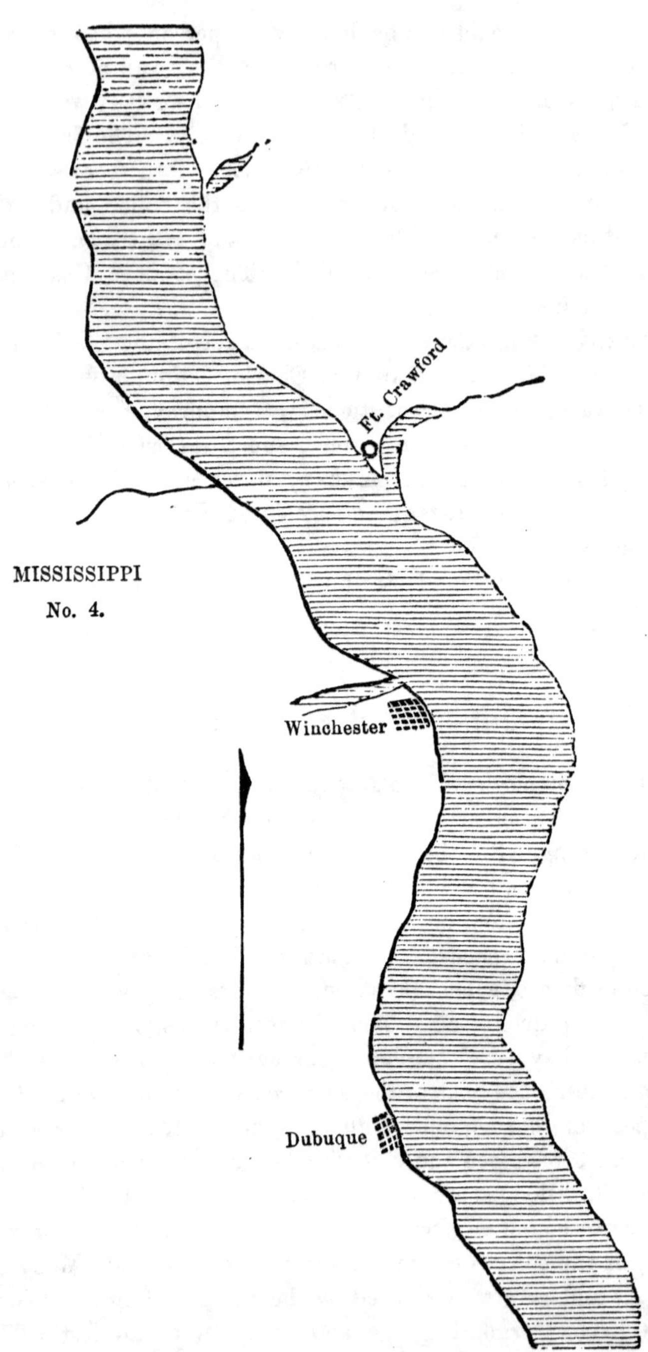
Ft. Crawford
MISSISSIPPI
No. 4.
Winchester
Dubuque

daughters, himself and wife, and two colored servants; D. M. Delmonico, New Jersey; wife of John Abrams, St. Louis; A. Dutcher and daughter, Mobile; E. Fitch, New Orleans; A. Barker and wife, Tenn.; Miss Snow, of Montgomery, Ala.; John Floyd, W. Smith, and Edward Young, Miss.; four colored waiters; nine firemen, Irish; a German family, six in number; besides thirty-one persons who were more or less wounded.

EXPLOSION OF THE EDWARD BATES.

A flue of the steamer Edward Bates collapsed on the Mississippi river, near Hamburg, Ill., on the 9th day of August, 1848, causing the death of fifty-three persons, and wounding forty others. The particulars are unknown, as few of those who witnessed the disaster survived to tell the melancholy story. The names of some of the killed and wounded have been preserved, and will be found in the following list:

KILLED—William Chamberlain, Mr. White, Mr. Rarridon, and Mr. Haines, deck passengers; Mrs. Bowen and nephew; Mrs. John Bowen and child; Mrs. Susan Bowen and child; Mr. Eades and two children; Master Eades, his nephew; John Brown, Andrew Hatfield, and Eli Delmay, deck hands; Geo. Matson and John Lenan, firemen; Henry Johnson, Wm. Parks, G. W. Lyons, J. Holliday, Wm. Amet, Frederic Smith, colored fireman, and Isaac Dozier.

Thirteen dead bodies, exclusive of the above, were afterwards picked up at Hamburg.

WOUNDED—George Blackwell, T. B. Ewing, D. E. Cameron, Samuel Simpson, Preston Leiper, Le Roy Jenkins, E. B. Morrison and wife, (badly,) M. Vansel, James Cook, J. H. Simpson, Master Bowen, Mr. Eades, E. T. Hudson, H. M. Swazy, J. Righter, and friend.

MORTALLY WOUNDED—George Watt, Samuel Dolsey, Wm. Wells, John Montague, Silas Bowman, Samuel Ferguson, T. M. McDonald, Joseph Morrison, Jacob Andrews, F. Turner, Jno. Swan, and Wm. Robinson.

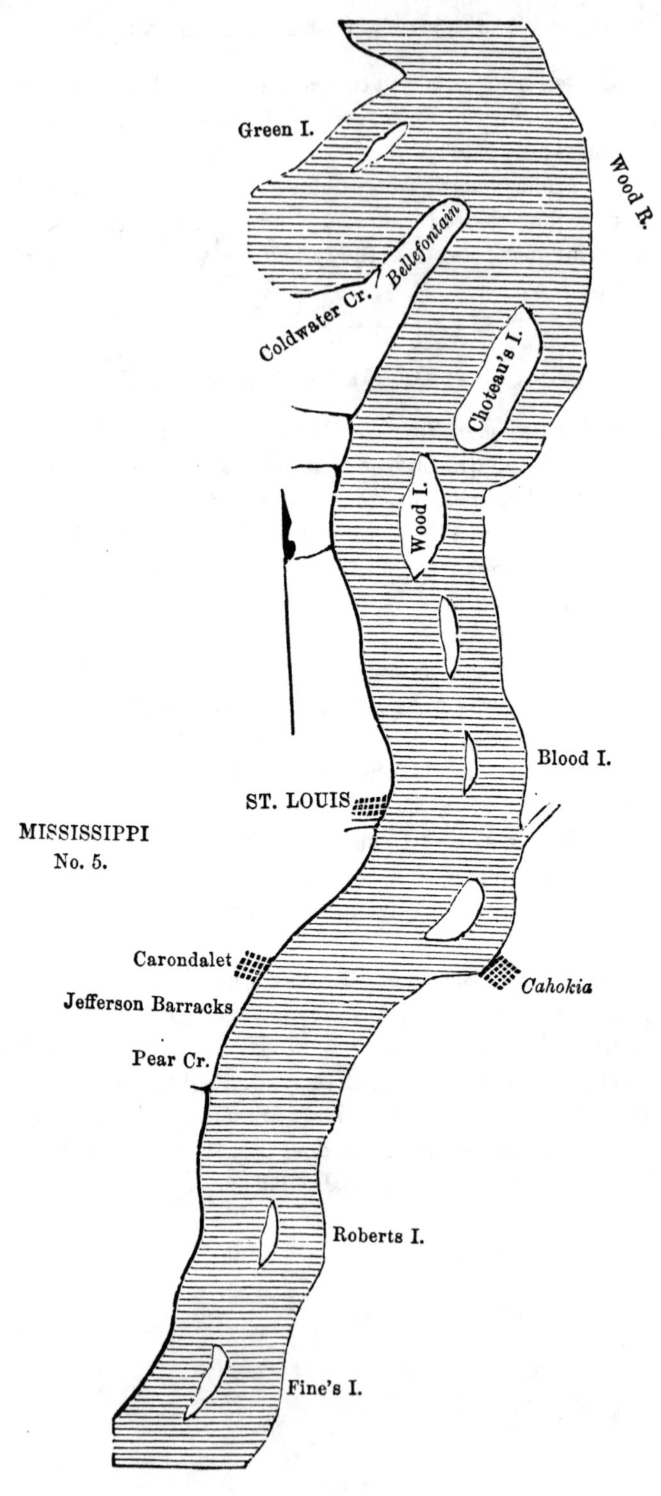
Green I.
Wood R.
Bellefontain
Coldwater Cr.
Choteau's I.
Wood I.
Blood I.
ST. LOUIS
MISSISSIPPI
No. 5.
Carondalet
Cahokia
Jefferson Barracks
Pear Cr.
Roberts I.
Fine's I.

BURNING OF THE PHŒNIX.

This terrible accident occurred about four o'clock on the morning of the 21st of November, 1847, on Lake Michigan, within seventeen miles of Sheboygan. The fire was first discovered under the deck, near the back end of the boiler; but it soon spread in every direction through the boat. There were more than two hundred passengers on board, and it soon became manifest that, with the means of escape which offered, not more than one-third of them could be saved. The excitement, consternation and despair which then prevailed among so many people doomed to a horrible death, cannot be depicted by any human language. About thirty of the passengers betook themselves to the small boats, which would contain no more, and they were taken up by the steamer Delaware, which soon hove in sight, but not in time to save those who remained on board the Phœnix, more than one hundred and sixty persons, all of whom were drowned or burnt to death.

The commander of the Phœnix, Capt. Sweet, was just recovering from a severe illness, and was still confined to his state-room, at the time the vessel took fire. He escaped, however, in one of the small boats, and was taken up by the Delaware. A large number of the passengers were Hollanders emigrating to the West. The following relation was given by Mr. House the engineer. Mr. House remained at his post until the flames fairly drove him into the water. Seizing a broad-axe, he separated with a single stroke a rope which sustained a piece of timber called a "fender," used to prevent the sides of the boat from chaffing against a wharf. As soon as this fender fell into the water, Mr. House leaped after it, but in his first efforts to get hold of it, he only pushed it further from him; and at that moment, a tall and vigorous emigrant jumped into the water, and endeavored to gain possession of the piece of timber, to which Mr. House trusted for his own preservation. However, the Hollander could not swim, and before he could reach the piece of wood he disappeared under the water, leaving Mr. House in uncontested possession of the frail support. When it is considered that this accident took place in the latter part of November, and that the water of the lake was almost in a freezing condition, some idea may be formed of the effort required when the chilled and benumbed passengers were laboring to keep themselves afloat on the various articles of cabin furniture, &c., which had been thrown overboard for that pur-

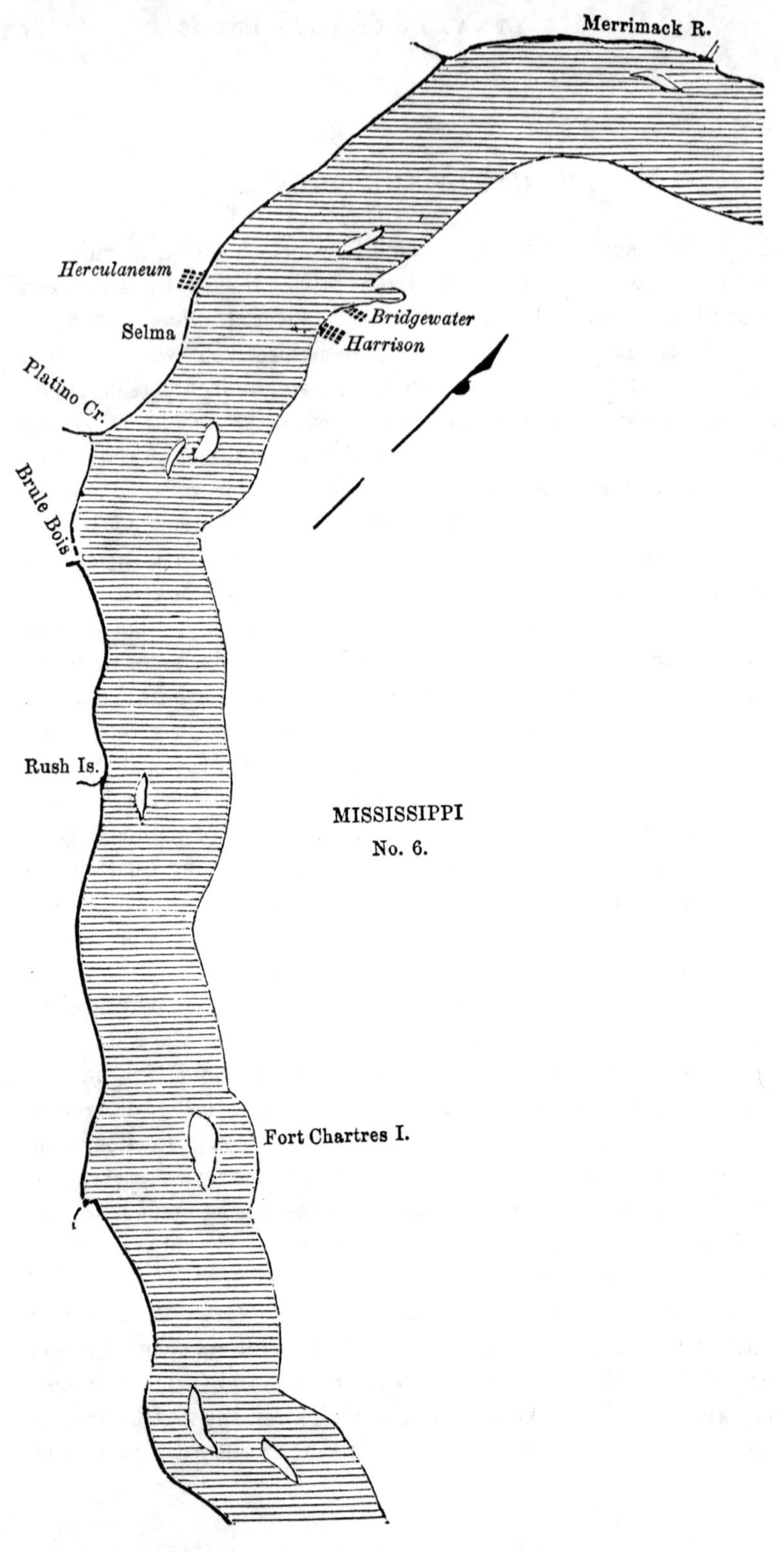
Merrimack R.
Herculaneum
Bridgewater
Selma
Harrison
Platino Cr.
Brule Bois
Rush Is.
MISSISSIPPI
No. 6.
Fort Chartres I.

BURNING OF THE PHŒNIX.

pose. Very few of them indeed were able, in such trying circumstances, to support themselves on the surface of the lake until assistance arrived. Mr. House soon discovered that the piece of wood which he had detached from the boat was not sufficient to sustain him, but he fortunately obtained possession of a state-room door, which drifted within his reach, and by attaching this with his neck-cloth to the fender, he formed a raft, large and buoyant enough to assure him of preservation from drowning; but his sufferings from the cold were almost insupportable. When he first betook himself to the water, he was surrounded by many others, who were striving hard to prolong their existence until relief might providentially be afforded; but one after another sunk, chilled and exhausted, into the long sleep of death. Very soon he found himself almost companionless on the bosom of the lake. In this frightful and agonizing situation, tortured almost beyond endurance, with both mental and corporal anguish, he remained for two hours. At last, when almost tempted to abandon his raft, and precipitate himself on that fate which seemed most likely to overtake him eventually, he discerned the lights on board of a steamboat which was rapidly approaching. Two or three persons were still clinging to settees, boards, &c., and he exhorted them in the most earnest manner to retain their grasp a little while longer, as relief was at hand. He addressed himself particularly to a lady, who had hitherto sustained herself on a floating settee with admirable heroism; he directed her attention to the approaching boat, which was now scarcely a furlong distant; but alas! her emotions at the prospect of deliverance seemed to overcome her more than the fear of death itself; for at this instant she swooned away, lost her grasp on the bench, and sunk to her final

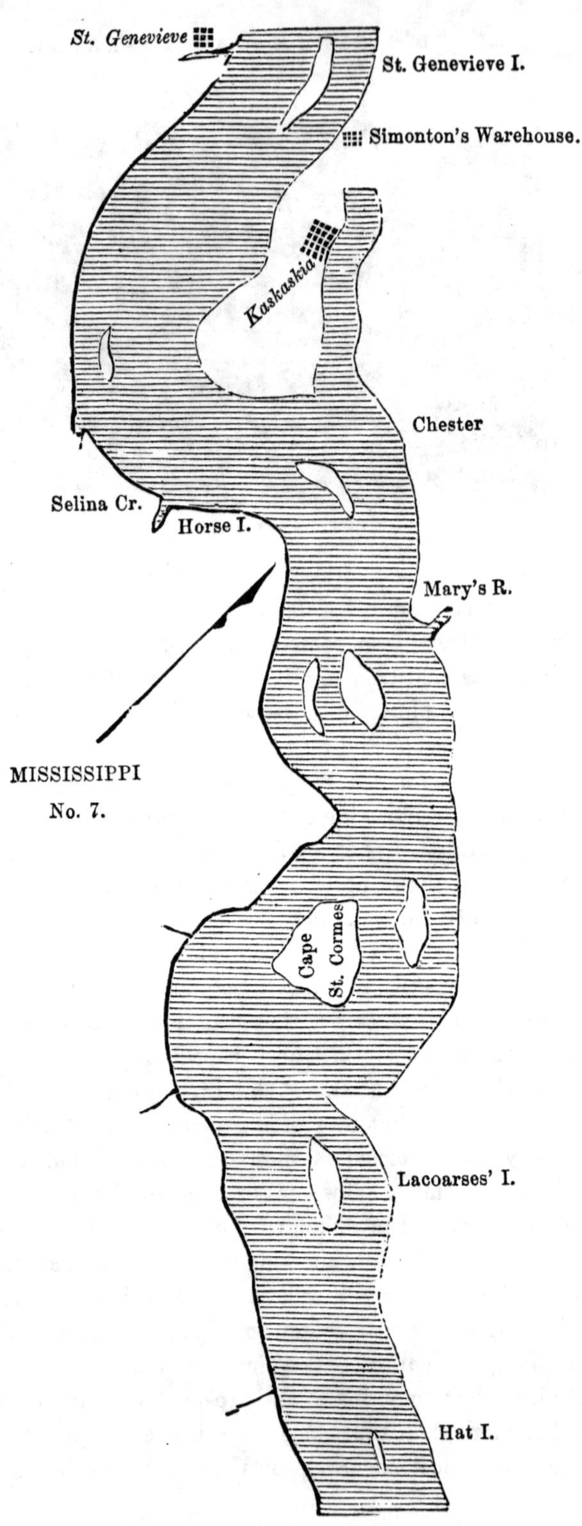
St. Genevieve
St. Genevieve I.
Simonton's Warehouse.
Kaskaskia
Chester
Selina Cr.
Horse I.
Mary's R.
MISSISSIPPI
No. 7.
Cape St. Cormes
Lacoarses' I.
Hat I.

resting place under the deep, blue waters. When the approaching steamer, which proved to be the propeller Delaware, arrived at the spot, Mr. House was the only person found alive. The propeller had already succored those passengers who had escaped from the burning steamer in the small boats. All who had remained on the Phœnix, and all who had thrown themselves into the lake, with but one exception, had perished.

At this time the blazing vessel presented a most awful and sublime spectacle. The hull was a complete bed of fire, which, bursting in flames from the sides, at times streamed far out over the waters, and then curled aloft, till flame meeting flame, the combined fiery current rushed furiously upward till it appeared to be lost in the clouds. When Mr. House, alone on his raft, beheld this grand, but dreadful object, the shrouds and rigging were covered with human beings, who sought safety there rather than in the waters. Their terror-marked features were lighted up by the ghastly glare of the flames, and as the fire reached them in their retreat, one after another fell, shrieking, into the fiery furnace below. One man reached the cross-trees (an elevated position on the mast), where he lashed himself, and there he remained till all his companions had fallen, and the mast went by the board; but in the mean-time he was roasted to death by the fervid heat. While the boat was burning, and all prospects of relief were cut off, some betook themselves to quiet prayer, others shrieked for aid, or uttered phrensied exclamations of despair, and others bowed in meek submission to the fiat of an overruling Providence. As the flames advanced, one voice after another was hushed in death, and finally a stillness, awful and profound, told the horrified spectator that the scene of suffering was finished.

This disaster is supposed to have occasioned a greater loss of life than any other steamboat accident which ever occurred on the American lakes. The greater number of those who perished were the Holland emigrants, whose names are unknown. Mr. House, the engineer, who related the particulars contained in this narrative, was personally acquainted with some of the American passengers who were lost, and their names only are preserved in the following list, given by Mr. H. himself.

Passengers Lost.—Mr. West, lady, and child, of Racine, Wis.; Mr. Heath and sister, of Little Fort; Mrs. Long and child, of Milwaukie; S. Burroughs, of Chicago; D. Blish, Southport; two Misses Hazelton, of Sheboygan; twenty-five other cabin passengers, names unknown to Mr. House; six or eight steerage passengers, and about one hundred and fifty Hollanders.

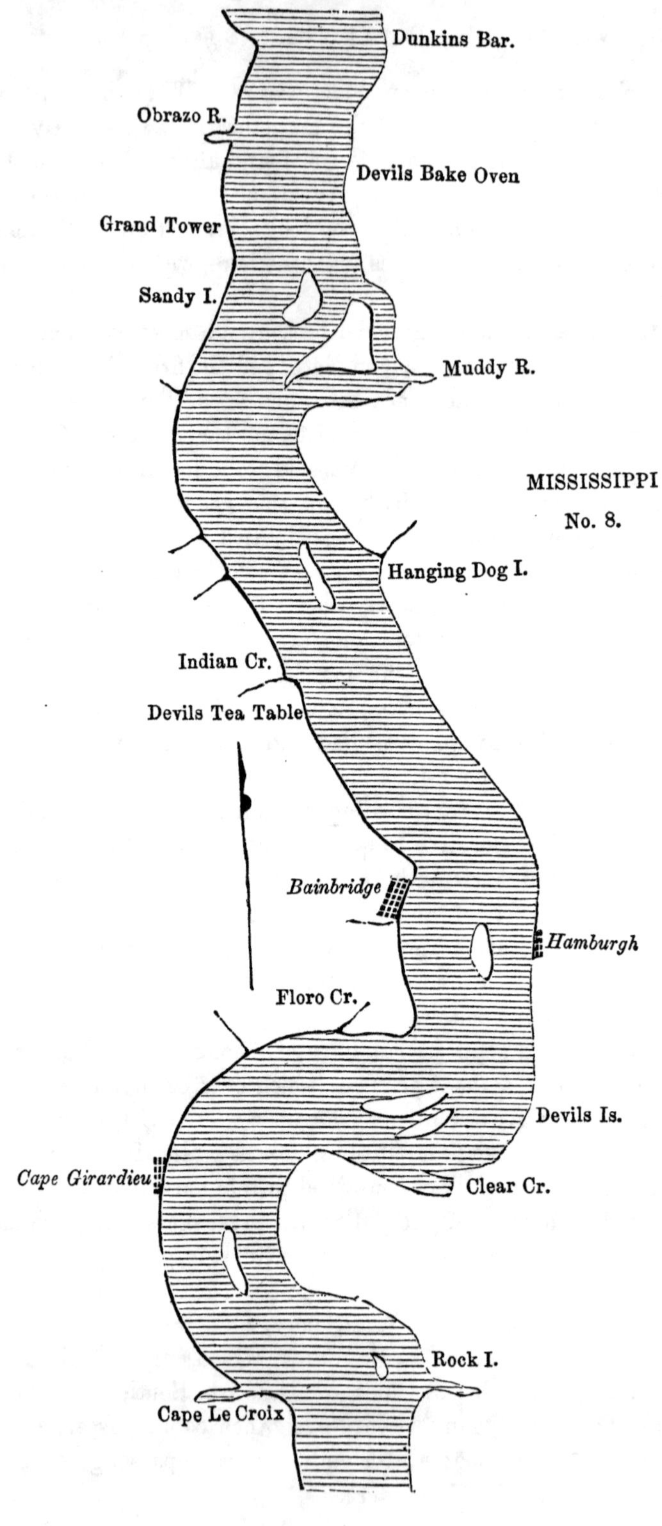
Dunkins Bar.
Obrazo R.
Devils Bake Oven
Grand Tower
Sandy I.
Muddy R.
MISSISSIPPI
No. 8.
Hanging Dog I.
Indian Cr.
Devils Tea Table
Bainbridge
Hamburgh
Floro Cr.
Devils Is.
Cape Girardieu
Clear Cr.
Rock I.
Cape Le Croix

Officers and Crew of the Boat Lost.—D. W. Keller, steward, of Cleveland, Ohio; J. C. Smith, saloon keeper, of Buffalo, N. Y.; N. Merrill, second mate, of Ohio city; W. Owen, second engineer, of Toledo, Ohio; H. Robinson, porter, Chicago; J. Nugent, fireman, of Buffalo. *Deck Hands.*—T. Harsey, T. Ferteau, of River St. Clair; J. Murdock and A. Murdock, of Canada; George ——, cabin boy; H. Tisdale, of Cleveland, (body found;) wheelsman, name not remembered; L. Southworth, of New Bedford; and two colored cooks, of Detroit.

The names of those *saved* were Capt. Sweet, Ohio city; Mr. Donihoe, clerk, River St. Clair; engineer, M. W. House, Cleveland; wheelsman, A. G. Kelso, Ohio city; deck hand, J. Moon, Cleveland; fireman, Michael O'Brien, Buffalo; second porter, R. Watts, Cleveland.

The Phœnix had as large a load of passengers and freight as she could carry.

The loss of life was the largest which ever occurred on the lakes, and the property lost was immense. It is supposed that those one hundred and fifty Hollanders had considerable money with them, as they were seeking a location in the West; but how uncertain is life! It is indeed mournful to record this sad catastrophe.

SINKING OF THE TALISMAN.

Before daylight on the morning of November 19th, 1847, the steamboats Talisman and Tempest came in collision on the Mississippi river, half a mile below Cape Girardeau. The Talisman was struck forward of the boilers, and sunk within ten minutes. The Tempest, which was but slightly damaged, rounded to, and came to the relief of the Talisman's crew and passengers. The officers and crews of both steamers exerted themselves to save life and property; but to the disgrace of human nature, it is related that a number of heartless and conscienceless scoundrels came in small boats to the scene of the disaster, and totally regardless of the supplications of the drowning passengers who implored their aid, they betook themselves to plunder, seizing on the floating baggage, and every other article of value which came within their reach. One of the villains engaged in these nefarious operations was a resident of Cincinnati, and bore the name of Barnes. His *Christian* name, (if he ever had any,) is not mentioned, or gladly would we give it to the public; still more gladly would we

> "Place in every honest hand a whip
> To lash the rascal naked through the world."

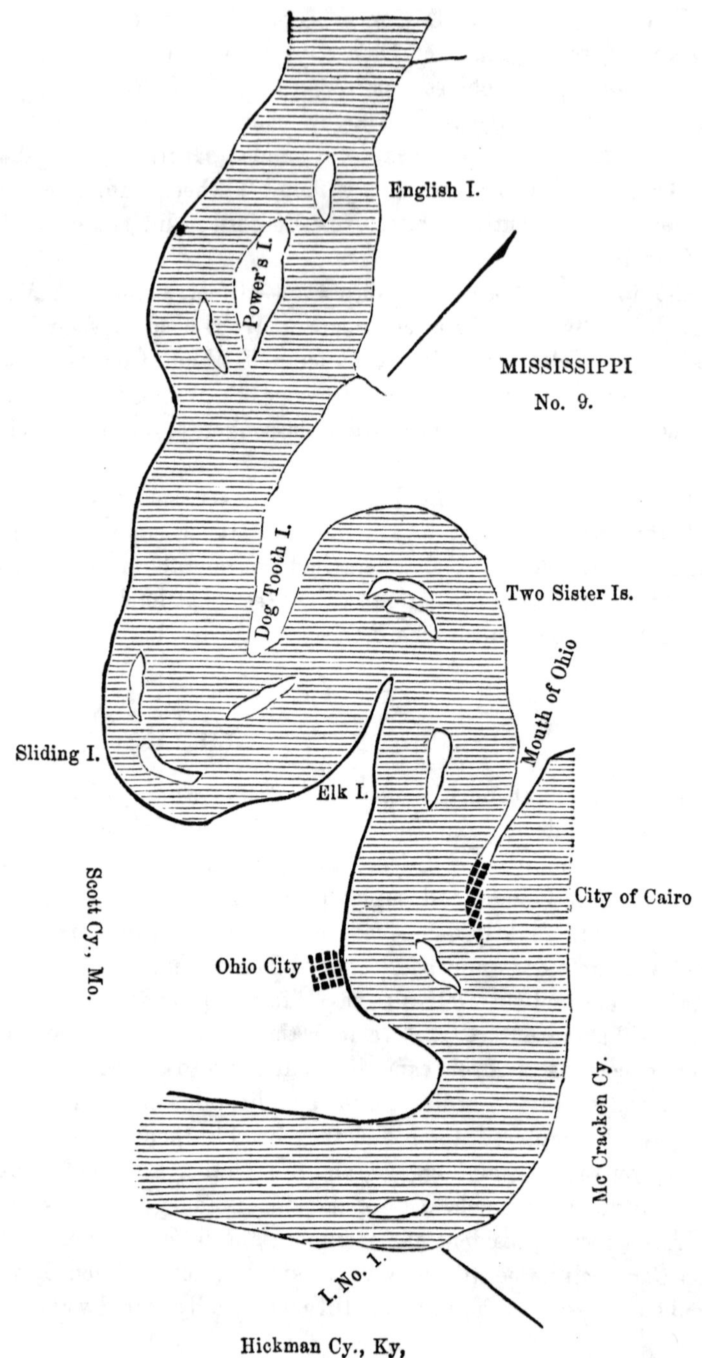
English I.
Power's I.
MISSISSIPPI
No. 9.
Dog Tooth I.
Two Sister Is.
Mouth of Ohio
Sliding I.
Elk I.
City of Cairo
Ohio City
Scott Cy., Mo.
Mc Cracken Cy.
I. No. 1.
Hickman Cy., Ky,

Several of the crew and many of the deck passengers were drowned. Two or three families of German emigrants, numbering about twenty-five persons, were among the passengers. Ten persons, all of one family, were lost. An effort was made to rescue the bodies of the persons drowned by means of the diving bell. A young German, who was unable to speak a word of English, continued to wander about the deck of the Tempest, wringing his hands and making exclamations of distress; his eyes were fixed upon the river, as if he expected the deep waters to give up the wife and children they had taken from him. The fate of Mr. Butler, the engineer, was particularly distressing. He

SINKING OF THE TALISMAN.

was on watch, and although he saw at once and was told repeatedly that the boat was sinking, he refused to leave his post until the water was up to his waist. It was then too late to save himself, and, being unable to withstand the rush of water, he was borne back among the machinery, and drowned. An interesting young married couple, whose names were unknown to the people of the boat and to their fellow passengers, were among the victims of this calamity. The young gentleman was a good swimmer and might have saved himself; but perished in a vain attempt to save the life of his bride. These two were the only cabin passengers lost; all the rest of the drowned were deck passengers, or persons belonging to the boat. Fifty-one persons, men, women and children, are known to have been drowned by this accident, and probably as many more, who are not designated in the annexed list.

Persons known to have been drowned.—Mrs. Nicholls, Mrs. Keziah Bennett, Sarah Bennett, her daughter, aged ten years, Belinda Bennett, another child of Mrs. B., aged eighteen months, Thomas Bennett,

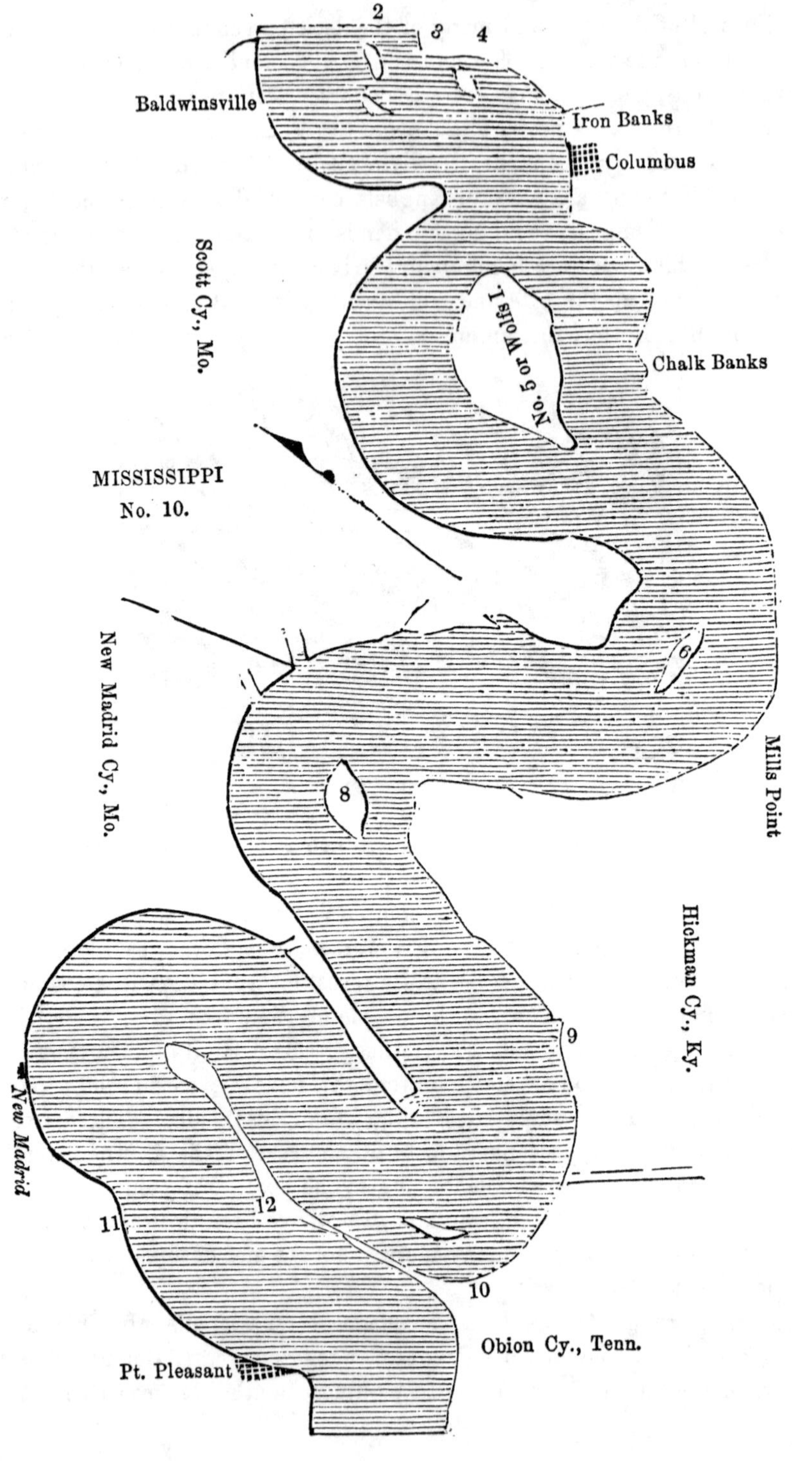
2
3
4
Baldwinsville
Iron Banks
Columbus
Scott Cy., Mo.
No. 5 or Wolfs I.
Chalk Banks
MISSISSIPPI
No. 10.
New Madrid Cy., Mo.
6
Mills Point
8
Hickman Cy., Ky.
9
New Madrid
12
11
10
Obion Cy., Tenn.
Pt. Pleasant

aged eight years, and Frances Bennett, aged six years, also children of Mrs. B., Miss Charlotte Cady, Miss Eleanor Cady, Eliza Stone, aged two years. (All of these were from Morgan County, Ohio, moving to Schuyler County, Ill. They were travelling under the protection of John B. Stone, whose little daughter was lost with the rest.) E. Williams, Johnson O'Neil, deck-hands from Pittsburgh; John Thomas Butler, chief engineer; two children of Mr. Thomas Pryor; sixteen German emigrants, whose names were not entered in the books; nine negroes belonging to Mr. R. R. Buchner, of Calloway County, Missouri; two young men from Armstrong County, Pa., and a family of ten persons from Illinois, names unknown.

An intelligent man, who was one of the survivors, stated that the deck was crowded with passengers, and the boiler deck was so thronged with passengers, freight, and live stock, that he (the narrator) could scarcely find a place to lie down. He estimated the number of deck passengers at one hundred and fifty, and supposed that half of them, at least, were drowned. Only four or five bodies, among them the two children of Mr. Pryor, were recovered by means of the diving-bell. Mr. Cady, the father of the two young ladies mentioned in the foregoing list, used many efforts to recover their remains, but did not succeed. It is conjectured that most of the bodies were carried to a great distance by the current.

EXPLOSION OF THE KATE FLEMING.

The steamer Kate Fleming, Captain Dunham, on her way from Louisville to Cairo, at the mouth of the Ohio river, exploded near Walker's Landing, on Saturday, October 5, 1850, at 12 o'clock, M. She had been aground on Walker's bar, but had got off, and the bell had given the signal to "go ahead slowly," when after a few revolutions of the water-wheel, the boiler exploded, dislodging the furnace, and setting fire to the boat which burned to the water's edge.

List of the Killed—E. Y. Bocock, Christian C. Odell, barkeeper; Annette, colored chambermaid; Jeffrey, colored steward; John, cabin boy; Hutchinson, a slave of Mr. Moore, of Miss.; a fireman and a deck-hand, and a Mr. Jennings, of New Albany.

Wounded—Capt. Dunham; J. Thornby, of Miss.; the steward of the Kate Fleming; the mate and second cook of do., and several of the deck passengers. Mr. Weld, of Louisiana, was badly bruised.

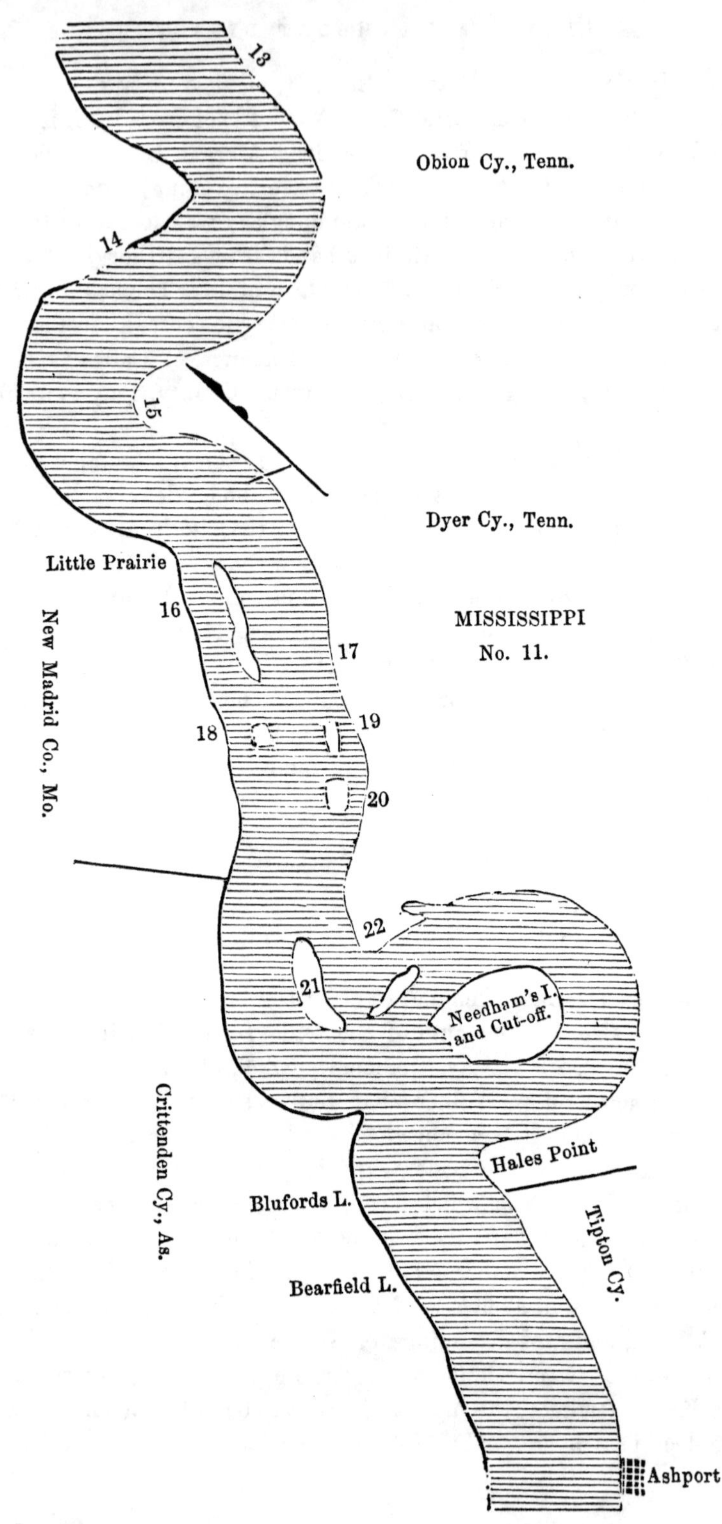
13
Obion Cy., Tenn.
14
15
Dyer Cy., Tenn.
Little Prairie
16
MISSISSIPPI
No. 11.
17
New Madrid Co., Mo.
18
19
20
22
21
Needham's I.
and Cut-off.
Crittenden Cy., As.
Hales Point
Blufords L.
Tipton Cy.
Bearfield L.
Ashport

Capt. Dunham, Capt. Quarrier, and Mr. Lowry, with several others, were standing on the hurricane deck, and were all blown up several feet in the air. Captains Dunham and Quarrier fell on the bow of the boat; the others fell into the river, and saved themselves by swimming.

The safe, containing a large amount of money, some of which belonged to the boat, and some deposited by the passengers, was blown into the river, and was supposed to be irrecoverably lost. Very few of the passengers saved their baggage and clothing, though some had sufficient presence of mind to throw their trunks overboard.

EXPLOSION OF THE ANGLO-NORMAN.

The new and beautiful steamer Anglo Norman, left New Orleans December 14, 1850, on an experimental trip, having on board a large "pleasure party," consisting of two hundred and ten persons. She proceeded in an admirable style some distance up the river, satisfying all on board that she was a first-rate sailer, and giving promise of a brilliant career in the future; but having tacked and directed her course back to the city, all her boilers exploded at the same moment, shattering a considerable part of the boat, and killing and wounding nearly half the people on board.

Mr. H. A. Kidd, editor of the New Orleans Crescent, was one of the excursionists, and was reported among the killed; but he lived to give a graphic account of his miraculous escape from death, which account he somewhat eccentrically entitled "The Experience of a Blown-up Man." Mr. Kidd says:

"Mr. Bigny, one of the editors of the Delta, and myself, took the only two chairs remaining unoccupied on the deck; his chair having the back towards the pilot-house, and mine with its back to the chimney. It will be seen at once that we had seated ourselves immediately over the monster boilers of the boat.

We had been engaged in conversation but a very few moments, when a jet of hot water, accompanied with steam, was forced out of the main pipe just aft the chimney, and fell near us in a considerable shower. I had never noticed anything of the kind before, and thought the occurrence very extraordinary. Just as I was about remarking this to Mr. Bigny, I was suddenly lifted high in the air, *how* high it is impossible for me to say. I have a distinct recollection of passing rather irregularly through the air, enveloped, as it seemed to me, in a dense cloud, through which no object was discernible. There was a sufficient

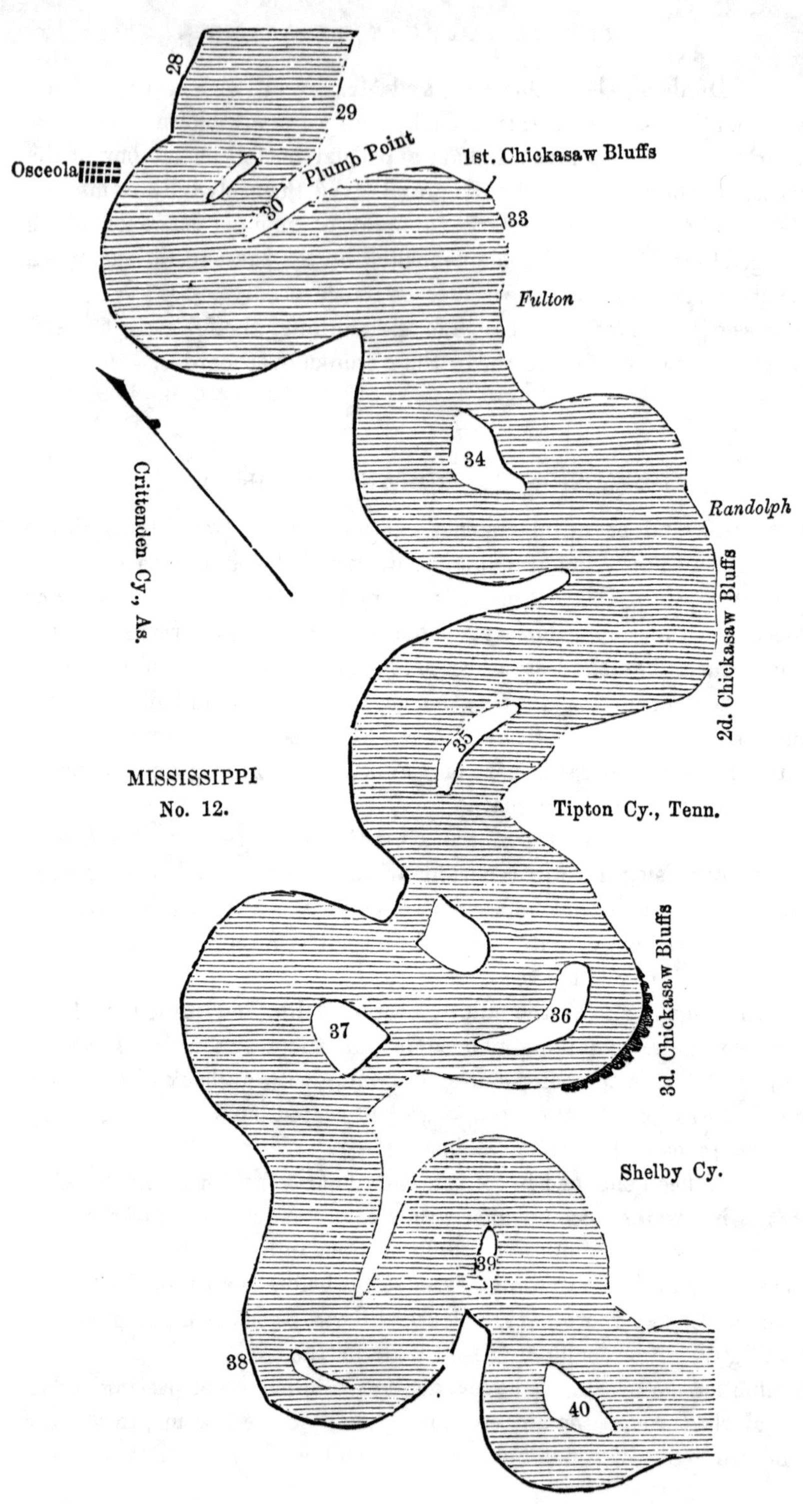

28
29
Osceola
Plumb Point
30
1st. Chickasaw Bluffs
33
Fulton
34
Crittenden Cy., As.
Randolph
2d. Chickasaw Bluffs
35
MISSISSIPPI
No. 12.
Tipton Cy., Tenn.
3d. Chickasaw Bluffs
36
37
Shelby Cy.
39
38
40

lapse of time for me to have a distinct impression on my mind that I must inevitably be lost. In what position I went into the water, and to what depth I went, I have not the slightest idea. When I arose to the surface, I wiped the water from my face, and attempted to obtain a view of things around me, but this I was prevented from doing by the vapor of steam, which enveloped everything as a cloud. This obscuration, however, lasted but for a short time, and when it had passed away, I had a clear conception of my situation. I found myself in possession of my senses, and my limbs in good working order. I looked around in every direction, and discovered that I was not far from the centre of the river, and in the neighborhood of some twenty or thirty people, who seemed to have been thrown into the water somewhat in a heap. They were sustaining themselves on the surface as best they could, many of them endeavoring to get possession of floating pieces of the wreck. I could see nothing of the exploded boat, and was fully satisfied in my mind that she was blown all to pieces, and that all my fellow passengers were lost, except those who, like myself, were struggling in the water. I will do myself the simple justice to say that, from the time at which I had risen to the surface, I had no apprehensions of drowning, though to a more disinterested spectator the chances might have appeared to be against me. I never

EXPLOSION OF THE ANGLO-NORMAN.

felt more buoyant, nor swam with greater ease. Still I thought it well enough to appropriate whatever aid was within my reach; so, like others, I began a race, which proved to be a tedious one, after a shattered piece of plank. I finally reached it, and putting my hands rather rudely upon it, I got a sousing for my pains. The piece was too small to render me any material service. I abandoned it, and turned in the direction of a steamboat, which I perceived advancing, and

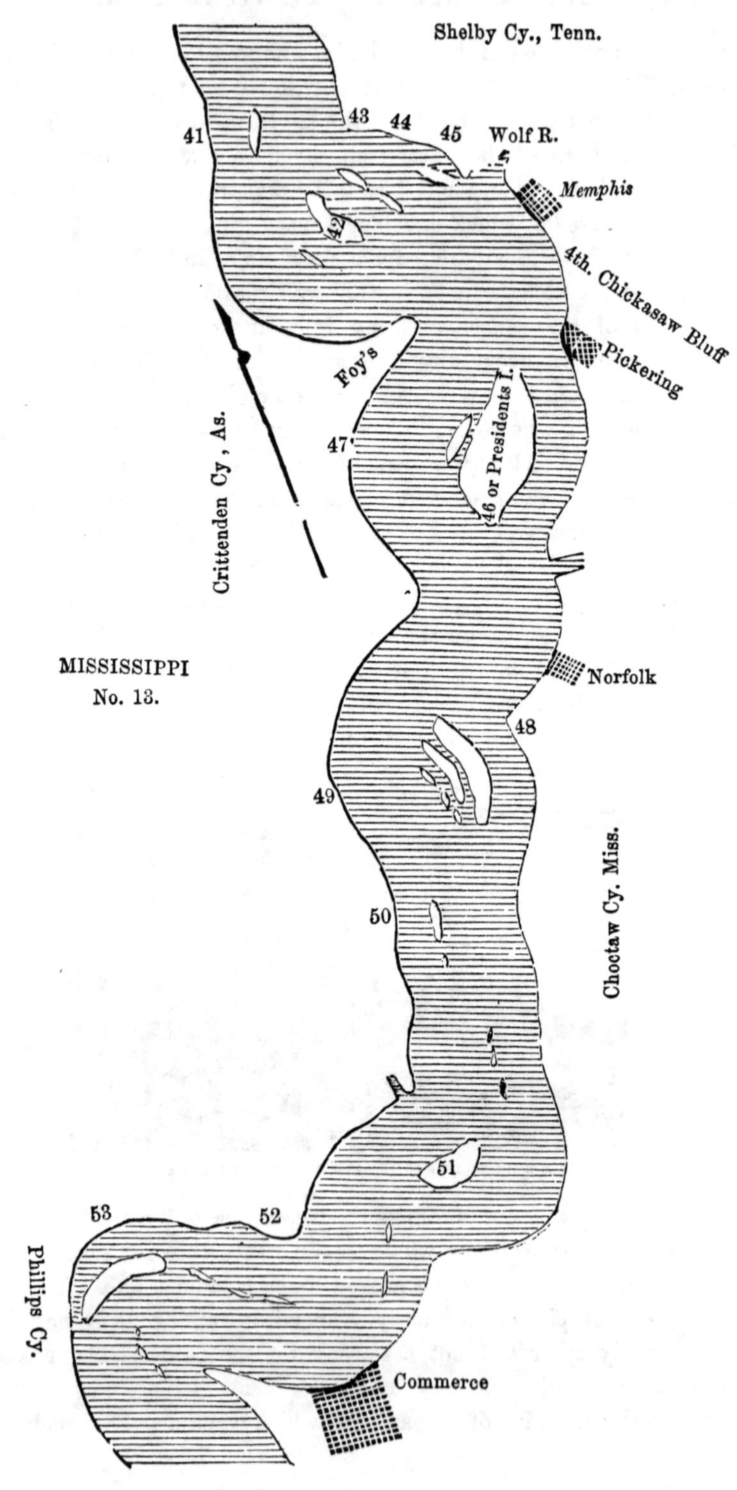
Shelby Cy., Tenn.
41
43
44
45
Wolf R.
Memphis
42
4th. Chickasaw Bluff
Pickering
Foy's
Crittenden Cy , As.
47
46 or Presidents I.
MISSISSIPPI
No. 13.
Norfolk
48
49
Choctaw Cy. Miss.
50
51
53
52
Phillips Cy.
Commerce

which I afterwards discovered to be the Naniopa. To keep my face towards the approaching steamer, I found that I had to oppose the strong current of the river. This, together with the coldness of the water, so exhausted my physical energies, that, for a brief space, I felt that I should not be able to keep afloat until the boat should reach me. As the steamer came near, there was a cry from my unfortunate neighbors in the water, 'Stop the boat! stop the boat!'

There was, indeed, great danger of our being run over by it. I however had no fears on this point, and made no effort to get out of its way. Fortunately for myself, I was one of the first which the boat approached. A sailor threw out to me a large rope, which I succeeded in grasping at the first effort. I was drawn to the boat's guards, which were several feet above the water. While drawing me up, the kind-hearted sailor cried, 'Hold on, partner! hold on!' But I could not, my strength being exhausted; the rope was slipping through my hands, and I should certainly have fallen back into the water, and been irrecoverably lost under the boat's guards, had not another sailor quickly reached down and seized hold of my arms. I was drawn on board as nearly lifeless as any one could be without being actually dead. Two stout men assisted me to reach the cabin. My chest, as I discovered from its soreness and my spitting blood, had been somewhat bruised, but a little bathing with whiskey soon have me relief. My friend Bigny was one of the first I met on board."

Both these editors had been in the most dangerous part of the boat, and their escape, almost without injury, was a remarkable instance of good fortune. One of the passengers who escaped, remarked, that of the immense boiler, weighing many tons, not a scrap as large as a man's hand remained. Very few of the names of those who were killed could be ascertained, but the general opinion was that the number of the victims could not be less than one hundred. Mr. Perry, who was attached to the office of the New Orleans Bulletin, was one of the killed. The Hon. James Bebee, a member of the Missouri State legislature, was believed to have been lost. The persons mentioned below were badly wounded. Messrs. Nathan, Jarvis, Stillman, and Storm, of the New York Novelty Works; Captain Ambol; Captain Thompson, of the Ship Lexington. Mr. Kidd, editor of the Crescent, and Mr. Bigny of the Delta, were both slightly injured.

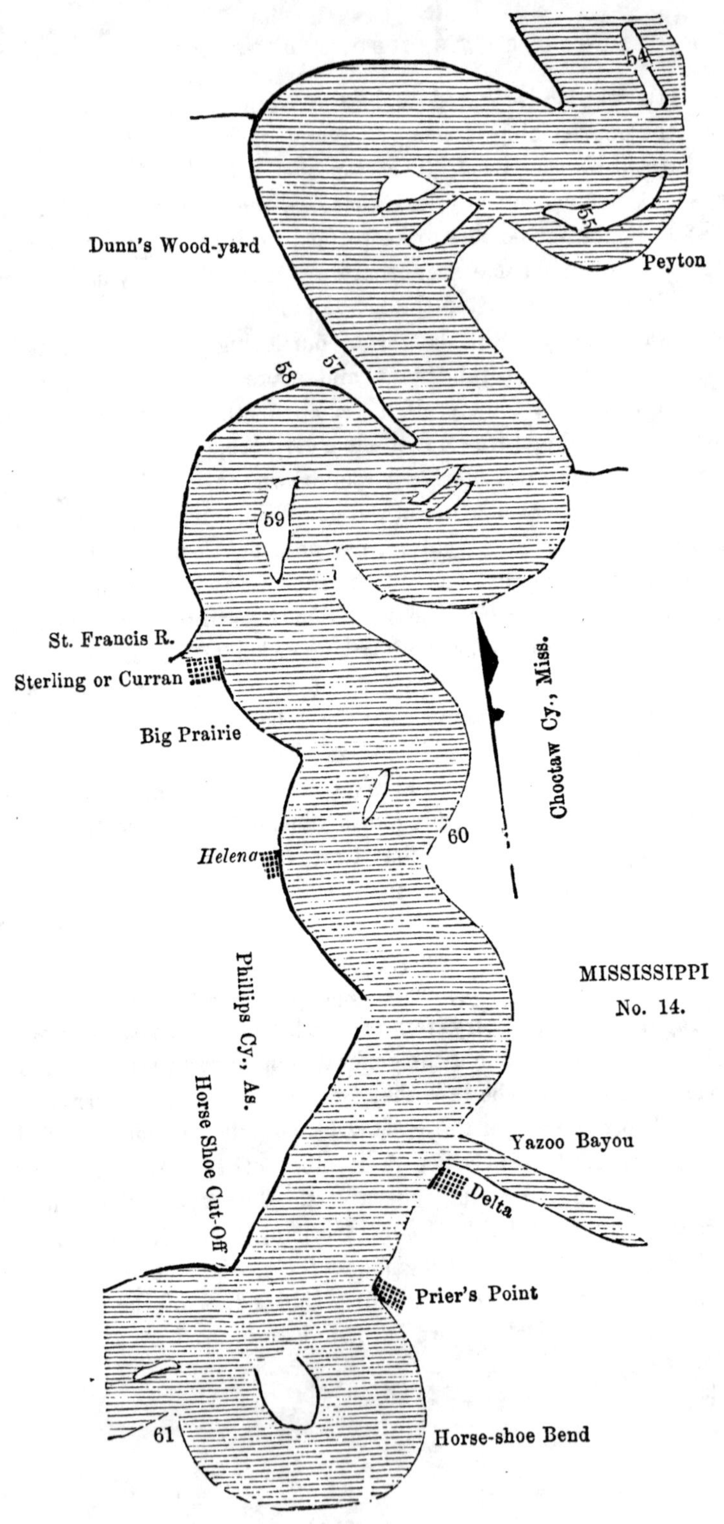
54
55
Peyton
Dunn's Wood-yard
57
58
59
St. Francis R.
Sterling or Curran
Big Prairie
Choctaw Cy., Miss.
60
Helena
Phillips Cy., As.
MISSISSIPPI
No. 14.
Horse Shoe Cut-Off
Yazoo Bayou
Delta
Prier's Point
61
Horse-shoe Bend

EXPLOSION OF THE OREGON.

The terrific explosion of the Oregon took place near island No. 82 in the Mississippi river, at one o'clock, P. M., on March 2d, 1851. All the boilers exploded at the same moment, carrying away the forward cabin, and killing, scalding or mutilating about sixty persons. The boat was heavily laden at the time, and carried about one hundred passengers.

Dinner was just over, and most of the passengers were in the social hall and on the forward guards. Immediately after the explosion the boat took fire, and burned to the water's edge. But for the timely assistance of the steamer Iroquois, which was about a mile off when the accident took place, all on board must have perished, as the Oregon was an unmanageable wreck in the middle of the channel. Capt. Lee, of the Iroquois, hastened to the assistance of the Oregon, but was obliged to stop to make some repairs. He succeeded, however, in reaching the Oregon, just as the flames were bursting through the hurricane deck. Men, women and children, almost surrounded by the raging flames, were collected on the after-part of the wreck. The shrieks of the affrighted women and children were heard far away over the waters, and as the Iroquois approached, the groans of the wounded and dying admonished the passengers and crew of that boat to prepare themselves for a ghastly and heart-rending spectacle. The captain of the Iroquois ran his boat aft of the Oregon; a communication was then made by placing ladders on the lower deck of the Iroquois and resting against the Oregon's upper deck; and on these ladders all the people on the wreck who were able to exert themselves, passed on to the Iroquois. Afterwards, with great exertion and risk, Capt. Lee succeeded in removing the wounded to his own cabin, the floor of which was soon covered with the most pitiable objects; scalded, charred and dismembered bodies, still panting and writhing in the spasmodic contortions of the last struggle. Some, who seem to have been less injured, appeared to endure equal or greater torment, or were enabled to give expression to their sufferings in frantic exclamations and prayers to heaven for a speedy death.

The cabin servants, who were at dinner, were nearly all killed. Eight white firemen, who were dining in the cabin at the same time, likewise perished. The clerk's office was entirely blown away, with all the books and papers of the boat. Owing to this circumstance, the

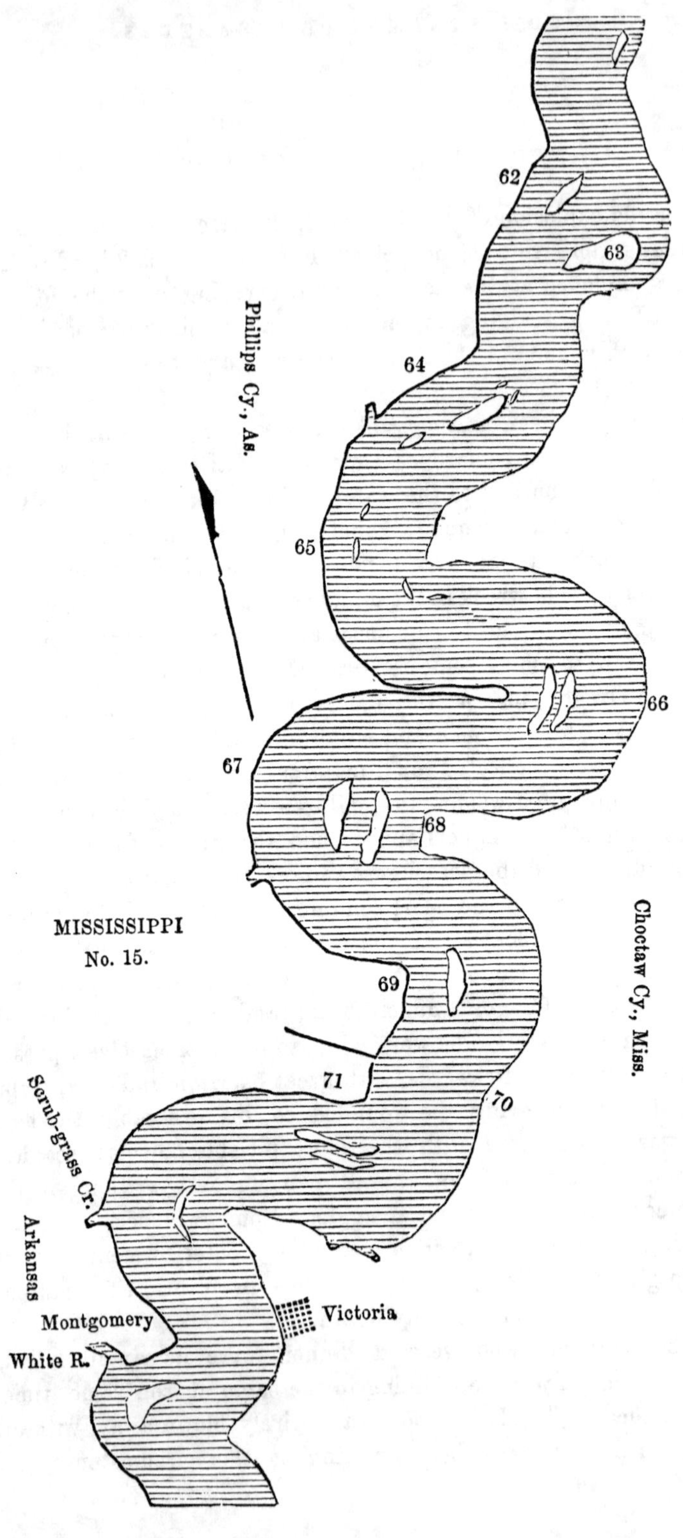
62
63
64
Phillips Cy., As.
65
66
67
68
MISSISSIPPI
No. 15.
69
Choctaw Cy., Miss.
71
70
Scrub-grass Cr.
Arkansas
Montgomery
Victoria
White R.

names of comparatively few of the passengers who were lost can be ascertained; and hence the list of killed must be regarded as very incomplete.

KILLED.—George Brown, first clerk; Richard Young, Shelby Co., Ky.; William Miller, Harrison Co., Ind.; Mrs. Asher, and Patrick Murphy, Louisville, Ky.; Patrick Lyons, deck-hand; William Larkin, Louisville, Ky.; six of the cabin servants, (colored,) six white firemen, and Mr. Love, engineer.

BADLY SCALDED.—Capt. Montgomery; Barrett Milliken, second clerk; Mr. Lyons, bar-keeper; Mr. Cannon, pilot, and J. M. Cox, Nelson Co., Ky.; besides eight or ten deck passengers who were unknown to the people of the boat, and too badly burnt to give any account of themselves.

SINKING OF THE JOHN L. AVERY.

The J. L. Avery, J. L. Robertson commander, was a new boat, built in the most substantial manner, and furnished with every necessary equipment for a first class passenger boat, being designed as a regular packet between New Orleans and Natchez. She left New Orleans, on her customary trip up the river, on March 7th, 1854. She stopped at Point Coupee and took in a large quantity of sugar and molasses; and on the 9th of the same month she passed the steamer Sultana, off Black Hawk point, forty miles below Natchez; and having left the Sultana, (with which she appears to have been racing,) about a mile astern, she struck what was supposed to be a tree washed from the shore by a recent freshet. A very large leak in the bottom of the boat was the consequence of this accident, and although the pilot immediately steered for the shore, the steamer sunk before she could get near enough to land the passengers. Mr. J. V. Guthrie, an engineer, and the carpenter, were standing just forward of the boilers when they heard the crash—the boat at the same time making a sudden surge to one side. The carpenter immediately lifted the scuttle-hatch and leaped into the hold, but finding the water pouring in too fast to admit of any attempt at repairing the damage, he made haste to get out again, at the same time giving notice to the engineer that the boat had snagged. Mr. Guthrie, perceiving that the boat was going down, hastened to the engine, but before he got there, he was up to his knees in water. The cabin passengers were hurried up to the hurricane-deck. Soon after, the boat righted, and the hull separated from the cabin and sunk in sixty feet of water.

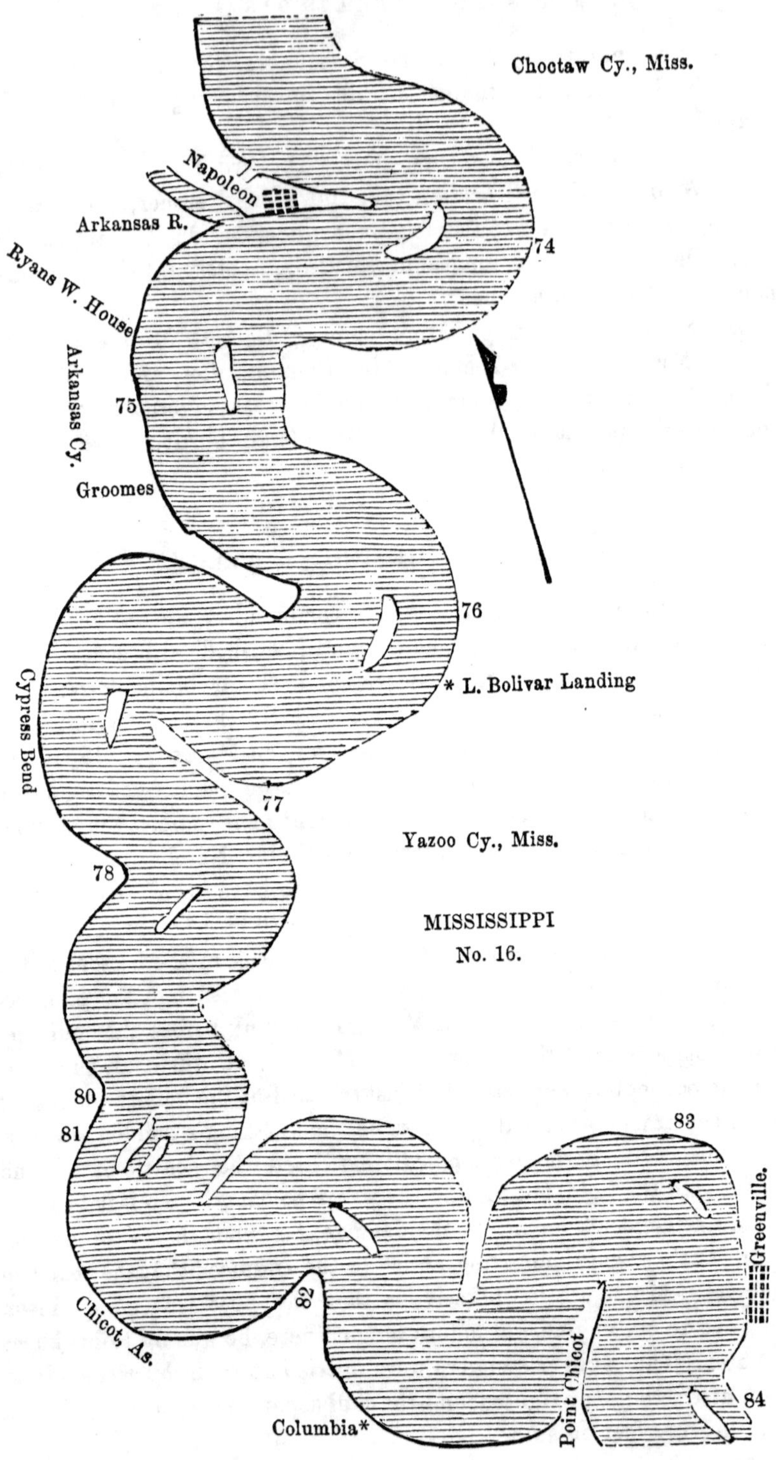
Choctaw Cy., Miss.
Napoleon
Arkansas R.
74
Ryans W. House
Arkansas Cy.
75
Groomes
76
* L. Bolivar Landing
Cypress Bend
77
Yazoo Cy., Miss.
78
MISSISSIPPI
No. 16.
80
81
83
Greenville.
Chicot, As.
82
Point Chicot
84
Columbia*

As the hull parted from the upper works, the surging of the waters caused the cabin floor to rise up against the hurricane roof, and six persons who remained in the cabin were dragged out through the sky-lights by Capt. Robertson and his two clerks. Mrs. Parmin, one of the six passengers rescued from that perilous situation, had her eldest child in her arms at the time, and was with difficulty prevented from plunging in again, as her babe was left asleep on the bed. But the situation of the deck passengers was the most calamitous; there was a large number of them crowded in their allotted place, where they were walled in by hogsheads of sugar, which would have prevented their escape, if escape had been otherwise possible. These unfortunate people were nearly all drowned.

SINKING OF THE JOHN L. AVERY.

There were many Irish emigrants on board, whose names were unregistered, and there is a great deal of uncertainty respecting the number of those who perished. Eye-witnesses testify that a large number of men, women and children could be seen drowning at one time. Of the twenty firemen on board, twelve were drowned. The second mate and another person launched the life-boat, but it was almost immedidiately upset, probably by the eager and ill-directed efforts of the drowning people to get into it. The steamer Sultana, with which the Avery had been racing, promptly came to the rescue of the drowning crew and passengers, and was the means of saving some of them; but the number lost is believed to be at least eighty or ninety.

Mrs. Seymour, one of the cabin passengers who escaped, relates the following incidents of the wreck:

While the passengers were at dinner, it was remarked that the atmosphere of the cabin was overheated, a circumstance which one of the

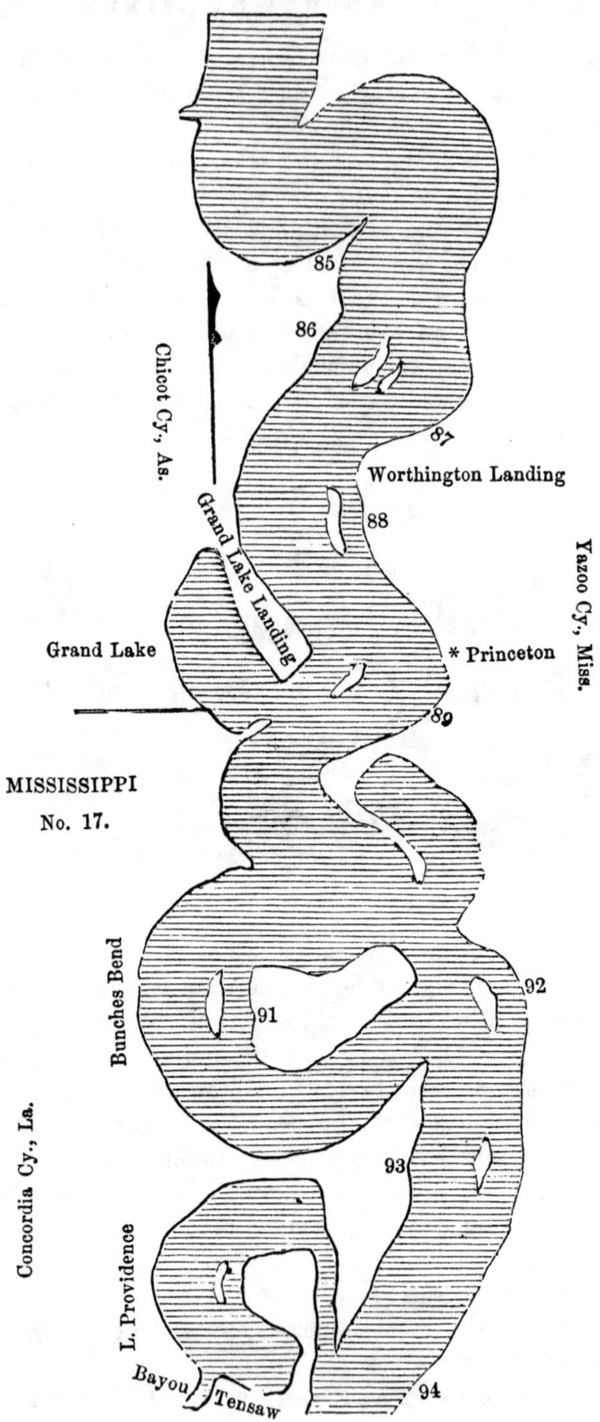

85
86
Chicot Cy., As.
87
Worthington Landing
88
Yazoo Cy., Miss.
Grand Lake Landing
Grand Lake
* Princeton
89
MISSISSIPPI
No. 17.
Bunches Bend
91
92
Concordia Cy., La.
93
L. Providence
Bayou
Tensaw
94

party accounted for by stating that some unusual means had been used to get up extra steam, as the officers of the Avery were resolved to outrun the rival steamer, Sultana. Mrs. Seymour had retired to her state room for an afternoon nap, from which she was aroused by the concussion when the boat struck; and soon after, she found herself in the water. She was drawn up into the floating cabin by one of the waiters, named John Anderson, who, as Mrs. Seymour testifies, was instrumental in saving the lives of several other passengers. She states that her pocket-book, containing nine hundred dollars, which had been placed under her pillow, was lost. She also lost a manuscript which she was preparing for the press, and which she valued still more highly than her pocket-book.

Mrs. Seymour continues:—I cast my eyes upon the water, which was covered with fragments of the cabin. To these frail supports human hands were clinging, while many human voices were crying, "Save me! oh, save me!" The water at first was dotted with human heads, sinking and rising, and then sinking to rise no more. A sudden splash drew my attention to the side of the boat, and I saw that a young lady, who had been drawn from the inundated cabin through the sky-light and placed in safety on the floating deck, in the delirium of the moment had plunged again into the water, from which she never again emerged. Several others followed her example, but appearing again on the surface, they were rescued by the waiter Anderson and two or three others of the boat's crew, who never slackened in their efforts to save human life. Two or three gentlemen leaped into the water and swam to land. A fine Texan poney, belonging to Mrs. Emerson, escaped from the deck, and endeavored to save himself by swimming. He reached the shore, but not being able to climb the bank, he fell back into the water and was drowned. In a faint but earnest tone, I heard a female voice say, "Oh, William, do save her!" On directing my gaze to the place from whence the voice came, I saw a woman sinking in the river. At the same time a child's voice exclaimed, "Oh, mother, he cannot save me!" I saw her fair hair, all wet, fall back from her young face as her little arms loosened their grasp on the neck of her brother, and the mother and her two children sank together.

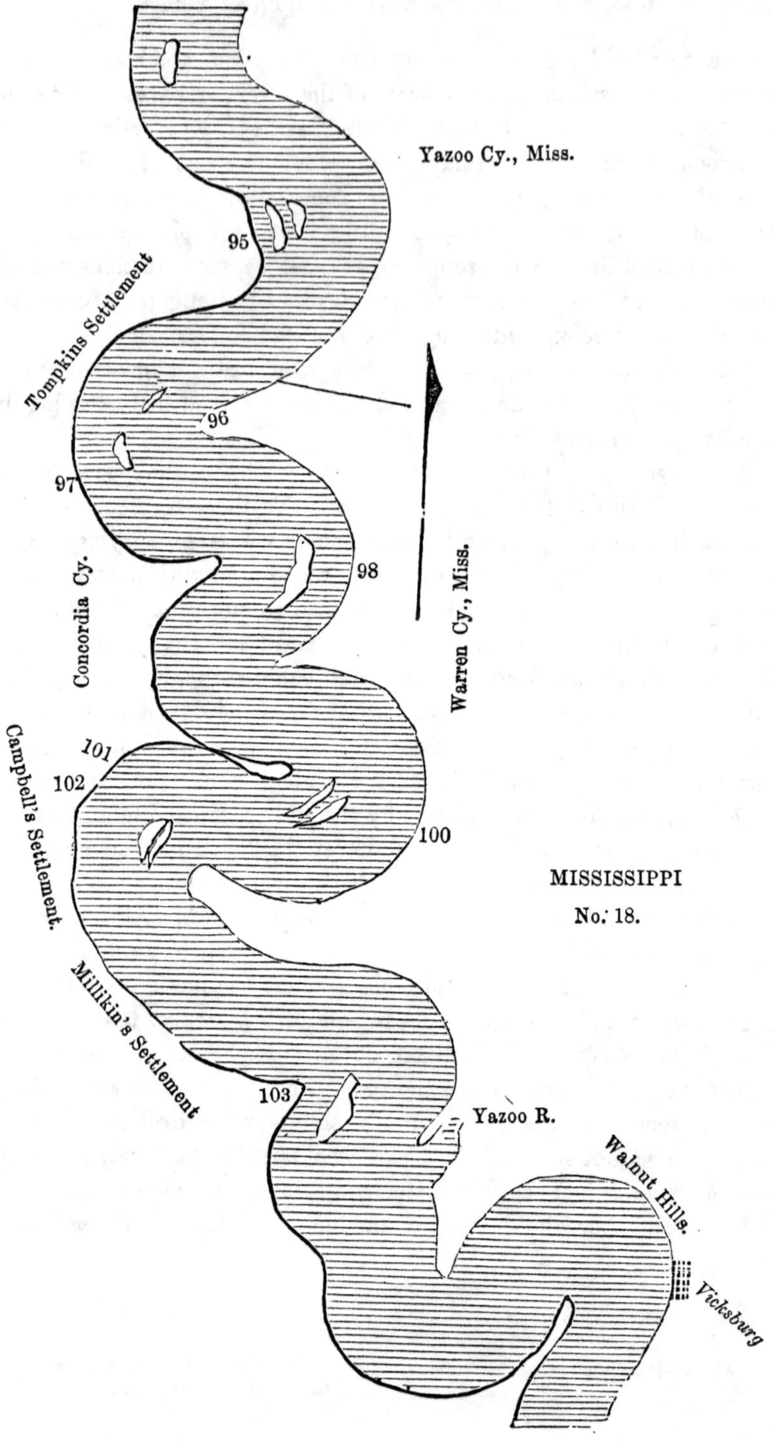
Yazoo Cy., Miss.
95
Tompkins Settlement
96
97
98
Concordia Cy.
Warren Cy., Miss.
101
102
Campbell's Settlement.
100
MISSISSIPPI
No. 18.
Millikin's Settlement
103
Yazoo R.
Walnut Hills.
Vicksburg

COLLISION OF STEAMER CHESAPEAKE AND SCHOONER PORTER.

The steamers Chesapeake and Constellation from Buffalo, were sailing in company on Lake Erie, June 9, 1847, and being off Conneaut about midnight, they met the schooner Porter, which turned aside to avoid the Constellation, and came in contact with the Chesapeake. It appears that the light on board the Chesapeake was mistaken by the helmsman of the schooner for a light on shore, and by some miscalculation of the distance, the schooner ran into the steamer, which she struck on the larboard bow. At the moment of collision, the crew of the Porter sprang on board the Chesapeake, and the latter continued her course out into the lake. Captain Waine of the Chesapeake, thinking that neither vessel was much injured, put about, and steered for the Porter in order to return her crew; but as she came nearer, it was perceived that the Porter was sinking, and by the time the small boat was lowered, she had disappeared. At this moment, the captain was informed that the steamer was leaking. All hands were called to the pumps, but the water gained on them, and the passengers were set to bailing. The firemen were driven from the hold by the rush of water. The Captain had ordered her to be run ashore; she was accordingly headed in that direction, but before she had proceeded far, the water had put out her fires, and the engine stopped. The anchor was then let go to maintain her position, as the wind was blowing freshly from the shore. From this time to the moment the boat sunk, all hands were employed in preparing floats for the conveyance of the crew and passengers to land. The Captain advised all to stick to the wreck, but some left it notwithstanding, hoping to swim ashore, or to float thither on pieces of plank, furniture, &c., but nothing was heard of them afterwards. Among those who left the boat in this way, was the chief engineer.

Within half an hour after the collision, the Chesapeake went down, head foremost, in seven fathoms water. The upper deck separated from the hull, and remained on the surface. On this floating platform, the passengers who remained alive, took refuge. Many of them were women and children, and their shrieks for aid are described by Captain Waine (who tells the story of the disaster) as most appalling. At this critical juncture, the steamer Harrison hove in sight, but soon passed them at a distance without hearing their cries for help. The

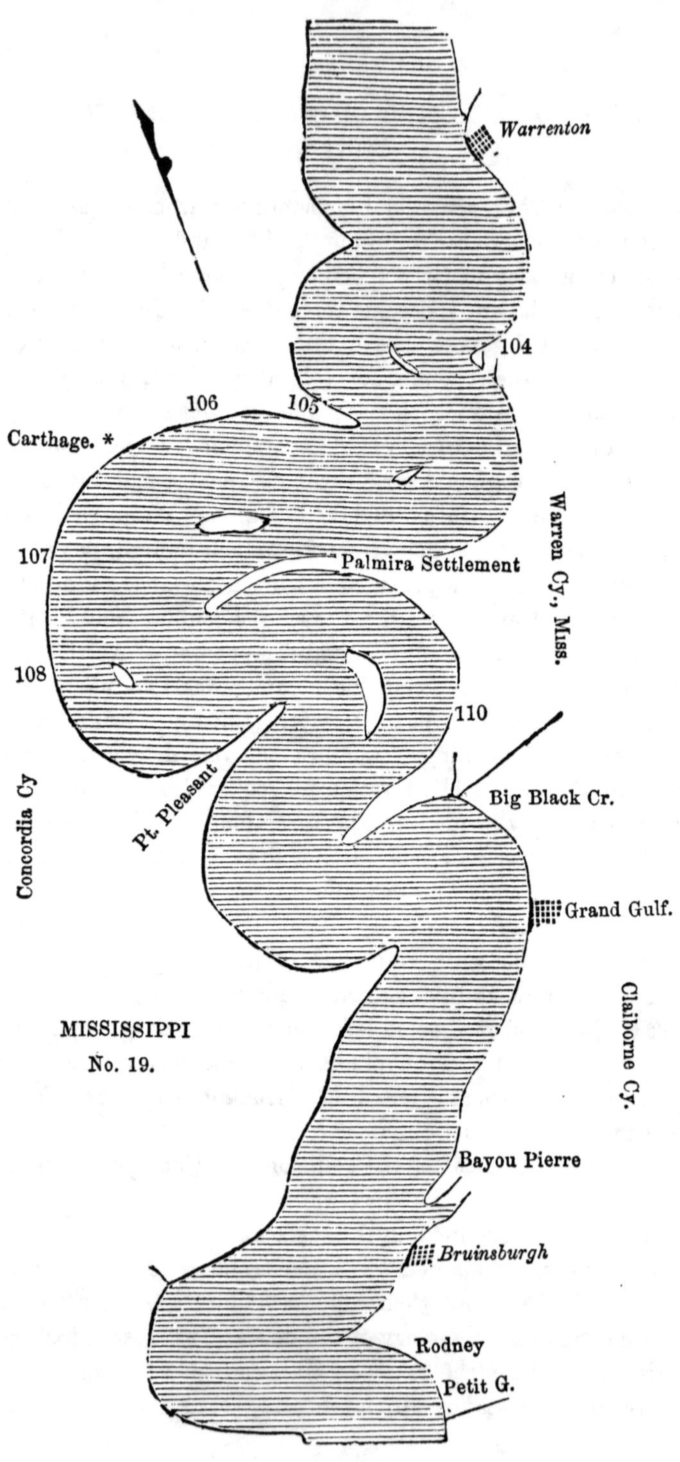

Warrenton
104
106
105
Carthage. *
107
Palmira Settlement
Warren Cy., Miss.
108
110
Concordia Cy
Pt. Pleasant
Big Black Cr.
Grand Gulf.
Claiborne Cy.
MISSISSIPPI
No. 19.
Bayou Pierre
Bruinsburgh
Rodney
Petit G.

Harrison stopped at Connaut, about a mile and a half distant from the wreck, and her captain was there informed by the clerk of the Chesapeake, who, with several other persons had reached the shore in a small boat, that his assistance was needed. The Harrison immediately started for the place, and rescued all who were still alive on the floating deck.

The persons named below are known to have been drowned:

Mrs. Houk, Waterton, N. Y.; G. Van Doren, Sandusky; E. Cone, Belle Air, Ohio; S. York, Tiffin, Ohio; R. Sutherland, chief engineer; Orson Ware, second porter; R. McNabb, deck-hand.

Besides these, many passengers whose names were unregistered, were undoubtedly lost. The clerk's books, and about $8000 in specie, sunk with the hull, and were never recovered.

During that awful half hour which preceded the sinking of the Chesapeake, the state of affairs on board was almost too horrible for description. The night was exceedingly dark; a high wind was blowing from the shore, precluding all hope of reaching land on floats; the boat was fast sinking, and death to all on board seemed inevitable. The captain preserved all his serenity, and advised the passengers that their only chance of safety consisted in remaining on the wreck. He assisted his wife and another lady to climb the mast, and fixed them on the cross-trees. Mr. Lytle, the steward of the boat, was very active and self-possessed, helping such as needed help, and often exposed his life to imminent peril in order to preserve the lives of others.

At length the bow began to fall, and the cry was heard, "She is going!" One loud, long, and unearthly shriek arose simultaneously from the despairing multitude; a shriek which the survivors say is still ringing in their ears, and such a shriek as they hope never to hear again. Many had betaken themselves to floating articles, settees, cabin-doors, planks, tables, &c. One man was seen to turn under his plank, where he remained, his fingers only visible, holding on with the grasp of death. A gentleman and his wife were seen on a float, sometimes sinking, and then rising again to the surface. The lady, not having presence of mind enough to guard against inhaling the water, soon became strangled and exhausted, and died beside her husband, who held out some time longer, but finally sunk into the same watery grave which had received his wife. "They loved in life, and in death they were not divided."

The most touching case was that of Daniel Folsom, his wife, and child. When the engine ceased to work, the yawl-boat was manned and sent ashore in charge of Mr. Sheppard, the clerk. Ten men

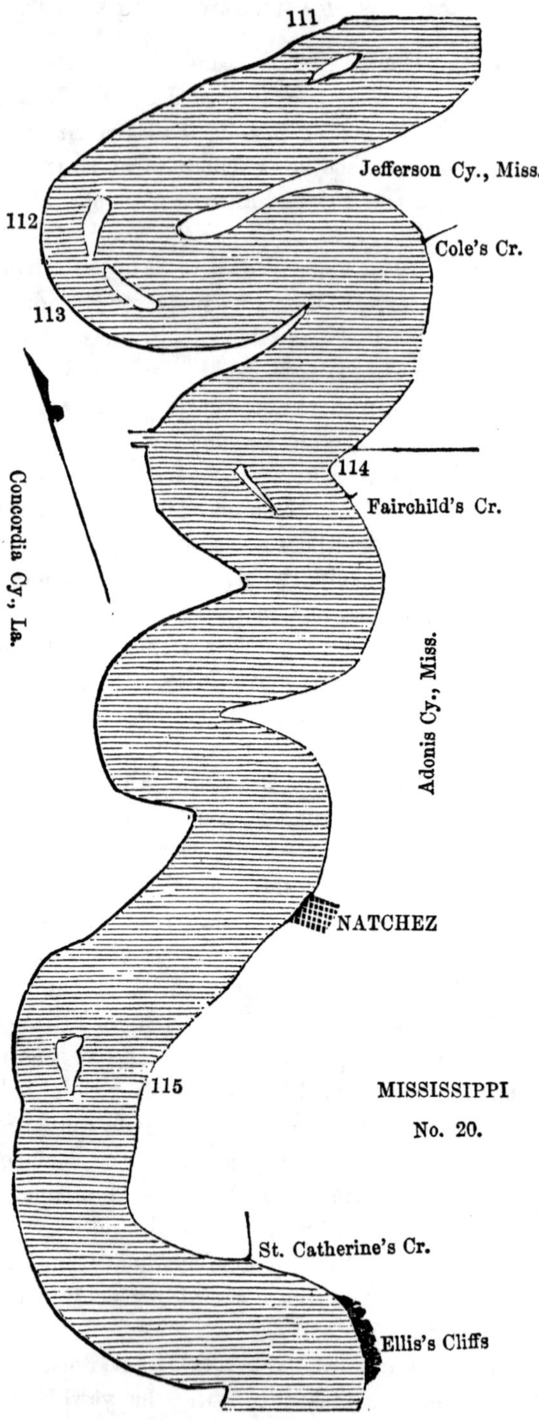

111
Jefferson Cy., Miss.
112
Cole's Cr.
113
Concordia Cy., La.
114
Fairchild's Cr.
Adonis Cy., Miss.
NATCHEZ
115
MISSISSIPPI
No. 20.
St. Catherine's Cr.
Ellis's Cliffs

were put on board, and four ladies, among whom was Mrs. Folsom. She at first refused to go without her husband. He knew it was not the time to debate such a question, and instantly resorted to the only argument which could prevail, by taking the child and putting it in the boat. She then followed, and the husband took an affectionate leave of her at the gang-way. All of this family were saved.

BURNING OF THE ORLINE ST. JOHN.

The steamboat Orline St. John left Mobile for Montgomery, Ala., on Monday evening, March 2d, 1850. On the fourth of the same month, when within four miles of her place of destination, she was discovered to be on fire on the larboard side, near the boilers. In less than three minutes from the time at which the first alarm was given, the whole cabin was enveloped in a sheet of flame. There were about one hundred and twenty human beings on board, and it is reported that not more than fifty of that number survived the destruction of the boat. As soon as the fire was discovered, the pilot steered for the shore, which the steamer fortunately reached before the tiller-ropes were severed by the flames. The boat was run ashore in a dense cane-brake on which her bow and waist rested, while the stern projected into the river. A few persons who happened to be on the forward part of the boat were landed without any difficulty, but the greater number of passengers ran aft, with the hope of getting into the yawl. But the deck passengers and a part of the crew had got possession of this small boat, and had already left the steamer. More than one hundred people were now collected at the stern, which, as mentioned above, projected into the deep water, which effectually cut off all means of escape in that quarter; and to go forward was now impossible, as the whole of the middle of the boat was completely wrapped in flame. To make the situation of these people still more critical, the cabin threatened to fall on them. "As the flames spread aft, (says an eye-witness,) the scene was indeed terrible. The ladies and children had gathered in the extreme after-part of the boat, and their screams for help can never be erased from my memory."

If the yawl had been brought back, all might have been saved; but the deck hands who had taken possession of it, ran it ashore in the cane-brake; and before the captain and second mate could bring it back, all who remained on the steamer, without a single exception,

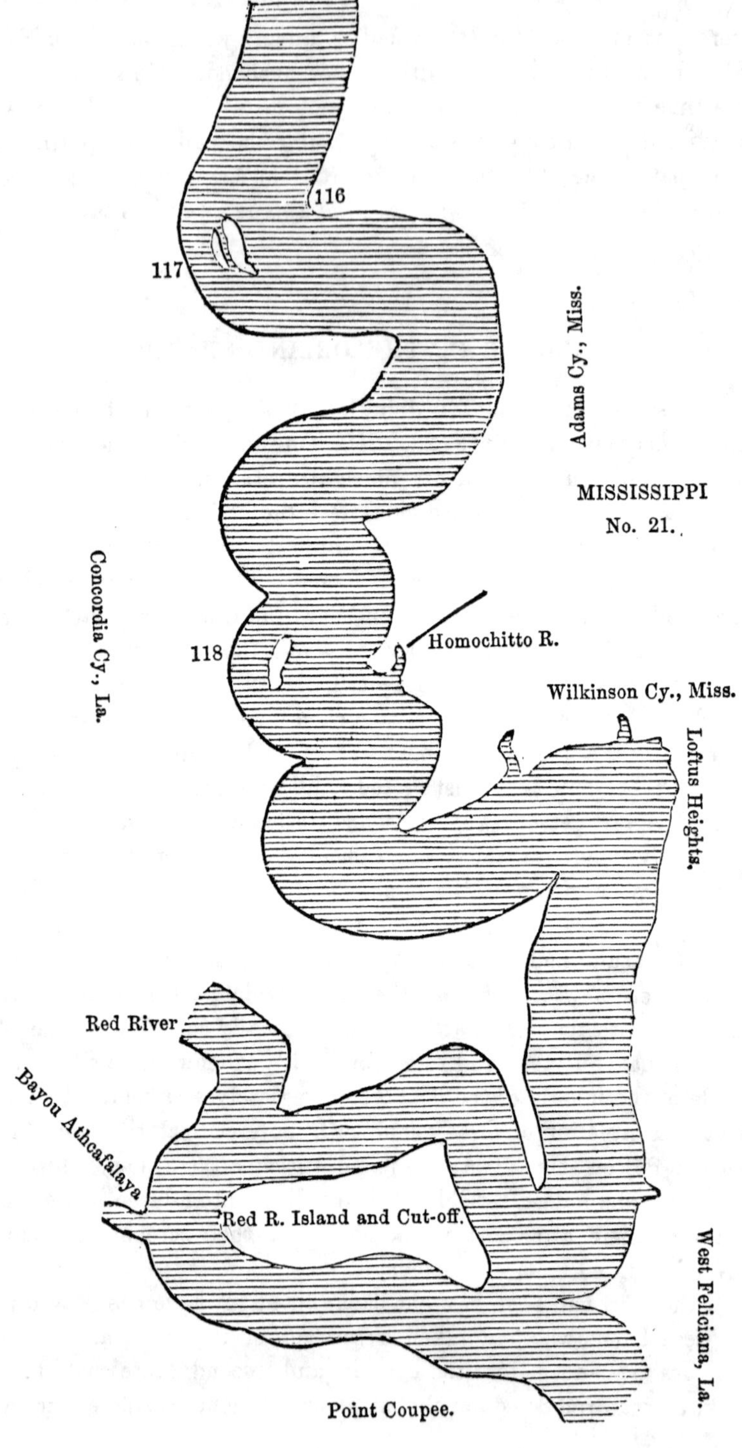
116
117
Adams Cy., Miss.
MISSISSIPPI
No. 21.
Concordia Cy., La.
118
Homochitto R.
Wilkinson Cy., Miss.
Loftus Heights.
Red River
Bayou Athcafalaya
Red R. Island and Cut-off.
West Feliciana, La.
Point Coupee.

were drowned or burned to death. Every woman and child who had been in the boat was lost; the only persons saved were those few who escaped over the bow when the boat struck, and the five or six deck hands who ran off with the yawl. There were a number of returned California gold diggers on board; such of them as saved their lives lost

BURNING OF THE ORLINE ST. JOHN.

all the produce of their toils. No property of any kind was saved, except a trunk belonging to Col. Preston, which his servant threw over the bow into the cane-brake.

List of Killed.—Mrs. Hall and daughter, Augusta, Ga.; Mrs. and Miss Vanhorn, and Mrs. Cain, S. C.; Thomas Stevens, printer, Camden, S. C.; Judge Tindslay, Hugh Hughes, second mate, and Peter Upson, steward, and wife, Mobile, Ala.; the second cook, colored, two white deck hands, eight colored firemen and slaves of passengers, and ten or twelve cabin passengers, names unknown.

Edward Maul, second clerk of the steamer Farmer, and a returned Californian, were severely burned. Purser Price, of the United States Navy, from California, lost two hundred and fifty thousand dollars in gold belonging to government. Mr. Noland, a Californian, lost ten thousand dollars, and several others from the gold region lost all they had. The boat, cargo, and baggage were entirely destroyed. There was an insurance on the steamer for twenty thousand dollars.

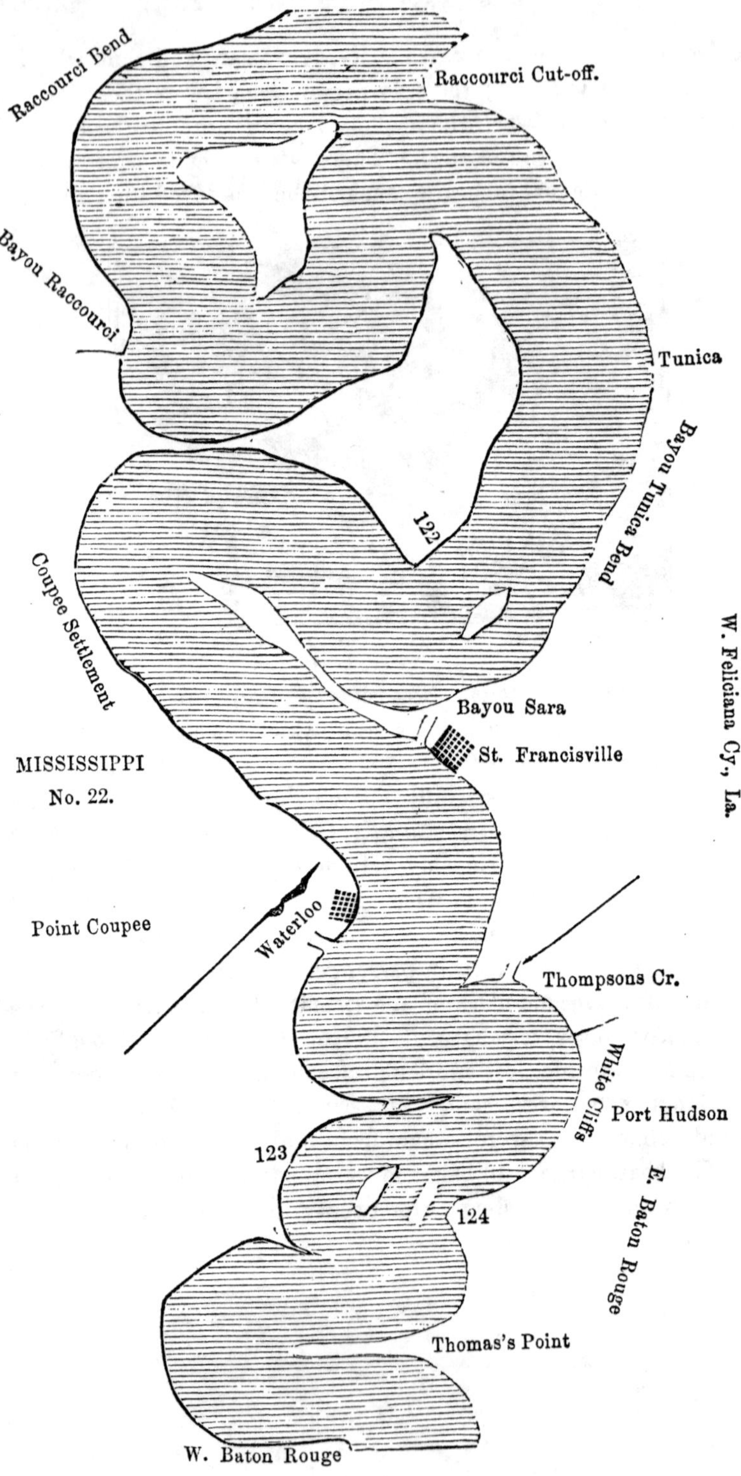

Raccourci Bend
Raccourci Cut-off.
Bayou Raccourci
Tunica
Bayou Tunica Bend
122
Coupee Settlement
W. Feliciana Cy., La.
Bayou Sara
St. Francisville
MISSISSIPPI
No. 22.
Waterloo
Point Coupee
Thompsons Cr.
White Cliffs
Port Hudson
123
124
E. Baton Rouge
Thomas's Point
W. Baton Rouge

EXPLOSION OF THE ANTHONY WAYNE.

The Anthony Wayne was an old steamer belonging to the regular line of Buffalo and Sandusky packets. On Sunday morning, at half-past one o'clock, April 28, 1850, while making one of her usual trips, this boat exploded, on Lake Erie, opposite the mouth of Vermillion river, and eight miles from the shore. Within twenty minutes after the explosion, the steamer sunk, the hull parting from the hurricane deck, and leaving the latter afloat on the lake. The surviving passengers and crew remained on this fragment of the wreck until daylight, when the schooner Elmira, Capt. Nugent, came up and took them off, together with the wounded, and all the dead bodies which could be recovered. There were eighty-four persons on the Anthony Wayne, about half of whom were saved alive, though some of these were badly wounded.

LIST OF KILLED.—Myron Tytus, of Dayton, Ohio; M. Hart, Perrysville, Ohio; wife and child of John Ellis, Mount Hope, Mich.; J. W. Doty, Warsaw, Ill.; J. J. Elmore, and J. Burchard, engineers; Henry Sturges, steward, Mount Clemens, Mich.; G. Franklin, fireman, of Detroit; A. J. Meade, bar-keeper; Wiley Robinson, John Williamson, and Henry Kelly, cooks; two waiters, colored; Alexander Cartwright, deck-hand; John Brainard, and James O'Neil, firemen; Whitney Parsons, porter; Henry Blane, deck-hand; John Falkner; Henry McDonough, and several others, names unknown.

DANGEROUSLY WOUNDED.—J. H. Josler, Crittenden County, Vt.; Robert Shay, Dayton, Ohio; John Terry, Louisville, Ky.; C. G. Lawrence, Angelica, N. Y.; A. W. Gray, Stillwater, N. Y.; a son of Mr. Ellis, Mount Hope, Mich.

SLIGHTLY WOUNDED.—John Beadley, Cleveland, Ohio; Matthew Faulkner, Sheffield, Mass.

The case of Mr. Archer Brackney, one of the passengers, is mournfully interesting. He was on his way from Lafayette, La., to Philadelphia, with the remains of his wife and child, recently deceased. Both the corpses were enclosed in one box. When the explosion took place, he succeeded in dragging his two living children from their berths, and with them plunged into the water. Finding himself unable to support the two children on the surface, he looked around for some piece of the wreck which might be useful in preserving their lives.

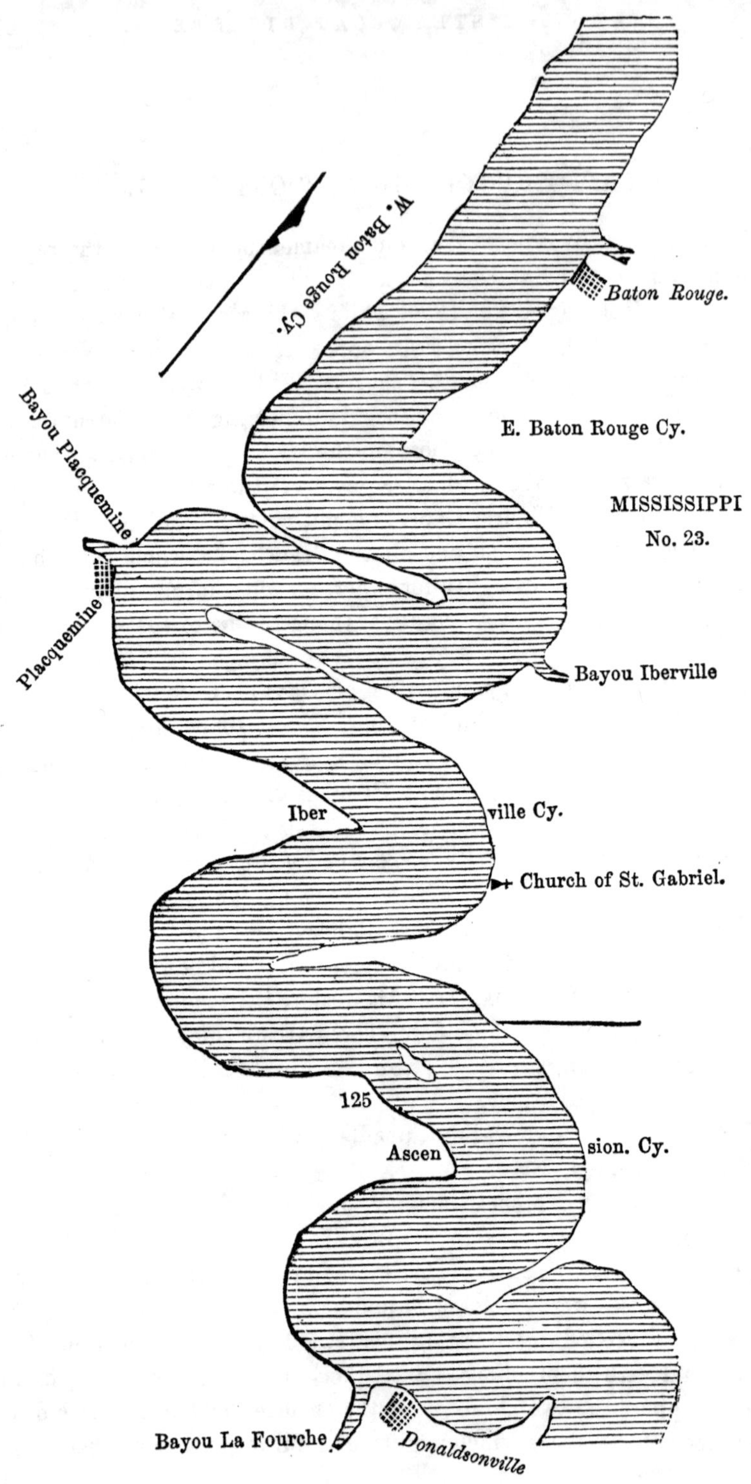
W. Baton Rouge Cy.
Baton Rouge.
Bayou Placquemine
E. Baton Rouge Cy.
MISSISSIPPI
No. 23.
Placquemine
Bayou Iberville
Iber
ville Cy.
Church of St. Gabriel.
125
Ascen
sion. Cy.
Bayou La Fourche
Donaldsonville

A floating object attracted his attention; it was the box which contained the bodies of his wife and child. On this he placed his little boy and girl, and endeavored to keep the box in an upright position, but the surges caused it to pitch and roll in such a manner, that his son, in spite of all his efforts, was washed off and drowned. He now turned all his attention to the preservation of the other child, and finally succeeded in gaining the floating part of the wreck with his little daughter, and both were saved.

EXPLOSION OF THE CLIPPER.

This explosion, of which a very vague account has been preserved, took place on Wednesday, September 19th, 1843, at about a quarter past twelve o'clock, M. One of the passengers, who lived to relate the story, and who appears to have powers of description peculiar to himself, states that the Clipper "blew up with a report that shook earth, air, and heaven, as though the walls of the world were tumbling to pieces about our ears. All the boilers bursted simultaneously; vast fragments of the machinery, huge beams of timber, articles of furniture, and human bodies, were shot up perpendicularly, as it seemed, hundreds of fathoms in the air, and fell like the jets of a fountain in various directions; some dropping on the neighboring shore, some on the roofs of the houses, some into the river, and some on the deck of the boat. Some large fragments of the boilers, &c., were blown at least two hundred and fifty yards from the scene of destruction. The hapless victims were scalded, crushed, torn, mangled, and scattered in every possible direction; some were thrown into the streets of the neighboring town, (Bayou Sara,) some on the other side of the bayou, three hundred yards distant, and some into the river. Several of these unfortunates were torn in pieces by coming in contact with pickets or posts, and I myself, (says the same credible witness,) saw pieces of human bodies which had been shot like cannon balls through the solid walls of houses at a considerable distance from the boat."

Every object in front of the wheel-house was swept away as if by a whirlwind. A gentleman who visited the place where the killed and wounded had been deposited, at Bayou Sara, says, "The scene was such as we never hope to look upon again. The floors of the two large ware-rooms were literally strewn with the wounded and dying, and others were pouring in as fast as it was possible to convey them to the spot. The sufferers were praying, groaning, and writhing in every contortion of physical agony.

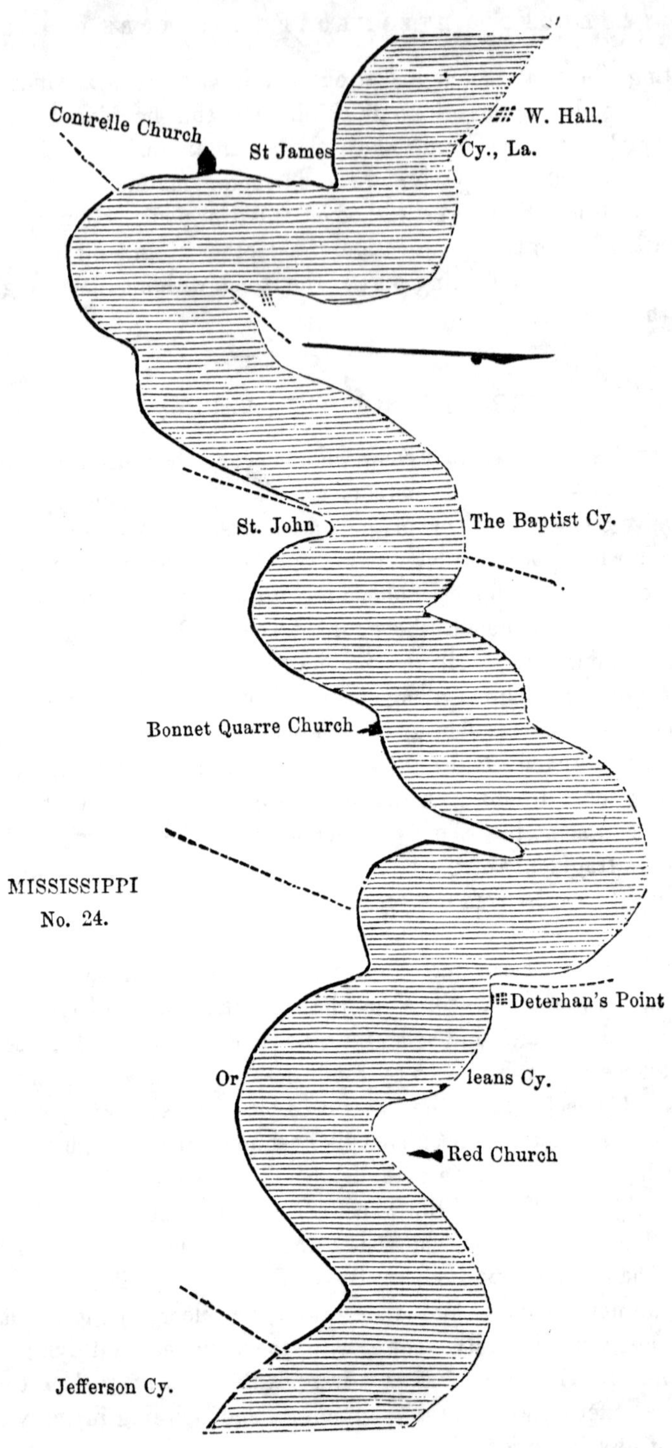

W. Hall.
Contrelle Church
St James
Cy., La.
St. John
The Baptist Cy.
Bonnet Quarre Church
MISSISSIPPI
No. 24.
Deterhan's Point
Or
leans Cy.
Red Church
Jefferson Cy.

KILLED.—Mr. Berry, chief clerk; second clerk, name not mentioned; William Sumpter, second engineer; (he was thrown more than one hundred and fifty yards, through the roof and gable end of a house, into the back yard against a fence; his body being completely dismembered, and crushed out of all resemblance to the human form;) William Nelson, third engineer; Arnault J. Laraud, pilot; William Wall, second pilot; the watchman; Gabriel Pool, carpenter; two colored cooks, the cabin boy and eight firemen, four deck hands and others, names not remembered.

WOUNDED.—John Tyson, chief engineer; John Peterson, mate; and a number of deck passengers, names unknown.

The watchman mentioned in the list of the killed, was thrown one hundred yards from the boat, through the solid walls of Bacon's hotel, and into a bed. He retained his senses perfectly, but expired within half an hour after the explosion. The cabin boy was thrown two hundred yards, through the roof of a shed; he was taken up dead and frightfully mangled.

LOSS OF THE GEORGE WASHINGTON.

The George Washington was on her way from Cincinnati to New Orleans, and at one o'clock, A. M., on January 14th, 1852, when she was a short distance above Grand Gulf, Miss., the boilers exploded, and the boat was burnt to the water's edge. She had in tow, at the time, two barges, heavily laden, both of which, with their cargoes, were totally consumed. But these losses are insignificant, when compared with the destruction of human life which was one of the effects of this accident. William Carroll, the first clerk of the George Washington, a Mr. James Treat, P. Supner, the cook, a fireman, six deck hands and six deck passengers were all killed at the moment of the explosion. Several passengers, names not known, are believed to have been burned with the boat. Mr. Chiswell, the carpenter, was badly scalded, and died within a few hours. Mr. Kuykendale, a passenger, was mortally wounded. Capt. Irwin, C. D. Clemone, passenger, and several others, were more or less injured.

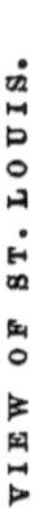

VIEW OF ST. LOUIS.

SKETCH OF ST. LOUIS.

St. Louis is situated on the right bank of the Mississippi river, eighteen miles below the entrance of the Missouri river, one hundred and eighty-two miles above the mouth of the Ohio river, eight hundred and forty-eight miles below the Falls of St. Anthony, eleven hundred and eighty-two miles above New Orleans, and one hundred and fifty miles below Jefferson city, the capital of the State of Missouri. St. Louis is a port of entry, and is situated in St. Louis County, lat. 38° 37′ 28″ N., long. 90° 15′ 16″ W. The site rises from the river by two plateaus of limestone formation, the first twenty and the second, sixty feet above the floods of the Mississippi river. The ascent to the first plateau is somewhat abrupt; the second rises more gradually, and spreads out into an extensive plain, affording excellent views of the city and the mighty river. The present site of St. Louis was selected by Laclede, in February 1764, as one possessing peculiar advantages for the fur trade, and for defence against the savage Indians, who at that time held almost undisputed sway, not only in Missouri, but in the United States. The confluence of the different rivers in the immediate neighborhood of St. Louis was a desideratum in the estimation of the trapper. It has become of vast importance to the place in establishing it as a centre for agricultural and manufacturing enterprises. The statistics of these early times show that for sixteen successive years, ending in 1805, the average annual value of the furs collected at this place, amounted to $303,750. The number of Deer skins was 190,000; of Beaver, 46,000; of Otter, 11,000; of Bear, 70,100; and of Buffalo, 1360. The population of St. Louis at this period was about 1500, more than one-half of whom were absent a great part of each year, engaged in trapping. It will readily be understood that the elements which gave this settlement an existence, were not of a character adequate to foster it beyond the limits of a small frontier village, and accordingly as late as 1820, the accession of population was only about 1600; up to this date the census only shows the population to have been 3,146. Military expeditions and establishments, together with a small emigration confined to those peculiar temperaments which delight in the wild and dangerous, still kept up a progressive improvement, which, centering here for personal security, as well as for trade, still fixed it as the seat of a commercial and manufacturing metropolis, destined in a few years to become an object of interest throughout the world. On the 11th of August, 1768, a Spanish officer by the name of Rious, with a company of Spanish troops, took possession of St. Louis and Upper Louisiana, as it was termed, in the name of his Catholic majesty, under whose control it remained until the final transfer to the United States by Napoleon, in 1804. In 1813, the first brick house ever put up on the banks of the Mississippi, was erected at St. Louis. In 1817, the first steamboat (Antelope) arrived here on her way to explore the great Missouri river, which at that time was almost as totally unknown as the Arctic ocean. In 1822, St. Louis was chartered as a city under the title given by Laclede, in honor of Louis XV. of France. From 1825 to 1830, the influx of population from all parts of the United States began to be of importance. It was then St. Louis received its first great impulse, and commenced extending its commerce from New Orleans to the Rocky Mountains, which has since given it the name of the Atlantic city of the Mississippi valley. In 1829, the keel boat entirely disappeared; the steamers Yellow-stone and Assinaboine about this time ascended to the great falls of the Missouri river, and from that day to the present, fine steamers have continued to make trips up the turbulent Missouri river, and the progress of St. Louis has been upward and onward.

The natural advantages which St. Louis enjoys, as a commercial emporium, are probably not surpassed by those of any inland port in the world. Situated midway between two oceans, and near the geographical centre of the finest agricultural and mineral region on the globe, almost at the very focus towards which converge the Mississippi, the Missouri, the Ohio and the Illinois Rivers, there can be no doubt that she is destined, at no distant date, to become the great receiving and distributing depot of most of the vast region drained by these rivers. Having already reached an enviable position among her sister cities, she is now looking westward, with a system of railways, intended not only to bring to her markets the agricultural and mineral treasures of the great Missouri Basin, but eventually to extend beyond the Rocky mountains to the valley of the Salt Lake, and finally to the golden shores of the Pacific Ocean. The Pacific railroad is now under full headway, being already completed to Jefferson city, a distance of one hundred and fifty miles from St. Louis. Her connection with the Atlantic cities, through Cincinnati and Chicago, is already secured. The Ohio and Mississippi railroad, extending in an air line from St. Louis to Cincinnati, was built by the great liberality and enterprise of Daniel D. Page and Henry D. Bacon, both citizens of St. Louis, without whose capital this great work would have fallen through, and the public would have been deprived of a direct and expeditious route between the east and west. Another railroad, leading to the Iron mountain, is rapidly approaching completion. The north Missouri and the Hannibal and St. Joseph's railroads are all chartered and under way.

The opening of these railways, and others proposed, will give St. Louis ready access to immense deposits of iron, coal, lead, and copper ores within a circuit of ninety miles, equal to the wants of the whole Mississippi valley for centuries to come, and which have not, to this time, been brought into use, simply because of the difficulty and expense of reaching the market; therefore, with all the commercial facilities which St. Louis now enjoys, facilities which have hitherto been productive of prosperity almost beyond example, what may she not become when the vast system of railways here contemplated shall have gone into operation?

St. Louis extends, in all, nearly seven miles by the curve of the Mississippi river, and about three miles back. The city is well laid out, the streets being sixty feet wide, and with but few exceptions intersecting each other at right angles. Front street, extending along the levee, is over one hundred feet wide, and built up on the side facing the river with a range of splendid five story wholesale stores and warehouses, which make an imposing appearance as the city is approached by water. Front, Main, and Second streets, parallel to each other, and to the river, are the seat of the principal wholesale business houses. The latter is occupied by heavy grocery, iron, receiving and shipping houses. Fourth street is the fashionable promenade, and contains the finest retail stores. The streets, parallel to Front and Main streets, are designated Second, Third, Fourth, Fifth, and so on. Large expenditures have been made from time to time in grading and otherwise improving the streets and alleys of St. Louis.

It may be doubted whether any city in the United States has improved more rapidly than St. Louis, in the style of its public buildings. But twenty-four years ago a Court House was erected at a cost of $14,000; it was then considered a handsome edifice, and sufficient for all future purposes; within a few years, however, this building has given place to a new structure, now nearly completed, the cost of which will exceed $500,000; it is constructed of St. Genevieve limestone, which is to be had in great abundance sixty miles south of the city. The Court House occupies an entire square, bounded by Market, Chesnut, Fourth, and Fifth streets; the style of architecture resembles that of the capitol, at Washington city. The fronts are adorned with porticos, and in the interior is a rotunda, lighted from the dome. The new Market and City Hall are of the first magnitude, corresponding to the present beautiful appearance of the city. A new Custom House is now being built at the corner of Third and Olive streets, at an estimated cost of $350,000. Of the four churches, the Catholic, the Presbyterian, the Episcopal, and the Baptist, which were all the town contained in 1827, not a vestige now remains, but in their stead has arisen up to date, sixty-four others, to wit, twelve Catholic, eighteen Methodist, eleven Presbyterian, seven Episcopal, three Unitarian, three Evangelical, and one Boatman's, besides three Jewish Synagogues. Several of these have cost above $100,000 each; of these St. George's, (Episcopal) at the corner of Locust and Seventh streets, the Catholic Cathedral, on Walnut street, and the Church of the Messiah. a magnificent Gothic edifice, recently erected by the Unitarians, at the corner of Olive and Ninth streets, are regarded as the finest. The Cathedral is one hundred and thirty-six feet long, and eighty-four feet wide, with a front of pure polished Freestone, fifty-eight feet high, adorned with a Doric portico, in the tower of which is a chime of bells, the heaviest weighing twenty-six hundred pounds. The United States arsenal, situated on Arsenal street, in the extreme South-east section of the city, is a large and imposing edifice, enclosed by handsomely ornamented grounds. Jefferson Barracks are located twelve miles below, on the bank of the Mississippi river.

Among the benevolent institutions may be mentioned the City Hospital, the Marine Hospital, situated three miles below St. Louis; the Sisters' Hospital, the Home for the Friendless, and the Orphan Asylums. The Home for the Friendless, designed for the benefit of aged indigent females, and opened October 4th, 1853, is situated on the Corondolet road, about five miles from the Court House; about $40,000 have been raised for the support of this Institution. The City Hospital has long been distinguished for the excellent accommodations which it affords to the sick, but of late has been found inadequate to the wants of the rapidly increasing population. A new edifice, intended as a House of Refuge, has recently been completed, and the building formerly occupied as a hospital, situated on land in the St. Louis common, known as the old County Farm, has also been fitted up for the reception of a juvenile Reform School. The Literary and Educational Institutions of St. Louis have, considering their recent origin, attained a high degree of excellence. The University of St. Louis, organized in 1832, under the direction of the Catholics, is a well ordered, well sustained, and most efficient institution. The Medical College connected with it, is also very flourishing. During the term of 1854, '55, it was attended by one hundred and twenty students. On the first of October, 1855, it is said that the number of matriculants enrolled for the ensuing season, was four times greater than any previous year.

The medical department of the Missouri University is also located here. It was founded in 1840, and during the winter of 1855, one hundred and forty students attended its lectures. The members of both these colleges enjoy excellent advantages for practice in the City Hospital. The Mercantile Library association of St. Louis was organized in 1846, and incorporated in 1851. The united size of the library and reading-room is eighty by sixty-four feet; lecture room, eighty by forty-four feet. In the third story is the largest and grandest hall in the western country, being one hundred and five feet long, and eighty feet wide. The cost of building was $95,000. The libraries contain upwards of eighteen thousand volumes, besides about one hundred and sixty magazines and other periodicals, independent of its newspapers.

St. Louis has about twenty-five publication offices, issuing newspapers and other periodicals. Ten or eleven papers are published daily, besides several weekly and tri-weekly papers. The press is generally characterized by talent and ability, and several of its issues have very large circulations. St. Louis has the best wharf of any city on the western waters. The levee, which a few years ago was a mere mudbank, is now widened, and handsomely paved from one end to the other, giving great facilities to the numerous boats in receiving and discharging their cargoes in good order. St. Louis is indebted to the Hon. L. M. Kennett for its present healthy and beautiful appearance. From the time this gentleman was elected mayor of the city, in 1850, to the time he retired, in 1853, he did nothing but improve the condition of the city. Innumerable sewers were built running from the low and damp portions of the city to the river, and all parts of this city have since been very healthy. It was during the administration of L. M. Kennett that the wharf was so vastly widened and improved; in fact he did more for the prosperity of the city than all his predecessors. In 1853 he declined serving any longer, preferring retirement; but in 1854 he was brought out for Congress against the Hon. Thomas H. Benton, being the only man of his party with whom they could hope to succeed against so formidable an opponent, and he was triumphantly elected to Congress.

The Manufactures of St. Louis, although in their infancy, are hardly less important than her commerce. The flouring business is carried on here more extensively than in any city of the west. The product of the mills of the city amounted in 1855 to 836,460 barrels; at Belcher's sugar refinery, which is one of the most extensive in the world, the yield for 1855 amounted to 24,563 boxes, 14,658 hogsheads, 24,457 barrels and 68,848 bags of refined sugar, besides

237,766 packages and 20,000 barrels refined from cane syrup. The manufacture of different kinds of chemicals and oils is very extensively carried on. There are, in St. Louis, twenty establishments for the manufacture of tobacco, yielding 16,000 packages, and consuming 1400 hogsheads of raw material. The manufacture of hemp into bale rope and bagging, and the distilling of whiskey, also employ a large amount of capital. Indeed there can be no doubt that the development of the vast mineral resources of the region tributary to her is destined to exert a controlling influence upon the future of this metropolis.

Her manufactures of iron already exceed those of any other city on the western waters. Numerous foundries annually turn out stoves, mill machinery, heavy railroad work, as well as large steam-engines, to an enormous amount. A large establishment went into operation here in 1853. Mining operations have already been commenced at Iron mountain. From this source Messrs. Chouteau, Valle and Harrison, obtain the material for their extensive rolling mill; in fact, thousands of tons of this superior iron, after passing through their establishment, are annually shipped to Pittsburgh. St. Louis has now about sixteen thousand establishments in operation in the city, comprising about two hundred different manufactories, which amount annually in value to $36,000,000.

St. Louis is by far the greatest shipping point on the Ohio or Mississippi rivers; there are constantly plying to and from this point over six hundred steamers. Each river which contributes to the commerce of St. Louis, has its regular packets, and for the most part a separate place of landing. The New Orleans, the Missouri, the Illinois, and the Upper Mississippi steamers, are as fine steamboats as float on the Western waters; some of them, in point of speed and accommodations, are equal to the best Lake or Ocean steamers. From St. Louis there are daily lines to New Orleans, Louisville, Cincinnati, and Pittsburgh; Peoria and Lasalle, on the Illinois river; Keokuk and St. Paul, on the Upper Mississippi river; Lexington, Kansas, and St. Joseph, on the Missouri river, and Nashville and Clarksville, on the Cumberland river, besides regular packets to Alton, Cairo, Memphis, and up the Tennessee river. With such an immense inland navigation, the commerce of the port requires a large number of steamers, and its tonnage exceeds that of every other Western city. The population of St. Louis in 1830, was 6,694; in 1840, 16,469; in 1850, 77,404; in 1852, 94,819; in 1856, 146,364.

EXPLOSION OF THE BRILLIANT.

This accident, which caused a frightful loss of life, took place on the Mississippi river, at Bayou Goula, six miles below Plaquemine, on the 29th day of September, 1851. The Brilliant, Capt. Hunt commander, left New Orleans two days before the accident, and was on her way to Bayou Sara, and the intermediate landings. She had stopped at Dr. Stone's plantation, and was about recommencing her voyage, when her boiler bursted, making a total wreck of the main cabin and state-rooms as far aft as the ladies' cabin, and sweeping away all the upper wood-work forward of the boilers. The boiler itself was projected forward among a crowd of the boat's crew and deck passengers, nearly all of whom were killed or wounded. The flues and parts of the machinery were thrown in the opposite direction, and made sad devastation among the cabin passengers.

As usual in the narratives of western steamboat calamities, the names of only a small number of the victims are recorded. Capt. Hunt stated that he had more than eighty deck hands and firemen on board at the time of the explosion. Of these, only twenty-five could be found after the accident. He could give no account of the number of deck passengers, but is certain that they were very numerous. There were thirty-five cabin passengers, ten of whom were ladies. Twenty-five of these were seen in the water after the explosion, three of whom were rescued by the steamer Natchez, and it is believed that the others all perished. The Natchez also conveyed to Plaquemine forty-two persons badly wounded who had been taken from the wreck. Of these, fifteen died within six hours. Fifteen others, badly wounded, were carried ashore in the yawl, and the steamer Princess took off three more in a similar condition. A majority of those wounded by this explosion did not recover.

Capt. Hunt furnished the names of a few of his boat's crew who were among the victims of this disaster, viz.: James Fullerton, mate; J. A. Cotton, first clerk; Robert Doyle, first engineer, was supposed to be mortally wounded; Mr. Falls, second pilot, was badly scalded. Capt. Hunt himself was in the wash-room when the boiler exploded, and he was uninjured. Mr. Lewison, editor of the Baton Rouge Advocate, was mortally wounded.

The accident is ascribed to the imprudent use of rosin among the fuel, in order to produce a more intense heat, and so to increase the speed of the boat. A wounded fireman stated that four barrels of rosin were burned at the landing, and the fifth was about to be consumed when the explosion took place.

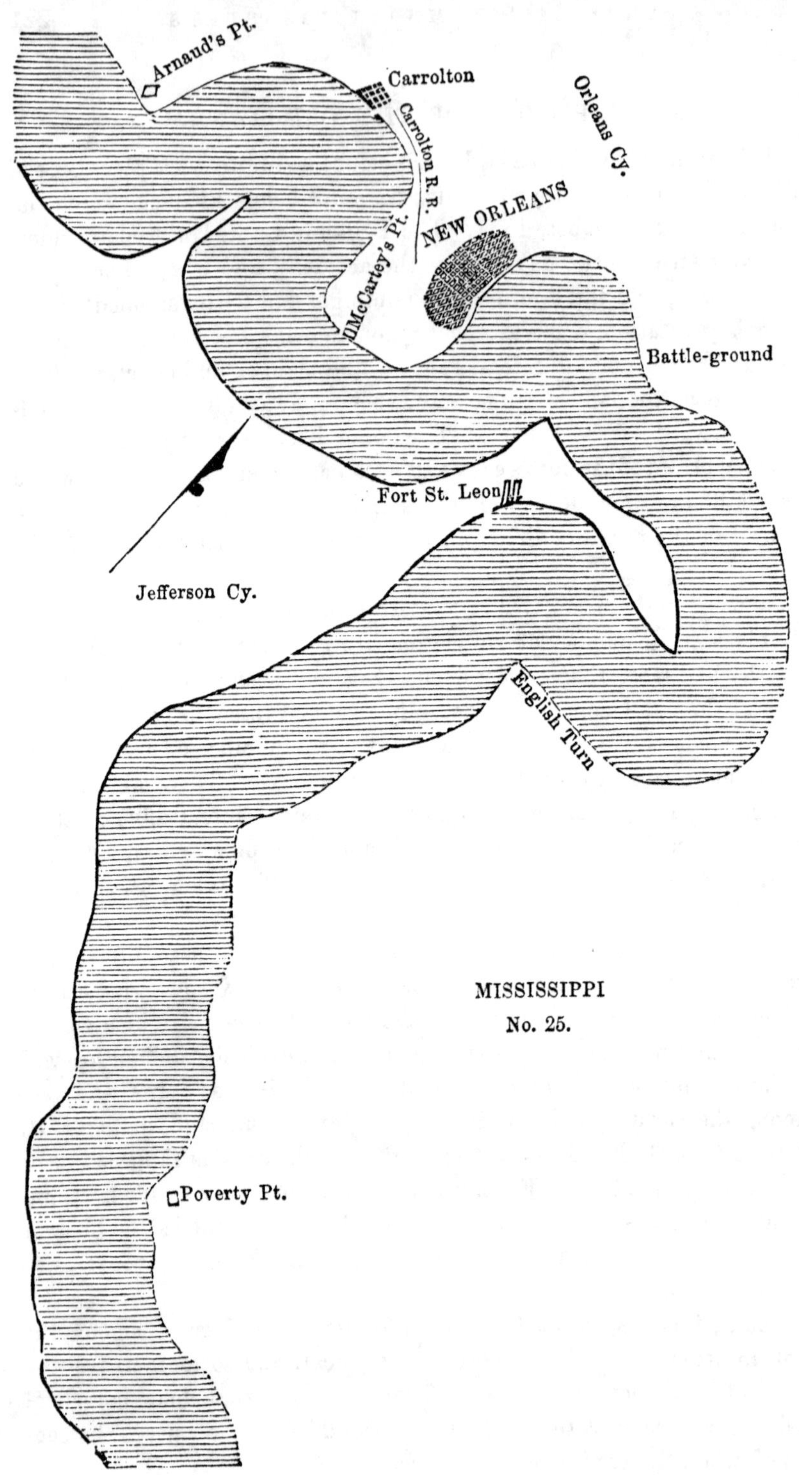
Arnaud's Pt.
Carrolton
Orleans Cy.
Carrolton R. R.
McCartey's Pt.
NEW ORLEANS
Battle-ground
Fort St. Leon
Jefferson Cy.
English Turn
MISSISSIPPI
No. 25.
Poverty Pt.

EXPLOSION OF THE REDSTONE.

The disaster we are about to record, took place on the Ohio river, a short distance above Carrollton, April 2, 1852. The Redstone was a small boat, about three years old, and was built at Pittsburgh for the Brownsville Slackwater Navigation. At the time to which we now refer, she was plying in the Madison and Cincinnati trade, in opposition to the regular line of Madison packets. She left Madison about noon on the day aforesaid, with thirty or forty passengers on board, and had stopped above Carrollton to take in a Mr. Scott. His parents accompanied him to the shore, and were looking at him when the boat began to move off; a moment after, they were horrified by seeing him blown high in the air, and then fall into the river. Two boilers exploded—one of them was blown on shore, and, in its course, prostrated a sycamore tree two feet in diameter. The trees and the shore, for hundreds of yards, were lined with shreds of clothing, sheets, blankets, and other vestiges of the wreck. A man's boot, ripped and torn, was picked up more than six hundred yards from the wreck, whither it had been blown, no doubt, from the foot of some unhappy victim. A passenger who had got on the boat at Milton, was taking a drink at the bar, and, after paying for it, was returning his purse to his pocket, when he was blown into the river and drowned. A lad from Madison was on board with his two little sisters; he was drowned, but the girls were saved. A Mr. Claxon, of Carrollton, was on the boat, and was blown ashore, but, strange to tell, he did not receive the slightest injury.

The following are the names of some of the persons killed:—E. G. Crossman, printer; E. N. Durbson, of New Philadelphia, Ind.; Mr. Coons; Rev. Henry A. Scott, (the young man whose parents stood on the shore and witnessed his death); Lewis Berry, of Brownsville, Pa., first engineer; Joseph W. Berry, of same place, second engineer; E. P. Durbin, Lawrenceburg, Ind.; M. Smith, Petersburg, Va.; seven cabin boys, names not known.

Badly Wounded.—Thomas W. Pate, captain; Sydney Longly and Charles M. Jackson, pilots: Samuel Fritz; George Breck, second cook; Henry Boezi, six firemen, and four deck hands.

Slightly Wounded.—Geo. Collard, mate; John Wilson, carpenter; Christman Wilson.

Twenty bodies, recovered from the water, were too much disfigured to be recognized. The boat was so completely shattered by the force of the explosion, that she immediately sunk in twenty feet water.

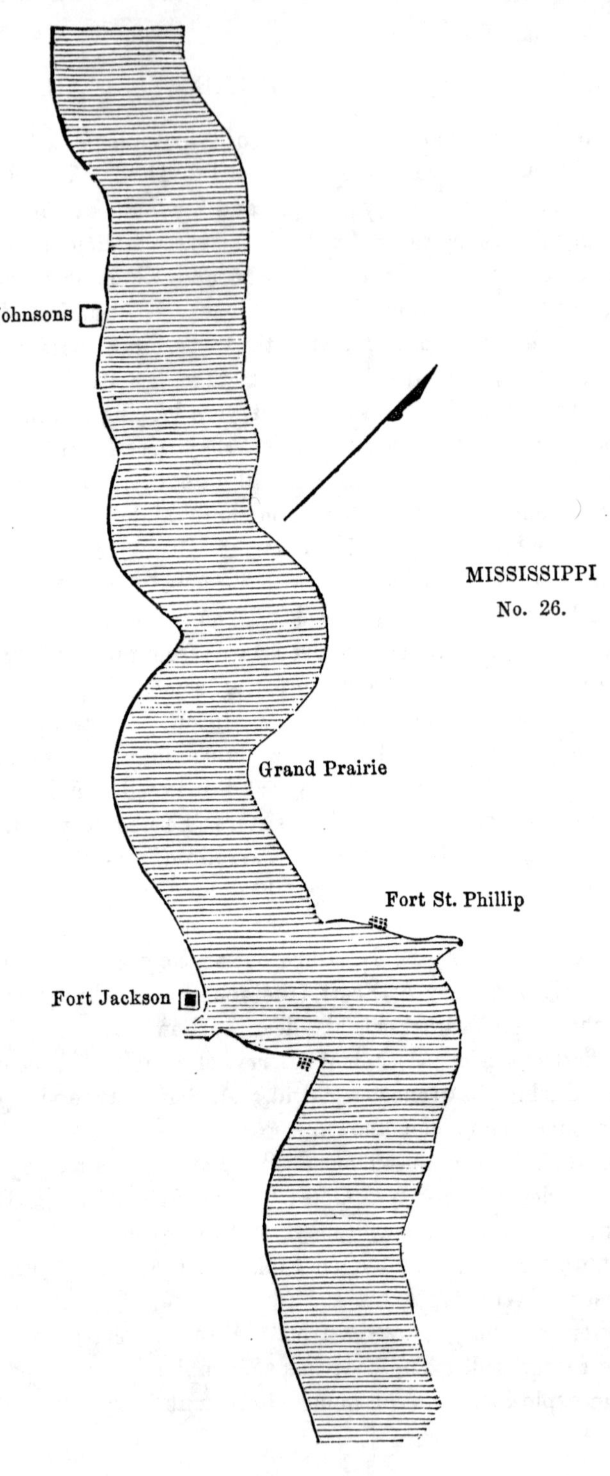
Johnsons
Grand Prairie
Fort St. Phillip
Fort Jackson
MISSISSIPPI
No. 26.

The captain was mortally wounded. This accident was thought to be the result of criminal negligence, as there was scarcely any water in the boiler at the time of the explosion. The engineer had stopped that part of the machinery, called the "doctor," which supplies the boilers with water, in order to produce "a high head of steam." In this he succeeded, and his life was the forfeit of his temerity and the recklessness with which he exposed the lives of others to unnecessary peril.

EXPLOSION OF THE LOUISIANA.

A few minutes after five o'clock, on the evening of November 15, 1849, the steamboat Louisiana, Captain Cannon, lying at the foot of Gravier street, New Orleans, had completed all the preparations for her departure for St. Louis. She was laden with a valuable cargo, and had on board a large number of passengers. The last bell was rung, and the machinery set in motion; but at the moment the boat disengaged herself from the wharf and began to back out into the river, all the boilers exploded with a concussion which shook all

EXPLOSION OF THE STEAMER LOUISIANA.

the houses for many squares around to their very foundations. The Louisiana was lying between two other steamers—the Bostona and Storm—the upper works of which were completely wrecked; their chimneys were carried away, and their cabins were shattered to small fragments. The violence of the explosion was such, that large pieces of the boilers were blown hundreds of yards from the wharf, falling on the levee and in different parts of the city. One of these iron

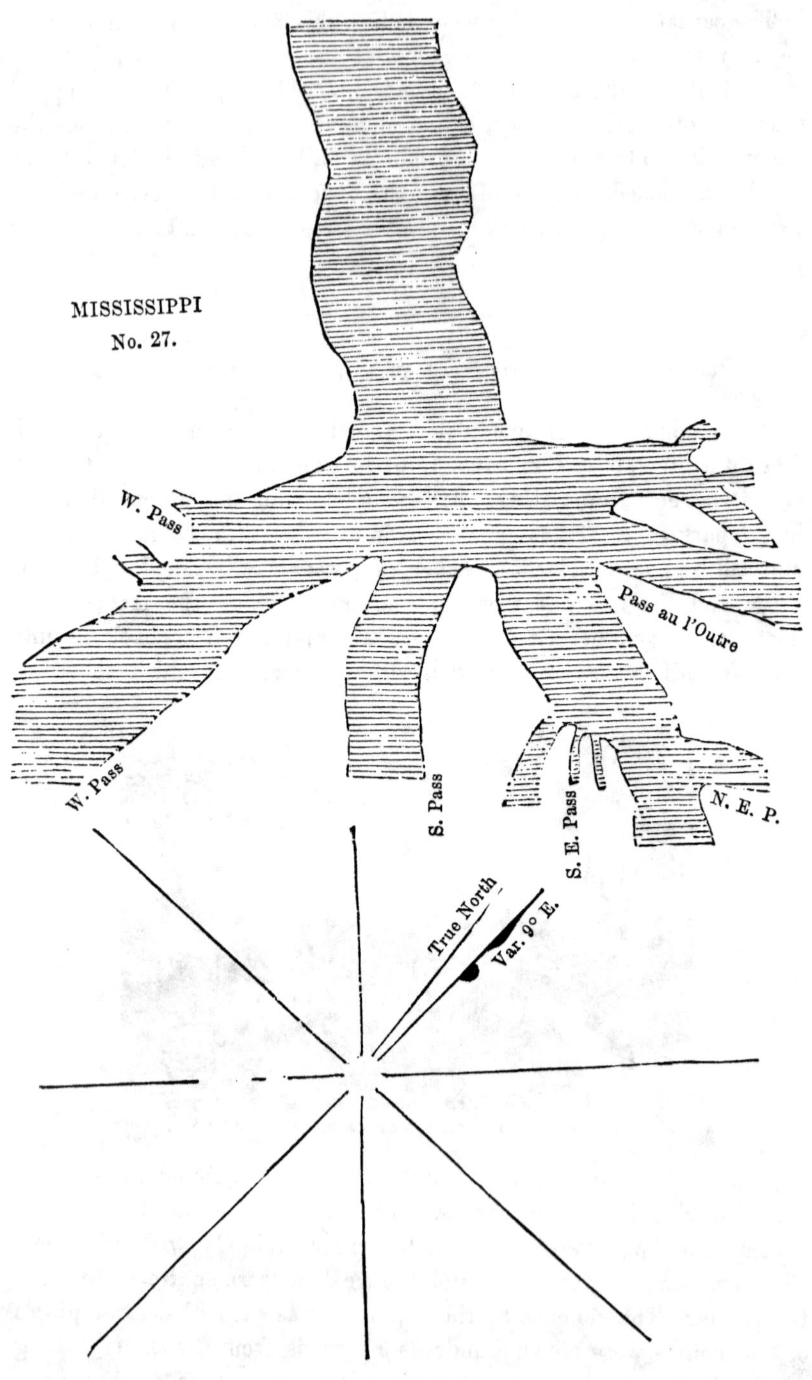
MISSISSIPPI
No. 27.
W. Pass
Pass au l'Outre
W. Pass
S. Pass
S. E. Pass
N. E. P.
True North
Var. 9° E.

fragments cut a mule in two, and then struck a horse and dray, killing both driver and horse instantly. Another mass of iron, of considerable size, was projected to the corner of Canal and Front streets, two hundred yards from the exploded steamer, where it threw down three large iron pillars which supported the roof of the portico of a coffee-house. Before it reached the iron pillar, this fragment passed through several bales of cotton which lay in its passage.

The tremendous detonation gave notice of the accident to the whole city, and soon all the levee near Gravier street was thronged with anxious and sympathizing spectators. A number of bodies, in every conceivable state of mutilation, had been dragged from the wreck, and were surrounded by the immense crowd which had assembled. Hacks and furniture cars were sent for, and the wounded were conveyed with as much despatch as possible to the hospitals. The sight of the mangled bodies on every side, the groans of the dying, and the shrieks of the agonized sufferers, produced a general thrill of horror among the multitude. The body of a man was seen, with the head and one leg off, and the entrails torn out. A woman, whose long hair lay wet and matted by her side, had one. leg off, and her body was shockingly mangled. A large man, having his skull mashed in, lay dead on the levee; his face looked as though it had been painted red, having been completely flayed by the scalding water. Others of both sexes, crushed, scalded, burned, mutilated and dismembered, lay about in every direction. Two bodies were found locked together, brought by death into a sudden and close embrace.

But it is utterly impossible to describe all the revolting objects which presented themselves to the view of the beholders. Suffice it to say, that death was there exhibited in all its most hideous forms; and yet the fate of many who still lived was more shocking and distressing than the ghastly and disfigured corpses of those whose sufferings were terminated by death.

A gentleman who was a passenger on the Louisiana, says that he was standing on the hurricane deck, abaft the wheel house, at the time of the explosion, and though his position was most perilous, he fortunately escaped unhurt. He distinctly saw the faces and arms of several ladies and gentlemen who were vainly struggling to free themselves from the falling planks and timbers. They were carried down with the boat when she sunk. The steamer went down within ten minutes after the explosion; and it is thought that many citizens who went on board to assist the wounded, sunk with the boat. The passenger mentioned above succeeded in saving a little negro boy. The river was covered with fragments of the wreck, to many of which persons who had been blown overboard were clinging, and a number of small boats were engaged in taking them up. The confusion was so great that it was quite impossible to ascertain the names of one quarter of those who were killed; and as a promiscuous crowd of strangers, emigrants, &c., were on board, the greater number of them could not be identified. It is generally admitted that this disaster caused a greater loss of life than ever took place on the Mississippi, before or since. The most authentic accounts make the number of killed one hundred and fifty, and some estimates extend the number to two hundred. The mayor of New Orleans judged from his own observations and diligent inquiries on the spot, that one hundred and fifty lives were lost, at the lowest calculation.

The steamer Storm, which lay in close proximity to the Louisiana, was almost as completely wrecked as the last-named boat itself, and was driven out fifty yards from the wharf by the concussion. Several persons on board of the Storm were killed or wounded. The captain himself was severely injured, but appeared on deck, his face covered with blood, and calmly gave directions for clearing the wreck and bringing his boat back to the wharf.

The fragments of iron, and blocks and splinters of wood, which were sent with the rapidity of lightning from the ill-fated Louisiana, carried death and destruction in all directions. Persons were killed or wounded at the distance of two hundred yards from the boat. There were many miraculous escapes. Dr. Testut, of New Orleans, was standing on the wharf, having just parted from his friend Dr. Blondine, of Point Coupee, who had embarked in the Louisiana, and was killed by the explosion. A fragment of iron struck a man down at Dr. Testut's feet; the poor fellow, while falling, stretched out his hands and convulsively grasped the doctor's palletot, tearing a pocket nearly out. His grasp was soon relaxed by death. Among the citizens who received severe injuries from the flying pieces of the wreck, was Mr. Wray, a clerk in the house of Moses Greenwood & Co., who had been on board of the steamer Knoxville, lying below the ferry landing, and was passing up at the time. He was struck on the thigh by a piece of wood, and so badly wounded that amputation was deemed necessary. Several newsboys, who had been selling papers on the Louisiana, and had just gone ashore, were killed.

The bodies of persons who had been in the steamer, were, in some instances, blown to the height of two hundred feet in the air, some of them falling on the wharf, and some into the river. Legs, arms, and the dismembered trunks of human bodies, were scattered over the levee. One man, it is said, was blown through the pilot house of the steamer Bostona, making a hole through the panels, which looked like the work of a cannon ball.

Among those who were killed on board of the Storm, was Mrs. Moody, the wife of the first clerk, who was standing on the guard, opposite the ladies' cabin. Twelve or fifteen other persons were killed in this boat, and several others were wounded, some of them mortally. The Storm had just arrived with passengers from Cincinnati, none of whom had been landed.

As stated above, a considerable number of those who were killed were emigrants, and other strangers. These are not included in the following list.

KILLED.—Robert Devlin, Baton Rouge; Capt. E. T. Dustin, of the Bostona; Mr. Gilmer, second mate, and Andrew Bell, pilot, La.; wife and child of Mr. Robert Moody, clerk of the steamer Storm; Capt. Edmonston, St. Louis; Mr. Roach, deck hand of the Storm; Mr. Knox, head steward of do.; a cabin boy of do., name unknown; two firemen of do.; John Sullivan, James Wolf, and a third, name unknown, newsboys; the coachman of St. Charles hotel; several negroes and deck hands of the Bostona; Dr. Thomas M. Williams, Lafourche; Dr. Blondine, Point Coupee; Robert McMackin, clerk of the Louisiana; J. J. Gillespie, Vicksburg; J. Merring, Cincinnati; Mr. Wilson, grocer, St. Louis; Mr. Edgar, Washington Co., Miss.; Sylvester Prescott and Æneas Craft, Memphis; Mr. King, of the firm of J. J. Grey & Co., St. Louis; Mr. Elliott, clerk of the firm of Marsh & Rowlett, New Orleans; Merrick Morris, clerk of the firm of Small & McGill, New Orleans.

WOUNDED.—Isaac Hart, New Orleans (supposed to be incurable); Mr. Ray, clerk of Moses Greenwood & Co., New Orleans; S. Davis, Mobile; Augustus Fretz, brother of Capt. Fretz, formerly of the steamer Memphis; A. Bird, planter, near Baton Rouge; Capt. Hopkins, of the Storm; John Meson, pilot of the Storm; Mr. Horrell, of the firm of Horrell & Gale, New Orleans; Mr. Price, clerk of the Bostona; chambermaid of do.; Harvey W. Bickham; Daniel Eckerle; Henry Livingston; Isaac Garrison; Hugh McKee; Henry, a slave; Samuel Fox; William Welch; Clinton Smith; Miley Mulley; a female slave of Moses Murray, and her two children; John Evans; William Burke; John Laws; Charles, a small negro boy; William Tucker; Henry Tucker; James Matthews; Juan Montreal; William Nee; Sandy, a slave of J. Adams; Sam, a slave of Captain Cannon; James

Welch; James Flynn; Patrick McCarthy; twenty or thirty other emigrants, whose names could not be ascertained; H. Rea, New Orleans; Thomas Harrison, Missouri; Frederick A. Wood, New Orleans; Samuel Corley, Ky.; Crocket Harrison, Missouri; George, a slave, and a negro child.

During the night, thirty bodies, all of strangers, were brought to the watch-house of the second municipality. Capt. Cannon, of the Louisiana, was on the wharf at the time of the explosion. He had stopped for a moment, to speak to an acquaintance, and this delay probably saved his life. A lady and her two children escaped from the wreck of the boat as it was sinking.

The effects of this disaster, unexampled in the history of steam navigation, were visible in every circle of society at New Orleans. Dismay was in every countenance, and the whole city seemed to be in mourning for the numerous dead; while every heart was deeply affected with sympathy for the surviving friends, and for all who were suffering in body or mind from the effects of the dreadful catastrophe.

COLLAPSE ON THE FRANKLIN, NO. 2.

This boat collapsed the outside flue of her starboard boiler, August 22d, 1852, on the Mississippi river, five miles above St. Genevieve. Thirty-two persons were killed, or so badly wounded that death in every case was the result. Every person on deck who happened to be aft of the engine at the time of the accident was scalded to death. None of the cabin passengers were injured.

List of the Killed.—Edward Levins, Galena; James Jones, Pa. M. Waggoner, Greensville, Ky.; Charles W. Williams, St. Louis; Patrick Murphy, boatman; P. Joy, St. Louis; J. Everett, and Mrs. Schriner and her son Charles, Louisville, Ky.; M. J. Steele, Jackson Co., Iowa; James Mosley, Floyd Co., Ind.; John Brown, Platteville Mo.; H. Dunn, fireman; M. Hainey; a fireman, name unknown; George Hardy, third engineer, Louisville, Ky.; and several others, whose names could not be ascertained.

Distances, Towns and Population

ON

THE MISSISSIPPI RIVER.

FROM ST. LOUIS, MISSOURI, TO

		Miles.	Pop.
Smith's Landing, Ill.,		20	48
Widow Waters's Landing, Mo.,	1	21	20
Sulphur Springs, Mo.,	2	23	100
Rattlesnake Springs, Mo.,	2	25	60
Dunkling's Lime Kiln, Mo.,	3	28	42
Harlow's Landing, Ill.,	2	30	60
Herculaneum op., Mo.,			100
Platin Rock, Mo.,	2	32	80
Selma Mo.,	3	35	140
Rushtower, Mo.,	5	40	80
John Brickey's, Ill.,	5	45	60
Salt Point, Mo.,	5	50	30
Fort Chartre, op., Ill.			80
St. Genevieve Mo.,	10	60	2400
Kaskaskia, Ill.,	5	65	400
St. Mary's, Mo.,	5	70	300
Rozier's Landing, Mo.,	1	71	80
Chester, Ill.,	9	80	2400
Maynard, Ill.,	1	81	100
Port Perry, Ill.,	1	82	30
Liberty, Ill.,	8	90	200
Underhill's Landing,	5	95	20
Herring's Landing,	1	96	16
Baily's Landing,	4	100	80
Wilkinson's,	5	105	30
Linhoop,	1	106	40
Wittenburg, Mo.,	14	120	46
Sellers' Landing,	1	121	40
Evans's Landing,	1	122	16
Birmingham,	6	128	38
Hines's Landing,	1	129	30
Sheffield, opposite,			140
Preston's Landing,	1	130	40
Bennett's Landing,	1	131	40
Neely's Landing,	1	132	41

		Miles.	Pop.
Vancil's Landing,	1	133	24
Willard's Landing,	2	135	16
Bainbridge,	1	136	20
Clear Creek,	9	145	10
Cape Girardeau, Mo.,	5	150	3000
Thebes, Ill.,	10	160	80
Walbridge Landing,	5	165	40
Commerce, Ill., op.,			100
Santafee, Ill., op.,			81
Thornton's,	3	168	20
Price's	2	170	18
Lane's,	3	173	17
Hunt's,	1	174	20
Rodney's	15	189	100
Cairo, Ill.,	5	194	1000
Columbus, Ky.,	26	220	200
Hickman, Ky.,	17	237	3000
New Madrid, Ky.,	38	275	500
Memphis, Tenn.,	165	440	18,000
Helena, Ark.,	85	525	500
Napoleon, Ark.,	100	625	1500
Columbia, Ark.,	65	690	500
Princeton,	50	740	300
Lake Providence,	25	765	1000
Vicksburg, Miss.,	75	840	6000
Grand Gulf, Miss.,	50	890	1400
Rodney, Miss.,	20	910	500
Natchez, Miss.,	40	950	10,000
Mouth of Red River,	65	1015	400
Bayou Sara,	35	1050	1000
Port Hudson,	12	1062	600
Baton Rouge,	23	1085	6000
Plaquemine,	20	1105	200
Donaldsonville,	35	1140	1500
New Orleans,	78	1218	225,000
Gulf of Mexico,	100	1318	

Distances on the Missouri River.

FROM ST. LOUIS, MISSOURI, TO

		Miles	Pop.
Mouth of Missouri River,		20	
Bellefontaine Bend,	5	25	
Jamestown,	2	27	50
Overall's Wood Yard,	2	29	20
Chasbonier,	6	35	10
St. Charles,	10	45	4000
Howard Bend,	12	57	
Bonhomme Island,	1	58	

		Miles.	Pop.
Cattleville Landing,	2	60	28
Howell's Ferry,	2	62	10
Dozier's	5	67	16
Port Royal,	1	68	8
Tavern Rock,	1	69	
Mount Albans	1	70	
Steel's Wood Yard,	2	72	8
Murdock's "	1	73	11

FROM ST. LOUIS, MISSOURI, TO

	Miles.		Pop.		Miles.		Pop.
Augusta,	3	76	100	Glasgow,	4	265	2000
Jones' Point,	2	78	4	Cambridge,	9	274	400
South "	4	82	4	Keysville Landing,	10	284	18
Basonia,	1	83	11	Buckhorn Point,	8	292	8
Washington,	1	84	400	Brunswick,	8	300	2000
Tuque Point,	1	85		Grand River,	1	301	
St. John's Island,	2	87		Windsor City,	7	308	80
Newport Landing,	2	89	16	Miami,	7	315	30
Patton's Wood Yard,	1	90	7	Thomas's Wood Yard,	6	321	12
Heatherley's "	7	97	7	Hill's Landing,	20	341	25
Miller's Landing,	1	98	13	Waverly,	5	346	700
Pinckney & Griswold's,	3	101	114	Dover Landing,	13	359	26
Bates' Wood Yard,	10	111	17	Lexington,	12	371	5000
Hermann,	10	121	2000	Farmville Landing,	1	372	28
Mouth of Gasconade,	8	129	30	Wellington,	7	379	150
Monning's Landing,	2	131	17	Camden,	10	389	600
Portland,	10	141	450	Napoleon,	8	397	50
Fisher's Wood Yard,	5	146	18	Cogswell's Landing,	5	402	20
St. Aubert,	5	151	150	Sibley,	5	407	300
Smith's Landing,	1	152	28	Richfield,	14	421	100
Shipley's "	3	155	30	El Paso Landing,	8	429	16
King's "	5	160	31	Blue Mills "	1	430	14
Bennett's "	2	162	45	Liberty,	6	436	2000
Mouth of Osage,	2	164	48	Wayne City,	7	443	200
Mouth of Moreau,	5	169	25	Randolph,	8	451	200
Jefferson City,	5	174	4000	Kansas,	6	457	1000
Claysville,	7	181	300	Kansas River,	2	459	
Stanley's Wood Yard,	2	183	21	Parkville,	13	472	1400
Marion,	8	191	640	Little Platte River,	1	473	
Eureka Landing,	5	196	26	Hout's Wood Yard,	6	479	12
Martin's "	2	198	14	Van Rankin's,	10	489	46
Nashville,	7	205	180	Fort Leavenworth,	10	499	600
Providence,	2	207	130	Platte City Landing,	3	502	300
Mount Vernon,	5	212	28	Weston,	4	506	3500
Rocheport,	8	220	680	Iatan,	13	519	100
Boonville,	12	232	3000	Independence Prairie,	25	544	30
Mouth of Lamine,	8	240	10	Columbus Landing,	6	550	20
Arrow Rock,	8	248	450	Maysville,	6	556	60
Little Arrow Rock,	7	255	40	Hart's Landing,	10	566	26
Bluff Port,	6	261	40	St. Joseph,	25	591	6000

Distances on the Upper Mississippi River.

FROM ST. LOUIS, MISSOURI, TO

	Miles.		Pop.		Miles.		Pop.
Mouth of Missouri River,		20		Warsaw, Mo.,	20	207	4000
Alton, Ill.,	5	25	5000	Churchville, opposite,			190
Grafton, Ill.,	18	43	200	Keokuk, Ill.,	5	212	6500
Gap au Gris,	27	70	100	Montrose,	12	224	1000
Worthington's	10	80	50	Nauvo o, opposite,			100
Hamburg, Ill.,	10	90	200	Fort Madison,	12	236	200
Clarksville, Mo.,	15	105	100	Pontoosuc,	6	242	100
Louisiana, Mo.,	12	117	400	Dallas,	2	244	180
Cincinnati, Ill.,	15	132	100	Burlington,	15	259	8000
Saverton, Ill.,	8	140	80	Oquawka,	15	274	300
Hannibal, Mo.,	7	147	5000	Kethsburgh,	12	286	300
Marion City, Mo.,	10	157	300	New Boston,	8	294	100
Quincy, Ill.,	10	167	12,000	Port Louisa,	12	306	80
Lagrange, Mo.,	10	177	200	Muscatine,	18	324	8000
Canton, Mo.,	8	185	100	Rock Island,	30	354	6000
Tully, Mo.,	2	187	180	Davenport, opposite,			5500

FROM ST. LOUIS, MISSOURI, TO

	Miles.		Pop.		Miles.		Pop.
Hampton,	12	366	100	Badaxe,	1	591	20
Leclair,	6	372	200	Warner's Landing,	10	601	30
Port Byron, opposite,			180	Wild-cat Bluffs,	12	613	14
Camanche,	18	390	200	Prairie La Crosse,	16	629	140
Albany,	2	392	500	Mouth of Black River,	12	641	80
Fulton City,	10	402	150	Hammon's Landing,	4	645	48
Lyons, opposite,			100	Fortune's "	2	647	80
Sebula,	18	420	100	Montoville,	4	651	180
Savannah,	2	422	400	Wenona,	7	658	300
Belle View,	18	440	100	Wabashaw Prairie,	4	662	100
Galena,	12	452	11,000	Homes' Landing,	10	672	48
Dubuque,	25	477	10,000	Hall's "	10	682	100
Wills's Landing,	12	489	140	Wabashaw Village,	25	707	300
Wapoton,	8	497	80	Nelson's Landing,	2	709	80
Buena Vista,	6	503	140	Reed's "	2	711	12
Cassville,	4	507	180	Lake Pepin,	1	712	480
Gottenburg,	10	517	200	Wells' Landing,	14	726	80
Clayton City,	10	527	300	Bullard's "	8	734	46
Wyolusing,	5	532	100	Red Wing,	8	742	60
McGregor's Landing,	7	539	40	Point Prescott,	22	764	85
Prairie du Chiene,	3	542	200	Point Douglass,	1	765	40
Red House Landing,	2	645	40	Red Rock,	25	790	180
Johnson's "	1	546	20	Crow Village,	3	793	300
Columbus,	29	575	200	St. Paul,	5	798	8000
Lansing,	2	577	80	Falls of St. Anthony,	8	806	4180
Winneshick,	8	585	200	Mendota,	6	812	350
Victory,	5	590	100	Fort Snelling,	1	813	400

FROM MOUTH OF LAKE ST. CROIX, TO

	Miles.		Pop.		Miles.		Pop.
Willow River,		22		Marine "	5	43	
Still Water,	8	30		Osciola "	20	63	
Arcola Mills,	8	38		Falls of St. Croix,	15	78	

Distances on the Illinois River.

FROM ST. LOUIS, MISSOURI, TO

	Miles.		Pop.		Miles.		Pop.
Alton,		25	5000	Bath,	12	167	100
Grafton,	15	40	200	Havana and Point Isabel,	12	179	180
Mason's Landing,	2	42	80	Liverpool,	10	189	160
Harding,	25	67	100	Copperas Creek,	12	201	50
Columbiana,	10	77	60	Lancaster,	8	209	30
Apple Creek,	4	81	40	Kingston,	2	211	40
Bridgeport and Bedford,	12	93	1400	Pekin,	10	221	3000
Montezuma,	4	97	300	Wesley City,	6	227	180
Florence and Harris's Landing,	6	103	200	Peoria,	3	230	10,000
				Spring Bay,	14	244	80
Griggsville,	6	109	100	Rome,	6	250	100
Naples and Perry,	4	113	3100	Chillicothe,	2	252	120
Meredosia,	6	119	1000	Lacon,	10	262	200
Lagrange,	10	129	200	Henry,	10	272	190
Beardstown,	10	139	1600	Hall's Landing,	4	276	40
Frederick,	4	143	1800	Hennepin,	8	284	200
Browning,	6	149	100	Peru,	18	302	4800
Sharp's Landing,	6	155	60	Lasalle,	1	303	4000

Landings and Distances

ON WHITE RIVER AND TRIBUTARIES.

(From Memphis to the Mouth of White River, 175 miles; from Napoleon to the Mouth of White River, 20 miles.)

FROM MOUTH OF WHITE RIVER TO

	Miles.
Richards', Landing,	1
Hortonbery's, "	11
Caroline,	3
Lerett's Wood Yard,	41
Big Creek,	20
St. Charles,	10
Anderson's Bluff,	2
Maddox's Bay,	9
Dugan's Bluff,	3
Crockett's,	1
Turgason's,	1
Adams',	8
Cascoe,	10
Pepper's,	0
Moreau's Wood Yard,	3
Smith's,	1
Maysville,	3
Aberdeen,	4
Rock Roe,	2
Widow Hatch's,	2
Walnut Ridge,	2
Clarendon,	6
Sawers',	7
Wolf's Wood Yard,	10
Pyburn's Bluff,	22
Bunt Bayou,	3
Arkapola,	3
Devall's Bluff,	5
Surrounded Hill,	2
Buena Vista,	3
Hidden Bluff,	6
Little Hill,	4
John Wright's,	2
Wattensaw,	2
Dr. McFadden's,	4
Weaks'	1
Jno. Underwood's	2
Capt. Taylor's,	4
Pittman's	6
Des Arc,	4
Ferguson's,	3
Arch. Hutchins',	5
McCartey's,	5
Pryer's Wood Yard,	4
Smith's,	2
Myers'	5
Ferguson's,	7
Peach Orchard,	5
Negro Hill,	5
Burnt Beach	6
	1
Mouth of Red River,	6
Gregory's Landing,	12
Gray's Bend,	10
Augusta,	8
Chambers'	4
West's,	1
Taylor's Bay,	1
Wilkerson's,	2
Cole's Landing	5
Morse's Camp,	20
Lewis Shadder's,	5
Mill Creek,	6
Grand Glaize,	5
Dr. Leach's,	4
Carpenter's,	2
Bell's,	3
Mrs. Husley's,	2
Village Creek,	3
Hunt's,	2
McJones',	3
Mrs. Jones',	1
Shon Smith's	½
Eschear's,	½
Love's Wood Yard,	1
Newport,	3
Elizabeth,	2
Jacksonport,	7
Batesville,	50
Buffalo City,	112
Forsyth,	120

BLACK RIVER.

FROM JACKSONPORT TO

	Miles
Powhaton,	90
Pocahontas,	60

CURRANT RIVER.

FROM POCAHONTAS TO

	Miles
Doniphan,	60

LITTLE RED RIVER.

FROM MOUTH TO

	Miles
Esquire Lindsey's,	1
Philip Crise's,	9
Goslin's,	2
Knight's,	4
Mat. Bowden's,	2
Harrison Brown's	4
Granny Aikin's,	1
Judge McDaniel's,	3
Joseph Wright's,	1
Mrs. Aikin's,	1
John Terry's,	2
West Point,	½
Kelly's,	1
Mosier's,	½
Kinder and Hutchin's,	½
Mark Young's,	2
John Cook's,	½
Kim. Harris's,	½
Alex. Crawford's,	2
William Lowry's,	½
A. Vanmetre's,	1
Prospect Bluff,	2
T. Young's,	½
Daniel Cook's,	½
Col. Prince's,	½
Buckley's Gin,	2
Searcy Landing,	3½

Distances on the Yazoo River.

FROM VICKSBURG TO

		Miles.			Miles.
Mouth of Yazoo River,		10	Montgomery's Landing,	7	161
Drumgoole's Bluff,	21	31	Head of the Island,	53	214
Big Sun Flower,	29	60	Sidon,	20	234
Satartia,	9	69	Rising Sun,	5	239
Liverpool,	5	74	Greenwood,	15	224
Yazoo City,	28	102	Le Flore,	3	257
Tcchula Lake,	52	154			

Distances on the Red River.

FROM NEW ORLEANS TO

		Miles.	Pop.			Miles.	Pop.
Mouth of Red River,		203	100	Mouth of Bondicue,	60	413	50
Mouth of Black River,	40	243	100	Clutcherville,	23	436	300
Gordon's Landing,	30	273	100	Natchitoches,	49	485	3000
Fulk's Landing,	12	285	80	Grand Ecore,	10	495	500
Capt. Wilson's Plantation,	25	310	100	Campti,	15	510	200
Alexandria,	25	335	2500	Shreveport,	110	620	5000
Cotile Landing,	18	353	120	Jefferson,	100	720	1800

Distances on the Ouachita River.

FROM MOUTH OF OLD RIVER TO

		Miles.	Pop.			Miles.	Pop.
Mouth of Black River,		40	100	Pigeon Hills,	6	416	150
Trinity,	75	115	1000	Morobay,	1½	417½	50
Harrisonburg,	20	135	1000	Wilmington,	6	423	100
Columbia,	75	210	300	Champagnole,	18	441	300
Monroe,	75	285	500	Eldorado Landing,	3	444	100
Trenton,	2	287	300	Miller's Bluff,	15	459	50
Ouachita City,	35	322	500	Beach Hills,	12	471	200
Alabama Landing,	18	340	300	French Port,	12	483	50
Mary Saline Landing,	35	375	300	Camden,	18	501	3000
Careyville,	35	410	200	Arkadelphia,	100	601	500

BURNING OF THE CAROLINE.

The Caroline was a Memphis packet, employed on the White river. She had ascended that river about twenty miles on Sunday, March 5, 1854, when, at 2 o'clock in the afternoon, the wood pile near the boilers, was discovered to be on fire. The pilot at the wheel, Mr. John R. Price, steered for the shore, which was overflown by high water. Before the shore was reached, some persons attempted to escape in the yawl, which, being overcrowded, speedily sunk, and all

BURNING OF THE CAROLINE.

who had embarked in it were drowned. The flames, in the meanwhile, rapidly overspread the steamer, which was soon consumed, down to the level of the water. There were many deck passengers on board, nearly all of whom were lost. The principal sufferers were women and children, who were not able to make the exertions required for their preservation.

The names of those of the crew and passengers who are known to have perished, will be found below:

LIST OF KILLED.—John R. Price and James Creighton, pilots; Lewis Pollock, assistant bar-keeper; eight deck hands and firemen, whose names the captain, in his report of the disaster, omitted to mention; wife and child of J. Haskins, Marshall county, Tenn.; four children of S. McMullen, of Madison county, Tenn.; Mrs. Haley and three children, Tippah county, Miss.; John Horton, wife, and two children, Mr. Karrell, Mr. Martin, Miss Susanna E. Pool, a son of Mr. Henshaw, Mr. Shelby, of Madison county, Tenn.; a son-in-law, a widowed sister, with her *thirteen* children, and another sister of Mr. Wortham; Mr. Harshaw, of Clarendon, Ark.; George Jones, clerk of the house of Poole & Co., Jacksonport, Tenn., and a number of deck passengers, names unknown.

It is a remarkable circumstance that scarcely any of the crew or passengers who escaped with life, were injured in the slightest degree. There was considerable amount of money on board. The safe, containing $5,000, sunk in the river, and never was recovered. Mr. Penn, one of the passengers, lost $3,500. The remains of Mr. Wilbank, who died a few days before at the Commercial Hotel, Memphis, were on board on their way to his former place of residence, where the funeral was to take place. The body, however, was doomed to find a grave beneath the waters of White river. A package of money which had belonged to the deceased, and which in his dying moments, he had directed to be sent to his widow, was lost with the other money in the safe.

The hull of the Caroline, having burned to the water's edge, broke in two, and sunk out of sight. The whole loss of boat, cargo, money, and other property belonging to the passengers, is estimated at $150,000. There was an insurance on the boat for $5,000. She was finished in the preceding summer, and cost $12,000.

EXPLOSION OF THE ST. JAMES.

The St. James was a high pressure boat, owned by Capt. W. H. Wright. She was built at Cincinnati in 1850, and was employed on the Mississippi river until about a month before her destruction, at which time she was engaged on Lake Pontchartrain. The accident took place on that lake, at Pointe Aux Herbes. The St. James left Rey St. Louis on Sunday night, July 4th, 1852, in company with the steamboat California, having on board a large number of persons who had been spending the anniversary of Independence at the watering places. Between two and three o'clock, on the morning of the fifth, the St. James stopped at the point designated above, fifteen miles from the Pontchartrain railway landing, and having taken in several passengers, started again on her course. Her companion, the California, was at this time a short distance astern; each boat, probably was endeavoring to outrun the other, and it is conjectured that the officers of the St. James, in their eagerness to beat their rival, exposed the lives of their passengers to very obvious danger.

EXPLOSION OF THE ST. JAMES.

The St. James had run scarcely two hundred yards from the point where she had stopped, when all the boilers exploded, and nearly at the same moment, the boat took fire. The staunchions being torn away by the explosion, the whole of the boiler deck fell upon the boilers and machinery, precipitating a great many persons into the lower part of the boat, which was now flooded with scalding water, or strewn with the ignited fuel, which had been scattered abroad. Owing to this circumstance, a number of passengers who had not been injured by the explosion itself, were severely scalded or burned when the deck fell in. As the time at which the disaster took place was long before daylight, many of the passengers were asleep. Some of them awoke in eternity, without knowing, perhaps, what cause had hurried them thither, and others were aroused from their slumbers by a sense of intolerable bodily anguish. Vainly would we attempt to picture the scene which now presented itself on the burning steamer. The shrieks of the affrighted passengers were heard on board of the California, and Captain Ensign, of that steamer, immediately steered for the wreck. The space between the two boats was lighted up by the conflagration to the brightness of mid-day, and the spectators from the California could see the terrified men and women on board of the St. James hurrying to and fro, wringing their hands, or seizing on such articles as they could use for temporary support, and jumping into the lake. The screams were awfully distinct and harrowing, as they arose not from the burning boat only, but from the water, in all directions, where many human beings were shouting for help, or gasping in the last agony. Voices were calling from all points, as the boats of the California went about swiftly, picking up all who could be reached. The horrified eyes of the people on the California could see men cease to struggle and go down, while those who saw them perish had no power to save. It was a scene to harrow the soul of humanity, a scene which could not be remembered without horror, and one that could never be forgotten.

As the California approached the burning wreck, the heat was so intense that Captain Ensign was compelled by a due regard for the persons immediately under his charge, to haul off a short distance. The boats belonging to the California were launched, manned, and sent to the aid of the sufferers. The flames rose from the centre of. the St. James, and Captain Ensign, while making a second attempt to reach the persons on the wreck, succeeded, by nice management, in getting under the stern, and a large number of ladies and gentlemen from the St. James were thus enabled to reach the deck of the California. All who were saved owe the preservation of their lives to Captain Ensign.

Among the passengers who were lost, was Judge Preston, of the Supreme Court of Louisiana, and several other distinguished citizens of that State. Judge Preston had his berth over the boilers. He was seen to retire to rest, and immediately after the explosion, the place where he slept was found shattered to pieces, and he was no where to be seen.

J. M. Wolf, Esq., a member of the New Orleans bar, and his son, a lad of fourteen, were seen standing together on the wreck. The boy was urging his father to jump into the water, declaring that he could save him. The father refused, and the boy threw himself overboard and swam towards the California, which was then approaching. He reached her in an exhausted state, and was saved. A rope was thrown to him just as he cried out that he could struggle no more. It is mentioned, as an illustration of this lad's coolness, that he placed his clothes on a small piece of plank and floated them with him to the California, having an eye to the safety of his wardrobe when his life seemed to be in the greatest peril. When taken on board the California, he had his rescued garments under his arm, and dressed himself with the greatest composure. Mr. Wolf, the father of this boy, who could not be induced to leave the wreck, was lost.

Captain Clarke, Commander of the St. James, was asleep at the time of the explosion. When awakened by the terrific report and the commotion on board, he ran on deck, and with the assistance of the pilot, Mr. Samuel Henderson, he took possession of the yawl, keeping back the crowd which was intent on the same object. Having launched this small boat, Captain Clarke placed in it Mrs. Asher, her daughter, (a young lady of sixteen,) and her two younger children; also Mrs. Sheed and Robert Smith, the steersman, who had an arm broken. With these persons, the yawl started for the California, but striking against that vessel, the little boat upset and all who were in it, except Mrs. Sheed were drowned. Mr. H. L. Sheed, the husband of this lady, was also one of the passengers of the St. James, and he was lost. Captain Clarke's two little sons saved themselves by swimming to the California. Captain Clarke himself was badly scalded, and Captain Wright, the owner of the boat, received severe injuries.

Many of the passengers had not registered their names. The persons named below are scarcely a moiety of those who perished.

List of Killed.—Hon. Isaac T. Preston, Judge of the Supreme Court of Louisiana; Mr. Richard Turner, late Commissary of the Fourth Ward, Second Municipality, New Orleans; J. M. Wolf, member of the New Orleans bar; John Molley and Nicholas Read, of New Orleans; Mr. Sheed, of the U. S. Branch Mint, of New Orleans; James M. Jones, mate of the St. James; the watchman of do., name not mentioned; a colored boy, slave of Dr. Penniston, of New Orleans; another slave, belonging to Captain Tuft; Mrs. Asher and her three children; Mr. Paul, engineer; John, a colored man, second steward of the boat; Robert Smith, steersman; S. Forrester; Mr. Gatchet Delisle; and about twenty others, whose names could not be ascertained.

Wounded.—Captain Wright, owner of the St. James, (badly scalded;) Captain Clarke, Commander of do., burned by a piece of blazing timber which fell on his head; Oliver Rout, second engineer, (badly scalded;) Francis Turner, Assessor of the First District; Wm. Collins, first engineer, (badly burnt;) Eliza Wilson; Wm. Deacon, (much injured;) Francois Francis, a passenger, (severely scalded;) Harry Harvey, passenger, (badly scalded;) J. G. Wheeler; Robert McMillar, deck hand, (scalded and right arm broken;) Gregory, colored boy, and Patrick, a colored man, slaves of Madam Isabel, (much hurt;) George, Bill, Patrick and Julius, firemen, all badly scalded.

Mr. Turner, the Assessor, who is mentioned in the list of wounded, had risen and dressed himself, and was walking about the cabin, thinking that he had been imprudent in venturing on a lake boat which used "high pressure;" and while his thoughts were thus occupied, the explosion took place. His injuries, however, were not of a very serious nature.

EXPLOSION OF THE AMERICA.

This afflictive event took place on Lake Erie, July 31, 1850. The head of one of the starboard boilers blew off, turning the boiler deck upside down, raising the upper deck about four feet, and making all the central part of the boat a complete wreck. As soon as the report was heard, several of the passengers jumped overboard and were

EXPLOSION OF THE AMERICA.

not seen afterwards. Many persons were killed or wounded, of whose names an imperfect list will be found below. The names of many of the passengers were not registered.

List of Killed.—J. McLaughlin, fireman; H. Brown, colored waiter, (he was literally torn to pieces by the pitman, a part of the steam engine;) Joseph Stancliff, Durham, Conn.; James Chancellor; Charles Porter; P. Welsh, fireman; Wm. Terry; M. Hagerty and James Chintstar, firemen; Patrick Kenby, deck hand; the third engineer, and several passengers, names unknown.

Wounded.—W. H. Burnitt, of New York, hands and arms scalded; Jeremiah Connor, wife and five children, of Missouri; all badly scalded; Wm. Livas, first cook, scalded; R. Retaliè, of Whitby, Canada, do.; Luther Kinney, of Washington, Macomb county, Michigan, do.; an old Frenchwoman, shoe-dealer of New York, badly scalded; Archibald Lindsey, steerage passenger, of Michigan, badly scalded; J. F. Lalor, L. G. Rumsey and Patrick Howley, (deck passenger,) of Cincinnati, slighly scalded; D. E. Terry, Norwalk, O., injured by a fall; B. Welsh, of Buffalo, badly scalded; J. Downing, of Albany, N. Y., slightly do.; Dennis Warren, deck passenger, much injured; Patrick Murphy, deck hand, do.; Thomas Purcell, fireman, do.; colored cook, name not known, slightly scalded.

A spectator of this disaster says, "It was a melancholy sight to go through the cabin, and see the terrible condition of the wounded. On some of them scarcely a particle of skin remained, and the flesh was frightfully burned. I have never witnessed anything to be compared with this awful catastrophe. One poor woman and all her five children were dreadfully scalded. Their sufferings cannot be imagined. The woman was perfectly exhausted with suffering, but seemed to care only for her children. One of them, a little girl, tried several times to jump overboard. Her screams were agonizing to all who heard them."

COLLISION OF THE DE SOTO AND BUCKEYE.

Between three and four o'clock, on Friday morning, March 1st, 1844, the steamboats De Soto and Buckeye came in contact on the Mississippi, near Atchafalaya. The De Soto was bound down, from Nachitoches, and the Buckeye was on her way to Ouachata, with about three hundred passengers on board, and a cargo of plantation supplies. The concussion was so violent that within five minutes after the accident, the Buckeye sunk to her hurricane deck, in twenty feet water. The passengers were asleep until awakened by the shock. They rushed on deck in the greatest consternation. A terrible commotion and confusion was produced by hundreds of people, in the wildest excitement, seeking their relatives; as many husbands and wives, parents and children, were separated by the universal disorder which prevailed in the fated vessel. All, or nearly all, were in their night clothes, and few were sufficiently self possessed to take proper means for their own safety, or for the safety of those who depended on them for assistance and protection.

A few brave spirits, forgetful of themselves, turned all their attention to the preservation of the women and children; but the boat went down so suddenly that few of those helpless beings could be saved. Mr. Haynes, of Alexandria, La., whose family was with him, lost his daughter, a beautiful little girl, about ten years old. His wife's sister, Miss Elizabeth Smith, an accomplished young lady, was likewise drowned. Mr. Haynes also lost sixteen slaves who were on the lower deck. Mr. Alexander McKinzie, formerly of Florida, lost his wife, seven children, and four slaves. Mr. John Blunt, who was also from Florida, lost his wife, child, and seven negroes. Col. King, of Louisiana, (afterwards Vice President of the United States,) lost two children. A young man named Pollard, supposed to be from Natchez, had a considerable sum of money deposited for safe-keeping in the clerk's office. When the boat was sinking he applied for his money; it was delivered to him, and he was not seen afterwards. A child of Mr. White, of New Orleans, was lost. Two sisters of a young man named Francis Larkin were drowned. Mr. Larkin and these young ladies had been taken on board at Red river landing. Mr. Beard, one of the unfortunate passengers of the Buck-eye, attempted to swim ashore with his young nephew on his back; but in the attempt both were drowned. The whole number who perished could not have been less than eighty. The night was clear, and the moon shed a brilliant light on the water, and to this happy circumstance the preservation of many lives may be ascribed. The De Soto remained by the wreck to the last, and the officers of that boat exerted themselves to the utmost in saving the lives and property of the Buck-eye's passengers. The mate of the De Soto rescued about forty persons from the water by taking them up into the yawl, conveying as many as the little boat could carry to the steamer, and then returning for more.

The surviving passengers of the Buckeye published a certificate exculpating the Captain and other officers of that boat, and ascribing the mischance to a combination of unfortunate circumstances which no precaution or foresight could have averted.

BURNING OF THE E. K. COLLINS.

Between ten and eleven o'clock, on the night of October 9, 1854, the steamboat E. K. Collins was burned to the water's edge on Lake Erie, nearly opposite the light house below Mauldin. At the time the fire broke out, she was on her way from Sault St. Marie to Cleveland. Before she could be run on shore, she was completely enveloped in flames. Twenty-three of the passengers and crew were either drowned or burned to death. The fire broke out on the boiler deck, and spread so rapidly that the passengers and crew, most of whom were in bed, had not time to dress themselves, before they ran on deck to seek the means of escape. As soon as the boat had reached shallow water she became unmanagable, and while the head was embedded in the sand the stern projected over the deep water, and all who happened to be abaft the machinery were reduced to the necessity of throwing themselves overboard, or remaining in the boat with the certainty of perishing in the flames. Had it not been for the timely arrival of the propeller Finertz, scarcely any would have been saved. The current set strongly from the shore, so that several men who attempted to save themselves by swimming were carried back and drowned. The Captain of the Finertz, seeing the light, hastened to the wreck, and had all his boats ready for service by the time of his arrival. Nearly all who were saved owe their preservation to the prompt assistance rendered by this vessel. As a surprising example of human depravity, it is mentioned that some wretch, in the very height of the consternation on board, stole eighty dollars, the hard earnings of a poor invalid, who had been working at Sault St. Marie, until his declining health obliged him to return to his family, at Cleveland. A purse of twenty dollars was contributed by the passengers for the relief of the unfortunate man who had been victimized by this atrocious and inhuman robbery.

Names of those who Perished by this Disaster.—Mrs. Dibble; Samuel Powell; Lawrence Whalom; Thomas Cook; Mrs. McNailly; Mrs. Watrums and child; a colored man from Virginia, name unknown; Charles Adams; John McNeely; John Ennis; P. Tinker; John Halstead; Mr. Lyman; Mrs. F. Lewis; Samuel Brown; A. Alwick; Thomas Anderson; J. A. Grinnan; James Grimmet; Nathanial Robins, and one of the pilots, name not mentioned.

EXPLOSION OF THE KATE KEARNEY.

One of the boilers of this boat exploded at St. Louis, on Thursday, February 14th, 1854. The Kate Kearney was about to start from the wharf and the last bell had just ceased ringing, when in a single moment the greater part of the boat was changed to a confused heap of ruins. There were fifty or sixty passengers on board, and the names of many, (as usual,) were not registered. It is quite certain that several persons, whose names were never ascertained, were blown overboard and lost. Fifteen persons, badly wounded, were taken to the Sister's Hospital, St. Louis; of these, several died within a few hours, namely:

the Rev. S. J. Gassaway, rector of St. George's church, St. Louis, F. Hardy, second engineer of the Kate Kearney, D. Keefer, a deck hand, and two colored men.

Among the wounded were Brevet Major D. C. Buel, of the United States army, Major R. C. Catlin, of the seventh, U. S. infantry, a son of that gentleman, and several other persons from Illinois and Missouri. Three persons, whose names are not mentioned, were seen to sink in the river.

Major Buel, one of the wounded passengers, gives the following account of his providential escape from a horrible death. He was overwhelmed among falling timbers and rubbish, from which, with great exertion, he extricated himself after the lapse of a few minutes. As soon as he felt himself at liberty he heard the alarm of fire; and although he had received several painful wounds, he united with others in an attempt to extinguish the flames. He continued in this active service until relieved by the arrival of the fire companies. He then went ashore, took a carriage, and drove to the Planter's House. It was only on his arrival there that he began to realize the serious nature of the injuries he had sustained, and from the effects of which he did not recover for several weeks.

The Kate Kearney was an old boat, having been engaged for eight or ten years in the packet trade between St. Louis and Keokuk. About three years previous, the same boiler which caused the disaster just related, collapsed at Canton, on the upper Mississippi, killing and scalding a large number of persons. The collapsed flues were taken out and new ones were substituted, but the shell of the old boiler remained. The boat was adjudged to be unfit for service several months before the explosion at St. Louis. She was withdrawn from the Keokuk trade, but as both the Alton packets had sunk, the Kate Kearney was chartered to do their duty; in which service she was engaged at the time of the explosion.

BURNING OF THE BELLE OF THE WEST.

The Belle of the West was burned to the water's edge, near Florence island, on the Ohio river, April 22d, 1850. Only an imperfect report of this disaster has been preserved.

List of the Killed.—Jeremiah Bamberger; John Anders and wife; Frederick Bretz, wife and three children; (two children belonging to this family were saved;) Mr. Keller, wife and three children; a lady, name unknown; a man, wife and six children, names unknown;

three children of Mr. Waggoner; two German deck passengers; and a family, consisting of two men, two women, and four children.

WOUNDED.—John Bamberger; Levi Yerdz; Miss Yerdz; and three or four others, names unknown.

A brave little boy, twelve years old, leaped into the river, and while swimming to the shore, saw his mother on board, overburdened with two small children, and trying to make her escape. He made her understand by gestures, that he wished her to throw one of the children into the water. She did so, and he swam with it to the shore. The mother escaped with the other child, and thus the whole family was saved. Several other families were less fortunate. A Mr. Waggoner, one of the passengers, was accompanied by his wife and eight children. Three of the children were drowned. Mr. Waggoner was emigrating to Iowa, having with him money, with which he intended to purchase land; but every dollar of it was lost. About fifty German Moravians, some of them with families, were on board. Many of these people perished in the flames, or in the water.

EXPLOSION OF THE VIRGINIA.

On Saturday, March 31, 1849, at 5 o'clock, P. M., the steamer Virginia, plying as a daily packet between Wheeling, Va., and Steubenville, Ohio, was torn into pieces and sunk by the explosion of her boilers, at Rush Creek, ten miles above Wheeling. Eight or ten lives were lost, and about fourteen persons were wounded. The explosion took place when the boat was about to land a passenger, Mr. Roe, who was killed. As almost the whole of the upper part of the boat was reduced to fragments, and the hull sunk immediately, there can be no doubt that all of the crew and passengers who were missing, perished in the wreck.

LIST OF KILLED.—Mr. Roe, Rush Creek; the chambermaid of the boat; William Ebert, Wheeling, Va.; a colored fireman, and eight or ten others, names unknown.

BADLY WOUNDED.—Mr. Boles and lady, Steubenville, Ohio; Mr. Collins, the pilot, one leg broken and otherwise badly injured; Henry Commons, Birmingham, Alleghany county, Pa.; John Taylor, first engineer, Wheeling, Va.; W. Barker, St. Louis; W. Althouse, Wheeling; the carpenter of the boat; James Zink, a boy, and A. Snyder, (both legs torn off,) Wheeling; and Mr. Atchison, Steubenville.

SLIGHTLY WOUNDED.—Mrs. E. Coen, Wheeling; Capt. Dawson,

Richetown; Mr. Beaty, Steubenville; and Mr. Burgess and lady, West Springfield, Ill.

Mr. Roe, the passenger who was going on shore at the time of the explosion, was on the plank, and was cut in three pieces by fragments of the boiler.

EXPLOSION OF THE ZACHARY TAYLOR.

This was an old boat employed in the transportation of hogs from Lawrenceburg to Cincinnati. On the 21st of December, 1853, she was towing two barges laden with hogs, and there were about three hundred of the same kind of animals on the deck of the steamer, abaft the engine. About day break, on the day aforesaid, when the boat was within ten miles of Cincinnati, one of the flues of the larboard boiler collapsed, projecting columns of steam and scalding water fore and aft, killing three of the boat's crew instantly, and scalding five others. The three men who were killed were lying asleep in front of the fire.

The first engineer, Moses Smith, was scalded in the face. The second engineer, John Everhart, was more seriously injured. Captain Prettyman had passed by the boiler a moment before the collapse. The hot water thrown back among the swine scalded many of them so severely that they jumped overboard.

There were thirty-five passengers on board, not one of whom was hurt. One of the deck hands who were killed was named Boyle; the names of the other two are not given.

VIEW OF NEW ORLEANS.

SKETCH OF NEW ORLEANS.

THIS great commercial emporium of the South and West is situated on the south bank of the Mississippi river, about 100 miles from its mouth, 1663 miles south-west of New York, 1438 miles south-west of Washington, 2025 miles south south-west of Pittsburgh, and 2000 miles south by east of the Falls of St. Anthony; lat. 29° 58′ N., long. 90° 7′ W. New Orleans is the seat of justice of Orleans Parish, La. It is built around a bend of the river, and from this circumstance it has acquired the *sobriquet* of the "Crescent City." The location of New Orleans is on a piece of land which inclines gently from the river to the marshy grounds in the rear of the city. The site is from two to five feet below the level of the river in the time of high water. To protect the city against inundations, an embankment, or levee, fifteen feet wide and six feet high, has been raised; it extends one hundred and twenty miles above the city, and to Port Plaquemine, forty three miles below it. This levee affords the citizens of New Orleans a delightful promenade, worthy of comparison with the boulevards of Paris.

The change in the course of the river at New Orleans causes vast alluvial deposits, particularly at that point where the commerce of the city chiefly centres. Here it has been found necessary to erect quays, extending from fifty to one hundred feet in the river. In consequence of the new alluvial formations at this point, the levee has been widened and an additional row of warehouses has been erected between the city and the river. The city was originally laid out by the French in an oblong, rectangular shape, 1320 yards in length, and 700 yards in breadth. Above this are the faubourgs of St. Mary, Annunciation, and La Course; below, are Marigny, Donnois, and Declouet; and in the rear, are Treme, and St. Johns. The suburbs, together with the village of Lafayette, which was formerly under a separate municipal government, are now incorporated with the city proper. In the year 1836, New Orleans was divided, by legislative enactment, into three municipalities, each with distinct municipal powers; but in 1852 this division was abrogated, and the faubourgs, the village of Lafayette, and all the other dependencies, extending about seven miles along the river, were consolidated under one charter, and one city government.

Algiers, which may be regarded as one of the suburbs of New Orleans, is a flourishing village, situated on the opposite side of the river, and is connected with the city by a ferry. It has several ship-yards and extensive manufacturing establishments.

New Orleans was settled by the French in 1717. The name was applied as a compliment to the Duke of Orleans, Regent of France, during the minority of Louis XV. In 1723, Charlevoix visited the place, and found about two hundred inhabitants, living chiefly in huts or cabins built without any orderly arrangement. There was a wooden warehouse and another wretched building which had been intended for a store, but was used as a chapel. In the same year, some German emigrants, after whom the "German coast" is named, arrived at this location, having changed their original intention to make a settlement in Arkansas. A memorable hurricane visited the place in this year, and destroyed nearly all the buildings. In 1727 the Jesuits and Ursuline nuns arrived; the former remained until the expulsion of their order from France, Spain, and Naples, in 1763, compelled them to leave Louisiana. Their entire property in this region was confiscated; their lands, which were then sold by the French government for $186,000, are now worth not less than $20,000,000. In 1730 two buildings which still remain on the upper side of the Cathedral were erected. The first visitation of the yellow fever occurred in 1769, being introduced, as it is said, by an English vessel, with a cargo of slaves from Africa. Four years before this time, the first British vessels visited this place, or rather came to anchor at Lafayette, where they traded with the planters and natives. In 1769 the colony was ceded to Spain, the population of the whole province being then 5,556 whites, and nearly as many blacks. In 1770 the river was frozen for several yards on both sides. In 1782 permission was obtained for the building of a custom-house. In 1785 the Americans of the West, and of Philadelphia began to trade with New Orleans. In 1788 nine hundred houses were destroyed by fire, which broke out on Good Friday, in a chapel on Chartres street. In 1789 many Americans settled in the neighborhood. In 1791 the first company of French comedians arrived. In 1792 the Baron Carondolet became governor of the province. He divided the city into four wards, established a night-watch, and lighted the streets. To defray the expenses of these improvements, a tax of $1.12½ was levied on each chimney. He erected several fortifications also, placing a fort where the mint now stands, another at the foot of Canal street, a redoubt in Rampart street, &c. Military training commenced this year. Five volunteer companies were formed, each company containing one hundred men. In 1794 the first newspaper, called the *Moniteur*, was printed. Much property in the city was destroyed in this year by fire, and by a hurricane. In 1801 Louisiana was ceded back to France. In 1803 the province was ceded to the United States by Napoleon. The city was incorporated in 1804. The population of the city was trebled within the first seven years after the Americans took possession of it. In 1812 the first steamboat, the New Orleans, arrived from Pittsburgh. January 8th, 1815, Gen. Packenham, commanding the English forces, made an attack on the city, but was signally defeated by the Americans under Gen. Jackson. The loss of the English, in killed and wounded, was nearly three thousand; the Americans had only seven men killed, and six wounded. In 1816 the levee gave way, nine miles above the city. The inundation did immense damage. In 1823 J. H. Caldwell was laughed at as a madman, for building the Camp Street theatre. It was quite out of town, and was accessible only by gunwales instead of pavements. From this date to the present time, the improvements have been so rapid, and are so much within the recollection of our readers, that it is unnecessary to mention them specifically. We will now glance at New Orleans as it is at the present day.

The streets of this city are sufficiently spacious, and for the most part, intersect each other at right angles. Canal street, which is the widest in the city, is 190½ feet in breadth. In the centre of this street is a grass plat 25 feet wide. The houses are generally constructed of brick, and those in the principal business locations are often six or seven stories high. There are many splendid dwellings, especially on the outskirts of the city. The houses have commodious basements, but no cellars, on account of the marshy nature of the ground. There are several handsome public squares in various parts of the city. Jackson Square, formerly called Place d'Armes, occupies the centre of the river front of the old town plot; it is ornamented with shell walks, shrubbery, statuettes, &c., and is a favorite place of resort. Lafayette Square, in the Second District, is finely laid out and adorned with a profusion of shade trees. Congo Square, in the rear of the city, is also a handsome enclosure.

New Orleans has a number of superb public buildings. The Custom House is a magnificent structure, and with the single exception of the Capitol at Washington, it is the largest building in the United States. Its dimensions are:—front on Canal street, 334 feet; on Custom House street, 252 feet; on New Levee street, 310 feet; and on Old Levee street, 297 feet; height 82 feet. It covers an area of 87,333 superficial feet. The United States Branch Mint is at the corner of Esplanade and New Levee street. It is an extensive building, 282 feet long, 108 feet deep, and three stories high. It has two wings, each 81 feet by 29. The Municipal Hall, at the corner of St. Charles and Hevia streets, is a beautiful marble edifice in the Grecian style of architecture. The Odd Fellows' Hall and the Merchants' Exchange are large and elegant buildings.

Many of the churches are spacious and beautiful buildings. There are 35 churches in the city—12 Roman Catholic, 7 Episcopal, 6 Presbyterian, 5 Methodist, 3 Lutheran, 2 Baptist, and 3 Jewish Synagogues.

New Orleans has many benevolent Institutions. The Charity Hospital is a magnificent edifice. The United States Naval Hospital is also a noble building. Stone's Hospital and the

Franklin Infirmary are likewise fine structures. The Literary and Educational Institutions are very numerous. Among these, we may mention the University of Louisiana, organized in 1849; it comprises a Law School and a flourishing Medical College.

The public journals of New Orleans are celebrated for superior ability. More than twenty newspapers are published in the city, among which, ten or twelve are dailies. Several of them are printed in the French language. There are also several periodicals specially devoted to literary and scientific objects.

There are eight banks in New Orleans, with an aggregate circulation of $8,127,846; deposits, $12,077,767. Cash assets:—specie, $8,195,295; loans and deposits, $17,409,767; foreign and domestic exchange, $3,857,612. The assessed value of real and personal proproperty in New Orleans for 1852, amounted to $70,194,930.

With respect to commerce, New Orleans possesses unrivalled advantages, especially for internal trade. This city is the grand emporium for the trade of the Mississippi and its tributaries, embracing 15,000 miles of navigable waters, and communicating with a vast extent of country of inexhaustible fertility and boundless resources. The levee of this city constantly presents an appearance of business activity which has scarcely a parallel in any other commercial city of the world. The steamboat trade is stupendous. The foreign and coastwise arrivals at New Orleans, for the year ending December 31, 1853, were:—ships, 782; barques, 447; brigs, 295; schooners, 596; steamships, 244; steamboats, 3,253;—total, 5,617. The shipping of the district, at the above mentioned date, amounted to 81,500 tons registered, and 184,512 tons enrolled and licensed;—total, 266,013 tons. The exports of cotton for the year ending August 31, 1852, were 772,242 bales to Great Britain; 196,254 to France; 75,950 to the North of Europe; 134,657 to the South of Europe and China; 128,629 to Boston; 101,938 to New York; 15.594 to Philadelphia, and 15,041 to other places in the United States. The other principal exports are flour, bacon, lard, grain, tobacco and sugar.

In addition to the several railroads communicating with various points in the State, are two extensive lines which are now nearly or quite completed—one called the New Orleans, Opelousas and Great Western Railroad—extending through Louisiana into Central Texas; and the other, the New Orleans, Jackson and Great Northern Railroad—designed to connect with the railway system of Tennessee, and of the Northwestern States. A charter has also been granted and a company organized for constructing a road to communicate with Mobile, through the Pontchartrain Railroad. In all these works, New Orleans has a primary and paramount interest.

In the year 1834, gas-light was introduced into the city, and machinery was constructed for supplying the inhabitants with water from the Mississippi. It is raised by steam-power to an elevated reservoir, whence more than 5,000,000 gallons are daily distributed to various parts of the city.

The cemeteries of New Orleans are a remarkable "feature" of the place. The burial of the dead is here managed on an unique plan: the bodies being not deposited underground, but above it. This method of interment is adopted on account of the damp constitution of the soil, which makes it impossible to dig a grave which will be free from the intrusion of water. The tombs are built from one to three stories high, and the coffins are deposited lengthwise in niches or cavities of a suitable size.

Owing to various sanitary measures adopted by the citizens, the health of this city has been much improved within a few years past, and the principal obstacle to the growth of the place, viz.: its supposed insalubrity, has thus been, in a considerable degree, removed.

Population of New Orleans 225,000.

BURNING OF THE GEORGIA.

On Saturday night, January 28, 1854, the steamboat Georgia was burnt on Alabama river, between Montgomery and Mobile. She had two hundred and thirty passengers on board, thirty or forty of whom are believed to have perished. When the fire was discovered, the boat was run ashore as speedily as possible. The scene which followed was one of indescribable confusion. One who saw it declares that women and children were "pitched on to the shore like logs of wood;" the necessity of getting them out of the burning boat with the greatest despatch seemed to require such rough and unceremonious handling. Several who were thus thrown out of the boat fell into the water and were drowned, and others struck the ground with such violence as to cause serious injuries. Mr. Jackson, of Barbour county, Ala., and one of his children, were lost. His widow and eight surviving children, who were on board with him, were left at Mobile, in destitute circumstances. Mr. Jackson had on his person checks or drafts to a considerable amount, which were also lost. Mr. Jolley and his family, of Randolph county, Georgia, were on the boat. The wife of this gentleman and one of his children were drowned. He lost besides, $900 in specie, and was left penniless. B. F. Lofton, of Lenoir county, N. C., lost two slaves. Rev. J. M. Carter, of Clinton, Ga., lost three negroes. His wife was badly burned. Dr. J. M. Young, of Hancock, Ga., lost a valuable slave, all his medical books, surgical instruments, and everything, in short, except the clothing which he wore at the time of the disaster. Mrs. Davidson, from Macon county, Ala., lost several negroes. Mr. Graham, from Williamsburg, S. C., lost two negroes and $500 in gold. Thos. J. McLanathan, of Bristol, Conn., was drowned. A gentleman from Stewart county, Ga., lost several slaves. A woman who fell or leaped from the cabin floor to the main deck was caught on the horns of an infuriated ox, and thereby received several severe wounds, but the animal threw her into the water and she was saved. A father, who had rescued his wife and six children, went back into the blazing wreck, hoping to save the seventh, but lost his own life. A young man who had escaped to the shore, returned to the boat to bring away his sister, but he was seen to fall into the blazing hull, from which he never emerged. Another man saved three of his children, but his wife and six other children were consumed on this funeral pyre. A young man, who had lost his wife in the wreck, sat on the wharf to all appearance an indifferent spectator of the frightful scene. It appeared afterwards that his grief had reduced him to melancholy madness, or idiotic apathy. Another young man who had seen his father and mother perish in the boat, loudly lamented the loss of $1,000 which the old gentleman had deposited in the safe. This bereavement seemed to be the only one which occupied his thoughts. W. B. Rhenn, of Newbern, N. C., saved himself, his wife, and his five children, but lost nine slaves.

Of the forty persons who perished in this conflagration, twenty-two were negroes belonging to the cabin passengers, and more than half of the others were children. From the moment the flames broke out until the fate of each person on board, for life or death, was decided, only three minutes elapsed; so quick was the work of destruction. Nearly all of the passengers were dressed, only two or three having retired to their berths. It was a fortunate circumstance that so many of the passengers were awake, otherwise the loss of life would have been still greater. Some were kept up by a desire to see the various landing places, and others were listening to the music of a violin which a young man was playing in the cabin.

BURNING OF THE G. P. GRIFFITH.

The fine steamer G. P. Griffith took fire on Lake Erie, about twenty miles below Cleveland, and was burnt to the water's edge, on June 17, 1850. The passengers were all in their berths when the alarm of fire was given, about three o'clock in the morning. The day had just begun to dawn, and the shore was in sight. At first very little alarm was felt on board, as the boat was rapidly approaching the shore, to which her head had been directed. But alas! the prospect of speedy deliverance soon vanished, and every heart was chilled with terror when the steamer, while yet half a mile from land, struck on a sand-bar and became immovable.

> "Then rose from sea to sky the wild farewell,
> Then shrieked the timid, and stood still the brave."

Many of the passengers then plunged madly into the lake, and few of these were saved. The scene on the burning vessel is represented as one which would have agonized any spectator who had no personal interest in the event. What must it have been to those whose lives, and lives even dearer than their own, were subject to the contingencies of a moment? The consternation of all on board may be estimated from the fact that scarcely any of the survivors were able to give a lucid account of the catastrophe. There were three hundred and twenty-six

BURNING OF THE G. P. GRIFFITH.

persons on the boat; of these, only about thirty, who were able to swim ashore, were saved. Every child perished, and every woman except one, the wife of the barber. One of the passengers, a Mr. Parkes, had secured a piece of the wreck, which was barely sufficient to support him on the surface, and he was reduced to the horrible necessity of pushing others away when they attempted to sustain themselves on the same fragment. He saw scores of people sinking around him, and heard many a voice exclaiming in piteous accents, "Save me! save me!" But who can be humane at such a moment? Who can feel pity for others, when his own life is exposed to the most imminent peril? Mr. Parkes says, that for a moment he felt like "giving up," and dying with his fellow passengers. But the instinct of self preservation was too strong for the emotions of sympathy. Soon he found himself almost solitary on the bosom of the lake. Most of the struggling people had disappeared, their wild supplications for aid had ceased and nothing was heard except the sullen sound of the waters as they beat against the charred hull of the steamer.

One of the passengers gives the following account of his escape. He was aroused from his slumber by the cries of fire and the screams of women and children. When he reached the deck he found that the boat was about three miles from land. The second mate gave orders for the boat to be steered towards the shore. She reached the bar half a mile from land, before the flames had made much progress; but as soon as the steamer grounded on that bar, the fire spread with appalling rapidity. One of the officers directed the passengers to save themselves, but did not point out any means of escape. Many of the passengers threw themselves overboard. The narrator says they leaped out of the boat in crowds, twenty at a time. The Captain remained on the upper deck, near his state room, forward of the wheel-house. When nearly all the passengers had jumped overboard to escape from the flames, the Captain threw his mother, his wife and child, and the barber's wife into the lake, and then plunged in himself. He remained a moment on the surface with his wife in his arms, and then both sunk together. The passenger who tells this story saved himself on a small piece of plank, supported by which he contrived to reach the shore.

The books of the boat were lost, therefore the names of very few of the victims can be given. But it is known that the loss of life was greater than in any previous disaster on the lake, except only in the case of the steamer Erie. One hundred and fifty-four dead bodies were recovered, and probably from thirty to fifty more remained at the bottom of the lake. The scene on the shore, after the awful tragedy was finished, was melancholy in the extreme. One hundred and fifty dead bodies were strewn along the beach. Boats had been employed in dragging for them at the spot where the wreck lay. A long trench was dug on the shore, and here the greater number of the dead were interred, unshrouded and uncoffined, and many of them unknown.

List of Killed.—William Daley; Capt. C. C. Roby, wife, mother and two children; Mrs. Wilkinson; Horace Palmer; Richard Palmer; Charles Brown; Theodore Gilman; Richard Mann; W. P. Tinkham and his two children; Daniel, a colored waiter; Hugh McLair; George Wilmen; P. Keeler; Mrs. Heth and Francis Heth and their four children; M. June; W. Tillman; A Ferguson; J. R. Manson; Thomas Wild; an unknown man, on whose person was found one thousand one hundred and sixty dollars; J. Marsh; another stranger, whose clothes were marked with the initials F. P.; Francis Huile; a great many English, Irish, and German emigrants, of whom only one, Robert Hall, was saved. Mr. Hall lost his wife and four children, his mother, two sisters and two brothers. Mrs. Walker and child; Selina Moony; and others not identified.

Henry Wilkinson, the clerk of the Griffith, swam ashore by supporting his chin on a piece of firewood. When about to leave the wreck, he first threw his mother and little niece overboard, and endeavored to save them, but was unable to do so, being nearly drowned in the attempt.

HIGH WATER AT CAIRO, 1844.

FLOODS OR FRESHETS ON THE WESTERN RIVERS.

Only those persons who have witnessed the devastation of a western flood can form any idea of the terrific nature of such a disaster. Sometimes the whole country, as far as eye can reach, is under water; while the strength of the current sweeps everything before it. In the year 1786, the Ohio river rose fifty-nine feet above low-water mark. As the surrounding country was but sparsely inhabited at that time, the damage done by this flood was comparatively trivial. In 1792 the Ohio rose 63 feet above low-water mark—four feet higher than the flood of 1786.

On the 11th of November, 1810, there was a great flood at Pittsburg. A brig which had been built at Plumb Creek, near that city, and which was ready to be launched, was floated off her ways by this freshet, so that the common process of launching was unnecessary. Fortunately the vessel was secured and made fast, or she would probably have made a long voyage down the river, without the usual equipments.

June 2, 1826, the Mississippi was three feet higher at St. Louis than it had been within the preceding forty years. It was up to Main street in that city—houses were swept away, and a vast amount of property was destroyed.

July 14, 1828, there was an extraordinary rise in the Ohio river, supposed to be as great as that of 1792. It carried desolation into the lower part of Wheeling, which was covered with water to the depth of six feet. There was a vast amount of property destroyed along the river.

In 1836 the Mississippi rose fifty-four feet above low-water mark, being nine feet ten inches higher than it was in the flood of 1810.

In 1844 the houses at Cairo, at the confluence of the Ohio and Mississippi, were nearly submerged. The swollen rivers were fourteen miles wide between the opposite shores of Kentucky and Missouri. Moveable property of every kind, fences, cattle, lumber, furniture, and entire houses, (wooden ones, of course,) were floated down the Mississippi and other rivers.

A building was seen driving down the Mississippi, while several persons from the windows were calling for assistance, which, on account of the torrent-like velocity of the stream, could not be afforded them. Many lives were lost, and the amount of property destroyed by this flood is beyond all estimate. Many drowning people and dead bodies floated down the Mississippi. A house, with a whole family inside of it, went over the Falls of Ohio. Boats passed over fields and plantations, far beyond the usual limits of the river, and took the frightened inhabitants from the upper stories and roofs of their houses, to which they had been driven for refuge from the waters. The levees or embankments made at different places, as defences against the river, were broken through. It is believed that more than four hundred human beings perished in this flood. Red River was higher in January of this year than ever it was before, within the recollection of man, and higher than ever it has been since. All the lands in the immediate neighborhood of that river were desolated, and every vestige of cultivation was destroyed. In June of this year, the Mississippi, at St. Louis, was eleven miles wide, and was on a level with the second story windows of the houses on the levee at that city. Many houses were swept away and great numbers of cattle were drowned. The loss of property was immense. An obelisk about twenty feet high has been erected on the levee below Market street, St. Louis, to designate the height of the water at the time of this flood.

In March, 1849, the water was ten feet deep in some of the streets of New Orleans. This was the most destructive flood that ever visited that city. The plantations above were overflowed, and the rush of the water over the fields, in some places, was perfectly irresistible, carrying away everything which opposed the current, which was believed to move at the rate of sixty miles per hour. The damage sustained by planters and others was estimated at $60,000,000.

In April, 1852, the Ohio, at Wheeling and Pittsburgh, rose as high as it did in 1832. There was a great destruction of property along the river, and many lives were lost.

EXPLOSION OF THE POCAHONTAS.

The disaster about to be related, took place on Arkansas river, ten miles below Dardanella, on the 14th day of March, 1852. While rounding out from a wood-yard, she collapsed both flues of her middle boiler, blowing out principally aft. Eighteen persons were scalded, of whom eight died before eleven o'clock on the following morning. The boat took fire immediately after the explosion, but was saved by the strenuous exertions of the officers and crew, assisted by the passengers.

KILLED.—Wm. Pettit, second engineer, Quincy, Ill.; Michael Maguire, fireman, Ireland; Henry Cook, first cook, Missouri; Lavinia Barker, Simon Barker and Mourning Barker, passengers, of Indiana; Joseph and John A. McDonald, passengers.

SCALDED.—Wm. Sanford, (badly,) third engineer, St. Louis; Wm. Blythe, fireman, Ireland; Wm. Morgan, deck hand, New Orleans; Matilda Housely, passenger, Indiana; Thomas Barker, infant, (badly,) Indiana; W. J. McDonald and son, Susan McDonald, and Amanda Housely, of Indiana, passengers, and the first engineer.

COLLISION OF THE GULNARE AND WESTWOOD.

While on her way from St. Louis to New Orleans, with a valuable cargo, the steamboat Gulnare, September 8, 1844, came in contact with the steamer Westwood, about twenty miles above Helena. The Gulnare was struck on the starboard side, opposite the main hatch, and was so badly broken up that she sunk within three minutes. The passengers and crew escaped, with the exception of two Germans and a United States soldier, who were deck passengers. These three persons were drowned. The soldier was much intoxicated. One of the Germans lost his life while attempting to save his baggage. The Gulnare was heavily laden, and only a small part of her cargo was saved.

EXPLOSION AND BURNING OF THE ST. JOSEPH.

This disaster took place at the mouth of Arkansas river, January 12, 1850. The St. Joseph was from New Orleans, bound to St. Louis, with a valuable cargo on board. This steamer and the South America were running side by side at the time of the accident. The larboard boiler of the St. Joseph exploded, and the boat soon after took fire. There were many deck passengers on board, some of whom plunged into the river. The boiler was blown backward, instantly killing a boy at the engine, and mortally wounding the second engineer, who died the next day. A Mr. Moore, of Glasgow, Mo., was also mortally wounded. He lingered in great agony for twenty-four hours, having every particle of skin pealed from his body. It is believed that eight or ten persons were drowned.

We have stated above that the steamer South America was near the St. Joseph at the time of the accident. Captain Baker, of the last named boat, took $3000 from the iron chest and handed it to the clerk of the South America for safe keeping. On the next day, Captain Baker, wishing to pay off his men, desired to have his money back, but the clerk of the South America would give him but $300, claiming the balance for salvage. Captain Baker stopped at Memphis, in order to take legal measures for the recovery of his money. The South America was attached at that port, and the Sheriff took possession and detained her for twenty-four hours. In the meanwhile, the facts of the case coming to the knowledge of the citizens, caused such a general feeling of indignation, that the officers of the South America being apprehensive of popular vengeance, agreed to refund the money to Captain Baker. The behaviour of Captain Greenlee to the crew and passengers of the St. Joseph's, is represented as inhuman in the highest degree.

LOSS OF THE STEAMBOAT MECHANIC.

(WITH GENERAL LAFAYETTE ON BOARD.)

The steamboat Mechanic had been chartered at Nashville for the conveyance of General Lafayette and suite to Marietta, Ohio. She departed from the former place on Friday morning, May 6th, 1825, having on board, besides her officers and crew, General Lafayette, General Carroll and staff, Governor Coles, of Illinois, General O'Fallon, Major Nash, of Missouri, and several other gentlemen as passengers. On the following Sunday, about 12 o'clock, midnight, while the steamer was ascending the Ohio, and when near the mouth of Deer Creek, about one hundred and twenty-five miles below Louisville, a severe shock was felt by the persons on board, and it was soon ascertained that the boat had struck some object under the surface of the

SINKING OF THE MECHANIC.

water. The commander, Capt. Hall, presently announced to the passengers in the cabin that the boat had snagged. Capt. Hall then caused the yawl to be made ready to convey General Lafayette and the other passengers ashore. In the meanwhile, the General had been aroused from his slumbers, and was soon prepared to leave the steamer. As the night was very dark, and great confusion prevailed on board, General Lafayette, while attempting to descend into the yawl, was precipitated into the river and would have been drowned but for the assistance of one of the deck hands, whose name we have been unable to ascertain. The General, although far advanced in age, was able to keep himself above water until help arrived. He lost eight thousand dollars in money, besides his carriage, clothing, &c., but finally reached the shore in safety.

While Capt. Hall was devoting all his attention to the preservation of his passengers, his desk, containing one thousand three hundred dollars, was lost overboard and was never recovered.

EXPLOSION OF THE PILOT.

The steam tow-boat Pilot, Capt. Brown, bursted all her boilers, on March 14th, 1845, a short distance below New Orleans, while engaged in towing the brig Pioneer up to that city. Some fragments of the boat were thrown into the air with such force as to carry away the top-gallant mast and fore top-gallant yard of the Pioneer.

List of Killed.—William B. Fagan, first engineer; Mr. Barry, a passenger; Mr. Davis, steersman; and a fireman, name not mentioned.

Wounded.—William Webster, branch pilot; William Reilly, second engineer; Capt. Brown; three deck-hands and four firemen.

Capt. Brown was thrown off the vessel by the concussion and was taken out of the water by the crew of the brig.

BURNING OF THE SOUTH AMERICA.

This steamer was destroyed by fire on the Mississippi river, nine miles above New Orleans, December 17th, 1850. About forty lives were lost. Sixteen of those who perished were United States soldiers; the rest were deck hands, and persons belonging to the boat. One woman was killed, viz: Mrs. White, the wife of the carpenter. In order to save her from the flames, her husband threw her into the river and then sprung after her, but could not save her.

List of Killed.—Jackson Knowles, head cook; William Sheppard, porter; a young man from Elizabethtown, Ill., name unknown; three firemen; a collier, wife and child; the following United States soldiers, viz.: Gilder, Hunt, Franks, Rean, Rosendale, Drury, Dumont, Dailey, Duyer, Gerard, Hyer, Johnston, Kimble, Loomis, Werther, Lind, and Donnie; several deck passengers, names unknown, were also lost.

All the baggage belonging to the passengers, and the boat's books and papers, were destroyed.

BURNING OF TWENTY-THREE STEAMERS AT ST. LOUIS.

AWFUL AND DESTRUCTIVE CONFLAGRATION AT ST. LOUIS.

TWENTY-THREE STEAMBOATS BURNED, SEVERAL SQUARES IN ASHES.

The prosperous and beautiful city of St. Louis, Mo., was visited on the night of 17th May, 1849, by a most terrible conflagration, which destroyed property to the amount of $5,000,000. The fire broke out about 10 o'clock, P. M., near the river, at the corner of Locust street and the Levee, where the corner house and the three buildings above on the Levee were destroyed. From thence the flames spread across Locust street, sweeping every house, (with but one exception,) in the blocks fronting on the Levee and Main street, and extending from Locust street southward to Chestnut street, a distance of three squares. The fire then advanced up Chestnut street and crossed over to the next block south, at the junction of Commercial alley with this street, then extending from the alley to Main street, and down that to Market street, consuming everything in its route, except two buildings at the corner of Market street and Commercial alley. At the intersection of Market and Main streets, the flames crossed diagonally to the Market Street House, and followed both sides of Market street up to Second street. Then, crossing Main street, the flames again swept every building, from Locust to Market street, except a row of four-story fire-proof warehouses just below Locust street. Thence the destructive element proceeded up Pine, Chestnut and Market streets, consuming every house in the two blocks between the streets just mentioned and Main and Second streets, together with nearly half the block north of Olive street.

At this point the ravages of the fire in this part of the city were stayed; but in order to produce this effect, it was found necessary to blow up two or three houses at the corner of Market and Second streets. Several persons were killed by the explosion, one of whom was Mr. Targee, a well known citizen of St. Louis. The fragments of one of the dead bodies were found on the opposite side of the street; one piece near the junction of Walnut and Second streets, and a thigh-bone and foot belonging to another body, near the lower end of Walnut street, two or three squares from the spot where the houses were blown up. These, with the body of a boy who was burned on the Levee, were supposed to constitute the remains of four persons who had perished in the conflagration.

Although the progress of the fire was arrested at the point designated above, the flames continued to spread southward; having made another start at the foot of Elm street, and spreading diagonally through the block, it again reached Main street, extending down to Spruce street, a distance, north and south, of two squares. Then crossing Main Street, it swept all before it to within a short distance of Third street, three squares to the west of its starting point. At Main street, the flames crossed Elm street, and consumed one fourth of the block north of Elm and west of Main streets. From the foot of Elm street, up its southern side to Second street, a distance of two squares, not a house was left standing. This dreadful calamity reduced many families from comfortable circumstances to perfect destitution. Hundreds of estimable people were made houseless.

"Cast abandoned on the world's wide stage,
And doomed in scanty poverty to roam."

About ten o'clock, P. M., the fire, by some means, was communicated to the steamer White Cloud. There was quite a fleet of steamboats moored at the Levee at this time. The Eudora was lying above the White Cloud, and the Edward Bates below it; the Belle Isle and Julia were moored below the Bates. A strong wind was blowing from the north-west at the time the fire commenced its devastations among the boats. The flames were soon communicated from the White Cloud to the Eudora, and the Edward Bates caught almost at the same moment.

The hawsers of this vessel were either cut or severed by the fire, and she then drifted into the current, carrying destruction to almost all the boats stationed south of her. As the wind set in towards the wharf, the cables were hauled in and they drifted out into the current, yet the flaming vessel followed them up with a speed from which it seemed impossible for them to escape. She appeared to be animated by some intelligent spirit, which prompted her to involve the others in that destruction to which she herself was doomed. The fleet of vessels being loosened from their moorings, were driven about, the sport of the wind and the waves, with nobody on board to control their motions.

Within half an hour from the time the conflagration commenced among the boats, twenty-three of them had been surrendered to the fury of the flames, and half a million dollars worth of property was destroyed. The spectacle was awful but magnificent; a spectacle to which no pencil could do justice, but not the less dreadful and horrifying to every spectator.

List of Boats Destroyed.—American Eagle, Cossan, Master, Keokuk and Upper Mississippi packet; valued at $14,000; total loss; insured for $3,500 at Pittsburgh; no cargo.

Alice, Kennett, Master, Missouri river packet; valued at $18,000; total loss; insured for $12,000.

Alexander Hamilton, Hooper, Master, Missouri river packet; valued at $15,000; total loss; insured for $10,500 in eastern offices; no cargo.

Acadia, John Russell, Master, Illinois river packet; valued at $4,000; total loss; fully insured in eastern offices; cargo valued at $1,000.

Boreas No. 3, Bernard, Master, Missouri river packet; valued at $14,500; total loss; insured for $11 500 in city offices; no cargo.

Belle Isle, Smith, Master, New Orleans trader; valued at $10,000; total loss; insured for $8,000 at New Orleans; no cargo.

Eliza Stewart, H. McKee, Master, Missouri river trader; valued at $9,000; total loss; insured for nearly the full value at Nashville; no cargo.

Eudora, Ealer, Master, New Orleans and St. Louis trader; valued at $16,000; total loss; insured for $10,500 at St. Louis; no cargo.

Edward Bates, Randolph, Master, Keokuk packet; valued at $22,500; total loss; insured for $15,000 at St. Louis; no cargo.

Frolic, Ringling, Master, tow-boat; valued at $1,500; total loss; no insurance; no cargo.

Kit Carson, Goddin, Master, Missouri river packet; valued at $16,000; total loss; insured for $8,000 at St. Louis; cargo valued at $3,000.

Mameluke, Smithers, Master, New Orleans and St. Louis trader; valued at $30,000; total loss; insured for $20,000 at Louisville, Columbus, &c.

Mandan, Beers, Master, Missouri river trader; valued at $14,000; total loss; insured for $10,500 at St. Louis; no cargo.

Montauk, Moorhouse, Master, Upper Mississippi trader; valued at $16,000; total loss; insured for $10,000 at St. Louis, &c.; cargo valued at $8,000.

Martha, D. Finch, Master, Missouri river trader; valued at $10,000; total loss; fully insured at St. Louis; cargo valued at $30,000; also insured.

Prairie State, Baldwin, Master, Illinois river packet; valued at $26,000; total loss; insured in eastern offices for $18,000; cargo valued at $3,000

Redwing, Barger, Master, Upper Mississippi trader; valued at $6,000; total loss; no insurance; cargo valued at $3,000.

St. Peter's, Ward, Master, Upper Mississippi trader; valued at $12,000; total loss; insured for $9,000 at Nashville and Louisville; no cargo.

Sarah, Young, Master, New Orleans and St. Louis trader; valued at $35,000; total loss.

Taglioni, Marshall, Master, Pittsburgh and St. Louis trader; valued at $20,000; total loss; insured for nearly the full value at Pittsburgh; cargo valued at $15,000.

Timour, Miller, Master, Missouri river trader; valued at $25,000; total loss; insured for $18,000 at St. Louis, &c.; cargo valued at $6,000.

White Cloud, Adams, Master, New Orleans and St. Louis trader; valued at $3,000; total loss; fully insured; no cargo.

And a Ferry boat, valued at $3,000.

EXPLOSION OF THE CONCORDIA.

On the 16th of September, 1848, the steamer Concordia burst all her boilers, when about to land passengers at Plaquemine, La. All the upper works were demolished, and some fragments of them were blown to the distance of three hundred yards. The cabin passengers all escaped uninjured. Twenty-eight of the crew and deck passengers were killed, and eight or ten persons were wounded.

KILLED.—B. M. McDowell, clerk ; Michael McQuaide, deck hand ; Henry Jordon, a colored fireman ; two cabin boys ; a fireman, name not mentioned ; Robert and Edward Davis, colored men ; and about twenty deck passengers, names unknown.

WOUNDED.—Capt. H. Pease (mortally) ; John F. Mosely, second clerk ; John Tabbot, colored fireman ; John Henderson, first engineer; F. W. Colles, book-keeper ; Samuel Bunnall, colored fireman. Capt. Pease died soon after the accident.

EXPLOSION OF THE TIMOUR NO. 2.

The steamboat Timour No. 2 exploded, September 25th, 1854, while lying at Edwards' wood-yard, on the Missouri river, three miles below Jefferson City. She was taking in wood at the time. All her boilers, three in number, exploded at the same moment, wrecking all the forward part as far as the wheel-houses, killing fifteen persons, and wounding five or six others. The boat sunk soon after the explosion. She had a valuable cargo, the greater part of which was lost. The names of the sufferers are not mentioned, with the exception of Mr. Charles Dix, the Captain's brother, who was blown overboard and drowned.

SINKING OF THE BELLE ZANE.

On the eighth of January, 1845, the steamboat Belle Zane, while on her way from Zanesville, Ohio, to New Orleans, struck a snag in the Mississippi, about twelve miles below the mouth of White river, and immediately turned *bottom upward!* This terrible accident took place in the middle of an exceedingly cold night. Of ninety persons who were on board a moment before the disaster, only fifty escaped drowning—and many of those who succeeded in reaching the shore were afterwards frozen to death. At the time the boat was snagged, the passengers were all in their berths; those who were able to extricate themselves when the boat suddenly turned over, had scarcely any clothing to protect them from the inclemency of the weather. No situation could be more wretched than that of the people who escaped to the beach, almost naked, unsheltered and drenched with water on a freezing night in December. They remained in this miserable situation for nearly two hours, when the steamboat Diamond came down and took off all who remained alive, sixteen in number. There were five ladies on board, all of whom were saved in the yawl. The feet and hands of some of the survivors were so badly frozen that amputation was necessary.

SINKING OF THE BELLE ZANE.

The following is a list of those who perished, as far as their names could be ascertained:—Dr. Brant, Ohio; Abner Jones, C. Banks, Mrs. Williams, two daughters and a colored slave, Miss.; Hettie Frazier and cousin, name unknown, Boston; Edward Bossing and son, Illinois; Mrs. Wilkes and family, consisting of eight persons; seven deck hands, fourteen slaves, and thirty other names unknown. Sixteen bodies were picked up, including four ladies, and buried on the banks of the Mississippi.

List of Steamboats Afloat

ON

THE WESTERN RIVERS.

Names.	Where Built.	When Built.	Tonnage.	Names.	Where Built.	When Built.	Tonnage.
Anglo Norman,	New Orleans,	1850	559	Aleonia,	Elizabeth,	1851	286
Alabama,	Cincinnati,	1851	298	Alliquippa,	Pittsburgh,	1845	306
Alice,	Cincinnati,	1852	130	Albertine,	Louisville,	1855	160
Aid, U. S.	Zanesville,	1852	125	Anawan,	Cincinnati,	1855	163
Audibon,	Murraysville,	1853	191	Alton,	Brownsville,	1847	345
Ariel,	Cincinnati,	1854	169	Aleck Scott,	St. Louis,	1848	710
Ambassador,	do.	1854	173	Atlantic,	Cincinnati,	1848	667
Anderson, Paul	Brownsville,	1850	310	Alliquippa,	Pittsburgh,	1844	214
Ambassador,	Monongahela,	1851	367	Antelope,	New Albany,	1854	600
Allegheny,	Shousetown,	1852	520	Bayard, Stephen	West Elizabeth,	1851	156
Alliance,	do.	1852	136	Barker, B. B.	McKeesport,	1852	83
Active,	Brownsville,	1852	52	Bayard, Col.	do.	1852	177
Arkansas,	California,	1852	246	Bedford,	Cristler's Ldg.,	1852	181
Alabama,	Elizabeth,	1852	213	Ben Bolt,	California,	1853	228
America, North	do.	1852	270	Bagaley,	Belle Vernon,	1854	396
Arctic,	Shousetown,	1852	351	Bay City,	Brownsville,	1854	228
Australia,	Brownsville,	1853	289	Baird, Wm.	Elizabeth,	1855	287
Adams, Alvin	McKeesport,	1853	592	Brown, Dick	McKeesport,	1855	57
Aubry, F. H.	Brownsville,	1853	247	Blake, Henry	Allegheny City,	1855	29
Adriance,	Shousetown,	1853	167	Buckeye,	Cincinnati,	1849	377
Arabia,	Brownsville,	1853	222	Boone,	do.	1848	196
Alida,	Belle Vernon,	1853	94	Bealer, C.	do.	1854	263
Altoona,	Brownsville,	1853	166	Bostona,	do.	1854	356
Adelia,	California,	1853	127	Boon, Dan'l.	do.	1854	381
Augusta,	Elizabeth,	1853	29	Bullitt, Fanny	Louisville,	1854	439
Admiral,	McKeesport,	1853	245	Black Locust,	Jeffersonville,	1853	106
Alice,	California,	1853	72	Boulder,	Louisville,	1854	78
Adriatic,	Shousetown,	1855	424	Buckeye,	Wellsville,	1853	48
Alma,	Belle Vernon,	1855	311	Buck, John,	California,	1854	111
Amazon,	do.	1855	410	Bridge City,	Wheeling,	1854	200
Argonaut,	Brownsville,	1855	229	Buckeye Belle,	Marietta,	1852	156
Adelaide,	Louisville,	1853	136	Bridges, H.	New Albany,	1855	176
Alada,	Belle Vernon,	1853	94	Beaty, Dr.	Louisville,	1851	281
Alabamian,	Alabama,	1853	198	Bella Donna,	do.	1852	468
Ariel,	Wheeling,	1855	31	Biebe, Junius,	Algiers,	1853	525
Albemarle,	do.	1855	186	Belle Godin,	Brownsville,	1854	189
Atlanta,	do.	1854	142	Billow,	Allegheny City,	1854	84
Alto,	Pittsburgh,	1850	37	Brazil,	McKeesport,	1854	211
Argyle,	Freedom,	1853	319	Beauty,	Newport,	1852	169
America, South	McKeesport,	1854	284	Bay State,	Cincinnati,	1852	210
Aubry, Major	Louisville,	1853	79	Banner State,	do.	1851	254
Amanda,	do.	1852	143	Buckeye Belle,	Marietta,	1852	156
Allegheny Belle,3	Brownsville,	1852	129	Buckeye State,	Shousetown,	1850	437
Alhambra,	McKeesport,	1854	187	Badger State,	California,	1850	127
Aunt Letty,	Elizabeth,	1855	304	Belle Quigley,	Brownsville,	1850	133
All Oak,	Chorester's Ldg.,	1854	57	Barker, B. B.	McKeesport,	1850	83
Atlanta,	Honey Comb, Ala.	1851	112	Bell, Jno.	Louisville,	1855	209
Antionette, Doug.	Cincinnati,	1854	242	Bluff City,	do.	1854	252
Anna,	New Albany,	1849	84	Burns, Lewis	Brownsville,	1855	62
Albree, Geo.	Brownsville,	1854	181	Blue Wing,	Louisville,	1850	170
Aquilla,	West Newton,	1854	59	Belle Key,	New Albany,	1853	525
Arkansas,	California,	1852	246	Baltimore,	Martinsville,	1853	637

Names.	Where Built.	When Built.	Tonnage.	Names.	Where Built.	When Built.	Tonnage.
Brown, Emma	Tennessee,	1854	108	Campbell, Ben	Shousetown,	1850	287
Belleville,	Algiers.	1851	128	Coursin, Ben	Cincinnati,	1854	161
Brunette,	Louisville,	1852	228	City of Cairo,	Louisville,	1855	199
Blanche Lewis,	Pittsburgh,	1855	200	Coosa Belle,	do.	1855	186
Brown, Emma	Memphis,	1854	108	Collier, Geo.	New Albany,	1851	540
Beardstown,	St. Louis,	1847	78	Darian, Major	Freedom,	1852	10
Black Hawk,	Rock Island,	1852	84	Diurnal,	Monongahela,	1850	199
Bluff City,	St. Louis,	1853	397	Daugherty, M. L.	Elizabeth,	1853	95
Belfast,	do.	1854	781	Delegate,	do.	1854	208
Bridge City,	Fish Creek,	1853	200	Done, J. H.	Shousetown,	1854	212
Colorado,	Monongahela,	1850	98	Denny, W. H.	California,	1855	276
Cleona,	West Elizabeth,	1850	204	Delta,	Cincinnati,	1849	396
Cataract,	do.	1851	283	Dunkirk,	do.	1851	377
Corn Planter,	McKeesport,	1851	178	Diana,	do.	1849	188
Colbert,	West Elizabeth,	1855	165	Delaware,	do.	1851	501
Clara,	Monongahela,	1851	248	Drennen, Col.	do.	1852	126
Clarion,	do.	1851	73	Duke,	do.	1853	348
Caspian,	West Elizabeth,	1851	249	Dutchess,	do.	1853	226
Calm,	McKeesport,	1852	26	Davenport,	do.	1855	138
Convers, Dan.	do.	1852	163	Downs, S. W.	Louisville,	1851	237
Cleopatra,	Monongahela,	1852	152	Defiance,	Cincinnati,	1849	544
Clara Dean,	Brownsville,	1853	190	Delia,	Louisville,	1851	311
Castle Garden,	McKeesport,	1853	162	Dean, Emma	Cincinnati,	1851	212
Caledonia,	do.	1853	239	Dean, Jennie	McKeesport,	1852	485
Crescent City,	Elizabeth,	1854	282	Day, D.	Cincinnati,	1852	213
Cassel, Kate	California,	1854	167	Dickinson, Col.	do.	1850	222
Convoy,	Freedom,	1854	123	Davis, A. L.	Nashville,	1853	102
City of Knoxville,	California,	1854	76	Daniel, Thos. M.	Madisonville,	1853	540
Conewago,	Brownsville,	1854	186	Dean, Jesse	Pittsburgh,	1855	186
Chicago,	California,	1854	219	Dubuque,	Elizabethtown,	1847	169
Chenoweth, J. S.	Haverhill,	1851	310	Enterprize,	Zanesville,	1850	200
Cloon, Sam.	Cincinnati,	1851	301	Echo,	Cincinnati,	1850	161
Charleston,	do.	1852	345	Europa,	do.	1850	349
Condor, 3.	Pomeroy,	1853	368	Empire State,	Elizabeth,	1849	303
Chouteau, Henry	Cincinnati,	1853	623	Eliza,	Cincinnati,	1852	349
Clark, B. E.	Fulton,	1853	200	Early, J. D.	do.	1853	348
Commodore,	do.	1853	129	Editor,	Brownsville,	1851	247
Crescent City,	Cincinnati,	1854	688	Elk,	Elizabeth.	1851	62
City Belle,	Murraysville,	1854	216	Excel,	McKeesport,	1851	79
Chambers, Col. A. [B.	Cincinnati.	1855	411	Elvira,	Brownsville,	1851	222
Cherokee,	New Albany,	1850	417	Elephant,	do.	1851	425
Creole,	Green Point,	1852	317	Envoy,	West Elizabeth,	1852	179
Caddo, 2	Louisville,	1851	274	Exchange,	Brownsville,	1852	128
Carrier,	Marietta,	1853	98	Empress,	Lowell,	1852	137
Capital,	Louisville,	1855	149	Eagle,	Shousetown.	1852	201
Cobb, R. L.	do.	1855	197	Equinox,	Monongahela,	1852	297
Clinton,	Elizabeth,	1850	34	Equator,	Beaver	1853	62
City of Wheeling,	Wheeling,	1853	439	Edinburg,	Brownsville,	1854	283
Crystal Palace,	Freedom.	1853	541	Endeavor,	Freedom,	1854	200
Colbert,	West Elizabeth,	1851	168	Eclipse,	California,	1854	1[illegible]6
Compromise,	Monongahela,	1851	270	Empire,	do.	1854	153
City of Huntsville	Elizabeth,	1852	238	Ella,	Elizabeth,	1854	173
Chevoit,	California,	1853	176	Evansville,	W. Brownsville,	1854	155
Cuba,	Brownsville,	1853	158	Empire City,	California	1854	268
Challenge,	Shousetown,	1854	229	Eaves, W. A.	Brownsville,	1854	146
Clipper,	Belle Vernon,	1855	68	Empress,	Louisville,	1853	693
Carson, J. B.	Shousetown,	1855	186	Eclipse.	New Albany,	1852	1117
Courier,	Parkersburg,	1852	165	Exchange,	Brownsville,	1849	110
C. D. Jr.	Louisville,	1853	347	Eclipse,	Belle Vernon,	1853	216
Ceres,	do.	1852	218	Embassy,	Wheeling.	1848	237
Clifton,	Glassgo, W.	1855	183	Eastport,	New Albany,	1852	570
Cline, J. G.	Madison,	1853	295	Eolian,	Brownsville,	1855	205
Cumberland Val.,	Louisville,	1850	199	Eunice,	Pittsburgh,	1855	206
Cabinet,	Wheeling,	1849	190	Effie Afton,	Cincinnati,	1855	400
Champion,	Cincinnati,	1854	147	Excelsior,	Brownsville,	1849	172
Cincinnati,	Pittsburgh,	1850	333	Eunice,	Brownsville,	1855	232
Champion, 1	Cincinnati,	1851	90	Empire,	New Albany,	1849	449

Names.	Where Built.	When Built.	Tonnage	Names.	Where Built.	When Built.	Tonnage
Frisbee, Kate,	Brooklyn,	1855	457	Guthrie, James,	Louisville,	1853	395
Forrest Rose,	California,	1852	205	Grapeshot,	do.	1855	179
Fawn,	Louisville,	1853	182	Given, D. A.	Paducah,	1853	184
Farrar, Fanny	Paducah,	1853	134	Glaze, Alice W.	Louisville,	1853	161
Florida,	Louisville,	1855	546	Grace Darling,	Madison,	1855	261
Falls City,	do.	1853	665	Graff, Henry,	Belle Vernon,	1855	250
Fort Henry,	Wheeling,	1853	157	Georgetown,	Lone Island,	1852	103
Freeman, Ra'dm.	Shousetown,	1850	493	Gaty, Sam.	St. Louis,	1853	296
Franklin,	do.	1851	19	Hartford,	Monongahela,	1851	144
Farward, Walter 2	Pittsburgh,	1851	39	Heroine,	Brownsville,	1851	95
Franklin, Jane,	Freedom,	1851	197	Harris, J. M.	Shousetown,	1851	123
Franklin,	Brownsville,	1851	181	Huron,	Christler's Ldg.	1851	168
Forest City,	do.	1851	207	Hays, C.	Elizabeth,	1851	240
Falcon,	McKeesport,	1851	180	Honduras,	Brownsville,	1852	296
Fanny Fern,	California,	1853	182	Herald,	do.	1852	295
Forrester,	Brownsville,	1854	188	Herron, Jno.	McKeesport,	1853	56
Fairfield,	Freedom,	1854	159	Henrietta,	California,	1853	179
Fairy Queen,	Belle Vernon,	1854	169	Hurricane,	Pittsburg,	1853	58
Franklin, Benj.	Brownsville,	1854	192	Hornet,	W. Brownsville,	1853	168
Fremont, J. C.	California,	1854	316	Hercules,	McKeesport,	1854	151
Falls City,	Wellsville,	1855	183	Hunter,	Allegheny City,	1854	42
Flora,	California,	1855	160	Hero,	Brownsville,	1853	60
Friendship,	Wheeling,	1851	98	Hawk Eye,	West Newton,	1854	46
Forest Queen,	Cincinnati,	1851	283	Harris, Fanny,	Brownsville,	1855	160
Fairy,	do.	1851	101	Hoosier State,	Cincinnati,	1850	344
Franklin, Benj.	do.	1848	473	Hungarian,	Elizabeth,	1850	279
Falcon,	McKeesport,	1851	441	Haverhill,	Haverhill,	1851	70
Flag,	Cincinnati,	1853	235	Harris, Maj. A.	Cincinnati,	1852	102
Fashion, 2	Elizabeth,	1849	88	Hickman,	do.	1855	228
Fire Canoe,	Lawrence,	1854	166	Highflyer,	Madison,	1854	492
F. K., Jr.	Ironton,	1854	61	Hope,	Louisville,	1855	193
Fulton,	Elizabeth,	1852	206	Hartsville,	Nashville,	1853	107
Farmer, W. W.	Louisville,	1854	207	Hill, H. R. M.	New Albany,	1852	603
Franklin, Benj.	do.	1855	733	Huntsville, City of	Elizabeth,	1852	238
Fashion,	do.	1853	408	Howard, E.	New Albany,	1852	390
Freighter,	Zanesville,	1855	93	Hercules,	Cincinnati,	1843	521
Flying Cloud,	Cincinnati,	1854	540	Humbolt,	do.	1855	513
Fusilier, A.	Parish St. Mary,	1851	358	Hawk Eye,	Davenport,	1852	32
Fanny Fern,	Shreveport,	1855	155	Harmon, Emma	Clarksville,	1854	125
Garth, Molly	Elizabeth,	1851	96	Illinois,	Brownsville,	1853	682
Georgia,	do.	1851	326	Illinois Belle,	McKeesport,	1854	148
Granite State,	W. Elizabeth,	1852	295	Ironton,	Cincinnati,	1850	189
Guadalupe,	do.	1853	139	Indiana,	do.	1850	369
Golden State,	McKeesport,	1852	298	Iris,	Rising Sun,	1852	87
Georgetown,	Lone Island,	1852	183	Irene,	Elizabeth,	1850	125
Gazelle,	Brownsville,	1854	205	Ingomar,	Louisville,	1854	731
Gray Cloud,	Elizabeth,	1854	246	Isabella,	Jeffersonville,	1849	249
Genoa,	California,	1854	227	Iowa,	Freedom,	1855	200
Grand Turk,	McKeesport,	1854	247	Ion,	Fox River,	1853	57
Great West,	California,	1855	230	Jefferson,	Elizabeth,	1850	94
Grapeshot,	do.	1855	153	Johnston, Mat,	do.	1851	45
Gipsey,	do.	1855	132	Justice,	West Newton,	1851	96
Gladiator,	Freedom,	1850	236	Jenkins, J.	Elizabeth,	1852	146
Gem,	Cincinnati,	1850	298	Juniatta,	Allegheny City,	1852	30
Gulnare,	do,	1849	347	Jefferson,	McKeesport,	1852	189
Grampus,	Rising Sun,	1851	97	Jeanette,	Elizabeth,	1854	145
Golden Era,	Wheeling,	1852	249	Jones, R. M.	Newport,	1851	193
Grand Prairie,	Gallopolis,	1852	261	Jacobs,	Maysville,	1854	74
Golden Gate,	Madison,	1852	317	Jones, Paul	McKeesport,	1855	354
Greenwood, Mos.	Cincinnati,	1852	268	Jake Sharp,	Sharp's Landing,	1854	34
Gazelle,	do.	1853	38	Jeanie Deans,	St. Louis,	1852	442
Glendale,	do.	1853	394	Kate,	McKeesport,	1851	180
Graham, N. W.	Covington,	1853	287	Keeling, Frank	Monongahela,	1852	115
Galena,	Madison,	1854	297	Keystone,	Brownsville,	1853	307
Gregoire, A. L.	Cincinnati,	1854	173	Kenton,	Cincinnati,	1848	271
Gales, Jo.	do.	1855	208	Kennett, L. M.	do.	1852	600
Garvin, Wm.	Louisville,	1853	269	Keys, Dick	do.	1853	369

Names.	Where Built.	When Built.	Tonnage.	Names.	Where Built.	When Built.	Tonnage.
Knox, Wm.	Point Harmer,	1852	200	Monongа. Belle,	Morgantown,	1854	74
Kimball, B. F.	New Albany,	1851	312	Minnesota Belle,	Belle Vernon,	1854	226
Kossuth, Gov.	Keokuk,	1852	89	Minerva,	Brownsville,	1854	199
Kentucky No. 2,	Evansville,	1851	149	Monongahela,	do.	1855	335
Keokuk,	Metropolis,	1855	435	May, Lucy,	W. Brownsville,	1855	172
Kimbrough, S.	L. Winnebago,	1852	66	Mason, A. G.	do.	1855	170
Lunette,	McKeesport,	1852	166	McNeal, E. P.	Cincinnati,	1850	204
Lake Erie,	Brownsville,	1851	130	Memphis, No. 2	do.	1852	303
Luzerne,	do.	1852	180	May Queen,	Monongahela,	1850	68
Liberty, No. 2	Alleghany City,	1852	30	Midas,	Cincinnati,	1851	309
Lookout,	Monongahela,	1853	176	Mediator,	do.	1852	422
Lyon, James,	Belle Vernon,	1853	190	Monarch,	Fulton,	1853	407
Latrobe,	Brownsville,	1853	159	Miller, Nettie	Smithland,	1554	146
Lazier, J.	do.	1854	73	Marion,	Louisville,	1854	133
Louisville,	do.	1854	155	Madona,	do.	1853	95
Lynch, D.	Elizabeth,	1854	50	Magnolia Banner,	do.	1855	151
Laimer, Gen.	do.	1854	92	Monticello,	Freedom,	1852	117
Lebanon,	Brownsville,	1855	226	Mosby, D. B.	Cincinnati,	1849	298
Laclide,	California,	1855	197	Music,	Louisville,	1850	473
Louisa,	Cincinnati,	1850	199	Magnolia,	New Albany,	1850	744
Lancaster, No. 2	do.	1848	168	Morrisetti,	do.	1849	650
Lelia, No. 2	do.	1851	134	McRea, R. W.	Louisville,	1853	323
Lady Pike,	Wheeling,	1851	240	Madison,	Cincinnati,	1853	399
Lee, Ben.	Cincinnati,	1852	122	Moses McLellan,	do.	1855	400
Lone Star,	Louisville,	1854	126	Martha, No. 2	Shousetown,	1849	180
Lind, Jenny	Zanesville,	1852	107	Movastar,	Naples,	1849	140
Logan,	Louisville,	1853	150	Minesota,	Elizabethtown,	1849	149
Lark,	Pittsburgh,	1853	45	Martha Jewett,	Hannibal,	1852	408
La Belle,	Wheeling,	1853	130	Mary C.	Rockingham,	1852	158
Louisa,	Paducah,	1851	81	Marengo,	Pittsburgh,	1855	325
Lecompte,	Louisville,	1855	238	Milburn, N. L.	Iowaville,	1853	76
Lake, Lizzie	Smithland,	1855	54	New York,	Monongahela,	1852	287
Latona, New	New Albany,	1850	397	Neptune,	Brownsville,	1852	214
Leathers, T. P.	Memphis,	1851	435	North Star,	Elizabeth,	1855	269
Lyon, Frank	Louisville,	1851	447	Northerner,	Cincinnati,	1853	400
Louisa,	Cincinnati,	1851	394	Natchez,	do.	1853	699
Laurel Hill,	New Albany,	1853	498	Nebraska,	do.	1854	683
Lancaster, No. 3	Cincinnati,	1855	257	National,	Louisville,	1854	248
Lincoln,	Monongahela,	1850	94	Niagara,	New Albany,	1855	798
Laughlin, James	Gallapolis,	1853	188	Nicholas, Jane	Wheeling,	1851	69
Linden,	do.	1853	140	Nashville,	New Albany,	1849	497
Landis, Joseph	Cincinnati,	1853	377	New St. Paul,	do.	1852	225
Lucas, Jas. H.	Louisville,	1854	476	Noble, Wm.	Cincinnati,	1849	350
Lewis, Henry	Cincinnati,	1854	480	Nominee,	Shousetown,	1848	213
Linda,	do.	1855	167	New Lucy,	St Louis,	1852	417
Lorentz, Fred.	Belle Vernon,	1855	236	Nile,	St. Joseph,	1853	26
Lewis F. Linn.	Pittsburgh,	1844	163	Obion,	Christler's Ldg.,	1851	62
Lady Franklin,	Wheeling,	1850	206	Oakland,	California,	1853	142
Luella,	Nashville,	1851	162	Oswichee,	Elizabeth,	1853	212
Lind, Jenny,	L. Winnebago,	1851	113	Ocean Wave,	do.	1854	235
Larkin, Thos. H.	St. Louis,	1855	1097	Ohio,	Cincinnati,	1849	348
Lodo,	Shreveport,	1855	60	Orb,	Wheeling,	1854	226
Messenger,	Pittsburgh,	1855	406	Oquawka,	Wellsville,	1855	48
McKee, John	McKeesport,	1850	140	Orion,	Wheeling,	1851	129
Magnolia,	Elizabeth,	1850	161	Odd Fellow,	Louisville,	1852	173
Meigs, Gov.	Freedom,	1851	145	Ophelia,	New Albany,	1850	289
Malone, Fanny	Elizabeth,	1852	87	Opelousas,	do.	1852	101
Mail, U. S.	do.	1852	196	Orleans,	do.	1852	401
Monticello,	Freedom,	1852	117	Ohio, No 2	Marietta,	1855	197
McFaden, Jno.	McKeesport,	1852	222	Ohio Belle,	Madison,	1855	406
Mar, Helen	California,	1852	180	Oceana,	St. Louis,	1854	609
Manchester,	Brownsville,	1853	293	Ogden, E. A.	do.	1855	400
Michigan.	Elizabeth	1853	482	Patton, R. M.	McKeesport,	1854	186
Morgan, Col.	Brownsville,	1853	83	Persia,	California,	1852	255
Magnolia,	Freedom,	1853	120	Prairie City,	do.	1852	302
Montauk,	California,	1853	237	Park, James,	do.	1851	258
Mansfield,	Belle Vernon,	1854	166	Philadelphia,	Shousetown,	1854	504

Names.	Where Built.	When Built	Tonnage.	Names.	Where Built.	When Built.	Tonnage.
Pennsylvania,	Shousetown,	1854	486	Star of the West,	McKeesport,	1855	435
Parthenia,	California,	1854	154	St. Louis,	Brownsville,	1855	192
Progress,	Shousetown,	1854	217	Sparhawk, G. W.	Wheeling,	1851	243
Prairie Rose,	Brownsville,	1854	248	Sciota, 2	Cincinnati,	1851	266
Princeton,	Wellsville,	1854	96	Sydonia,	do.	1851	235
Pringle, J. S.	Brownsville,	1854	307	Swallow,	do.	1851	337
Poe, Jacob	Freedom,	1855	201	Stokes, K.K.,Gen.	do.	1852	140
Prairie Bird,	Jeffersonville,	1853	65	Sparhawk, Fanny	do.	1852	259
Paull, James	Fulton,	1853	70	Susquehanna,	Elizabeth,	1852	404
Philips, Wm.	Elizabeth,	1852	67	Sun,	Cincinnati,	1852	158
Princess,	Cincinnati,	1855	716	Strader, Jacob	do.	1853	906
Planter,	New Albany,	1852	182	Seventy-six,	do.	1854	257
Pittsburgh,	Shousetown,	1851	509	Switzerland,	do.	1854	413
Pontiac,	Cincinnati,	1850	269	Stark, Molly	do.	1855	128
Post Boy,	do.	1851	158	St. Paul,	Wheeling,	1852	226
Pearl,	do.	1851	184	Somers, H. M.	Evansville,	1851	116
Philips,	Pittsburgh,	1849	67	Summit,	Brownsville,	1850	144
Pike,	Cincinnati,	1852	245	Southerner,	Jeffersonville,	1853	393
Powell, R. W.	New Albany,	1855	350	Sherman, W. A.	New Albany,	1855	195
Polar Star,	St. Louis,	1852	310	Sophia,	Louisville,	1852	42
Pounder,	Marietta,	1853	31	Scott, Thos.	Elizabeth,	1849	50
Quaker City,	California,	1853	214	Swan, Thos.	Wheeling,	1853	651
Queen of the West	Cincinnati,	1854	407	Shylock,	Nashville,	1852	45
Retrieve,	Elizabeth,	1850	204	Simpson, John	Louisville,	1850	228
Rockaway, 2	do.	1850	325	Shriver, Thos.	McKeesport,	1850	154
Ranger 2	West Newton,	1850	38	St. Charles,	Cincinnati,	1850	311
Regulator,	Shousetown,	1851	156	Storm,	do.	1848	247
Ruby,	West Elizabeth,	1851	163	Southern Belle,	Louisville,	1851	525
Ray, Thos. P.	Brownsville,	1852	66	Stacy, D. S.	do.	1852	377
Return,	do.	1852	219	Sweney, W. P.	do.	1852	200
Royal Arch,	West Elizabeth,	1852	213	St. Paul,	St. Louis,	1846	358
Rescue,	Shousetown,	1853	169	Sonora,	do.	1851	363
Rosalie,	Brownsville,	1854	158	Sass, R. F.	Pittsburgh,	1855	238
Ranchero,	Freedom,	1854	207	Sovereign,	Shousetown,	1855	337
Rochester,	Belle Vernon,	1855	199	Sarchet. Kate	Louisville,	1855	184
Reliance,	Shousetown,	1855	157	Swan,	do.	1855	192
Red Fox,	Pittsburgh,	1855	78	Sangamon,	New Albany,	1853	86
Red River,	Marietta,	1851	277	Stella Blanch,	Paducah,	1853	203
Raymond, James	Cincinnati,	1853	294	St. Mary,	St. Louis,	1855	276
Republic,	Brownsville,	1854	110	Trenton,	Monongahela,	1851	144
Rainbow,	New Albany,	1854	487	Twin City,	California,	1852	197
Reindeer,	do.	1851	409	Troy,	Brownsville,	1852	97
Raven,	McKeesport,	1852	96	Tornado,	do.	1853	93
Rodolph,	Madison,	1855	273	Time and Tide,	Freedom,	1853	131
Rock City,	Nashville,	1854	147	Tropic,	Brownsville,	1853	242
Robertson, Dr.	do.	1854	226	Tennessee,	Belle Vernon,	1853	69
Relf, J. M.	Louisville,	1851	158	Tampa,	W. Brownsville,	1853	190
Rosa,	do.	1851	265	Two Brothers,	California,	1854	193
Runaway,	Alexandria,	1853	91	Tigress,	Brownsville,	1854	176
Republic,	New Albany,	1854	747	Tweed, J. P.	Cincinnati,	1851	315
Statesman,	Brownsville,	1851	250	Tiber,	Marietta,	1851	184
Saranak,	do.	1851	352	Tecumseh,	Cincinnati,	1852	418
Salem,	Monongahela,	1851	149	Telegraph, 3	do.	1853	750
Swamp Fox,	Shousetown,	1851	281	Thomas, N. W.	do.	1853	419
Susquehanna,	Elizabeth,	1852	289	Tennessee Belle,	Paducah,	1855	248
Simonds, John	Freedom,	1852	1024	Tishomingo,	New Albany,	1852	188
St. Clair,	Elizabeth,	1852	321	Tatum, David	Louisville,	1855	374
St. Nicholas,	do.	1853	667	Trabue, James	do.	1854	244
Snowden, Sam.	McKeesport,	1853	175	Tompkins, John	do.	1855	191
Streider, Jno.	California,	1852	235	Trenton,	Monongahela,	1851	154
South Carolina,	Brownsville,	1853	194	Trabue, S. F. J.	New Albany,	1854	577
San Antonia,	Freedom,	1854	129	Touro, Judah	do.	1854	333
Sultan,	McKeesport,	1854	339	T. C. Twichell,	do.	1855	456
Sea Gull,	Jeffersonville,	1854	187	Tempest,	St. Louis,	1846	211
Shangiss,	California,	1854	185	Tiger,	Sauk County,	1849	84
Swallow,	do.	1854	198	Toledo, No. 2	Jersey City,	1851	81
Silver Wave,	Glasgo, W.	1855	245	Unicorn,	Brownsville,	1853	189

Names.	Where Built.	When Built.	Tonnage.	Names.	Where Built.	When Built.	Tonnage.
Union,	Cincinnati,	1852	209	Walsh, Edward,	Madison,	1855	598
Umpire,	do.	1855	111	White, David	do.	1853	636
Uncle Sam,	do.	1853	261	Ward, Robt. J.	New Albany,	1853	931
Umpire,	Nashville,	1854	125	Wathen, A.	Jeffersonville,	1853	158
Union,	Wellsville,	1846	31	Watts, Emma	Paducah,	1853	111
Uncle Sam,	Louisville,	1848	741	Wallis, P. C.	Louisville,	1855	230
Vinton, S. F.	Lawrence Co.,	1850	284	Wide-awake,	Wellsville,	1855	40
Venture,	Elizabeth,	1851	87	Woodruff, Jas. E.	New Albany,	1855	512
Virginia,	West Elizabeth,	1852	643	West, Sallie	Louisville,	1853	286
Vienna,	Monongahela,	1853	170	Wright, H. M.	Jeffersonville,	1852	356
Vermont,	West Elizabeth,	1848	161	Wenona,	St. Louis,	1852	247
Virogua,	Monongahela,	1849	92	Woodside, W. G.	Moundville,	1855	197
Victoria,	Louisville,	1855	161	Wallace, Sir Wm.	Pittsburgh,	1855	255
Vernon, Die	St. Louis,	1850	447	Wenona,	St. Louis,	1852	249
Winchester,	Freedom,	1851	222	Wave,	Elizabethtown,	1848	89
Watt, James	Monongahela,	1852	79	Westener,	St. Louis,	1853	462
Washington City,	Freedom,	1852	282	Winchester,	Freedom,	1851	180
Wilson, Alex.	Belle Vernon,	1854	215	Wisconsin,	Rock Island,	1849	140
Winefred,	Elizabeth,	1854	126	White Cliffs,	Little River,	1854	160
Wenona,	Belle Vernon,	1855	171	Yeatman, W. T.	Freedom,	1852	165
Whiteman, Lewis	Cincinnati,	1851	319	York State,	Brownsville,	1852	247
Winslow, R. H.	Newport,	1851	335	Young America,	Monongahela,	1853	127
Wilcox,	Cincinnati,	1851	260	Yorktown,	Pittsburgh,	1853	144
White River,	do.	1852	71	Young Sam.	Shousetown,	1855	155
Wetumpka,	do.	1852	313	Yorktown,	Cincinnati,	1848	298
Wood, Aurilla,	Wheeling,	1852	91	Yuba,	Murraysville,	1852	348
Wayne, Mattie,	Cincinnati,	1852	335	Young, Wm. C.	Louisville,	1854	199
West, Charlie	do.	1853	286	Yazoo Belle,	Jeffersonville,	1855	138
War Eagle,	Fulton,	1854	297	Zanesville,	Zanesville,	1850	71
Windsor,	Fulton,	1854	200				

A List of Steamboats at Mobile.

Names.	Where Built.	When Built.	Tonnage.	Names.	Where Built.	When Built.	Tonnage
Wilson,	Cincinnati,	1851	260	Sallie Spann,	Jeffersonville,	1852	190
Emma Watts,	Paducah,	1851	111	Magnolia,	do.	1852	326
Jeanette,	Elizabeth,	1855	144	Cuba,	Louisville,	1855	286
Advance,	Shousetown,	1853	166	Messenger,	do.	1852	390
Benj. Lee,	Cincinnati,	1852	122	Heroine,	Brownsville,	1851	94
Bloomer,	Louisville,	1852	70	Octavia,	Jeffersonville,	1852	185
Pink Toney,	do.	1852	206	Forest Monarch,	New Albany,	1848	215
S. S. Prentiss,	do.	1854	272	Sallie Carson,	do.	1852	206
Rescue,	Cincinnati,	1854	76	P. Dalman,	Louisville,	1851	365
Impire,	California,	1854	153	Col. Fremont,	Elizabethtown,	1850	75
Fairfield,	Freedom,	1854	157	Emperor,	Jeffersonville,	1848	397
Isabella,	Jeffersonville,	1849	249	Coreo,	New Albany,	1847	90
Azile,	New Albany,	1852	132	Clara,	Baltimore,	1841	94
J. R. Thompson,	New Orleans,	1851	160	Champion,	Cincinnati,	1853	158
Madison,	Memphis,	1852	169	W. W. Fry,	Jeffersonville,	1849	165
Illinois Belle,	McKeesport,	1854	148	Fashion,	New Albany,	1851	296
Cuba,	Mobile,	1855	42	Belle Gates,	do.	1851	278
W. Jones. Jr.,	do.	1853	391	Lucy Bell,	do.	1853	170
Wild Duck,	Bilori,	1850	26	Col. Clay,	New Orleans,	1851	296
Montgomery,	Cincinnati,	1854	315	Magyar,	Jeffersonville,	1849	125
Jennie Beale,	New Albany,	1852	231	Junior,	Smithland,	1852	192
Empress,	do.	1850	304	Pratt,	Report,	1847	293
Aerial,	Jeffersonville,	1854	169	Swan,	Louisville,	1850	444
Eliza Battle,	New Albany,	1852	316	Natchez,	New Orleans,	1853	388
Cremona,	do.	1852	263	Canouchet,	Providence,	1855	147

Besides forty-one boats on the stocks nearly completed. The actual carrying capacity of the boats here given, are about one-third more than the Custom-house measurement, which would make at a low estimate, the total tonnage in the Western rivers, 442,663 tons, and costing over $19,000,000.

Number of Boats on the Lakes.

120 Steamers, - - - - -	68,400 Tons.	
118 Propellers, - - - - -	41,000 "	
40 Barques, - - - - -	14,821 "	
211 Brigs, - - - - - -	51,212 "	
608 Schooners, - - - - -	148,120 "	
290 Sloops and Scows, - - -	111,140 "	
Tonnage, - - - - - -		434,693
Total tonnage on the Western Rivers, - - - - -		442,663
Total Tonnage, - - - - - - - -		877,356

Costing $16,198,421.

DIMENSIONS OF THE AMERICAN LAKES.

The greatest length of Lake Superior is 438 miles. The greatest breadth is 166 miles. Mean depth, 988 feet. Elevation, 620 feet. Area, 33,000 square miles.

The greatest length of Lake Michigan is 364 miles. Its greatest breadth, 110 miles. Mean depth, 869 feet. Elevation, 590 feet. Area, 24,000 square miles.

The greatest length of Lake Huron is 300 miles. Its greatest breadth, 163 miles. Mean depth, 811 feet. Elevation, 578 feet. Area. 21,000 square miles.

The greatest length of Lake Erie is 256 miles. Its greatest breadth, 81 miles. Its mean depth, 86 feet. Elevation, 560 feet. Area, 68,000 sqare miles.

The greatest length of Lake Ontario is 184 miles. Its greatest breadth, 65 miles. Its mean depth, 510 feet. Elevation, 264 feet. Area, 61,000 square miles. The total length of all five Lakes is nearly 1600 miles, covering an area altogether of upwards of 900,000 square miles.

EXPLOSION OF THE GLENCOE.

On the 3d day of April, 1852, the Glencoe, Captain Lee, from New Orleans, arrived at St. Louis, and had just been moored at the levee, foot of Chestnut street, when three of the boilers exploded, with the most appalling and destructive effects. The sound of the explosion was heard in the most remote quarters of the city; in the neighborhood of the levee the shock was like that of an earthquake, the houses for several squares around appeared to reel under the force of the concussion. The boat was crowded with people at the time; the passengers were engaged in looking after their baggage, and numbers of citizens, hotel-runners, hackmen, &c., had pressed into the boat. There was a fearful loss of life, but the names and number of the killed are beyond the scope of inquiry, as many of the victims were strangers; the bodies of a large number blown overboard were not recovered from the water, and many of the dead were so shockingly disfigured or torn to pieces that all recognition was out of the question. Fragments of wood, iron, and dead bodies were thrown to a surprising distance.

The shock of the explosion drove the steamer far out into the river, and immediately afterwards she took fire, the furnaces having been dismantled, and the burning fuel scattered over the decks. As the

EXPLOSION OF THE GLENCOE.

Glencoe floated down the stream, she presented a frightful spectacle. The whole forward part of the boat to the wheel-house, and down to the water line, had been swept away, and all the after-part was a commingled mass of timbers, freight, and human bodies heaped together in the wildest confusion. The fire burned fiercely and spread rapidly. The spectators on the shore beheld men, women and children running, with phrensied gestures, from one part of the burning steamer to another, seeking some means of escape from the dreadful death which threatened them—some who had been caught between the falling timbers were writhing in agony, making ineffectual efforts to extricate themselves, and imploring others to assist them. Numbers of the crew and passengers were compelled by the advancing flames to throw themselves overboard; some of these succeeded in reaching the shore, but many of them were drowned.

In the meantime, several small boats were actively engaged in rescuing the drowning people, and a considerable number were saved in this manner. The wreck finally lodged at the foot of Poplar street, where it burned to the water's edge, and then sunk, carrying down with it the ashes and bones of the dead. Near the spot where the explosion took place many dead bodies and dying persons were extended on the levee. Thirteen mutilated corpses were soon after removed to the office of the Board of Health, that being the most convenient place where they could be deposited. Twenty or thirty of the wounded were conveyed to the Sisters' Hospital. Others who were less injured, some with their faces scalded or blackened by the fire, were running about the levee in a frantic manner, crying for assistance. The dead bodies of five persons who had been blown from the deck of the Glencoe were found on the steamer Cataract. They were dreadfully mangled, the limbs in some cases being torn from the trunk—heads were mashed and disfigured to a degree which defied all attempts at identification. The body of a woman was found on the levee stretched across a marble slab, (the top of a table which had also been blown from the boat;) every bone in this corpse was broken, and "the limbs," says an eye-witness, "were so badly mangled that they could scarcely hang together."

The body of Mr. John Denny, first clerk of the Glencoe, was found on the hurricane deck of the steamer Western World. Few external injuries were found on this body, but life was totally extinct. The body of a little girl, with the legs torn off, was recovered from the river. The dissevered leg of a man was picked up on the side walk in Commercial street; the boot which remained on the limb, led to the recognition thereof as a part of the mortal remains of William Brennan, one of the engineers. Of the thirteen wounded persons who were sent to the hospital, three died during the night, and scarcely any of the others were believed to be curable.

Capt. Lee, his lady and one of his children, left the boat as soon as she landed, and a very few minutes before the explosion. The Captain's little son, ten years of age, who remained on board, was killed. Mr. A. R. Jones, a merchant of St. Louis, was instrumental in saving a great number of lives. He obtained a yawl, and approached the burning boat near enough to take off a great many passengers. As an acknowledgment of his humane services in the time of danger and affliction, the steamboat men of St. Louis presented Mr. Jones with a handsome silver mug, bearing a suitable inscription.

List of the Killed.—John Denny, first clerk of the Glencoe; Henry Balsar, pilot; John Curtis Lee, son of the Captain, aged ten years; Edward McCarty, hack driver, St. Louis; Mrs. Schenil, passenger, Memphis, Tenn.; (every bone in her body was broken, as mentioned in the preceding narrative;) John Grey, aged 12 years, a pedlar boy, from Memphis; William Brennan, assistant engineer; a family, consisting of a man, his wife and three female children, names unknown; George W. Rolfe, runner at the American Hotel, St. Louis; David Cree, Belfast, Ireland; George Reeder and James Wile, runners at the Virginia Hotel; a woman, name unknown; and many others, whose bodies could not be identified; making a total of sixty killed.

Badly Wounded.—William Callahan, fireman; Jesse H. Harrington, passenger, Cook county, Ill.; Samuel High, a citizen of St. Louis, who went on board after the boat arrived; Thomas Carroll, passenger, Liverpool, England; Frederick W. Burlog, German emigrant; Thomas Donahoe, Dubuque, Iowa; Patrick McLaughlin, New York; Daniel B. Henman, Gibson county, Ill.; James McLean, Ohio; Michael Dunn, one of the boat's crew; Sarah Matthews, passenger, aged thirteen, mortally wounded; W. B. Catherwright, passenger, Mississippi; William Brathwed, an Englishman; (he had with him $1,900 in specie;) George Buchanan, engineer.

Slightly Wounded.—Mr. Lane, bar-keeper; Mr. Studdiford, Ohio; Francis Cafferty, hotel runner; Thomas Foley, assistant engineer.

Very few of those who were badly wounded lived twenty-four hours after the accident. In addition to those mentioned in the foregoing list, some of the wounded were conveyed away by their friends, and their names were not ascertained.

Two or three steamboats which lay near the Glencoe, were much damaged by the explosion. A lady from Illinois was killed in her state-room in the steamer Cataract, which lay next to the Glencoe.

EXPLOSION OF THE SALUDA.

The Saluda exploded on Missouri river, near Lexington, April 9th, 1852. It appears that this boat had been detained in the neighborhood of Lexington for four days, by a strong tide. Several of her passengers left her to seek other conveyance. On the day above mentioned, the Captain made another effort to stem the current. The steamer left the landing at half past one o'clock, A. M., and five minutes after, the boilers exploded with such tremendous effect that the

EXPLOSION OF THE SALUDA.

cabin and all the wood-work forward of the wheel-house were completely demolished, and not a piece of timber was left above the guards. The boat sunk within a few minutes. The books were all lost, and the names of all the passengers who were killed by the explosion or who sunk with the boat could not be ascertained. The number of those who perished is estimated at one hundred.

The commander, Capt. Belt, who was on the hurricane roof, was blown high in the air, and fell against the side of a hill in Lexington, at least one hundred feet from the wreck. The second clerk, Mr. John Blackburn, was standing on the boiler-deck, and was also blown on shore, to a considerable distance from the boat. He was taken up dead. It may be mentioned as a melancholy coincidence, that a brother of this gentleman, (E. C. Blackburn,) was killed by the accident on the Pacific railroad in November, 1855. They were both highly esteemed by all who knew them. The mutilated bodies of a large number of the passengers of the Saluda were found in the streets of Lexington. Charles Labarge and Louis Gareth, the pilots, and Messrs. Clancy and Evans, the engineers, were lost. Their bodies were blown into the river, and were never recovered. One of the surviving passengers lost his wife and seven children. A lady was deprived of her husband and three children. Such was the force of the explosion, that a part of the boiler passed through a warehouse on the wharf, and quite demolished it. The citizens of Lexington subscribed $1,000 for the relief of the sufferers. The accident is ascribed to the negligence of the engineer.

KILLED.—Mr. Laynell, second bar-keeper; Mr. Nash and Mr. McClency; E. S. Halfer, second engineer; Mr. Leggett; Mr. Wayley; J. Brick; Mrs. Dunbar and child; Mrs. McGehas and child; two children of Mr. Rollins; two Messrs. Bayley; two second clerks; a first engineer; two pilots; Mr. McAllister; W. H. Bridges; five firemen, and many others, names unknown. Many of those who perished were Mormons.

Sixteen persons were wounded, two of them mortally; names not mentioned.

COLLISION OF THE SULTANA AND MARIA.

These boats came in collision on the Mississippi, seven miles below Natchez, November 21, 1846. The bow of the Sultana struck the Maria opposite her boilers, throwing them out of their place, and breaking the connection pipe and much of the wood-work, causing the

COLLISION OF THE SULTANA AND MARIA.

boat to sink within five minutes. About thirty lives were lost, and several persons were scalded with more or less severity.

KILLED.—Garret Bennis, James Slemmon, Wm. Moreland, John Ross, Dennis McArtney, John Steamlon, Wm. English, Frank Roberts, Peter Mattis, Peter Valenier, and perhaps twenty others, names unknown.

WOUNDED.—Wm. Leahey, Samuel Buzzy, Patrick Kenney, John B. Fleming.

Fast Time Made by Steamboats

ON

THE WESTERN RIVERS.

FROM NEW ORLEANS TO LOUISVILLE—DISTANCE 1480 MILES.

				Days.	Hours.	Minutes.
May, 1815,	Steamer	Enterprise	made the Trip in	25	2	40
April, 1817	"	Washington	"	25	—	—
Sept., 1817	"	Shelby	"	20	4	20
May, 1819	"	Paragon	"	18	10	—
Nov., 1828	"	Tecumseh	"	8	4	—
April, 1834	"	Tuscarora	"	7	16	—
Nov., 1837	"	General Brown	"	6	22	—
" "	"	Randolph	"	6	22	—
" "	"	Empress	"	6	17	—
Dec., 1837	"	Sultana	"	6	15	—
April, 1840	"	Edward Shippen	"	5	14	—
" 1842	"	Belle of the West	"	6	14	—
" 1843	"	Duke of Orleans	"	5	23	—
" 1844	"	Sultana	"	5	12	—
May, 1849	"	Bostona	"	5	8	—
June, 1851	"	Belle Key	"	4	23	—
May, 1852	"	Reindeer	"	4	20	45
" "	"	Eclipse	"	4	18	—
May, 1853	"	A. L. Shotwell	"	4	10	20

And in the same month and year, the steamer Eclipse, E. T. Sturgeon, Master, made the quickest time on record; and when we take into consideration the low water, swift current, and other obstacles she met with, we may safely set her down as the fastest boat in the WORLD.

ECLIPSE'S TIME FROM NEW ORLEANS TO

	Days.	Hours.	Minutes.
Donaldsonville - - - -	—	5	42
Baton Rouge - - - - - -	—	9	27
Natchez - - - - - -	—	19	46
Grand Gulf - - - - - -	—	24	25
Vicksburgh - - - - - -	—	28	11
Columbia - - - - - -	—	40	8
Napoleon - - - - - -	—	44	12
Helena - - - - - - -	2	3	38
Memphis - - - - - -	2	9	55
Cairo - - - - - - -	3	4	4
Evansville - - - - - -	3	18	24
Louisville - - - - - -	4	9	30

FROM NEW ORLEANS TO ST. LOUIS—DISTANCE 1200 MILES.

	Days.	Hours.	Minutes.
1840, Steamer J. M. White made the Trip in	3	23	—

FROM NEW ORLEANS TO NATCHEZ—DISTANCE 300 MILES.

				Days.	Hours.	Minutes.
May, 1814,	Steamer	Orleans	made the Trip in	6	6	40
July, 1814	"	Comet	"	5	10	—
May, 1815	"	Enterprise	"	4	11	20
April, 1817	"	Washington	"	4	—	—
Sept., 1817	"	Shelby	"	3	20	—
May, 1819	"	Paragon	"	3	8	—
Nov., 1828	"	Tecumseh	"	3	1	20
April, 1834	"	Tuscarora	"	1	21	—
Aug., 1838	"	Natchez	"	1	17	—
" 1840	"	Edward Shippen	"	1	8	—
" 1842	"	Belle of the West	"	1	18	—
" 1844	"	Old Sultana	"	—	19	45
" 1851	"	Magnolia	"	—	19	50
May, 1853	"	A. L. Shotwell	"	—	19	49
" 1853	"	Southern Belle	"	—	20	3
" 1853	"	Princess, No. 4	"	—	20	26
" 1853	"	Eclipse	"	—	19	47
Aug., 1855	"	New Princess	"	—	18	53
" 1855	"	New Natchez	"	—	17	30

FROM NEW ORLEANS TO CAIRO, MOUTH OF THE OHIO RIVER—DISTANCE 1000 MILES.

				Days.	Hours.	Minutes.
May, 1853,	Steamer	Eclipse	made the Trip in	3	4	4
"	"	A. L. Shotwell	"	3	3	40

FROM LOUISVILLE TO CINCINNATI—DISTANCE 150 MILES.

				Days.	Hours.	Minutes.
1818,	Steamer	General Pike	made the Trip in	1	16	—
1819	"	Paragon	"	1	14	20
1822	"	Wheeling Packet	"	1	10	—
1837	"	Moselle	"	—	12	—
1843	"	Duke of Orleans	"	—	12	—
1843	"	Congress	"	—	12	20
1846	"	Benj. Franklin, No. 6	"	—	11	45
1852	"	Alleghany	"	—	10	38
1852	"	Pittsburgh	"	—	10	23
1853	"	Telegraph, No. 3	"	—	9	52

FROM LOUISVILLE TO ST LOUIS—DISTANCE 750 MILES.

1843,	Steamer	Congress	made the Trip in - - -	49 hours.
1854	"	Pike	" - - -	47 "
1854	"	Northerner	" - - -	46½ "
1855	"	Southerner	" - - -	43 "

FROM ST. LOUIS TO ALTON—DISTANCE 25 MILES.

1853, Steamer Altona made the Trip in 1 hour and 25 minutes.

FROM ST. LOUIS TO ST. JOSEPH, (MO. RIVER,)—DISTANCE 590 MILES.

1853, Steamer Polar Star made the Trip in 64 hours.

FROM CINCINNATI TO PITTSBURGH—DISTANCE 480 MILES.

1850,	Steamer	Telegraph, No. 2,	made the Trip in	41 hours.
1851	"	Buckeye State	"	40 "
1852	"	Pittsburgh	"	39 "

MINOR DISASTERS.

Convoy.—The steamboat Convoy was burnt ten miles above Natchez, April 29th, 1849. Two persons, who jumped overboard, were drowned. The boat was a total loss.

Andrew Fulton.—The steamboat Andrew Fulton, on her way from New Orleans to St. Louis, was wrecked on the Plateau Rocks, March 1st, 1849. Three passengers were drowned.

Keokuk.—The steamboat Keokuk was snagged at the foot of St. Genevieve island, on the Mississippi, August 29th, 1844. She sunk in three fathoms water. One cabin passenger, and ten or twelve deck passengers, names unknown, were drowned.

Glide.—The steamboat Glide, Capt. Delzell, exploded on the Mississippi, August 10th, 1844. A passenger was blown overboard by the explosion, and no effort was made by the crew to save him, although he floated for some time, and called for assistance. The Glide had no small boat.

St. Charles.—The steam ferry boat St. Charles, exploded near the Levee at St. Louis, December 7th, 1844. Mr. Bell, a passenger, was mortally wounded; and several other persons were slightly injured.

Western.—The steamboat Western, on her way from Pittsburgh to St. Louis, came in collision with the steamer Aliquippa, which struck her in the middle and nearly cut her in two. Several children were drowned. The boat cost $16,000, and was insured for $10,000.

Shark.—The tow-boat Shark exploded near New Orleans, January 6th, 1846. The Captain's brother, Mr. Whon, was instantly killed. Mr. Kew, first engineer, and a fireman, were mortally wounded. Three other persons were badly scalded.

Syren.—The steamboat Syren exploded near Chattahoochie, February 8th, 1845, while taking in freight. Ten of the crew were killed. The boat sunk and the cargo was all lost.

Red Rover.—The steamboat Red Rover came in collision with the steamer Ruby at Fort Stoddart, on the Alabama river, forty miles above Mobile, March 9th, 1845. The Ruby sunk immediately, with all her freight and $10,000 in specie. Two persons were drowned.

Persian.—The steam tow-boat Persian exploded twenty-two miles below New Orleans, October 24th, 1845. C. Cruler, first engineer, and George Clinton, mate, were killed instantly; and eight persons were badly scalded.

Potomac.—The steamboat Potomac, from New Orleans, bound for Nashville, exploded at Choctaw Pass, January 9th, 1845. Two deck hands were killed, and three other persons seriously injured.

Simon Kenton.—The steamboat Simon Kenton burst a connection-pipe, August 28th, 1847, while lying at the wharf at St. Louis. A German woman attempted to jump into the yawl with her infant in her arms. The child fell into the river and was drowned. Four persons were scalded severely.

Cleveland.—The steamboat Cleveland, running between. Pittsburgh and Beaver, collapsed two flues, June 14th, 1844. The cook and a colored man were killed, and five persons were dangerously wounded.

New Hampshire.—The steamboat New Hampshire, on her way from New Orleans to Little Rock, Ark., May 1st, 1849, exploded all her boilers, forty miles below the place last mentioned. Twelve persons were killed, viz.: George T. Allen, first clerk; Alexander McComas, pilot; James Van Dyke, mate; four negro firemen, a wheel man, the second steward, a cabin-boy, Charles Radcliffe, carpenter, Mr. Berring, a cabin passenger, and a deck hand, name unknown. The boat was totally wrecked.

Louisiana.—The steamboat Louisiana exploded one of her boilers, August 12th, 1844, killing seventeen persons, viz: William Smith, Henry Finley, J. Goodman, John Henry and Jacob Cross, and twelve U. S. soldiers, names unknown. The explosion took place fifteen miles above Bayou Sara.

Swan.—The steamer Swan burst two of her boilers near New Orleans, August 16th, 1844, killing William Andrews, pilot, Robert Elliott, bar-keeper, Peter Aimes, steersman, and a negro fireman. The Captain and several other persons were badly scalded.

Caspian.—The steamboat Caspian struck a snag at the foot of Island No. 25 on the Mississippi, December 11th, 1845. She sunk in fifteen feet water. Forty German emigrants were drowned.

Denizen.—The steamer Denizen, Capt. Rhodes, exploded thirty miles below Vicksburg, November 30th, 1845. Capt. Rhodes was killed, and a cabin passenger badly wounded.

Malon.—The steamer Malon sunk in the Ohio river, near Paducah, September 12th, 1854. Thirty-five deck passengers and one cabin passenger were drowned.

Phœnix.—The steam tow-boat Phœnix blew up near New Orleans, May 20th, 1843, killing a Mr. Hall, and two other persons, names unknown.

Peruvian.—The steamer Peruvian burst all her boilers, June 7th, 1833, while on her way from New Orleans to Louisville More than fifty persons were killed.

Fashion No. 2.—The steamboat Fashion No. 2 collapsed a flue on the Monongahela river, near Pittsburgh, December 20th, 1850, killing Joseph Carroll and A. Lightle, passengers, Isaac Peebles, assistant engineer, a son of the Captain, and James Louderback, fireman. Several persons were scalded.

Fusileer.—The steamer Fusileer exploded both boilers near Attakopas, on the Mississippi river, December 30th, 1852. The first mate was killed; the Captain was badly wounded.

Hercules.—The steam tow-boat Hercules was badly damaged by coming in contact with the brig Ermon, December 26th, 1828, on the Mississippi river, below New Orleans. Three of the crew were drowned.

Financier.—The steamboat Financier exploded on the Upper Mississippi, October 2d, 1850, killing Mr. King, son of the Captain, and William Greene, second engineer. The carpenter and cabin-boy were scalded.

Meteor No. 3.—The Meteor No. 3, on her way from Red River to New Orleans, was burned to the water's edge and sunk fifty miles above the last named city, October 11th, 1850. Three colored men were drowned.

Tippah.—The steamboat Tippah, on her way from Tallahatchie river to New Orleans, was burned twenty-five miles above Vicksburgh, January 7th, 1852. The second engineer was drowned. Mrs. Butler, the Captain's wife, swam ashore.

Columbus.—The steamboat Columbus collapsed a flue on the Mississippi, May 6th, 1850, killing one man and wounding twelve others.

May Queen.—The steamboat May Queen collapsed her flues on the Arkansas river, on February 16th, 1852. Twelve persons were killed, and seven were badly wounded.

Mary Kingsland.—The steamboat Mary Kingsland exploded, for the third time in her history, on the 1st of March, 1852. George Hainey, second engineer, and two others, names unknown, were killed; George Swiler, pilot, was mortally wounded; and several other persons were severely injured.

Princess.—The steamer Princess was burned, two miles below Fort Adams, on the Mississippi, October 8th, 1854. The persons killed were, Mrs. Weise and child, and Miss Wilson, passengers; George Brantz, a deck hand, and five negroes.

Magnolia and Malumka.—The steamers Magnolia and Malumka came in collision on the Alabama river, February 16th, 1854. Three lives were lost.

Sylvester Webster.—The steamer Sylvester Webster capsized August 18th, 1854, on the Mississippi river, thirty-five miles below New Orleans. The captain and two female passengers were drowned.

Buckeye State.—The steamer Buckeye State burst a steam-pipe on the Ohio river, March 25th, 1852, scalding three passengers severely. One of them jumped overboard and was drowned.

GIPSEY.—The steamer Gipsey was burned, December 7th, 1854, near the mouth of New river. Dr. Harker and his son and daughter perished in the flames. Four other persons were burned to death or drowned.

MEDORE.—The steamer Medore blew up on the Mississippi, April 12th, 1842. John R. Boone was killed.

DOUGLASS.—The steamboat Douglass burst a steam-pipe, near New Madrid, mortally wounding a child of Dr. Hoffman, and two children of Mrs. Montgomery. Mr. C. Lemard of Louisville, and a slave of Dr. Hoffman, were killed instantly. Several passengers were badly scalded.

WEST WIND.—The steamer West Wind collapsed a flue at the mouth of the canal near Louisville. *Killed.*—Mrs. Dothart and sister, St. Louis; Mr. Sadwood; an old man from St. Louis, name unknown; Mr. Vidonc, St. Louis. Several passengers were wounded.

COLLISION OF THE FARMER AND SCIOTO VALLEY.—The steamers Farmer and Scioto Valley came in collision, November 20th, 1842, twenty miles below Louisville. The Farmer was sunk and three deck hands were drowned.

MUNROE.—The steamer Munroe was sunk in the night of March 20th 1854, ten miles above Natchez. Thirty persons were drowned.

COLLISION OF THE METEOR AND PARIS.—The steamboat Meteor was struck by the Paris, abaft the wheel-house, August 24th, 1848, when five miles below Stevensport. The Meteor sunk immediately. Four or five German deck passengers were drowned.

BROOKLYN.—The steamboat Brooklyn collapsed a flue, March 6th, 1847, twenty miles below Vicksburg. P. Feinan, fireman, and H. Concle, German passengers, were killed.

CLINTON.—The steamer Clinton was burned, March 23d, 1847, five miles above Bonne Caro, on the Mississippi. Two deck passengers, the second mate, (Mr. Weaver,) the bar-keeper, the cook and the chambermaid, were lost.

SIMON KENTON.—The steamer Simon Kenton, on her way from Quincey to St. Louis, April 4th, 1847, broke a connection-pipe. A. Mead, deck hand, was mortally wounded.

COLLISION OF THE WM. R. KING AND WINONA.—The steamers Wm. R. King and Winona came in collision on the Tombigbee river, February 5, 1847. The former was sunk and two persons were drowned.

MEDORA.—The steamer Medora exploded below Point Hudson, on the Mississippi river, March 18, 1847. Four persons were killed and three others were wounded.

NATIONAL.—The steamer National was burned at the mouth of Kentucky river, March 20, 1847. The clerk was killed.

PALMYRA.—The steamer Palmyra struck a rock near the Upper Rapids, Mississippi river November 3, 1838. One life lost.

JAMES PITCHER.—The steamer James Pitcher was burned to the water's edge, November 29, 1846. One person killed.

WAVE.—The steamboat Wave was burned near Pern, on the Illinois river, June 21, 1837. A French gentleman, name unknown, was drowned.

DE WITT CLINTON.—The steamboat De Witt Clinton, on her way from New Orleans to Pittsburgh, January 25, 1852, struck a snag eight miles below Memphis, and sunk in 15 feet water. All on board were drowned, except one fireman and the officers of the boat. Thirty-six lives were lost.

LOUISIANA.—The steamer Louisiana, while racing with another boat on Lake Pontchartrain, May 7, 1849, collapsed a steam pipe. Four persons were killed instantly, and six others were badly scalded.

GOVERNOR BENT.—The Governor Bent, an Arkansas river boat, exploded all her boilers near Island No. 76, on the Mississippi, May 12, 1849. One fireman was killed. A few moments before the explosion, all the crew were seated on the boiler-deck, when their attention was attracted to a rat, which they all pursued, except one man, and he was killed. Had the rat not appeared at that moment, many lives would have been lost.

WYANDOTTE.—The steamer Wyandotte was totally wrecked on the Mississippi, above Vicksburg, November 21, 1848. Thirty of the passengers and crew perished.

COLLISION OF THE MARENGO AND HARRY HILL.—The steamers Marengo and Harry Hill came in violent contact, on the Mississippi, below Natchez, November 30, 1848. The Marengo sunk and three of her crew were drowned.

AMERICA.—The steamboat America exploded fifteen miles below Madison, Ind., on the Ohio river, December 19, 1848. Four persons were mortally wounded, and ten others were much injured.

CHARTER OAK.—The steamboat Charter Oak was destroyed by fire, near Bailey's Landing, on the Mississippi river, April 12, 1848. Many of the passengers were lost, and others severely wounded.

KENNEY.—The steamer Kenney exploded in the Tombigbee river, (Alabama,) June 5, 1848. Fifty of the crew and passengers were killed or missing.

COLLISION OF THE SULTANA AND GRAY EAGLE.—A collision took place between the steamers Sultana and Gray Eagle, at Island No. 35, on the Mississippi, June 13, 1848. Two men belonging to the Gray Eagle were killed and five were wounded.

HARDEE.—The steamer Hardee burst her connection pipes, on Missouri river, thirty miles above Weston, September 6, 1849. Captain G. Fishback was instantly killed; Geo. Martin the pilot, was mortally wounded, and several others were badly scalded.

CARROLLTON.—The steamer Carrollton, going from New Orleans to Vicksburg, was blown up near Baton Rouge, October 1, 1835. Eight persons were killed instantly, and seven others were mortally wounded.

BIG HATCHIE.—The steamboat Big Hatchie exploded one of her boilers at Harmon's Landing, 100 miles above St. Louis, on the Mississippi, July 25, 1845. A passenger, named Hoyle, was instantly killed, and a son of Mr. Ludlow, Manager of St. Charles Theatre, New Orleans, mortally wounded. Several other persons, names unknown, are supposed to have been killed.

COLLISION OF THE R. B. GILMORE AND DELAWARE.—The steamboat R. B. Gilmore was wrecked and sunk by coming in collision with the steamboat Delaware, on the Ohio river, below Louisville, April 15, 1838. Several passengers, names not reported, were drowned.

EUTAW.—The mail-boat Eutaw, running between Wheeling and Steubenville, collapsed a flue, April 23, 1838, causing the death of a fireman. Several persons were badly scalded.

DACOTAH.—The steamboat Dacotah exploded at Peoria, Ill., August 20, 1851. She was bound for Minnesota. Eleven persons were killed, viz.:—Mr. Haywood and three children; Wm. Baker, wife and child; H. Foster; C. Van Sycle; three children of B. Wordsworth; H Bains and Wm. Moffatt.

ECHO.—The steamboat Echo collapsed two flues at Bayou Sara, May 20, 1851, killing three of the crew, and wounding five others.

FINANCIER.—The steamer Financier exploded on the Mississippi, near Alton, October 12, 1850. The mate and the Captain's son were killed. Several of the crew were badly scalded.

DUNCAN.—Tne steamer Duncan blew up on Savannah river, June 8, 1841, killing three negroes. The boat was burned and sunk.

PIKE.—The steamboat Pike was sunk, September 5, 1840, by coming in contact with the steamer Fayette, two miles below Alton, Ill. Seven persons were known to be lost.

FARMER.—The steamboat Farmer collapsed a flue, on the Mississippi, above New Orleans, Nov. 27, 1840. Mr. Berry, second engineer, and a german deck passenger were killed.

CHESTER.—The steamer Chester, Captain Cable, on her way from New Orleans to St. Louis, collapsed two flues, twenty miles above the first-named place, on the first of July, 1840. The mate and a deck hand were blown overboard and drowned.

EDNA.—The steamboat Edna exploded, July 3d, 1842, at the mouth of Missouri river. Fifty passengers, (German emigrants,) were mortally wounded.

AMOS CROCKER.—The steamer Amos Crocker was sunk, April 27th, 1849, in Red Bayou. One life was lost.

EMBASSY.—The steamboat Embassy, from Pittsburgh to St. Louis, collapsed two flues at Three Mile Island, June 9, 1849. Ten persons were killed and twenty-five wounded.

IRON CITY.—The Iron City struck some floating ice near St. Louis, December 31st, 1848. Her bow was broken so as to cause her to sink immediately. Five of the crew were drowned.

Cora.—The steamboat Cora, on her way to Council Bluffs, May 5th, 1850, was snagged and sunk, drowning fifteen persons.

Columbus.—The steamboat Columbus collapsed one of her flues, May 7th, 1850, near Island No. 4, on the Mississippi. Eight deck passengers and two firemen were scalded to death, and five other persons were drowned.

Ironton.—The steamer Ironton collapsed a flue on the Mississippi, May 9th, 1850. One man was killed, and eight persons were wounded.

Belle Creole.—The steamer Belle Creole bursted one of her boilers near New Orleans, November 16th 1849. Five persons were killed or wounded.

Josephine.—The steamer Josephine exploded on the Mississippi, April 18th, 1845. Mr. James Ellis, of Alleghany county, Pa., was mortally wounded.

Charleston.—The steamboat Charleston exploded on the Chattahoochie river, May 11th, 1845. One of the deck hands was dangerously wounded.

Tiger.—The steam tow-boat Tiger exploded all her boilers, six in number, on the Mississippi river, November 10th, 1854, killing three persons.

Edna.—The steamer Edna, while starting from the wharf at Columbia, June 12th, 1847, exploded all her boilers, killing twenty persons, and wounding eight or ten others.

Cutter.—The steamer Cutter, when about to leave Pittsburgh, March 17th, 1843, collapsed a flue, killing Joseph Hughes, one of the engineers, and mortally wounding another.

J. M. White.—The steamer J. M. White, the finest boat of her day, was snagged and sunk thirty-five miles above Cairo, March 28th, 1843. One woman was drowned.

Simon Kenton.—The steamer Simon Kenton collapsed a flue at St. Louis, June 29th, 1847. Six persons were killed.

Star Spangled Banner.—The steamer Star Spangled Banner struck a snag fifteen miles below Baton Rouge, July 12th, 1847. About one hundred and twenty-five deck passengers were drowned.

Prairie State.—The steamer Prairie State exploded at Pekin, Ill., April 25th, 1852. Twenty of the crew and deck passengers were killed.

Capitol.—The steamer Capitol was burned at St. Mary's landing, seventy miles below St. Louis, December 30th, 1844. A Mr. Dalrymple, his wife and son, perished in the flames.

Path-Finder.—The steamboat Path-Finder was burned near Vicksburg, February 12th, 1845. Eight lives were lost.

Queen City.—The steamer Queen City collapsed a flue, on Ohio river, May 6th, 1846, scalding about twenty-five Germans, some of whom died in consequence.

General Scott.—The steamer General Scott, plying on the lakes, exploded one of her boilers, June 9th, 1846. A fireman was killed, and two others were dangerously wounded.

Majestic.—The steamer Majestic collapsed a flue twenty miles above Memphis, December 5th, 1837. Three persons were killed.

Native.—The steamboat Native exploded at Eddyville, December 15th, 1828. Two negroes were killed.

Shamrock.—The steamer Shamrock exploded on the St. Lawrence river, July 9th, 1837. Fifty-four passengers were lost.

Nick Biddle.—The steamer Nick Biddle struck a snag in the Mississippi, forty-five miles above Vicksburg, July 25th, 1837. Ten deck passengers were drowned.

Collision of the Daniel O'Connell and William Bayard.—The steamer Daniel O'Connell ran afoul of the William Bayard, December 18th, 1837. The latter was sunk, and all the people on board were lost.

Louisiana.—The steamboat Louisiana, the largest American boat afloat at that time, August, 1841, exploded opposite Baton Rouge, killing twenty-three persons, most of whom were U. S. soldiers.

St. Charles.—The ferry boat St. Charles exploded on Missouri river, December 7th, 1841, killing Ann Bell and four other persons.

Westward.—The steamer Westward exploded near New Orleans, December 12th, 1847, killing twelve of the crew and dangerously wounding the Captain.

Iron City.—The steamer Iron City was crushed and sunk by the ice at St. Louis, December 31st, 1849. The cook and steward were killed.

Decatur.—The steamboat Decatur was burned near Island No. 66, on the Mississippi, December 20th, 1845. A colored woman was drowned.

Collision of the Congress and Buckeye.—The steamer Congress was sunk by coming in collision with the Buckeye near Island No. 26, on the Mississippi, February 10th 1846. Twenty-six lives were lost.

St. Louis.—As this fine boat was ascending the Mississippi, in November, 1838, she struck a bar, which caused her to burst a connecting steam pipe, by which Jno. Suthern, the cook, and a deck passenger named Chas. Robbins, were scalded to death. Another deck passenger named Ubanks, in the noise and confusion, jumped overboard and was drowned.

Union.—As the steamer Union was ascending the Ohio river, on Saturday morning, Dec. 2, 1826, five miles below Big Bone, and fifty miles from Cincinnati, she burst her boilers, killing the engineer, Robert Simmons, Jno. Williams, Theodore Frazier, Simon Smithers, Alonzo Duble, and scalding several others. The explosion was deafening, and the boat was torn almost to pieces; the boiler jumped out forward about sixty feet, and sunk in the river.

Stranger.—The steamboat Stranger burst her boiler on the morning of Dec. 17th, 1832, when opposite Plaquemine, by which six lives were lost, John Suner, Wm. Dible, N. Long, and three deck hands, names unknown.

Dolphin.—The steamer Dolphin was burnt to the water's edge on the 27th of April, 1832, when about twenty-five miles below Wheeling; the sight was grand to behold, and fortunately but one life was lost by this disaster. A deck hand perished in the flames while asleep in his berth.

Crusader.—The steamer Crusader exploded on the morning of the 20th June, 1837, near Mobile, spreading death on all sides. J. C. Duncan was instantly killed, and eleven fatally scalded. Immediately after the accident she anchored, and waited till the U. S. Mail boat Mobile came along, and was towed to Mobile. Three of the scalded died before reaching Mobile, and the others the next day. Most of the killed were deck hands. One Frenchman, Jean Edeor, was mortally wounded, and from letters found upon his person, must have belonged to a noble family. He was buried with the rest, and his fate will probably never be known by his family.

Nimrod.—This boat burst her steam-pipe on Sunday night, August 19th, 1834, while under way, and when near Maysville, the steam came rushing out with great force and heat, scalding six persons in a shocking manner, four of whom died. Names of those killed.—Benjamin Iser, Maysville; —— Blanton, Louisville; Oscar Lee and Theodore Snigleton, Rochester, New York. The Nimrod was a regular Maysville and Cincinnati packet.

Reaper.—This ill-fated boat sunk in April, 1833, about sixty miles below Fort Adams, on the Mississippi, in seventy feet water, going entirely out of sight. Mr. Livingston Harrison, engineer, the pilot, mate, and thirty slaves chained together, lost their lives. Mr. Harrison was a citizen of Cincinnati, where his family and numerous friends still live.

Yazoo.—This boat, bound from Mobile to New Orleans, exploded one of her boilers on Monday morning, May 7th, 1838, while off Breton Island. A passenger named Keeler, who was formerly engineer on the Roanoke, was instantly killed. The Yazoo sustained little damage.

Collision of the Algonquin and Warren.—The steamer Algonquin run into the Warren near New Orleans, December, 1837, breaking the connection-pipe on the Warren, by which seven persons were scalded to death. *Killed*—Patrick Murphy, Enos McFaul, Jonathan Eller, William Jones, and three women, names unknown.

Rolla.—The steamer Rolla collapsed a flue near Rock Island, on the Mississippi river, November, 1837, killing a fireman, and severely injuring the engineer.

Siren.—The steamer Siren exploded on the night of the 17th of February, 1845, and was one of the most terrible explosions that ever occurred on the western waters. Ten of the crew were instantly killed and many wounded. Capt. Sharpless was thrown fifty feet in the air, but fortunately fell into the water, swam ashore, and was not seriously injured. The passengers very fortunately were not exposed to the force of the explosion, or the catastrophe would have been more terrible. *Killed*—Mr. Imbus, pilot; black boy; Charles Bordenrider, bar-keeper; and his son, a cabin boy; George Tully, cabin-boy. Wash. McGougan was blown overboard and was picked up by the mate of the boat on a cotton bale, but died before he reached shore. Thomas White, Patrick Murphy, a deck hand, Green, a black boy, Wilkins, a black man, George, a black boy, passenger, belonging to Dr. Harrison, and Jack McGougan were all killed, and forty wounded. The accident occurred on the Chattahoochie river. The U. S. mail was lost.

COLLISION OF THE RUBY AND RED ROVER.—On the 9th of March, 1845, the steamers Red Rover and Ruby came in contact; the accident occurred near Fort Stoddart, Alabama river; the Ruby immediately went down in sixty feet water, carrying down with her Mr. John Carter Knight, and a negro servant.

SALEM.—This fine boat, on her voyage to New Orleans struck a snag near Vicksburg, on the 13th of May, 1841, and immediately went down. The steward was carried under with her.

TOMOCHICHEE.—This boat left New Orleans, April 23d, 1843, bound for Mobile, and when near the English Turn, struck a snag and sunk immediately. One passenger, a Mr. Southgate, of New Hampshire, was drowned.

COLLISION OF THE OREGON AND TENNESSEE.—These boats came in collision on the Mississippi river, just above St. Louis, on the evening of the 27th April, 1841, by which accident the boilers of the Tennessee were knocked down, and her engineer and several others were mortally scalded.

BEDFORD.—On the evening of the 25th of April, 1840, the steamer Bedford, from St. Joseph, was descending the Missouri river, near its mouth, bound for St. Louis, with a large crowd of passengers, when she struck a snag and sunk in less than five minutes in deep water. Seven or eight persons were drowned, including a Mr. Moore, an old volunteer Revolutionary soldier, a negro woman and three children, a white infant whose mother was saved, Mr. John Buck, of Pennsylvania, and Wm. Morton, of New Orleans. During the excitement of the Bedford going down, a young lady jumped overboard and swam near fifty yards, reaching the shore in safety, the first time she ever knew she could swim. Her name was Lucy Wimer, of Belleville, Illinois.

BUCKEYE.—This disaster was one which spread terror throughout the southern and western states. It occurring in early times, made a profound impression upon the minds of travellers, and for years after this accident, the main talk was the explosion of the Buckeye. On Wednesday evening, May 10, 1839, as she was under way, and near Randolph, Tennessee, the Buckeye, Capt. Thompson, exploded with a terrific noise, scattering death and desolation all around. The boat was completely smothered in steam and smoke, which caused many inhaling the hot steam, to die. Charles Gretzinger, pilot, killed; Mr. Randolph, do.; second pilot was dangerously wounded; Thos. Rogers, of Cincinnati, was never found; Mr. Pretis, of Portland, first engineer, killed; Mr. Barkly, the clerk, and Capt. Thompson, were both injured; six firemen were killed, Pat Donahue, Michael Finch, John Dunn, Wm. O'Flarety, Dennis Megan, Samuel Dunbar. Six passengers missed at the time, were no doubt drowned. Mr. Overton Atkinson, of New Orleans, was on the Buckeye at the time, but escaped with a few bruises. The Sultana towed the Buckeye to Louisville.

MASSILON.—This boat, by some accident, burst her connection pipe on the 5th of June, 1339, scalding two persons to death, and knocking two overboard, who were drowned. Names of killed, Samuel Swan, Alabama; Geo. Hite, Nashville, Tenn.; Benjamin Jonson, and a deck hand.

FLORA.—The steamboat Flora burst her steampipe on Friday morning, November 18, 1836, when near Rising Sun, Indiana, scalding and killing sixteen or seventeen persons. The explosion made a great noise; the passengers rushed to the side doors and opened them, when the hot steam rushed in, scattering death to all who inhaled it. Had the cabin doors remained closed, none would have lost their lives. *Killed*—Benj. Myrich, of Charlestown, Mass.; Saml. Donelly, of Washington, Pa.; E. McLaughlin, Columbiana Co., Ohio; Hon. G. L. Kinnard, of Indiana; Geo. Fisher, supposed to be a resident of Louisville, Ky.; Saml.

Watterbury of Madison, Ind.; Miss Lucy Wing; Allen Wilhoite of New Castle, Ky.; Alonzo Piercing. Mr. Phillips of Pittsburgh was dangerously hurt; Miss Ward and sister, mortally wounded. Several jumped overboard and thus perished.

Bonnets of Blue.—The steamer Bonnets of Blue sunk near Montgomery, Ala., on the 30th of Feb., 1836, drowning C. B. Turner of Mobile, and J. Wilbur of Kentucky.

Albert Gallatin.—The steamer Albert Gallatin, on her way from New Orleans to Galveston, Texas, blew up in January, 1842, killing five, and wounding nine. *Killed*—C. D. Crooks, of Galveston; A. B. Jones, Ohio; Amos Longsheet, Texas; Wm. Deets, Maine; and a deck hand, name never known. *Wounded*—Miss Brierly, Miss Young, both of New Orleans; Mrs. Johnston, and Miss Wilmer in her care; Adam Dunkin and nephew; carpenter and engineer, and several others, names unknown.

Star.—This boat blew up near Mobile, March 1st, 1842, killing Isaac Mix, A. B. Dunn, G. C. Simpson, Alexander Millton, Simon Drew, Alfonso Garasche, Miss Eliza Clarke, Mrs. Jones, Mrs. Finch, Miss Annie Smith and Andrew Girtz, and wounding seven others, several mortally.

Hermitage.—As this steamer was descending the Cumberland river, January 13th, 1840, she came in contact with the steamer Hugh L. White, and immediately sunk in ten feet water. The accident occurred near Harpeth Shoals. The boat was crowded with passengers, but only one life was lost, that of a fireman, named Hugh Pratt.

Navy Express.—This boat exploded near Mobile, July 25th, 1838, while waiting for the mail. The explosion was fearful, but fortunately no lives were lost. The chimney was thrown at least one hundred feet into the air. The cause of the explosion is attributable to the thinness of the boiler; not being thicker than common sheet iron.

Home.—The steamer Home blew up at the wharf at Cincinnati, Ohio, on the evening of the 18th of January, 1838, killing seven or eight persons, mostly belonging to the boat. She had just arrived a few hours previous to the accident, and the passengers had all left the boat. *Killed*—John Clancey, Patrick Roony, Michael Allen, Samuel Sinter and William Hoyt, deck hands. Four were blown into the river, but were saved.

Boreas No. 2.—This fine St. Louis and Missouri river packet was burnt near Hermann, on the Missouri river, May, 1846, proving an entire loss to her owners. Messrs. Wetherland & Co., Santa Fee traders, lost $60,000 in gold by this accident, and a man named Jones, from Chicago, Ill., was lost.

Belle of Hatchie.—The Belle of Hatchie, a Memphis Packet, struck a snag about eight miles above Helena, on the 30th of July, 1848, and sunk in less than two minutes out of sight. The hurricane deck parted from the hull as it went down, or every soul on board would have been lost. There were about forty passengers on board at the time, and they remained on the floating wreck. Immediately after striking the snag, one of the deck hands took the yawl and went ashore alone, leaving the passengers to take care of themselves. The watchman of the boat was washed overboard and swam ashore; the mate climbed up the jackstaff as the boat settled down, and was thus saved; four deck hands went overboard and were drowned. Passengers in their fright, jumped into the river, and were drowned. One lady, wife of Capt. Joyce, of Memphis, as the boat was going down, gave her infant child to a man named Nathaniel Harbert, and told him to save it, even if she should be lost. He leaped overboard with it immediately and swam ashore, a distance of three hundred yards below the wreck—he was almost exhausted, but saved his precious freight intrusted to him by a fond mother. The lady was afterwards got out of the cabin on to the hurricane deck, and was saved.

Collision of the Melodeon and G. W. Kendall.—These boats came in collision on the Mississippi river, near Plaquemine, December, 1850, the Melodeon going down in a few moments, drowning two persons—deck passengers—names unknown. The Melodeon was bound from New Orleans to Nashville, with a heavy cargo.

Newark.—This boat was bound from Zanesville, Ohio, to Pittsburgh, with a valuable freight, and crowded with passengers. On Thursday evening, April 15th, 1847, when under way, the flue in the front end of one of her boilers collapsed, blowing off the head of the boiler, which passed up through the cabin floor, tearing it up about twenty feet, and then passing through the hurricane roof, killing and wounding eleven persons:—George Nixon, carpenter; Christopher Castle; L. Hubble, engineer; James Coyle; Adam Everett, steward; John Day; T. Harris; C. Hyatt, and Wm. Tignar were all severely scalded—the four first named persons died soon after the accident.

PINEY WOOD.—The steamer Piney Wood caught fire on her trip from Springfield to the Lake end of the Ponchartrain Railroad, in October, 1848, and was totally consumed, with several passengers. *List of Persons Burnt*—Mr. Duncan, a merchant of Springfield; D. Brown; two families, consisting of one gentleman named Watkins, his wife, his sister-in-law, two young ladies and two children, and two servants belonging to them; two negro men and the chambermaid of the boat, and a man named Wilson, from New York, and a D. Minter, were all consumed.

PLANTER.—This ill fated boat and Captain will long be remembered on the Western waters. The Planter was an Illinois river packet, more of a freight than passenger boat, or the disaster would have been more terrible. On the 5th of January, 1848, while at Jones' Ferry, Illinois river, taking on a cargo of grain, her boilers exploded, tearing the cabin to fragments; the wreck then took fire, and but for the great exertions of the crew, would have been consumed. Five persons were instantly killed, and the Captain, clerk, and engineer and many others severely scalded. Several of the scalded died soon after the accident. The Captain was afterwards killed at Lexington, Mo., in 1852, by the explosion of the ill fated Saluda.

MONEDO.—This boat exploded her boilers on the 15th of November, 1848, when about eight miles below Little Rock. One deck hand was instantly killed, and four badly scalded.

COLLISION OF THE CHICKASAW AND CLIFTON.—These boats came in collision on the 26th of March, 1852, by which accident the Chickasaw immediately went down in forty feet of water. Her cabin parted from the hull, and floated down the river with the crew and passengers in it. The following is a list of those known to have been lost by this calamity; Thos. Todd, carpenter, Penna.; Wm. Smith, Cincinnati; one cabin passenger, name unknown; J. McKee, deck hand; John Thompson, Covington, Ky.; Wm. Asher, and Samuel Beers, New Orleans; six firemen who were asleep at the time, were all drowned. One old man, deck passenger, from Pennsylvania, was lost.

COLLISION OF THE YORKTOWN AND WABASH VALLEY.—These boats came in collision on the Mississippi River, near New Orleans, April, 1846, by which the Wabash Valley was lost. Three cabin passengers and one deck passenger were lost. The following are the names of the cabin passengers drowned: Wm. Alter, Samuel Allington, Abraham Sutton.

SWAN.—The tow-boat Swan exploded on the 16th of August, 1841, on the Mississippi, killing Wm. Andrews, pilot, Robert Elliot, Peter Ames, and a colored fireman of Mobile. Mason Altage, the engineer, was slightly scalded; Geo. Brawdy badly, do.; and the cook, fireman, and steward, slightly do.

PALESTINE.—The steamer Palestine caught fire on the 19th of June, 1844, when just above the mouth of the Ohio. She was crowded with passengers, and when the alarm of fire was given, the wildest confusion prevailed. Ladies were screaming, and men rushing to and fro hunting their wives and friends. A rush was made for the yawl which was suspended at the stern of the boat. Fourteen crowded into it, when the ropes were cut to prevent others from getting into it, and all in it were precipitated into the water, and out of the whole number only two were rescued, the remaining twelve meeting a watery grave. *Drowned*—Charles Harrington, of Pittsburgh; Messrs. Snodgrass, Findley, Smith, and Moore, of Platte county, Mo.; Geo. W. Stephens, Wm. Hopson, and Mrs. Levina Horn, of Haskill county, Ky.; Jos. Neal, a colored man, and three firemen, making twelve in all.

COLUMBUS.—The steamer Columbus, Capt. Post, left New Orleans, May 1, 1850, for St. Louis, having a heavy freight, and about two hundred deck passengers; and when under full headway in an island schute about fifteen miles below the mouth of the Ohio, one of her boilers burst with a loud report, killing and scalding many. The deck passengers were so terribly frightened that many of them jumped overboard and were drowned. The shrieks of the women and children were heart rending in the extreme. All thought the boat was lost, and women crowded around the crew, imploring protection, so that they could not do their duty in casting anchor. Two men and a woman were killed outright, and seventeen persons scalded, including one of the engineers. The steamer Magnolia was in sight at the time of the explosion, and took her in tow, and landed her at Cairo. The steam and hot water fortunately blowed out the forward end of the boiler, otherwise the loss of life would have been fearful indeed.

St. Louis.—The New Orleans and St. Louis packet St. Louis collapsed a flue when near the Jefferson Barracks, on the 23d of May, 1850, at ten o'clock at night, killing ten or twelve instantly, and scalding twenty-five others so badly that sixteen of them died the next day. They were mostly deck passengers, on their way to New Orleans. The St. Louis was a new and splendid boat, and on her first trip. Her engineer, Mr. Donahoe, was tried at St. Louis for manslaughter, but after a lengthy trial was acquitted. The St. Louis never proved a profitable boat after this accident.

Collision of the Commerce and Dispatch.—The steamers Dispatch and Commerce came in collision on the night of May 6th, 1850, near Port Martland, on Lake Erie, the Commerce sinking in eight fathoms water. She had on board a portion of the twenty-third regiment of British troops, twenty four of whom were drowned, with one officer and sixteen passengers, making a total of forty-one souls.

Collision of the Luna and Duchess.—These steamboats came in contact with each other May 17th, 1850, the Duchess striking the Luna abaft of the boilers, causing her soon to go down, drowning three negroes, and two deck hands, Patrick Jones and William Wilson.

Collision of the Buckeye State and Saratoga.—The passenger steamer Buckeye State, on Lake Erie, October 23d, 1851, run down the schooner Saratoga, a short distance above Long Point, on the Canada side. Three lives were lost by this disaster.

Montgomery.—This fine boat took fire on her downward trip to New Orleans, November, 1851, and was totally consumed with twenty-five hundred bales of cotton. Three deck hands perished in the flames.

Greenwood.—As the steamer Greenwood was leaving the wharf at Kanawha Salines, August 24th, 1850, one of her boilers exploded with terrific violence, making a complete wreck of the boat. *Injured*—Capt. E. Williams, thigh broken and slightly scalded; Jacob Smith, passenger, scalded; George Montgomery, and a young man named Yonce, badly scalded; Henry Burch, of Buffalo, badly scalded, and was carried to the house of A. E. Sargent, where he lingered till Sunday, the 28th, and expired in the greatest agony.

Hercules.—The tow-boat Hercules exploded at the mouth of the Mississippi river, April 10th, 1850, killing six men and mortally wounding five more. The boat was blown almost to pieces. *Killed*—B. F. Miller, pilot, James Riddle, William Hammond, John Warren, William Haren, Thomas Murphy, and Rufus Tarbott.

Collision of the Mercury and Pittsburg.—These boats came in collision on the Ohio river, near Guyandotte, on the 3d December, 1823, by which accident John Williams, pilot, of Wheeling, was killed, and six passengers slightly injured.

Tiger.—On Wednesday afternoon, the 6th of November, 1844, the steam tow-boat Tiger exploded her boilers, six in number, while having in tow a barque near the Southwest Pass of the Mississippi river, tearing the boat all to pieces, and killing three persons and wounding several others. The reason no more were killed, the captain had just called all hands to haul in the spring cable. *Killed*—Captain David B. Clark, pilot, of New Orleans; David Brown, first engineer, of New York; A. Snyder, second do., of Canada. The remains of the two engineers were recovered and buried at Hitchcock's Island. The body of Mr. Clark was seen flying through the air at the time of the explosion, and was never recovered. Captain Carwell, the Master, was severely hurt, but recovered in a few weeks. The Tiger was owned by Mr. Joseph Clark, of New Orleans.

Potosi.—This Upper Mississippi river packet collapsed a flue when backing out from the landing, at Quincy, Ill., on Friday evening, October 4, 1844, killing a Mr. N. Perrin, a cabin passenger, who was blown by the concussion out among some horses on the forecastle of the boat, and trampled to death. Mr. Perrin resided at New York, Minnesota Territory, and was the third brother who have lost their lives by steamboat explosions. He left a large family to mourn his untimely end. Phillip Miller was blown overboard, and his body never found. The steamer Monoma towed the Potosi to St. Louis.

COLLISION OF THE OTTER AND ATLAS.—The steamer Atlas, descending the Mississippi, and the Otter ascending it, bound for the Missouri river, came in collision on the night of September 14, 1846, killing one passenger, John Duffy. The boats were not seriously injured.

COLLISION OF THE CALIFORNIA AND ISAAC NEWTON.—These boats came in collision on the Ohio river, above Cincinnati, February, 1847, the California going down in less than two minutes, drowning six persons, three of whom were named Wm. Watson, Augustus Thompson, and D. Irvin. After striking her, the Isaac Newton came up nobly to the rescue, and took off all her passengers and crew, and after breakfasting them, took them to Guyandotte without charge. The California was a total loss.

DANIEL WEBSTER.—The tow-boat Daniel Webster burst one of her boilers on the 6th of January, 1847, on the south-west bar, killing Mr. Wm. Taylor, a Balize pilot, and a fireman.

CAROLINE.—The steamer Caroline burst one of her boilers at the foot of Wabash Island, on the Ohio river, on the 20th of November, 1847, killing John Jones, Humphrey Davis, and Dennis Clarke, and wounding six others severely.

EDNA.—The steamer Edna, Capt. Phillips, when opposite Columbia, on the Ouachita, on the 4th of June, 1847, burst all four of her boilers, killing fifteen or twenty persons, and wounding many others. *Killed*—Judge Mayo, Louisiana; Mr. Hill, Arkansas; Mr. Odell, South Carolina; Mr. King, do.; Mr. Daily, Louisiana; Mr. Jones, Florida; Dr. Watt, New Orleans; E. Rodgers, Ohio; S. Minter, Georgia. *Boats Crew Lost*—Mr. Donaldson, Ga.; Jim Watson, Jim Thompson, P. Gordon, Thos. Plunkett, D. Anderson, bar-keeper; J. H. Voss, James Pool, pilot; S. Steager, Mr. Oliver, engineer, and four deck passengers.

CHAMPLAIN.—The steamer Champlain burst her boilers on the morning of the 3d of November, 1847, at Bridgewater, on the Mississippi river. Three men scalded.

LUNA.—The steamer Luna broke one of her shafts, and burst a cylinder head, on the 3d of November, 1847, killing the cook, and seriously injuring several others.

HARRY HILL.—The steamer Harry Hill burst one of her boilers at Louisville, on the 11th of January, 1847, severely scalding the first engineer.

MEDORA.—The steamer Medora burst her boilers on the 12th of February, 1847, while on her way from New Orleans to Natchitoches, killing Charles Martin, and severely scalding sixteen passengers, among them Major Blake, of Miss.; Dr. John Evans, and Mr. R. Flynn, of Miss.; Dr. Henroy, Mr. Caruthers, and Mr. Moise, residences unknown.

QUEEN CITY.—The steamer Queen City while lying at Natchez, Miss., on the 27th of May, 1846, burst one of her steam pipes, killing seven passengers and wounding ten mortally, and twenty others seriously.

COLLISION OF THE RAINBOW AND AMERICAN EAGLE.—The steamers Rainbow and American Eagle came in collision on the Mississippi river, when about fifty miles above New Orleans, on the 14th March, 1844, by which accident five persons were seriously scalded and one passenger killed outright. The Rainbow was descending the river.

YAZOO.—The steamer Yazoo, Captain Culver, struck a snag on Monday night, August 9th, 1847, on the Mississippi river, which tore away her wheel-house. Lieutenant Nile, of the 2d Illinois Regiment of Volunteers, who had just returned from Mexico, was carried away by the snag and lost.

CLINTON.—The steamer Clinton was burnt up, on the Mississippi river, on the 21st March, 1847. Seven lives were lost, and the U. S. mail.

GENERAL HARRISON.—The steamer General Harrison, running on the Chattahoochee river, burst her boiler on the 14th of November, 1842, killing five persons.

DISPATCH.—The boiler of the tow-boat Dispatch exploded at Pittsburgh, on the 18th of August, 1846, seriously scalding a Mr. Pearce, whose father resides opposite Monongahela.

COTTON PLANT.—The steamer Cotton Plant, bound for Upper Red, sunk in Red river on the 17th of April, 1845, drowning three persons and two children.

HUNTRESS.—The steamer Huntress burst her boilers on the Ohio river, one hundred and twenty miles below Louisville, on the 10th of April, 1830, killing the first engineer, three firemen and the second steward. A negro fireman jumped overboard and was drowned.

Tally-ho.—The steamer Tally-ho exploded her boiler on the Ohio river, on the 1st of May, 1830, just as she was leaving Dover Landing, killing the engineer and two deck hands.

Ramapo.—The Ramapo burst her boiler on the 4th of March, 1826, when about fifty miles above New Orleans, mortally scalding Wm. Mathews. The unfortunate man, just before he died, prayed fervently. His parents resided in Rochester county, New York.

Patriot.—The Patriot collapsed a flue, on the Ohio river, when near Owensboro, Kentucky, on the 13th of April, 1829, scalding four men severely.

Island Packet.—The steam ferry boat Island Packet exploded at Wheeling, Va., December 9th, 1847, killing a son of Hugh Clarke and a traveller, name unknown. Two other persons were wounded.

Eliza.—The steamer Eliza going from St. Louis to New Orleans, was snagged and sunk in the Mississippi, five miles from the mouth of the Ohio, October 8th, 1842. About forty persons were drowned.

Hector.—The steamboat Hector was burned on the Mississippi, near Island No. 74, two miles above Napoleon, Ark., November 16th, 1842, while on her way to New Orleans. A passenger and one of the crew perished in the flames.

Cutter.—The steamboat Cutter, Capt. Collins, collapsed a flue at Pittsburgh, March 17th 1843. *Killed*—Andrew McClelland, second engineer, three of the crew and ten deck passengers. The first engineer was mortally wounded.

Rob Roy.—The steamer Rob Roy collapsed a flue on the Mississippi river, four miles above Columbia, Ark., May 19th, 1836. Eight persons were killed, and fourteen others were badly scalded.

Cahawba.—The steamer Cahawba, Capt. Curtis, struck a snag in the Mississippi, eight miles above the mouth of Arkansas river, November 21st, 1836. One man was killed.

Post Boy.—The steam tow boat Post boy exploded near the mouth of the Mississippi, December 19th, 1840. The engineer was killed, and two of the crew were badly scalded.

Collision of the Archer and Die Vernon.—The steamboats Archer and Die Vernon came in collision five miles above the mouth of Illinois river, November 27th, 1851. The Archer was cut in two and immediately sunk. Most of the passengers on the lower deck were drowned, The names of those who perished, as far as could be ascertained, are given below. *Drowned*—Jane Smyers and six children; Susan Dick; Peter Maloney and family, consisting of eight persons; Albert Teesdale; Walter Sniker; Mr. Abbott; Felix Arthur and family, consisting of five persons; Andrew Hardy and sister; Dennis Corcoran; Samuel Mulholland, Alton, Ill.; Anna Sherman, and ten others, names unknown.

Collision of the Collier and Domain.—The small steamboat Collier was run into by the steamer Domain, on the Ohio river, a few miles above Wheeling, November 7th, 1844. The Collier sunk, and one of her crew was drowned.

Volant.—The steamer Volant was burned on Yazoo river, thirty miles above Vicksburg November 15th, 1853. A drunken passenger was burned to death.

Collision of the Detroit and Marion.—The steamer Detroit ran into the Marion on the Detroit river, August 8th, 1841. Several persons were drowned, but no names are given.

Troy.—The steamer Troy exploded on Lake Erie, at the mouth of Niagara river, March 19th, 1850. Fifteen persons were killed. The only names given are, John Buckley, Thomas Gant, William Allen, William Worthington, Nicholas Leland and Peter Leland.

James Robb.—*A man frightened to death*—The steamboat James Robb took fire on the Mississippi river, January, 1852. Great consternation prevailed in the boat. The passengers were running to and fro, doing all in their power, as usual, to increase the confusion, when a gentleman named Moore, from Memphis, Tenn., who had about $6,000 in a belt fastened around his waist, seized his trunk and made for the forecastle, but after running a few yards, he fell down dead. There was every reason to believe that he was literally frightened to death. His trunk contained a large amount of money in addition to that which he carried about his person, all of which was delivered to the friends of the deceased. The fire was soon extinguished, and the boat was but slightly damaged.

Buckeye Belle.—Tne steamer Buckeye Belle exploded on the Ohio river, near Marietta,

November 12th, 1852. Several members of the Ohio legislature were killed or badly wounded. Senator Covey died in consequence of his wounds on the next day. Twenty-two lives were lost.

MAGNOLIA.—The steamboat Magnolia exploded at St. Simon's island, Georgia, January 9th, 1852. Thirteen persons were killed, and eleven injured.

GEORGE WASHINGTON.—The steamboat George Washington exploded near Grand Gulf, Miss., January 14th, 1852. Sixteen persons were killed, and ten wounded.

PITSER MILLER.—The steamer Pitser Miller exploded at the mouth of White river, January 23d, 1852. Three persons were killed.

DE WITT CLINTON.—The steamer De Witt Clinton struck a snag near Memphis, Tennessee, January 25th, 1852. Forty lives were lost.

CADDO.—The steamer Caddo was sunk near New Orleans, February 14th, 1852. Five lives were lost.

MARY KINGSLAND.—The steam tow-boat Mary Kingsland exploded February 29th, 1852. Five persons were killed, and three wounded.

INDEPENDENCE.—The steamer Independence was wrecked in Matagorda Bay, Texas, March 26th, 1852. Seven lives were lost.

REDSTONE.—The steamer Redstone exploded near Carrolton, Ind., April 3d, 1852. Twenty-one persons were killed, and twenty-five were injured.

POCAHONTAS.—The steamer Pocahontas exploded near Chocton Bend, Mississippi river, April 11th, 1852. Twelve lives were lost.

PRAIRIE STATE.—The steamer Prairie State collapsed her flues on the Illinois river, April 25th, 1852, killing and wounding twenty persons.

PITTSBURGH.—The steamer Pittsburgh broke her cylinder head, May 19th, 1852. One man killed.

FOREST CITY.—The steamer Forest City collapsed a flue at Cleveland, Ohio, June 14th, 1852. Three persons killed.

ST. JAMES.—The steamer St. James exploded near New Orleans, July 5th, 1852. Forty lives were lost.

CITY OF OSWEGO.—The propellor City of Oswego sunk near Cleveland, Ohio, July 12th, 1852. Twenty lives lost.

HENRY CLAY.—The steamer Henry Clay was burned near Yonkers, on the Hudson river, July 28th, 1852. Eighty persons were killed, and twenty more were more or less injured.

NORTH STAR.—The steamboat North Star, on her way from Tuscaloosa to New Orleans, was destroyed by fire Feb. 28th, 1842. Sixteen persons were killed, among whom was Col. C. D. Connor, of Marengo, Mich., and Mr. Tannyhill of Tuscaloosa.

ANTOINETTE DOUGLASS.—This boat blew up on the Alabama river, November 26th, 1850, killing thirty persons and wounding 16 others.

GEN. BENT.—This boat struck a snag below Memphis, in January, 1854, causing her to sink in a few moments. Twenty-one deck passengers were lost.

PEARL.—This boat was sunk by coming in contact with the steamer Natchez, on the Mississippi river, near Conrad Point. Two deck hands were crushed to death, and three others lost. Captain Stanley was also lost.

COLLISION OF THE OHIO AND W. B. CLIFTON.—The steamers Ohio and W. B. Clifton came in collision on the Mississippi river, on the 2d of April, 1854, near Columbus, and the Clifton sunk in twenty-five feet water, drowning seven deck passengers.

CHARLES BELCHER, LIAH, TUNA, SAXON, CRESCENT, AND NATCHEZ.—On the night of the 3d of February, 1854, the steamers Charles Belcher, Liah, Tuna, Saxon, Crescent and Natchez were consumed at the wharf at New Orleans. Fourteen negroes, Captain James Leathers, of the Natchez, the chambermaid and her child, all perished in the flames; Mrs. Carlisle, of St. Louis, (wife of Captain Carlisle, of the steamer Charles Belcher,) was sick in bed at the time of the accident; but leaped, with great presence of mind and heroism, from the hurricane deck, with her child in her arms, and was saved; Captain James Leathers was a young man, and highly esteemed by all who knew him; he was with General Lopez in his first expedition against Cuba, and fought like a lion.

ST. LOUIS.—The ferry boat St. Louis exploded her boilers at St. Louis, March 23, 1851, killing Wm. W. Benson, first enginer; Paul Trundley, second do.; Alex. McKean, pilot; Sebastian Smith, fireman; John W. James, aged about sixteen years; a daughter of Mr. Louis Jarvis, aged fifteen years; Albert Wells, Ernest Augustus Smidt, Isaac Coop; Meriwether S. Smith; a boy, name unknown; Dr. Truitt, Illinoistown; an Irish boy, name unknown; a young man named Robert Hardin or Harding, whose body was blown about one hundred yards on the levee, and seven others drowned—sixteen badly wounded.

COLLISION OF THE LOWELL AND VINTON.—These steamers came in collision on the Ohio river, just below Wheeling, on the night of the 24th of March, 1851, the Lowell sinking in a few moments. *Drowned*—J. B. McKeon, first engineer; two firemen, and a family of twelve persons from Bedford, Pa. Mr. D. Evans, carpenter, and part owner of the Lowell, had a very narrow escape from death, being cut out from the deck as the boat was going under.

MINSTREL.—The steamboat Minstrel, Capt. McComer, from Cincinnati bound to Nashville, struck a floating log, and sunk on the 3d day of February, 1844, ten miles below Madison, Ohio. One deck passenger was drowned.

HUGH L. WHITE.—This steamboat collapsed a flue, a few miles below Demopolis, Alabama. A colored boy, the property of W. R. Hardaway, was killed. One passenger and the second engineer were badly scalded.

BEAVER.—A small steamboat, called the Beaver, plying on Bayou Plaquemine, was burnt, February 10, 1844. A negro child was killed.

ATLAS.—The boiler of the steam tow-boat Atlas burst on the 1st day of April, 1828, at the mouth of the Mississippi river. She had came alongside of a vessel which was to be towed up to New Orleans. When the steamer had made fast to this vessel, the bell gave the signal to proceed; but, as soon as the machinery was put in motion, the head of the boiler was blown off. This boiler-head was of cast iron, and in an unsound condition before the explosion. The second engineer was killed.

PHŒNIX.—About 12 o'clock, M., on the 24th day of May, 1843, the tow-boat Phœnix, Captain Annable, having in tow the ship Flavius, from Liverpool, burst three of her boilers, a short distance below Carrollton, on the Mississippi river. There were twenty men on the Phœnix, four of whom were immediately killed, and three others were more or less hurt. *Killed*—Charles Davis, an Irishman; John, a Portugese; George Granger, an American fireman; and another fireman, name not mentioned. *Wounded*—John Clarke, the pilot of the Phœnix. He was severely scalded, and was not expected to live. James Skinner, second engineer, dangerously scalded; five firemen were also scalded, three of them very severely. The Captain of the British ship in tow, was struck and slightly injured by a piece of plank hurled from the Phœnix by the force of the explosion.

GENEVA.—The explosion of the steamer Geneva took place on the night of December 2, 1852, twenty miles above St. Louis, on the Mississippi river. All the boilers burst simultaneously, and the boat was totally wrecked. The cause of the explosion remains a mystery to this day. The engineer was tried for manslaughter, and acquitted. *Killed*—Captain Dean, a passenger; Captains Johnson and Perry; Mr. Johnson, the clerk; John Ingraham; and Mr. Miller. *Wounded*—Alex. Kelsey, first engineer; second do., and the mate; and several others whose names are not mentioned. The body of Captain Charles Dean was found burnt to a crisp. He was a highly esteemed citizen of St. Louis. He had been, at different times, commander of several boats, but had quit the river and entered the commission business, as a partner in the firm of Carson & Dean. The Geneva had stopped to take in wood at the time of the disaster.

KANAWHA PACKET.—One of the boilers of the Kanawha Packet exploded on the 27th day of June, 1829, at Guyandotte, on the Ohio river. The boat was detained there for a few minutes to land passengers, and when about to leave the wharf some other business gave occasion for a delay of half an hour. When the steamer was shoved out from the shore, the engineer discovered that the water in the boilers had sunk below the guage-cocks, and as the steam was high, he appeared to be alarmed. At this moment, another detention was caused by sending a passenger ashore in the yawl. As soon as this was done, the engineer started the machinery again, and as the motion began, both heads were blown out of one of the boilers. Eight persons, including the two engineers, were killed.

PHŒNIX.—The steam tow-boat Phœnix exploded January 21, 1847, at the head of South-west Pass, Mississippi river, while engaged in towing the ship Manchester and the barque Leontine. *Killed*—Samuel Dill, second engineer of the Phœnix; James Lathrop, pilot; Joseph Lancaster, mate; Henry Haick, steersman; Charles Smith and John Ricardiff, deck hands; Owen Jones and Martin Boyle, firemen. Twelve persons were killed on board of the Manchester, the ship in tow, and two on board of the barque Leontine. *Wounded*—Mr. Fisk, first engineer of the Phœnix; eight passengers of the Manchester, and two of the Leontine Both of the vessels in tow were considerably damaged, and the Phœnix likewise was much injured.

MAJESTIC.—The steamer Majestic, when about to start from Memphis, on her regular trip to St. Louis, May 25, 1835, met with a deplorable accident. The passengers, of whom there was a large number, were attracted to the starboard side of the boat to witness some interesting object on shore, and the crowd collected on that side caused the boat to careen considerably. As soon as the throng dispersed, and the boat resumed her right position, the larboard boiler collapsed. Forty persons were more or less scalded; and, although some were killed instantly, eight or ten died on the following day, and several of the others were believed to be incurable.

LANCASTER, No. 3.—This boat burst a steam pipe while lying at Stepstone, Ky., above Cincinnati, July 1855, scalding to death John Kenney, James Kelley, and Thos. Joyce, deck hands, of Cincinnati, besides severely scalding three others.

OCEAN WAVE.—This boat took fire August 1855, while on Lake Ontario, about forty miles above Kingston. At the time of the discovery of the fire she was nearly two miles from shore, which she was immediately headed for, but so intense was the heat that the machinery gave out, and she drifted to sea. The entire cabin was consumed, and the hull sunk out of sight in fifteen minutes. *Lost*—Mr. Trumbull, first engineer; Julias Santers, barkeeper; the cook of the steamer; Mrs Donald; the nurse and three children of the cashier of the Gore Bank, Hamilton, C. W.; three ladies, names unknown; Mr. Lyman B. Fisk, of the firm of H. S. Humphrey's, of Ogdensburg; besides sixteen others, no names given.

WESTERN WORLD.—This boat was sunk on a dark night, January, 1853, by coming in collision with H. R. W. Hill. The accident occurred on the Mississippi river, just below Princeton. The Western World was crowded with passengers, and over twenty-five lives were lost—deck passengers. The World was turned bottom upwards, and sunk in fifty feet of water, proving an entire loss to her owner, Capt. Alexander Norton. A part of the wreck floated for fifteen miles, when it was caught, and one woman and child was rescued from it.

FARMER.—This boat blew up on the night of the 23d of March, 1853, when about ten miles from Galveston, in the bay, on her way from Houston, Texas. *Killed*—S. E. Hart, W. Hubby, T. Hale, the barkeeper, and several others. *Missing*—Capt. Webb, the commander of the Farmer; Thos. Prichard, clerk of do.; Caleb Robertson, of Galveston, Texas; Mr. Dunlevy, carpenter; Philip Mandus, Mexican, from Gaudalajara; Mr. Warner, second engineer; and C. H. Sterns. *Wounded*—Mr. Dixon; Blakeman, mate; Mr. Curtis, the engineer; Mr. McCormick, the pilot; G. Hunter, of Cincinnati; and John Mc Reynolds. The ladies all escaped unhurt. The steamer Neptune was about one hour employed in taking off the killed and wounded. The scene was horrible. The United States mail books, and money of the boat was lost.

COLLISION OF THE PAUL JONES AND MAJOR BARBOUR.—The steamer Paul Jones from New Orleans to Louisville, and the steamer Major Barbour, Capt. H. J. Spotts, came in collison on the morning of the 3d of February, 1848, about 4 o'clock, near Troy, on the Ohio river, sinking the Major Barbour to her hurricane roof in a few minutes, causing the loss of the second clerk, who resided at Henderson, Ky.; two ladies and two children lost, and several other persons missing and supposed to have been drowned. The boat took fire, while sinking, from the lamp in the cabin, which consumed the principal part of the cabin that remained above the water. The hull was afterwards raised. The Paul Jones received but slight injury.

List of U. S. Licensed Pilots and Engineers

AT CINCINNATI.

BY ACT OF CONGRESS, 30TH AUGUST, 1852.

PILOTS.

NAMES.	FROM
Anshutz, William J.	Cincinn. to N. Orleans.
Ayres, Monroe	Cin. to Pitts'gh, Zanes.
Albert, Adam,	Cin. to New Orleans.
Armstrong, John L.	" "
Aldrich, Aquilla	Cin. to St. L., Laf'tte.
Attenborough, W. M.	Cin. to New Orleans.
Autenheimer, F. A.	" "
Ambrose, James	Cin. to N. O., St. L's.
Andrews, J. M.	Cincinnati to Cairo.
Attenborough, Rich. H.	Cin. to New Orleans.
Ballinger, Jerry S.	" "
Brashears, Henry C.	Cincin. to Louisville.
Brashear, Charles B.	Cin. to N. O., Ft. Sm.
Brashear, Benjamin F.	Cin. to New Orleans.
Broker, John	Louisv. to N. Orleans.
Birch, John R	" "
Biddle, Boulden	Pittsburgh to St. Louis.
Barton, Wm. H.	Big S., Nash., Laf'tte.
Birch, Richard E.	Cin. to New Orleans.
Bruce, Thomas J.	Cin. to Nash., Ky. R.
Burks, George	Kn. R. Nash., St. L's.
Bryson, Isaac	Pitts'gh to Louisville.
Boss, Robert	Cin. to Cairo. Laf'ette.
Blinn, Orra	Cincin. to Lafayette.
Bell, George W.	Pittsb'gh to Louisville.
Ballinger, Daniel H.	Cin. to New Orleans.
Blinn, Lorenzo	Cincin. to Lafayette.
Blashford, David	Pittsb'gh to St. Louis.
Burt, William E.	Cincin. to St. Louis.
Brickell, Samuel	Cin. to New Orleans.
Burt, Samuel W.	Cin. to St. Louis.
Burks, Samuel	Cin. St. L's, Nashville.
Birch, Hiram,	Pitts. " "
Boughner, Peter	Cincin. to Portsmouth.
Blinn, Enos M.	Pitts. Cairo, Lafay'te.
Boss, Alexander	Cin., N. O., St. Louis.
Burne, Andrew	Pomeroy to Louisville.
Baldwin, Robert G.	Cin., N. O.. St. Louis.
Chapman, William S.	Cincin. to St. Louis.
Cullum, George W.	Cincin. to Nashville.
Connor, John,	Portsmouth to R. Sun.
Corns, James,	Cincin. to Big Sandy.
Collier, Wheeler-2 Cl's	Cin. to New Orleans.
Case, John	Cincin. to Portsmouth.
Conway, John L.	Cincin. to St. Louis.
Clark, James A.	" "
Christ, George W.	Pitts. to New Orleans.
Clark, George W.	Pitts. to St. Louis.

NAMES.	FROM
Campbell, George W.	Cin., St. L., Lafayette.
Collier, Thomas	Cincin. to Portsmouth.
Carroll, James	" St. L's., Memphis.
Craig, DeKalb	" to Louisville.
Crawford, Thomas R.	Pitts. to Louisville.
Case, Loyd	Cincin. to Portsmouth.
Collier, Joseph	" "
Cox, William B.	" New Orleans.
Cooper, Jocomus	Wheeling to Lafayette.
Coleman, John R.	Cincinnati to St. Louis.
Collier, Edmond	" "
Crawford, Jacob	Pitts. to Louisville.
Corns, Wesly D.	Cincin. to Big Sandy.
Canada, James O.	" N. Orleans.
Caffrey, Barnett J.	Pom., Nash., M. A. R.
Cooper, Robert	Cincin. to Manchester.
Conner, Andrew,	" Foster's L'ng.
Davidson, Peyton G.	Cincin. to Pomeroy.
Dugan, Alonza	N. Rich to Patriot.
David, Charles	Cincin. to Louisville.
Dickerson, Jefferson	" to St. Louis.
Doxen, John R.	" to N. Orleans.
Dean, Alexander	Pittsburgh to St. Louis.
Dodson, Charles	Cin., N. O., St. Louis.
Dugan, Hugh	Cin., New Orleans.
Deunis, Ambrose	" Wheeling.
Davis, Lewis	Pitts., Louisv., Zanes.
Downing, John B.	Cincin. to N. Orleans.
Davidson, Wm. F.	" Pom'y, B. San.
Dunseth, David	" N. O., St. Louis.
Dittman, Charles H.	" Louisville.
Dugan, William	" Madison.
Dean, John W.	" New Orleans.
David, John	" Madison
Devinney, Osburne	" Cairo, Lafay'te.
Emmerson, Allison	Cin. to New Orleans.
Echols, Marcus A.	Cin., St L's and Nash.
Fawcett, Snelling, P.	Cin. to Louisville.
Frazier, Benjamin A.	Cin. to New Orleans.
Frazier, Anthony J.	Cin. to Nashville.
Ford, Alexander	" New Orleans.
Frazier, Alexander	" Mem, Nash.
Fraim, Archibald	" N O., St. L's.
Fainey, Riley	" Kan Salines.
Fyffe, Robert	" Nashville.
Farrow, Thornton J.	" St. Louis.
Fainey, Charles J.	" Kan Salines.
Ford, William	" N. O., St. L's.

PILOTS.

NAMES.	FROM
Fleming, Andrew	Cin. to N. O., St. Louis.
Gilleland, Jacob	Cincin. to Pittsburg.
Gray, John	" N. Orleans.
Gough, Isaac D	" N. Orleans.
Golden, James S.	" K Salines.
Gardner, Amos	" Nash., L'te.
Garrett, William	" Ky. River.
Gosney, William J.	Pitts. to Louisville.
Golden, Warren	Cin., Pom., K. Salin.
Guthrie, Joseph S.	Cin., Louisv., K. R.
Gregg, William A.	Cin., N. O., St. Louis.
Hicks, William	Pitts. to Louisville.
Howard, Thomas H.	Cin. N. O. and St. L's.
Holloway, John W.	Cin. to Pom., K. Riv.
Holden, Daniel L.	N. Rich. to Patriot.
Holton, Wm. J.	Cincin. to Louisville.
Hughs, Charles	" Pomeroy.
Hanselman, Henry	" N. Orleans.
Harrison, John A.	" "
Hildreth, Samuel F.	" Louisville.
Hukill, George M.	" Nashville.
Hukill, Francis M.	" St. L., Nas.
Hinton, William	" N. Orleans.
Hopkins, David O.	Pittsburg to St. Louis.
Harrison, Wm. H.	Cincin., N. O., Nash.
Hawk, Columbus B.	Cin., N. O., St. Louis.
Hiner, James	Cin. to Big Sandy.
Handlin, Alex. H.	" N. O., St Louis.
Harrison, Henry B.	" New Orleans.
Hoel, William R.	" "
Hall, Joseph W.	" St. Louis.
Hiner, David A.	" N. O., St. Louis.
Henderson, John	" Foster's Landing.
Hales, Hugh R.	" Nash., Laf., Ca'o.
Halloway, Charles M.	Mariett., Louis., K. R
Honshill, Wm E.	Cin. to Guyandotte.
Jenkins, Napoleon	Cin. to Louisville
Jacobs, John	Cin. to St L., Nash.
Jolly, Alsibad	Cin. to New Orleans.
Jacobs, Josiah	Pittsburg to St. Louis.
Jones, James L.	Cin. to St. Louis.
Jordon Aaron M.	Cin., N. O., St Louis.
Johnson, James	Pitts., St L., Laf'tte.
Jolly, Oscar B.	Cin., St. Louis N. O.
Keating, Loftus,	Cin. to N. O., St. L's.
Kavenaugh, Daniel J.	Cin. to St. Louis.
Knowles, Leverett	Pitts. to Louisville.
Kerr, William M.	" "
Kelsey, Naaman	Cin. to N. O., St. L's.
Knox, James	Cincin. to Louisville.
Keeler, Edwin	" St. Louis.
Kavenaugh, Dennis	" St. Louis.
Kane, James V. O.	" St. Louis.
Kelburn, Charles C.	" Memphis.
Kavenaugh Patrick	" St. Louis.
Laughlin, William W.	" N. Orleans.
Litterell, William	" N. Orleans.
Lallance, William T. A.	" Parkersburg.
Logan, Linas	Cin., St. Louis, Laf'te.
Larew, Edwin W.	Cin., St. Louis, N. O.
Laughlin, Samuel	Cin., Nash., S. L., La
Louderback, J. H.	Pitts. to Louisville.
Litterell, Bejamin F.	Cin. to New Orleans.
Melvin, John	Napo'on to Ft. Gibson.
Montague, William J.	Cin. to St. Louis.
Matthews, James H.	" New Orleans.
Myers, Michael	" St. Louis.
Morgan, Evan	Pitts. to Louisville.
Myers, William M.	Cin. to New Orleans.
Moore, Jesse	Pitts. to Louisville.
Murry, Francis H.	Cin., St. L., Lafayette.
Madison, James H.	Cin. to St. Louis.
Marshall, Alfred	" St. Louis.
Morrison, Abraham B.	" St. L. & N. O.
Marshall, Isaac	" St. Louis.
Mace, Ellis	" Pomeroy.
Murdock, David J.	" St. Louis.
Mullen, Samuel	" St. L. & N. O.
Miller, Joseph	" Pomeroy.
Miller, James M.	" New Orleans.
Malone, George	" New Orleans.
Minick, Hiram	" New Orleans.
Morledge, John	" New Orleans.
McFall, John	Cin. to N. O., St. L's.
McCammont, Joseph	" N. O., St. L.
McBride, James	" New Orleans.
McFall, Charles R.	" N. O., St. L.
McGee, Wylie	" Nash, La., St.L.
McBride, Matthew	" Marietta.
McFall, Edward	" N. O., St. L.
McMasters, Gilbert	" St. Louis.
McGuire, Richard	" Lafayette.
McBride, Samuel	Pitts. to St. L. & N. O.
McLean, William	Wheeling to Louisv.
McKinley, William	Cin. to N. O. & St. L.
McKay, Rowley S.	" N. O & Ft. S.
McComas, Harry G.	" Nashville.
Nelson, Robert T.	" New Orleans.
Oursler, Charles—2 C's	" New Orleans.
Owen, Charles F.	" Memphis.
O'Neal's, George	" Pittsburgh.
Parker, William F.	Cincin. to N. Orleans.
Parker, Samuel	Pomeroy to Louisville.
Parsons, J. R. B.	Cincin. to Big Sandy.
Prather, James H.	" " Maysville.
Purcell, Bryson	" " N. Orleans.
Purcell, Joseph R.	" " "
Pierce, Lewis	" " "
Pierce, Duter J.	" " "
Patterson, James	" N. O. & St. L.
Patterson, Edwin	" N. Orleans.
Phillips, Thomas	" Lou. & Ky. R.
Riley, John C.	" N. Orleans.
Rowley, James H.	" Pittsburgh.
Runyon, James D.	" Louisville.
Rairdon, Nathaniel	" N. B'd, L'k R.
Robinson, John T.	" Madison.
Ross, Oliver S.	" N. Orleans.
Rogers, Wm. 2d class.	" "
Ross, Oliver	" "
Rhodes, Sam'l C.	Pitts. to Louisville.
Riley, Francis A.	Cincin. to N. Orleans.
Reed, Hiram	Pitts. to St. L. & Mem.
Randolph, Wm. F.	Pitts. to St. Louis.
Ruckman, Shepard	Cincin. to N.O. & St.L.
Roush, Francis	Cincin. to Pomeroy.
Smith, John T.	" St. Louis.
Smith, Albert H.	" "
Stout, John	" N. Orleans.
Smith, Madison	" N. O. Ft. Smith.
Seeds, James M.	" N. Orleans.
Smith, Hezekiah	Pitts. to Louisville.
Sebastion, John	Cincin. to N. O. & St. L.
Stewart, Daniel V.	" N Orleans.
Shinkle, Josiah	" Portsmouth.
Symmes, Henry	" N. O. & St. L.
Stewart, Coleman W.	" " "
Stewart, William A.	" " "
Scott, Moses A.	" Cairo & Lafay'e.
Smith, Edward J.	" to St. Louis.

PILOTS.

Names.	From	Names.	From
Seeds, Charles	Cincin. to St. Louis.	Woodward, Benjamin	" Louisville.
Smith, Joseph C.	" N. Orleans.	Weaver, Daniel	Cincin. to Memphis.
Sebree, Mathias	" "	Wade, Josiah P.	" N. Orleans.
Smithers, John R.	Pitts. to Louisville.	Warman, James	" "
Smith, John F.	Cincin. to St. Louis.	Weaver, B. J. B.	Cin. to Mem. & Nash.
Sebree, John W.	Cin. Aurora, & L'k R.	Wells, Christopher	Pitts. to Louisville.
Shinkle, Oliver P.	N. Richm'd to Louisv.	Woolf, George	Cincin. to Ft. Smith.
Simpson, A. W.	Cin., St. L., Mem.. Nash.	Whitney, Robert	" N. Orleans.
Tatman, Theodore	Cincin to N. Orleans.	Whitten, Joseph W.	" "
Tong, William H.	" "	Williamson, Euclid	Cin. to N. O. & St. L.
Trunnell, Thomas	" "	Williamson, Elbert W.	Pitts. to St. Louis.
Whittan, Oscar D.	" "	Weaver, John J.	Cincin. to Louisville.
Webber, Charles	" Memphis.	Wiley, William	Louisv. to Kan Sal's.
Wilson, A. D.	" Pittsburgh.	Weaver, Davis G.	Cincin. to Memphis.
Wood, Andrew	" Pom., K. R.	Wade, Richard M.	" N. Orleans.
Woolf, Daniel D.	Pomeroy to Louisville.	Wykoff, Milton J.	" Portsm'th.
Wade, David E.	Cincin. to N. Orleans.	Williamson, John A.	Cin. to N. O. & St. L.
Wright, William	Cin. to Kan. Salines.	Young, Thomas E.	Cincin. to N. Orleans.
Williamson, Arch.	" Pomeroy.	Young, Finley	Cin. to Pom. & L. R.
Williams, Harrison S.	Pitts. to St. Louis.		

ENGINEERS.

Names.	Class.		Names.	Class.		Names.	Class.	
Arthur, William	2d	"	Cammitz, Joseph W.	1st	"	Hillings, Lewis G.	"	"
Ashford, Tebulon,	1st	"	Clements, Anderson	"	"	Homan, James	1st	"
Andrews, Chas. B.	"	"	Cornell, George W.	2d	"	Hirst, Samuel B.	2d	"
Anspaugh, John	"	"	Carver, Sylvester	"	"	Hollman, Jasper	"	"
Andrews, Edwards	"	"	Deon, Alexander	"	"	Hunter, Wm. A.	"	"
Anstead, John A.	"	"	Davis, Joseph H.	"	"	Homan, Wm. T.	"	"
Arthur, Robert W.	2d	"	Davis, Paul	1st	"	Hand, Jeremiah	"	"
Andrews, William	1st	"	Doty, James	2d	"	Irwin, James	1st	"
Bloxen, Elisha	"	"	Doty, John	"	"	Jewett, Decatur S.	2d	"
Bowers, Joseph	2d	"	Downey, William	"	"	Johnson, Wm.	1st	"
Bagby, Abner	"	"	Estep, Joshua	1st	"	Jones, Rich'd H.	"	"
Burdge, Henry R.	1st	"	Everhart, John H.	2d	"	Johnson, John	"	"
Benninger, W. H.	"	"	Everson, Benjamin	1st	"	Keen, Philip	2d	"
Brown, Hiram A.	"	"	Estep, Wm. H.	2d	"	Ketchum, Jacob	1st	"
Black, Ambrose	2d	"	Fleming, James	1st	"	King, Wm. R.	"	"
Ballard, Stephen	"	"	Falkner, Charles S.	"	"	Keys, James L.	"	"
Batcheldor, Andrew J	"	"	Farrall, Thomas	"	"	Kelly, Andrew J.	2d	"
Batterson, John A.	1st	"	Falkner, Lemuel	"	"	Kelly, Michael	"	"
Brashear, Moses	"	"	Fleming, John C.	"	"	Kountz Josiah	1st	"
Burns, Andrew	2d	"	French, John	"	"	Kirkpatrick, David	2d	"
Buffington, Edwd J.	"	"	Fox, Irwin	"	"	Ketchum, Myers	"	"
Barnett, Abraham	"	"	Green, Caleb	"	"	Kidwell, Wash.	1st	"
Brown, Wm. D.	"	"	Goble, Stephen	"	"	Kinniston, James	"	"
Bennett, John	"	"	Garrison, John	"	"	Kerns, Thomas	"	"
Brooks, John T.	"	"	Goble, Samuel B.	"	"	Kennelly, Harman	2d	"
Baynum, Edward	2d	"	Griffith, Samuel	2d	"	Krantz, Geo. H.	"	"
Burtnett, Spencer	"	"	Gough, John	"	"	Lionberger, Wm.	1st	"
Clements, Daniel B.	1st	"	Goble, David	"	"	Lober, Jacob	"	"
Coffin, William	"	"	Harrison, Wm. D.	"	"	Lester, Marcus	"	"
Couch, John R.	"	"	Hedges, Samuel	"	"	Lanning, Paul	"	"
Case, Joseph	"	"	Horner, John	1st	"	Lane, Lewis L.	2d	"
Conly, Peter	"	"	Hershberger, L. C.	"	"	Mix, Wm. F.	1st	"
Christopher, Charles	"	"	Harbaugh, Lemuel	"	"	Miller, Wm.	"	"
Clements, Enoch	"	"	Holmes, Perry B.	2d	"	Mills, Wm.	"	"
Crumlish, Daniel	"	"	Henry, John B.	1st	"	Maddox, Richard	"	"
Carroll, Randolph	"	"	Hurst, William,	"	"	Minor, Robert	"	"
Clements, Ambrose S.	"	"	Hanselman, John B.	2d	"	Middlecoff, John G.	"	"
Curtis, William G.	"	"	Hartwig, Henry	1st	"	Miller, John	"	"
Carroll, De Witt	"	"	Hand, Benj.	"	"	Manning, John	"	"
Cox, John	"	"	Hayman, Benj. F.	"	"	Martin, Wm. J.	"	"
Cockayne, Dowden	"	"	Hardin, Wm. M.	2d	"	Montgomery, J. D.	"	"
Clark, William	2d	"	Hunter, Wm. N.	"	"	Manear, Samuel	2d	"

ENGINEERS.

NAMES.	CLASS.	NAMES.	CLASS.	NAMES.	CLASS
Malone, Thos. W.	1st "	Rensford, Henry	1st "	Thompson, Daniel L.	1st "
Martin, J.	" "	Rensford, Thomas	2d "	Tolle, Micaiah	" "
Maralta, J.	" "	Rose, Thomas	" "	Toucher, Timothy J.	2d "
Metcalf, James T.	2d "	Ridley, William H.	1st "	Taber, Oscar J.	" "
Marshall, J.	" "	Reed, Thomas J.	" "	Van Forsen, A. C.	" "
McClury, Hobson	2d "	Roan, John	2d "	Van Birkalew, F.	" "
McCullough, John	" "	Roup, Jonas T.	1st "	Voorhees, Com. D.	1st "
McGinnis, Thomas	1st "	Rose, J. J.	2d "	Vaughn, James P.	2d "
McLean, Robert L.	" "	Radcliff, John	" "	Willey, William A.	" "
McLean, Jesse	" "	Simmons, Benj.	" "	Webb, John A.	1st "
McNabb, Melvin R.	2d "	Smith, William B.	" "	Woodward, Henry	" "
McFarland, W. D.	1st "	Spronse, James A.	" "	Webb, Stephen W.	" "
McCloskey, George	" "	Stagg, Jesse	" "	Whittaker, James	" "
McCoy, Cornelius	2d "	Smith, Snelling	" "	Wasson, William	" "
Nesbitt, John S.	" "	Squires, Presly	1st "	Woodward, Amos	" "
Nye, Edward M.	1st "	Squires, Henderson	" "	Wilson, Nathan W.	" "
Naylor, Henry	2d "	Stickney, Paul	" "	Wood, William	2d "
Nichols, James	" "	Saunders, Asa M.	2d "	Wagner, James J.	" "
Nelson, Thomas	" "	Scott, Thomas	" "	Warden, Americus	1st "
Osenton, John T.	" "	Senior, George	" "	Washington, John T.	" "
O'Riely, William A.	" "	Summons, David P.	1st "	Wright, Edgar W.	" "
Parker, Benj. F.	1st "	Summons, Frank. E.	2d "	Walton, George	" "
Prather, Edward G.	" "	Simmons, John J.	1st "	Whipple, George	" "
Prather, John G.	" "	Stapp, Edwin	" "	Ward, William W.	" "
Prather, Benj. P.	" "	Smith, Moses B.	" "	Wegman, David	" "
Phillips, William B.	1st "	Smith, John W.	2d "	Watson, Charles	" "
Powell, H. F.	2d "	Smith, George W.	" "	Ward, John	" "
Power, William S.	1st "	Strattenheld, Joseph	2d "	Wagner, William	" "
Prichard, Douglass	2d "	Shaw, Dennison H.	1st "	Weaver, Lewis	2d "
Porter, James B.	" "	Sebree, Norman	2d "	Wright, William	" "
Prather, Grafton O.	" "	Stephenson, Lem. (rev.)	1st "	Williams, Thomas	1st "
Porter, William H.	1st "	Toplas, William W.	2d "	Wasson, Garrison	2d "
Preston, Daniel H.	" "	Trew, James W.	" "	Watson, Elisha	1st "
Robinson, Chas. D.	" "	Troxton, William	1st "	Young, Seneca W.	2d "

List of Pilots and Engineers at St. Louis.

PILOTS.

NAMES.	FROM	NAMES.	FROM
Arrington, T. H.	Mem. to Nap. & W. R.	McKee, Moses	Nap. to Ft. Gibson.
Bateman, Morgan M.	" " "	Montany, Ferd. B.	" White R.
Bowman, Thos. R.	Mem. to St. Frnn. R.	Nixon, Hugh B.	Mem. to Nap. & W. R.
Cabbell Samuel C.	Quincy to Keokuk.	McDonald, Daniel	Mem. to Nap.
Drew, Nathaniel F.	Nash. to. N. O.	Odell, Francis C.	Quincy to Keokuk.
Dearing, Robert	Mem. to White R.	Owens, Wm.	Keo. to Rock Island.
Dearing, John	Mem. to Bol. &. W. R.	Patterson, Tillman D.	Florence to Paducah.
Dupree, Wm. C.	Mem to Bolivar.	Prichard, Hanson R.	Nap. to White R.
Elliott, John	Nash. to Memphis.	Partin, James A.	Mem. to Jackson Pt.
Fletcher, Frs. M.	Mem. to Nap.	Patty, Thomas	Quincy to Keokuk.
Goad, Alexander	Nap. to White R.	Sprout, Thomas	St. Louis to Lasalle.
Huey, Lazarus	Mem. to St. Fran. R.	Scales, Washington	Desmoines River.
Hicks, James	Mem. to Bolivar.	Spain, John D.	Randolph to St. He.
Haight, Silas	Lower Rap. of Miss.	Westley, Robert	St. Louis to Laselle.
Jones, Wm. M.	Mem. to White R.	Whiting, Elijah	Ft. Gibson to N. O.
Jones, John R.	" "	Whiting, Presley	Nap to Ft. Smith.
Joiner, Rufus	" Napoleon.	Waters, Zachariah	" "
Jennings, Robt. J.	" "	Waters, Vincent L.	Mem. to Nap. & W. R.
Kinman, Riley	" Nap. & W. R.	Whiteside, Jonathan	" " "
Lamb, Enos	Louisville to N. O,	Wilds, Wm. R.	Mem. to Ft Gibson
Lainer, Wm. B.	Mem. to Nap.	Whitson, Carter	Mem. to Bolivar.
Mason, Richard M.	" "	Young, John	Nap. to Ft. Smith.
Melvin, John	Nap. to Fort Gibson.		

PILOTS.

Names.	Trade.	Names.	Trade.	Names.	Trade.
Abrahams, James	Ill	Davis, Granville	N O	Holland, Jos B	Mo
Atchison, John W	Ill	Duffy, D F	N O	Hart, Samuel	Ill
Armstrong, Joseph L	U M	Davis, Ira C	N O	Hunter, Thos	Ill
Asbury, D R	Keo	Daugherty, William D	Ill	Howard, Wm	U M
Annis, Asa	Mo	Deans, James C	N O	Hodges, Jno D	N O
Amos, Thomas B	U M	Douglass, Thomas	Ill	Hopkins, Alpheus	O
Atchison, Samuel	U M	Devinney, F K	Ill	Holliday, Wm	U M
Ashbury, D R	U M	Dewitt, Wm L	Ill	Hagerty, Geo W	N O
Allen, James	N O	Dozier, F	Mo	Harbison, Jno	Cairo
Bowen, William	N O	Douglass, Jas M	Mo	Hall, Wilford P	U M
Benton, E G	Ill	Dozier, John	Mo	Henderson, Edward T	Mo
Bacon, George R	O	Davis, Jas A	N O	Hight, Washington	U M
Baker, Barton W	Mo	Drips, Chas A	Mo	Humphries, John B	Mo
Burk, Samuel	Mo	Davis, Wm B	U M	Hernandes, F	Mo
Bell, Squire B	N O	Delphiavelyn, B	N O	Harrington, Jno L	U M
Belt, Lloyd F	Ill	Denoia, Jas	Mo	Homans, Jas B	N O
Brady, James L	N O	Doming, Cyrenius	Ill	Hayden, Jas H	N O
Badger, Alexander	N O	Dozier, Jas	Mo	Harris, John G	N O
Becket, Charles	Ill	Downing, John B	O	Hannum, Philip	Mo
Blunt, Charles W	Mo	Delancy, James C	N O	Humphries, Jno H	Ill
Baker, C W	Mo	Dickson, Phineas	U M	Hale, Jas N	U M
Burk, William	N O	Delisle, John	U M	Henley, Wm T	N O
Blakesley, Willis	U M	Dickson, Jeptha	U M	Herndon, E T	Mo
Barclay, John	N O	Edds, Wm	Mo	Hiner, David	O
Bryan, Joseph W	N O	Ewing, Henry	Ill	Hooper, Jno D	Mo
Baker, Robert	Mo	Ealer, H A	N O	Hale, Thomas	Mo
Baily, Bobert B	Mo	Elton, Henry	U M	Hickcox, Asher N	Mo
Baker, Wlliam B	Mo	Earley, Wm H	O	Johnson, Jas H	Keo
Baaber, Jesse	Mo	Ealer, Geo	N O	Jones, Jno R	Naples
Bryant, William S	Ill	Ealer, Geo	Nas	Jolly, Zobriskie	N O
Bowen, B W S	Ill	Eairchild, Oliver H	Ill	James, Willy	N O
Bersie, Hiram	U M	Fowler, Oscar	Mo	Jamison, Wm C	Mo
Burt, Frank W	Ill	Fowler, Benj	N O	Jackson, Jno H	Mem
Berry, David	U M	Finley, Jas	N O	Jamison, Jesse T	O
Brady, Morris	N O	Fairchild, O H	Ill	Kirkham, H	U M
Bell, Henry C.	Mo	Fisher, Jacob	Ill	Kane, James V O	Mo
Burton, R P	Ill	Farris, Willson	N O	King, Enoch P	N O
Burdeau, Joseph	Mo.	Gere, Wm E	U M	King, John P	U M
Burk, John H	N O	Graham, Jas A	U M	Keating, Wm W	N O
Buchanan, John	N O	Ginggray, Wm	N O	Kelly, J	N O
Cunningham, Alex G	N O	Grant, A M	U M	Kennett, D H	N O
Carroll, Jo W	Cairo	Gallagher, Wm	N O	Kirkham, Samuel	U M
Clay, Littlebury B	Ill	Gray, Wm T	N O	Kellogg, Ira	Ill
Cartwright, Judson	Ill	Goll, Cephas B	U M	Keaser, John	Mo
Chipley, Benton	Ill	Grant, Alex	Ill	Kriban, Wm	N O
Carson, H G	U M	Goll, Wm A	Ill	La Barge, Charles	Mo
Cable, Isaac C	N O	Gordon, Wm P	N O	Lisle, William J	Cairo
Callahan, Edward	U M	Grammar, John J	U M	Lowery, John	Ill
Cromwell, A	Ill	Gregg, Benj W	U M	La Barge, Joseph	Ill
Connoyer, C	Mo	Garrett, Aurin	Ill	Lindell, Peter	U M
Curtis, Samuel	U M	Gray, Edward	O	Lambert, John	Ill
Claymor, Lewis	U M	Grimes, Wm P	U M	Lockridge, Samuel	N O
Criddle, Alex	N O	Grammer, Miles	U M	La Barge, Joseph, Jr	Mo
Cayton, F M	N O	Goll, William	Ill	Leech, James W	Ill
Coleman, James	U M	Goll, Cephas	U M	Lynn, Thomas M	Mo
Colter, William	Ill	Guylick, Samuel	U M	La Ventre, D	Mo
Carroll, George	Osage	Grimes, Absalom	U M	Lee, Hinton L	Mo
Carroll, John	O	Gunsollis, James	Mo	La Barge, Stephen	Mo
Carlisle, John	N O	Gale, John	U M	LeClair, Anto D	U M
Clements, Abner	N O	Gunsollis, John	Mo	La Barge, Allen	Ill
Campbell, J M	U M	Hardy, David H	Napo	Lane, John C	N O
Dudgeon, John T	Mo	Harris, A R	N O	Lamothe, Wm P	Alton
Dickson, James D.	Ill	Harris, Jno J	N O	Lapage, Akin	Ill
Deming, John	N O	Hight, W P	U M	La Barge, John B	Mo

NOTE.—In the above list of pilots, Mo stands for Missouri river; U M for Upper Mississippi river; Ten for Tennessee river; Keo for Keokuk; Mem for Memphis; N O for New Orleans; and O for Ohio.

PILOTS.

Names.	Trade.	Names.	Trade.	Names.	Trade.
Mortimore, James O	Ten	Parker, N W	U M	Stewart, Charles	U M
Mullen, Samuel	N O	Purdew, Jos F	Cairo	Simpson, W C	U M
Miller, Wm A	Mo	Parker, Joseph	U M	Stewart, James	Ill
Morrison, Mort	Mo	Petit, Jeremiah W	N O	Scott, John	N O
Mortineau, John	Ill	Parker, Thomas	U M	Smoot, Wm	Osage
McKenney, James P	Mo	Penney, David	O	Tipton, David	U M
Mundy, Wm	N O	Quick, Jackson	Ill	Thrasher, J N	U M
Montgomery, James	O	Reeder, Alhambra	Mo	Thornburg, Wm O	O
McGarrah, Gales	Mo	Rose, James	Mo	Thomas, James B	Ill
Merrill, John	Mo	Risley, D R	Mo	Taylor, Thomas H	U M
Mulford, Chas	U M	Reese, David E	Ill	Thornburg, Benjamin T	U M
Merrick, Alfred	U M	Redman, Miles T	O	Tennison, John S	N O
Massie, Wm R	Mo	Randolph, Wm W	O	Townsend, James H	N O
Mulloy, Wm C	N O	Russell, James	N O	Tebeau, Edward	Mo
Morrison, Chas	U M	Remlin, Jacob	O	Veits, Luke	Ill
McCloy, John	Mo	Reid, James B	Mo	Vickers, George	U M
Moore, Enos B	N O	Russell, Isaiah	N O	Van Houten, G	N O
McKenney, James A	Ill	Rudd, Leonard	N O	Weaver, John B	Mo
Marsh, Waldo	Ill	Root, Adolphus M	U M	Wolf, A D	Mo
McGinnis, John	U M	Riley, Wm C	Napo	Wright, Wm G	Mo
McQuiggin, Madison	U M	Reed, James	N O	Wilcox, E P	U M
McGinnis, James C	U M	Smith, Cartright	Ill	Wesley, John	Ill
Maloney, John	U M	Scott, Thomas W	Mo.	Wetherow, M	Mo
Matison, Samuel	U M	Strong, Sneed	Cairo	Welborne, Joel H	Mo
McKee, Isaac H	Mo	Stanley, Abraham	Ill	Weaver, Tobias E	Mo
Mines, Wm	Ill	Sutton, J T	N O	Way, John	N O
Matison, Wm	U M	Smoot, Wm	Mo	White, Hugh L	U M
Newhouse, George	N O	Stewart, Wm P	N O	Williams, Demetrius L	U M
Oliver, Joseph G	Mo	Smith, Charles H	Ill	Wright, Robert	Mo
O'Hara, Wm	Ill	Switzer, Henry	N O	Wilson, James	U M
Ohlman, Joseph	Mo	Smith, Erasmus A	N O	Woolford, James	Mo
Ohlman, Lawrence	Mo	Smith, Robert H	N O	Waddle, Jno C	Mo
Owens, Elias H	U M	Sousley, J R	Mo	Wemper, Alfred	U M
Owens, Ephraim	U M	Stephen, Edward	N O	Wetherill, Alex	Ill
Ohlman, Michael	Mo	Stephen, Richard	U M	Willie, A N	N O
Phillips, Henry S	Ill	Sutton, J C	U M	Wilcox, Wm P	Mo
Perrin, Thomas M	N O	Sargent, James S	Ill	Williams, Jno A	Cairo
Price, Robert P	Mo	Scott, John	Ill	Watson, Jno S	N O
Parkinson, John T	Mo	Sargent, Y Z	Ill	Woodward, Cordan R	Ill
Parkinson, Wm	Mo	Stephen, Josiah W	Cairo	White, Henry	U M
Phillips, Richard	N O	Sharp, Lewis	Mo	Wright, Daniel	U M
Parker, James H	U M	Schelmeter, Gasper	Ill	Wellman, Chas V	U M
Postal, Wm C	Mo	Shaw, George	U M	Wetherow, Wm B	Mo
Pratt, C H	N O	Stephens, James A	N O	Woolfolk, R F	N O
Pomroy, David	O	Smith, Robert	N O	Yore, James A	Mo
Postal, Oscar	Mo	Scott, Charles	N O	Yore, Wm A	Mo
Packard, Bryant	Ill	Stephen, Allen	O	Youngblood, Wm C	N O

ENGINEERS.

Names.	Class.		Names.	Class.		Names.	Class.	
Ackerman, Thos	2d	"	Blessing, Ira M	2d	"	Belvin, James	2d	"
Allison, Erasmus	1st	"	Blasdell, Wm A	"	"	Baldwin, John A	"	"
Arbuthnot, Cochran	2d	"	Brannon, Joseph	1st	"	Bostwick, Samuel	"	"
Ackley, John	"	"	Brandon, Wm	"	"	Bennett, Wm A	"	"
Armstrong, James	"	"	Bacon, Hobert C	2d	"	Boles, John C	"	"
Allison, Joel	1st	"	Benson, Jesse W	1st	"	Bartlett, Edward	"	"
Avery, Edward E	"	"	Bail, John	2d	"	Beadle, James H	1st	"
Ainsworth, Wm H	2d	"	Briggs, Wm	"	"	Coonce, John W	1st	"
Burt, Wm B	1st	"	Bruce, John A	"	"	Cook, James W	"	"
Bergaw, Moses	2d	"	Benning, Frederick	1st	"	Corbey, Wm H	"	"
Blessing, Fdk B	1st	"	Black, Zeneas W	"	"	Coy, Abraham	"	"
Baker, Theodore	"	"	Bean, Joseph	2d	"	Carver, Leroy	2d	"
Buffington, Wm	2d	"	Blasdell, Charles W	1st	"	Cranmer, Thomas E	1st	"
Bishop, Preston W	1st	"	Bowen, John L	2d	"	Curtiss, Wm H	"	"

ENGINEERS.

Names.	Class.	
Copley, Milton W	1st	"
Chalfant, Lewis P	"	"
Coyle, Joseph C	"	"
Crole, Martin	2d	"
Cabbell John	1st	"
Cory, Charles F	"	"
Cox, Swepston	"	"
Chaplin, Charles	"	"
Congar, Carlos W	2d	"
Coy, Wm C	1st	"
Collins, Henry H	"	"
Carter, Thornton	2d	"
Cobbs, Thomas	"	"
Coulson, Martin	"	"
Clark, Tilghman	1st	"
Cabbell, Samuel	"	"
Chappell, Wm C	2d	"
Church, Anson W	1st	"
Conley, Charles	"	"
Cox, Wm R	2d	"
Chalton, Edmund	"	"
Condit, David R	"	"
Cooper, John P	"	"
Cheek, Thomas	1st	"
Carlin, Samuel E	"	"
Clemons, Englehart	"	"
Clauburg, Frederick R	"	"
Christman, Abner	2d	"
Deeter, George W	"	"
Duel, Edmund C	"	"
Darby, William	"	"
Dovener, William	1st	"
Donahue, James R	"	"
Dewitt, Charles C	"	"
Davis, Edward	"	"
Davis, Robert	"	"
Detering, Wm	2d	"
Deakin, Lemuel K	1st	"
Dearing, Joseph	"	"
Dale, Isaac A	"	"
Edwards, John S	"	"
Fairfowl, Hector W	"	"
Folcroft, George	2d	"
Fitzgerald, Lewis	1st	"
Fulton, George	"	"
Few, William	"	"
Fulton, Thomas C	2d	"
Furch, Frederick	"	"
Fraim, John	1st	"
Foster, Michael	2d	"
Forbes, William	1st	"
Gay, John	2d	"
Genung, Alfred	1st	"
Grissmore, Nathan	"	"
Grapevine, Frederick	"	"
Gray, Thaddeus	"	"
Goble, George S	"	"
Grisby, Basil G	"	"
Grazier, George	2d	"
Garwood, James	"	"
Griffey, Wm C	1st	"
Gills, John B	2d	"
Gibson, Wm D	"	"
Gray, John	"	"
Graham, John	"	"
Hardesty, John	"	"
Harman, Richard	"	"
Henricks, William	1st	"
Hamilton, William	"	"
Hyatte, Fielding B	1st	"
Hill, David	"	"
Hickman, Nathaniel P	"	"
Harrison, Charles	"	"
Hanfield, Thomas	"	"
Hicks, Wm W	"	"
Hovey, Wallace	2d	"
Hill, William	"	"
Hill, Thomas B	1st	"
Harrison, Nathan C	"	"
Holmes, John	"	"
Herzog, Andrew	2d	"
Handlin, Constant S	1st	"
Hardy, Albert W	"	"
Hill, Samuel G	"	"
Hall, Samuel H	"	"
Harrison Reuben	"	"
Hughes, Joseph H	2d	"
Hawdon, George	1st	"
Harris, Benj W	2d	"
Hamilton, Jacob	1st	"
Habb, Louis	"	"
Hughes, Wm B	2d	"
Hinkle, Wm B	1st	"
Haffey, John	2d	"
Henson, Gustavus A	"	"
Hendricks, Henry B	"	"
Hughes, Patrick	"	"
Ivester, Enoch T	1st	"
Ivers, Charles	2d	"
Johnson, Henry A	"	"
Johnson, Robrt	"	"
Jones, Edwin L	"	"
Jenks, Jacob	2d	"
Jones, Thomas H	1st	"
Jones, Robert	1st	"
Jamison, David S	2d	"
Jones, Emanuel M	"	"
Kelsey, Alexander	1st	"
Knapper, Henry	2d	"
Kintnor, John A	"	"
Kramer, George H	"	"
Kimber, Job V	1st	"
Kimber, George W	2d	"
Keech, Amos	1st	"
Keller, Jacob	2d	"
Kennett, Presly G	1st	"
Lovejoy, Samuel H	"	"
Leftwich, Wm	"	"
Lewis, James H	"	"
Levis, George M	"	"
Lingo, Thomas D	"	"
Lynn, John T	"	"
Ledlie, John	2d	"
Lumpkin, Geo W	"	"
Landerdale Sam	"	"
Lauderdale, Lycurgus	1st	"
Lindsay, David	"	"
Marsh, Wm	"	"
Massott, Julius	"	"
Morgan, Charles	"	"
Miller, Wm	"	"
Montinge, Joseph	"	"
Myers, Wm H	"	"
Mock, Levi	"	"
Mitchell, Thomas T	2d	"
Mislong, Nicholas	"	"
Morgan, Edward	1st	"
Moore, Wm H	"	"
Mitchell, Montefore	1st	"
Mackall, Samuel	2d	"
Mosher, Samuel	"	"
Murray, Charles T	"	"
Morgan, George P	1st	"
Marsh, Frank	"	"
Mead, Wm	"	"
Miller, Thomas	"	"
Moore, Francis H	2d	"
Massott, Oscar	"	"
Merriman, Edward	2d	"
Montgomery, Theodore	"	"
Matthews, Calvin	"	"
Montgomery, Pearson	1st	"
Moffit, Hiram	"	"
McCann, Washington	2d	"
McNeal, Wm	1st	"
McGinnis, James	"	"
McDonald, Samnel	"	"
McCory, John B	2d	"
McKnight, Benj J	"	"
McCarron, Dennis G	"	"
McKnight, J W A	"	"
McCabe, Wm B	1st	"
McGuire, John	"	"
McCord, Arthur C	"	"
Newell, Lewis	"	"
Newell, Charles	"	"
Newcum, Samuel	2d	"
Norris, James	"	"
Nearns, Hamilton C	1st	"
Norman, Andrew J	"	"
Nelson, Thomas	2d	"
Owen, Austin	1st	"
Owen, John W	"	"
Orr, David A	"	"
Owens, James G	"	"
Oram, John	"	"
Oldenburgh, Wm	2d	"
Overton, Harman	"	"
Owens, Huntington	"	"
Owens, Elias W	"	"
Oakley, Thomas	"	"
Pyatte, James A	1st	"
Peyton, Charles S	"	"
Packard, Timothy A	"	"
Pyatte, Larkin	"	"
Peyton, George W	"	"
Packard, Charles W	"	"
Pratt, H R	2d	"
Price, Joseph M.	"	"
Perault, Fabien	1st	"
Parker, Eliphalet	2d	"
Pierce, Ephraim	1st	"
Purcell, George C	"	"
Quick, Luke	"	"
Rose, Wm S	2d	"
Richardson, R H	1st	"
Rossell, James M	"	"
Roff, George	"	"
Ritchy, Lazarus K	"	"
Rambo, Joseph	"	"
Reeder, Alhambra	2d	"
Riter Dewitt C	1st	"
Rose, James	"	"
Reed, John F	"	"
Robirds, Oby	"	"
Richardson, Wm B	"	"
Rodgers, John C	"	"

ENGINEERS.

Names.	Class.		Names.	Class.		Names.	Class.	
Reed, John S	2d	"	Stephenson, Albert	1st	"	Wyley, Samuel P	2d	"
Roe, Wm S	1st	"	Sutton, Abram	"	"	Walker, Alexander	"	"
Rowe, Albert M.	2d	"	Seely, Austin	"	"	Wanny, Bernard	"	"
Reed, Hugh	1st	"	Shultice, Simon	2d	"	Wilthrow, Robert B	"	"
Reeder, Wm H	2d	"	Stackhouse, Wm H	1st	"	Woodville, Alex T	1st	"
Sanford, George S	2d	"	Summerville, Samuel	"	"	Wilson, John W	"	"
Stewart, James G	"	"	Sherman, Wm W	2d	"	Warner, John H	2d	"
Stearns, Ruel J	1st	"	Sheddon, James	"	"	Weaver, Daniel I	"	"
Schofield, William	"	"	Shindle, John	"	"	William, E P	1st	"
Smith, John T	"	"	Stoze, Frederick	1st	"	Ward, Wells	"	"
Scroggs, Wm C	"	"	Skillman, John	"	"	Wolfe, Hiram	"	"
Sherman, Wm W	"	"	Starr, Job V	2d	"	Wagoner, Henry C	"	"
Speckernagle, Wm T	2d	"	Sheppard, Wm	"	"	Woodworth, James	"	"
Sanford Wm W	1st	"	Siefert, Christian	"	"	Wilson, John	"	"
Smith, Wm B	"	"	Toureville, Joseph T	"	"	Winton, William	"	"
Sanders, John Jr.,	2d	"	Tanner, James M	1st	"	Willison William	"	"
Saltmarsh, Charles W	1st	"	Trainor, Philip	"	"	Winnton, James	"	"
Sterrett, Wm	"	"	Thorpe, John	2d	"	Webb, Wm W	2d	"
Singley, Samuel	"	"	Turner, Walter J	1st	"	Waring, George	1st	"
Spargo, Stephen	"	"	Tenny, Warren	2d	"	Williams, Joseph B	"	"
Smith, John W	"	"	Turner, Napoleon	"	"	Wise, Henry	"	"
Sanford, Wm T	2d	"	Tedford, John	"	"	Whipple, Lucius S	"	"
Stanley, George W	"	"	Taylor, Francis	"	"	Wilson, Matthew F	2d	"
Summers, Harrison	1st	"	Vanhorn, William	1st	"	Yohn, George	1st	"
Sanford, George W	"	"	Wright, Samuel F	2d	"			

List of Pilots and Engineers at N. Orleans.

PILOTS.

Names.	From		Names.	From	
Auld, Edward	N O and	Balize	Brown, D E	N O and	R R
Alban, W	"	R R	Baxter, P	"	St. Louis
Arnold, James	"	Balize	Broman, P	"	Atk'ps by Sea
Ashford, W J	"	St. Louis	Blouin, O J	"	Bayou Laf
Abrams, W H	"	Y R	Bendif, H	"	R R
Alexander, Edward	"	P R	Bell, R	"	Cumberland
Alcove, Richard	"	St. Louis	Bishop, A F	"	Y R
Ayles, James	"	B R	Benedict, Joseph M	"	Y R
Anter Sidney	"	Y R	Bixby, H C	"	Cincinnati
Austin, E S	"	R R	Brindle, Joseph	"	St. Louis
Alban, George	"	R R	Blanchard, H	"	Bayou Sara
Arteburn, Benjamin	"	Louisville	Bloys, D D	"	St. Louis
Ankrim, P	"	R R	Bales, John W	"	Plaquemine
Allen, Ellsworth	"	Mobile Lks	Brown, J C	"	Y R
Alban, J P	"	R R	Browder, John J	"	R R
Ashbury, Israel	"	Louisville	Bail, Hiram	"	R R
Atkinson, J J	Lake Verret and	Last Island	Bradenbury, Green	"	Cairo
Agnada, J D	" "	R R	Curran, P	"	R R
Bordman, W T	N O and	Mobile Bay L	Challener, J H	"	P R
Broadwell, J M	"	Louisville	Carter, O D	"	O R
Bernard, Joseph	"	Y R	Capps, J	"	R R
Blanchard, Chas B	"	Vicksburg	Crooks, James	"	R R
Brown, E A	"	Y R	Cunningham, John	"	St. Louis

NOTE.—In the above list of Pilots, Y R stands for Yazoo River; O R for Ouachita River; T R for Tennessee River; B L for Bayou Lafourche; P R for Pearl River; R R for Red River; B R for Black River; W R for White River.

PILOTS.

Names.	From	Names.	From
Casder, N	N O and Ouachita	Hughes, John	N O and R R
Collins, W	" Plaquemine	Harris, T L	" R R
Cooper, James	" Cumberland	Howe, A J	" Cairo
Cable, William H	" O R	Herron, H H	" Grand Lake
Castillo, Edmond	" Attakapas	Hale, N B	" Attakapas
Collins, James	" "	Hooper, H C	" Balize
Chamange,	" R R	Hall, J W	" R R
Carlton, James S	" Louisville	Huggins, Z J	" Attakapas
Cavalia, Edmond	" Balize	Hazr, E E	" Y R
Collins, Jesse H	" Attakapas	Hardwick, W C	" Millik's Bend
Cessier, H V	" R R	Hill, Henry	" R R
Cotton, C C	" R R	Hulim, C	" R R
Carrell, Thomas R	" Cincinnati	Jones, David H	" Ohio River
Cooper, T R	" Ouachita	Jackson, Wm D	" Y R
Case, George W	" Purcetor	Jamerson, R	" Louisville
Chambers, W A	" Bayou Laf	Jacobs, James	" R R
Cary, A B	" Plaquemine	Johnson, W H	" Bay Plaq'ne
Dorsey, R J	" Attakapas	Jones, George T	" Mobile
Dessaps, A	" Bayou Sara	Johnson, W S	" Attakapas
Doherty, J J	" Louisville	Johnston, J W	" Plaquemine
Demperoolf, Anty	" Memphis	Joffroin, J C	" Ouachita
Droillard, L A	" St. Louis	Kendall, R G	" R R
Daymon, Isaac	" Louisville	Kercheval, Thos C	" St. Louis
Duval, Theron	Mouth of Arkansas, and on River.	Kay, G	" R R
		Kirby, Thos C	" Y R
Dias, W C	N O and R R	King, T L	" Ouachita R
Dunlevie, S	" Y R	Kay, B W	" R R
Dickey, S B	" Attakapas	Kroger, M	" Chefuncta
Daugherty, S	" White R	Klarke, H	" W River
Dessarp, C	" Plaquemine	Kay, Wm	" R R
Davis, J	" Louisville	Kinney, D	" G'lf of Mexico
Daniel, W H	" R R	Leonard, W H, H	" St. Louis
Duke, J	" Balize	Leadbeater, T G	" Y R
Davis, Wm M	" Ouachita	Le Blanc, A	" Plaquemine
Davis, John F	" Ohio	La Barth, I	" Lafourche
Dent, J L	" Vicksburg	Lodwick, L T	" R R
Denelow, A D	" Attakapas	Livingston, R	" Ouachita
Denty, W A	" R R	Lawles, James	" Balize
Derker, T	" R R	Lambert, Wm H	" Balize
Davis, Martin	" Balize	Lawles, J T	" Balize
Edward, R	" R R	McKay, R S	" Fort Smith.
Easly, J R	" Y R	Miller, A	" Balize
Elliott, W	" Y R	Morton, J F	" Vicksburg
Fulton, John F	" R R	Mony, J. B	" Balize
Ferrio, Edward	" R R	Mouchon, John A	" R R
Ford, J	" Cincinnati	McKinney, John	" R R
Fearing, Charles H	" R R	Martin, John W	" R R
Freeman, A S	" R R	McMahon, B F	" Cincinnati
Forbes, Charles	" Balize	McDonald, John	" Black River
Guartney, G M	" Y R	Miller, R	" Balize
Gibson, Wm A	" R R	Miller, E	" T R
Gerard, N H	" Cairo	McCullough, E S	" W R
Green, W G	" R R	Melvin, Alandria	" Fort Gibson
Gardner, Wm	" Cairo	Miller, R D B	" Louisville
Graham, R	" R R	Miller, Wm P	" Louisville
Glascock, D	" Attakapas	Mollier, F	" R R
Goslee, T R B	" St. Louis	McKinney, H B	" R R
Gibson, J D	" Ouachita	McLaughlin, A L	" Ouachita
Hedeman, H	" Balize.	Mitchell, F M	" Ohio
Harrison, C F	" Attakapas to New Iberia	Milliken, U	" Tennessee R
Hoffman, J W	"	Milliken, W	" Florence, Ala
Hymel, S	" Bayou Sara	McLaughlin, N M	" B R
Hanover, W	" Mobile by Lk	Moore, Joseph	" B R
Hurt, Nathan	" Louisville	Manscoe, B	" St Louis
Harrison, Benj G	" Louisville	Maulding, W H	" Y R
Hill, Orville H	" C R	Millikin, S	" Tenn R
Hudson, P	" Ouachita R	McClure, Silas	" R R
Haring, H	" Louisville	McCoy, J D	" St Louis

PILOTS.

NAMES.	FROM
Miller, R B	N O and St Louis
McPherson, John	" Gulf of Mex
Martin, J M	" R R
Mears, H F	" R R
Morgan, Thos G	" R R
McGregor, J C	" Y R
Moore, Thos	" R R
Napier, Wm J	" T R
Neal, W C	" Gross Tate
Neal, C C	" Alexandria
Nelson, W L	" Key West
Ostrander, T F	" Louisville
Ostrander, J H	" Louisville
Ognere, R	" Bayou Laf
Oldham, J P	" Y R
O'Daniel, James	" Rio GrandeR
Okey, Charles	" Louisville
Osgood, Geo	" Balize
Portevent, T B	" Pearl R
Peters, James R	" Louisville
Prindle, Geo B	" R R
Pierce, Chas	" Cincinnati
Pell, Allen	" Florence, Ala
Parker, A	" Louisville
Plumner, J L	" Y R
Pell, James	" Louisville
Place, M Y	" Galveston
Porter, S	" Balize to Sea
Potter, S	" Balize
Quig, Edward	" Y R
Reinhardt, L	" Balize
Robb, James M	" R R
Robb, Joseph	" Louisville
Robertson, H	" Mobile
Richardson, Wm B	" Col's & Ark
Rogers, H H	" Tennessee
Robinson, Jones	" R R
Robichaud, J S	" Opolousas
Rollins, C H	" Ouachita
Risher, W W	" R R
Salls, Felix H	" Bayou Teche
Sammons, Jacob	L Verett & New Iberia
Smith, Jacob	N O and Balize
Streck, H Y	" Lafourche
Stephenson, W L	" Vics'bg toY R
Sellors, J.	" Louisville
Saul, H	" Balize
Sissen, N	" Y R
Smith, E	" Vicksburg
Smith, N C	" O R
Switzer, Wm	" Vicksburg
Schooles, Wm	" R R
Smith, M H	" R R
Smith, W C	" R R
Sutton, James	" Mobile
Swain, Wm	" R R
Smith, Geo	" Ouachita
Scovel, M H	" Bay de Glaize
Smith, J R	" Y R
Smith, Joshua	" Louisville
Shields, S M	" "
Sweeney, Geo	" Red River
Sparhawk, G M	" Louisville
Shoomaker, Wm	" Red River

NAMES.	FROM
Sargent, A W	N O and Red River
Sanford, Alfred	" Yazoo River
Strong, S	" Nashville
Smith, T J	" Balize
Sheppard H	" "
Thompson, J S	" Galveston, T
Turner, Wm H M	" Bayou Sara
Terrebonne, O	" Lafourche
Taylor, D	" Balize
Turner, T B	" B Lafourche
Taffier, D	" Atk'ps & B Pl
Thompson, J Wm	" Red River
Tabot, Wm H	" Balize
Tayloy, P D	" Cincinnati
Turner, Z	" Bayou Sara
Vincent, J L	" "
Walder, L T	" Red River
Willie, J C	" Yazoo River
White, E G	" Memphis
Wood, G A	" St. Louis
Withers, A G	" Ohio River
Willenbry, J	" Balize
Watson, R	" Red River
Walker, J D	" "
Whitworh, Y J	" "
West, J M	" "
Wood, J H	" Yazoo River
Waples, T C	" Red River
Wilie, J	" Yazoo River
Wells, J C	" "
Whipple, J B	" Ouchita R
Whiteworth, J H	" Opelousos
Woodferk, R J	" St. Louis
Wright, Isaac	" Red River
Wilson, Wm A	" Louisville
Wilder, M	" Key West
Wilson, Miram	" Red River

IN THE COLLECTION DISTRICT OF VICKSBURG, MISSISSIPPI.

Dew, M P	Yazoo River
Futerue,	"
Powell, A J	"
Pleasants, F P	"
Pamsate, S H	"

IN THE COLLECTION DISTRICT OF FRANKLIN, LA

Broad, A	Attakapas and L Island
Hanson, C F	" "
Stevens, A	" "
Stevens, J	" "
Smith, Abr	" "
Trellind, L W	" "

IN THE COLLECTION DISTRICT OF POINT ISABEL TEXAS.

Armstrong, J B	Rio Grande
Anderson, Charles	"
Brown, A M	"
Dalsell, R	"
Kennedy, M	"
King, K.	"
Martin, J	"
Ward, J M	"

ENGINEERS.

Names.	Class.
Allabaugh, John	1st “
Allen, Isaac	2d “
Adams, Wm	“ “
Armor, Charles	“ “
Armstrong, James	1st “
Atkinson, James M	“ “
Anthony, Samuel D	“ “
Bradshaw, Geo H	“ “
Broduck, James	2d “
Bowman, Harry	“ “
Brett, Benjamin M	“ “
Bryan, Wm	1st “
Brotherton, William	“ “
Burgett, Joseph D	“ “
Brinn, G B	2d “
Bowman, Joseph	“ “
Bell, James	1st “
Borland, James	2d “
Bagless, D B	1st “
Bass, Wm	“ “
Buchanan, John	“ “
Beatty, William	“ “
Bickerstaff, S	“ “
Brooks, Thos	“ “
Barringer, Samuel	2d “
Boyle, Edward	“ “
Bags, Geo	“ “
Bobb, John Jr.	1st “
Baswell, T C	“ “
Bobb, Charles	2d “
Boutte, Zenon	“ “
Birkerstaff, Andrew J	“ “
Briggs, James H	“ “
Baslue, John	“ “
Berry, Washington	1st “
Crowley, Cornelius	“ “
Constantine Dominick	2d “
Carlile, Abraham	“ “
Calaway, David	“ “
Covert, Ellison	“ “
Cook, Thomas	1st “
Cook, Eugene L	“ “
Casey, George H	“ “
Childs, Alfred	“ “
Cherry, Joseph	“ “
Caldwell, J D	“ “
Cristic, John	“ “
Crockett, Hampton	2d “
Chapman, Levi	1st “
Conner, John	“ “
Cole, Patrick	2d “
Chambers, D B	“ “
Camden, John S	“ “
Caswell, William	1st “
Cornover, John D	“ “
Champagne, Victor	2d “
Conklin, C G	“ “
Clements, A S	“ “
Chapman, Levi,	1st “
Creighton, Alexander	“ “
Clanton, Lewis L	“ “
Cristian, Charles	2d “
Cline, Wm	1st “
Clark, L W	“ “
Clayton, Samuel S	“ “
Crawford, John	2d “
Collins, Bernard C	“ “
Chambers, Wm W	“ “
Coleman, George	1st “
Clegg, Wm	1st “
Constantine, D	2d “
Dawson, John H	1st “
Dare, James	“ “
Dovener, Franklin	“ “
Dwyer, John	2d “
Dearing, Willis	1st “
Dawson, Charles	“ “
Davidson, John W	2d “
Daniels, David	“ “
Davis, Wm	“ “
Doyle, Joseph	1st “
Evans, Isaiah	2d “
Eakin, David R	1st “
Ellis, Chas D	“ “
Evans, Wm H	“ “
Evens, D	“ “
Fisk, Chas A	2d “
Fluke, Henry	1st “
Frost, Henry	“ “
Finn, Richard	2d “
Finney, G H	1st “
Goodwin, Joseph	2d “
Green, Martin	1st “
Geary, Alexandria	“ “
Gower, Ephraim H	“ “
Goodrich, Hiram G	“ “
Goald, Henry	“ “
Goold, Jacob L	2d “
Gross, John Eli	1st “
Green, Wm	“ “
Gould, Wm	“ “
Gorsuch, A P	“ “
Griffin, Levi	“ “
Grace, John	“ “
Goss, Richard	“ “
Green, Jerry R	2d “
Gilman, Wm	“ “
Harrington, L	1st “
Hansell, James D	2d “
Hughes, Charles	“ “
Hershey, Peter	1st “
Harden, Warner	2d “
Harris, James	1st “
Hudson, S M	“ “
Hawley, Wm	“ “
Hall, David J	2d “
Homer, Henry B	“ “
Hewitt, Joseph	“ “
Harrison, Peter	“ “
Holmes, Wm H	“ “
Hamilton, James	1st “
Henry, Alexander	“ “
Hall, Wm L	2d “
Harden, Jess S	1st “
Hendricks, Warren	“ “
Hughes, J T	2d “
Harkinger, C	1st “
Hornberger, P T	“ “
Heirn, Frank	“
Harser, W	2d “
Holden, J C	“ “
Halstead, D C	1st “
Hart, Henry B	2d “
Haines, Quinlars	1st “
Hayes, Samuel	“ “
Harper, James	2d “
Hughes, Z J	1st “
Harrington, Samuel	“ “
Hawkins, Henry J	2d “
Harper, John H	“ “
Hahn, G A	1st “
Hughes, George	2d “
Inkster, John	“ “
Isbester, Wm	“ “
Jackson, Frank	1st “
Jolly, Henry	“ “
Johnson, Fargus	“ “
Jones, Wilson	“ “
Kidd, Elijah H	2d “
Kerns, David	1st “
Kinkead, Wm H	2d “
Kinykendoll, Henry	1st “
Keeper, Alexander	
Kingkead James	
Kerns, Joseph W	
Kerns, Louis B	
Kirkpatrick, J	
Knight, Richard A	
Kidd, E H	
Kelly, R G	
Kerns, David	1st “
Lacey, John S	2d “
Luff, John	“ “
Luther, David	1st “
Lyon, Thomas	“ “
Lee, Louis	“ “
Lee, Andrew P	2d “
Lester, Charles	1st “
Lampton, W	“ “
Littleton, J W	“ “
Love, John M	“ “
Long, George W	2d “
Luke, Alexander	1st “
Miller, John B	“ “
Moore, John	2d “
Myers, Jacob	1st “
Murry, John	2d “
Mix, Arnos B	1st “
Matthew, John	2d “
Marrs, Thomas	“ “
Munch, Philip	1st “
Metzler, Thomas	“ “
Mitchell, T F	“ “
Meslerman, H	“ “
Milburn, W	“ “
Magovern, B	“ “
Marsh, Anderson	“ “
Mackisin, R	“ “
Murray, Thomas H	2d “
Marsh, J C	1st “
More, John	“ “
Moore, J B	2d “
Mastorson, J	“ “
McDermott, Michael	“ “
McDonald, John	“ “
McClelland, T W	“ “
McKinney, James	1st “
McFarland, J	“ “
McChesney, G C	2d “
McMillen, W	1st “
McFarland, Jackson	“ “
McGarety, James	“ “
Neff, Jacob	“ “
Nolan, Joseph	“ “
Neeld, James S	2d “
Newell, Hiram,	1st “
Oxley, Charles W	2d “

ENGINEERS.

Names.	Class.
Orr, John	1st "
Odell, Thomas B	2d "
Parker, Charles W	1st "
Peterson, Thomas F	" "
Perter, Seward	" "
Park, Geo W	" "
Patterson, Wm	" "
Perkins, Willis	" "
Pettis, David D	" "
Pohlman, A	2d "
Phillips, J A	" "
Perkins, Wm	" "
Pawson, Milton	1st "
Phelon, Wm H	" "
Preon, Joseph	" "
Price, Allen	" "
Patterson, P T	" "
Peltes, David	" "
Pillow, Jeremiah	2d "
Reynarod, H S	1st "
Rollins, Able	2d "
Rav, Patrick	" "
Robinson, G	" "
Rose, A J	1st "
Rose, W P	" "
Reed, J F	" "
Rayal, William	2d "
Rose, Jacob M	1st "
Riggle, B	" "
Richardson, R N C	" "
Roup, Gliver	2d "
Resor, Napoleon	1st "
Ramsey, John	" "
Resor, Leonedus M	2d "
Roberts, Charles	" "
Russell, George	1st "
Rose, Wm	" "
Smith, Wm H	2d "
Scott, Wm R	1st "
Scott, Arthur	" "
Scott, John	2d "
Shaneyfelt, Peter	" "
Simpson, Andrew J	" "
Seay, D	" "
Sherman, Hugh M	1st "
Seymour, Caleb	" "
Scott, John W	" "

Names.	Class.
Skinner, James M	2d "
Smith, John M	1st "
Seeley, Chas	2d "
Sinnott, Richard	1st "
Shaffer, T J	2d "
Saunders, J W	1st "
Smith, J F	" "
Sisson, Henry C	2d "
Squires, Thomas	1st "
Simmons, A J	2d "
Stevens, W	" "
Smith, Jesse R	1st "
Swift, J M	2d "
Streck, Alexander	1st "
Suberville, A	2d "
Scott, Wm	1st "
Savage, Albert G	" "
Swift, J M	" "
Stoddart, David	2d "
Stout, W C	1st "
Stilman, Brown	2d "
Swift, Samuel	" "
Smith, Wm M	" "
Shield, M J	3d "
Skinner, H	2d "
Taylor, John	" "
Turner, Lawrence	3d "
Tull, Telemachus	1st "
Taylor, John M	2d "
Tumbleson, Thomas	1st "
Thompson, T A	" "
Trahant, L	" "
Thompson, H F	" "
Tucker, James	2d "
Taliver, Wesley	1st "
Tyson, John	" "
Turner, Richard	2d "
Ulrich, John	" "
Vetter, George	1st "
Voris, John	" "
Van, Veventes N	" "
Waldron, A P	" "
Whittier, Charles	" "
Whitten, Robert F	2d "
Williams, W L	1st "
Wilson, James	2d "
Williams, A R	1st "

Names.	Class.
Watson, John C	1st "
Wood, Elias	" "
Woodengton, Geo W	" "
Watson, R G	" "
Wade, George	" "
William, J W	2d "
Wilson, F C	1st "
Welch George W	2d "
Wilcox, S F	" "
Winteringer, Alex	1st "
Wilkens, S C C	2d "
Woodard, J J	" "
Wetson, John	" "
Winship, T J	1st "
Winnas, Nelson	3d "
Walker, John	2d "
Waters, E L	" "
White, David	" "
Walsh, Joseph	1st "
Wise, C M	2d "
Weaver, George J	1st "
Wise, E M	2d "
Witham, Gideon	1st "
Wall, D G	" "
Wadsworth, B	" "
Whitmore, W A	" "
Youngblood, Wm	2d "
Zerns, John	1st "

IN THE COLLECTION DISTRICT OF VICKSBURG, MISS.

Names.	Class.
Brown, T R	2d "
Gordon, Frances	" "
Mitchell, E P	1st "
Tuyford, Charles	2d "

IN THE COLLECTION DISTRICT OF FRANKLIN, LA.

Names.	Class.
Dickson, G R	1st "
Kendall, G M	2d "

IN THE COLLECTION DISTRICT OF POINT ISABEL, TEXAS.

Names.	Class.
Brown, John	1st "
Mercier, R A	" "
Martin, Edward	2d "
Ocomu, A	1st "
Righter, Charles	2d "

List of Pilots and Engineers at Galveston.

PILOTS.

Names.	Names.	Names.
Peter Stockholm	Thomas Jordon	Joseph Klanke
James S Graham	Isaac H Wicks	Geo W Wheat
Eli A Stephens	Wm J Ward, (dead)	J H Sterrett
M McCormack	James Montgomery	W J Whitfield
Samuel T Roach	H L Conner	Jacob Watson
William Jenkins	Andrew Thompson	Samuel P Christian
J W L Roach	John Clement	Shadrick Roach
R O W McMannis		

ENGINEERS.

Names.	Class.		Names.	Class.		Names.	Class	
Joseph W Taylor	1st	"	Joshua Stevens	1st	"	Washington Clark	2d	"
Wm L Enslow, (dead)	"	"	Irwin R Ward	"	"	Sanford Gregory	1st	"
A McGill	"	"	Numa McMoustin	"	"	A C Ashworth	"	"
D F Gerrish	2d	"	Abel Coffin, Jr.	2d	"	Wm Hibert	2d	"
Wm Sapeyn	1st	"	Peter L Lapeyre	"	"	John H Wright	1st	"
Fredk Clipper, (dead)	2d	"	Thomas Peacock	1st	"	Richard Lacock	2d	"
Victor Favrur	"	"	Oliver Lampton	2d	"	H B Quch	1st	"
James W Taylor	"	"	Charles Callway	1st	"	Henry Schroder	2d	"
James A Gray	1st	"	Daniel E Connor	"	"	James Myers	"	"
Israel Clark	"	"	Edward P Hemmeway	"	"	Charles Martin	"	"
R Roles	2d	"						

RAILWAY ROLLING STOCK.

In our sketch of Cincinnati, published in this volume, we made some incidental allusions to the extensive manufacturing establishments of that city. We are aware that many of those establishments deserve a more extended notice, and we wish it were in our power to do them full justice, but this our straightened limits will not permit. But, as a specimen of the enterprise and industry of Western capitalists, we subjoin a short account of one of the largest and most complete steam engine and locomotive manufacturies in the Western States. We speak of the manufacturing establishment of Messrs. Moore & Richardson, Cincinnati. These extensive works cover nearly one entire square of the city, near the bank of the river. Here are manufactured both marine and locomotive engines, and for the prosecution of this work, there is a foundry attached which is capable of casting twenty tons of metal at one time, and steam hammers suitable for the performance of the heaviest forging. This manufactory was originally established in the year 1828. The present proprietors are practical men, of great experience in the business; one of them, Mr. Moore, has been connected with the establishment from its commencement. When in full operation, the manufactory employs about three hundred workmen. It is under the most skilful direction, and possesses every possible facility in the way of machinery for the manufacture and repair of engines, whether locomotive or marine, as well as the various kinds of machinery required for the construction and repair of railways.

The manufacture of locomotives was commenced at this establishment in 1846; since which time it has produced about one hundred engines of that class, numbers of which may be seen in constant operation on the Little Miami and Cincinnati, and the Cincinnati, Hamilton and Dayton Railroads; among which is the celebrated and unrivalled passenger locomotive "Nat Wright," running on the Little Miami Railroad. Specimens of the workmanship of this establishment may also be found on various other railways in Ohio, Kentucky, Tennessee and Indiana, and in all cases they have given ample satisfaction.

The engines of the magnificent low pressure steamer Jacob Strader, were also constructed at these works, from designs by Mr. Moore, one of the proprietors. Here, likewise, was made the machinery of the splendid steamers Northerner and Southerner, and in respect to beauty, efficiency and durability, this machinery will not suffer in comparison with any which has ever been produced in the United States or in Europe.

BURNING OF THE BULLETIN NO 2.

The steamboat Bulletin No. 2, Capt. C. B. Church, was burned on the Mississippi river, near Islands No. 96 and 97, March 24th, 1855. A large quantity of cotton was among the freight, and this highly combustible article caused the flames to spread rapidly. The boat was run ashore as quickly as possible; but as soon as she struck the bank, she bounded back again, and floated down the river until consumed to the level of the water. The surface of the river was covered with floating bales of ignited cotton; and many persous who had leaped overboard, while attempting to save themselves by clinging to these fiery masses, were severely burned. One of the cabin passengers stated that he was

BURNING OF THE BULLETIN NO. 2.

sitting on the hurricane deck when the fire first appeared, and before he could get a bucket of water to throw on it, the whole boat seemed to be in a blaze. If the force pumps had been in good order, (which was not the case,) the flames could easily have been suppressed. An eye-witness thinks that the boat and the lives of many passengers could have been saved, if gum elastic hose had been provided for such an emergency. Certainly it shows shameful and criminal neglect on the part of the Captain or owners, when a steamer is without such apparatus. While the boat was burning, the passengers were greatly excited and dismayed; but we have one instance of surprising coolness, whether it proceeded from courage or stupidity, we will not pretend to say. A gentleman was standing in the cabin with perfect composure and apparent unconcern while the fire was making rapid progress in every direction. Capt. Church advised this stoical person to take off the door of a state room and endeavor to save himself thereon. "Make yourself easy, Captain," was the calm response, "I am safe enough!" And, sure enough, he was saved. This anecdote reminds us of one which is told of a celebrated gambler, who leaped from a burning boat into the Mississippi, exclaiming, "Now, gallows, save your own!"

Some of the passengers of the Bulletin succeeded in leaping on shore from the forecastle at the moment the steamer struck the land; but a large majority, who were in the after-part of the boat, were cut off from this means of escape. Capt. Church and all the other officers of the boat faithfully used every effort to save the passengers, and the Captain remained so long on board for this purpose, that his own life nearly became the sacrifice of his fidelity. When driven by the flames from the last refuge on the wreck, he threw himself in the water. The boat had drifted out to such a distance from the shore, that he would infallibly have been drowned, had not a skiff, which happened to be near, come to his assistance.

List of those who Perished.—Mr. Swick, Boston; C. Denny, deck hand; J. B. Williamson, New York; Jesper Brown, Friar's Point, Miss.; Orville Hill, Nashville; B. Handwerkt, Memphis, Tenn.; John McConican, North Carolina; Evans Gwynn, Columbus, Ohio; a negro girl belonging to J. M. Craig, Arkansas; Nathaniel Carter, barber; Stephen Tareter, cabin-boy; four negro firemen, belonging to Capt. Church; several do. belonging to W. L. Porter, New Orleans; one negro fireman belonging to Mrs. Reinhart, Memphis, Tenn.; one do. belonging to J. R. Upsham, of same place, and an assistant engineer.

PRINCIPAL RAILROADS IN THE UNITED STATES.

CAMDEN AND AMBOY RAILROAD.

The Camden and Amboy Railroad Company was chartered by the legislature of New Jersey in 1830. With the exception of the Albany and Schenectady railroad, this was the first railroad of any magnitude in the United States. At that time the manufacture of locomotive engines was still in its infancy, even in England; nor was it generally known or believed on this side of the Atlantic, that steam power could be successfully applied to the motion of cars on railroads. This being the fact, the charter of the Camden and Amboy Railroad Company, it will be found on examination, actually provides for the use of horse power as the agent of transportation. Before the road was completed, however, the locomotive had come into general use on the English roads, and the Messrs. Stevens, the projectors and principal stockholders in the Camden and Amboy Company, imported for experiment on this road the first steam locomotive engine brought to the United States. When this road was first projected, the public had no confidence in the probability of its being ever completed. They were equally incredulous of its even producing sufficient revenue to pay the interest on the cost of its construction. Its successful progress was, however, insured in 1831–2, by a subsequent contract with the State, which provided, in consideration of certain concessions on the part of the Railroad Company, for ample protection against competition for the limited period of thirty years. The Camden and Amboy railroad was completed in the years 1832, '33; since which time, also, they have, by connection with the Philadelphia and Trenton railroad, and the construction of a railroad from Bordentown through Trenton and New Brunswick to a junction at the latter place with the New Jersey Railroad and Transportation Company, given the public another medium of communication between New York and Philadelphia.

The Camden and Amboy Railroad Company have likewise, in conjunction with the Delaware and Raritan Canal Company, constructed the Trenton and Belvidere Railroad, about sixty-eight miles, connecting at Easton with the Pennsylvania railroads, which penetrate the extensive coal fields of that State. They have constructed, likewise, a plank road from the Belvidere railroad, eleven miles to Flemington; also the Jamesburg and Freehold railroad, which extends fourteen miles in length to the marl beds of Monmouth county, and will probably soon be further extended to the sea shore, near Long Branch. The Burlington and Mount Holly railroad was likewise constructed by the aid of the Camden and Amboy railroad company.

Besides constructing these branch railroads, the joint companies contribute, by means of transit duties on passengers and freight, a handsome revenue to the State. These transit duties have been erroneously represented to be a tax levied on the citizens of other States. They apply to all passengers, whether citizens of the United States or elsewhere. They are no more a tax, than the tolls on the New York and Pennsylvania canals. These companies, relieved from the payment of these duties, they would not vary their charges from what they are at present. The fact is, that the State, instead of taxing the *capital* of the companies, which is fixed and inviolate, has seen proper to tax their *business* and *revenue*, which is constantly augmenting. The transit duties are not therefore a charge on the citizens of other States, but a tax on the Companies' revenue. They are taxed in proportion to the number of passengers and tons of freight they transport. But the charge on passengers and freight is no greater than it would be, were the Companies' *capital* taxed, or were they exempted from all taxation.

If there were no railroads through New Jersey, passengers and freight would have to pay, in tolls over bridges and ferries, a far heavier amount than the transit duties now paid by the companies.

The Camden and Amboy railroad extends from Camden, opposite Philadelphia, to South Amboy, on the bay of Amboy, thirty miles from New York. Commodious steamboats take the passengers at South Amboy through Staten Island Sound to New York; affording a picturesque view of that island, whose shores are studded with flourishing villages, and adorned with the magnificent country residences of the New Yorkers. In clear weather these steamboats often take the route outside of the island, through the narrows, by which the traveller enjoys a view of the ocean, and the forts and harbor defences of our commercial metropolis.

The other route, via. Tacony, or (in the winter) Kensington, transports the traveller through Trenton, the seat of government of New Jersey, within sight of Princeton, through New Brunswick, Rahway, Elizabethtown, Newark and Jersey city, to New York. Both routes are about ninety miles long. By a recent act of the legislature, and the consent of the joint companies, the average fares of the different railroad lines cannot exceed two and a half cents per mile.

The average time of passage between New York and Philadelphia, is from four to four and a half hours. Eight or nine passenger lines leave each city daily. The price of passage is from $1.50, $2.25, to $3.00. The cars are spacious and elegant, and the engines of the first class. In fact, all the equipments and appointments of the road are of the first order.

The principal Agents at Philadelphia and New York cities, are Wm. H. Gatzmer and Ira Bliss, celebrated for their courtesy and strict attention to their duties. The officers of this company are Robert L. Stevens, President; Robert R. S. Van Rensaelaer, Superintendent; James S. Green, Treasurer; Saml. J. Bayard, Secretary; W. H. Gatzmer, Agent, Philadelphia; and Ira Bliss, Agent, New York.

LITTLE MIAMI, COLUMBUS AND XENIA RAILROAD.

On this road, four passenger trains are in daily operation. The main line of the road extends from Columbus, on the Sciota river, in a southwesterly direction through Xenia, Ohio, to the Little Miami. It has the following connections:

1. At Columbus, it connects with the Cleveland and Columbus and Central Ohio Railroads for Cleveland, Dunkirk, New York, Boston, Pittsburgh, Philadelphia, Zanesville, Wheeling, Baltimore, Washington, D. C., Newark and Steubenville.

2. At London, Ohio, it connects with the Springfield and Columbus Railroad.

3. At Xenia, it connects with the Dayton, Xenia and Bellefere Railroads for Dayton, Indianapolis, Chicago, St. Louis, and other points in Western and Southern sections, and also with Springfield and Delaware, Ohio.

4. At Morrow, it connects with the Cincinnati, Wilmington and Zanesville Railroad, for Circleville, Lancaster and Zanesville.

5. At Loveland, it connects with the Marietta and Cincinnati Railroad, for Hillsborough, Chilicothe and Marietta.

6. At Cincinnati, it connects with lines of steamers on the Ohio

river, and by the Ohio and Mississippi and Covington and Lexington Railroads, with St. Louis, Louisville, Memphis, Nashville, New Orleans, and all other points of the South and West. The President of the Little Miama Railroad is Jacob Strader. The President of the Columbus and Xenia Railroad is Wm. Dennison, Jr.; Superintendent, Wm. H. Clement; General Agent, P. W. Strader.

CLEVELAND, COLUMBUS AND CINCINNATI RAILROAD.

On this Railroad, three trains run daily between Cleveland, Columbus and Cincinnati. The accommodations for trávellers are of a very superior order, combining speed, safety and convenience.

The Cleveland, Columbus and Cincinnati Railroad connects as follows:

1. At Cleveland, with the Lake Shore Railroads and the line of steamers for Buffalo, New York and Boston, and with a series of steamers for Detroit, Sault Marie and Lake Superior.

2. At Grafton, with the Cleveland and Toledo Railroad, for Toledo, Chicago and the West.

3. At Shelby, with the Sandusky, Mansfield and Newark Railroad, for Sandusky, Mansfield and Newark.

4. At Crestline, with the Ohio and Indiana Railroad, for Fort Wayne and the Wabash Valley, and with the Ohio and Pennsylvania Railroad for Pittsburgh, Philadelphia and Washington City.

5. At Galeon, with the Bellefontaine and Indiana Railroad for Indianopolis, St. Louis and the Southwest.

6. At Delaware, with the Springfield, Mount Vernon and Pittsburgh Railroad for Springfield and Dayton.

7. At Columbus, with Little Miami and the Columbus and Xenia Railroads

From this view it will appear that the Cleveland, Columbus and Cincinnati Railroad communicates by its various branches, directly or indirectly, with every section of the country, and offers a convenient mode of access to all the principal cities of the United States. The President of this Railroad Company is L. M. Hubby; Superintendent, E. S. Flint.

CLEVELAND AND PITTSBURGH RAILROAD

Runs Three Trains. Daily, (Sundays excepted,) and makes immediate connections with all Roads at CLEVELAND, PITTSBURGH, and WHEELING.

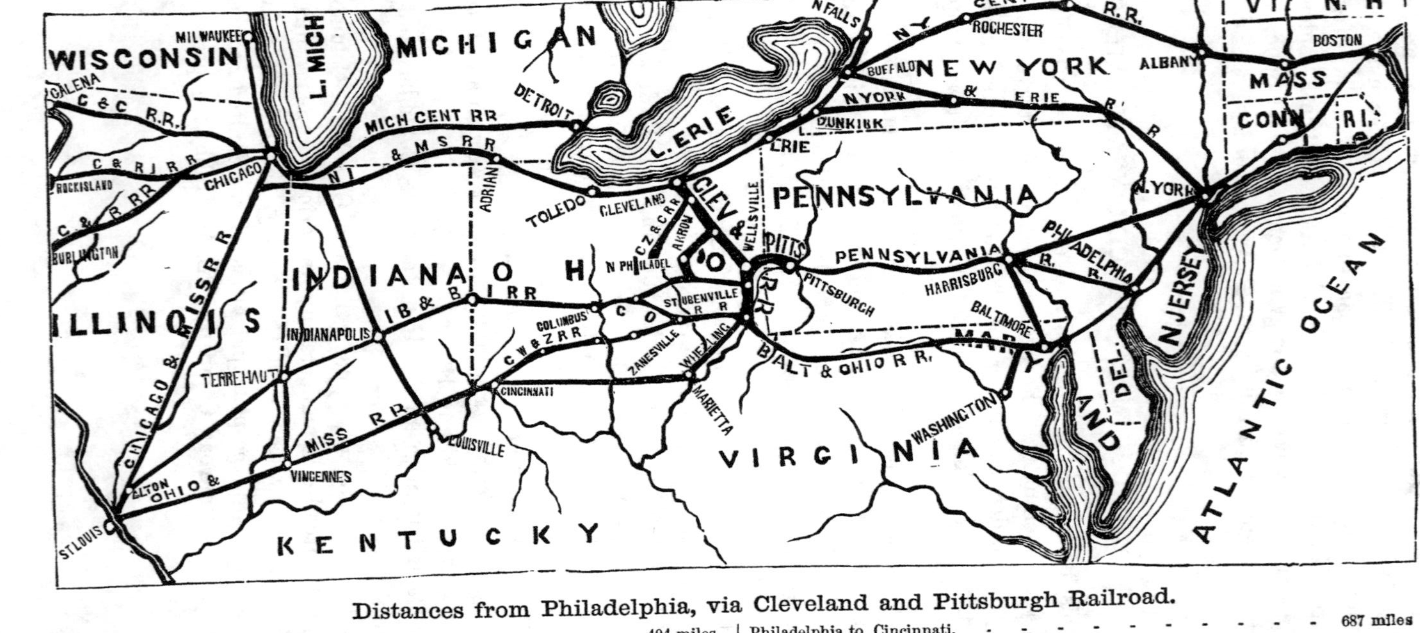

Distances from Philadelphia, via Cleveland and Pittsburgh Railroad.

Philadelphia to Cleveland, Ohio, - - - - - - - - - - - - - - -	494 miles.
" " Chicago, Illinois, - - - - - - - - - - - - - - -	849 "
" " Wheeling, Virginia, - - - - - - - - - - - - - -	438 "
" " Columbus, Ohio, - - - - - - - - - - - - - - -	575 "
Philadelphia to Cincinnati, - - - - - - - - - - - - - -	687 miles
" " Indianapolis, Indiana, - - - - - - - - - -	753 "
" " St. Louis, Missouri, - - - - - - - - - - - - -	1042 "

H. C. ROCKWELL, President.
J. DURAND, Superintendent.

THE NEW YORK AND ERIE RAILROAD.

The internal improvements of the United States, like the rivers, lakes, mountains, and other natural features of the country, are on the most magnificent scales. The Egyptian pyramids, the Roman aqueducts, and the famous Chinese wall, were indeed stupendous undertakings; they are astonishing monuments of human enterprise and industry; but, with respect to real utility and adaptation to the purposes required, some of the railroads of the United States are the greatest results of human energy that the world has ever witnessed. Among these enduring records of our country's greatness—records traced in lines of iron on the most substantial tablet—the great work, whose title appears at the head of this article, deserves special attention. Not to mention it in a book of this kind, would be a sin of omission which would certainly be unpardonable.

The New York and Erie railroad has the unrivalled length of four hundred and sixty miles, extending from the Hudson river to Lake Erie. It communicates with the Hudson by three *termini*, viz.: 1. At Jersey city, opposite the city of New York. 2. At Parmont, where it has another connection with New York city by a ferry of twenty-four miles. 3. At Newburgh, where it is connected with New York city by a sixty mile ferry.

On Lake Erie and Niagara river it has three *termini*. 1. The most western *terminus* is at Dunkirk, on Lake Erie, forty-two miles west of Buffalo. 2. It has a terminus at Buffalo, via the Buffalo and New York city railroad, branching off at Hornellsville. 3. It has a third terminus at Niagara Falls and Suspension bridge, via Conandaigua and Niagara Falls railroad branch, connecting with the New York and Erie railroad at Elmira, Chemung county, New York.

The New York and Erie railroad keeps in operation three daily express trains, and one mail train, in addition to its numerous stock and freight trains, making direct connection with all the steamboat lines on Lake Erie, and with all the railroad trains running on the northern and southern shores of that lake. It connects with its various branches as follows:—

1. With Buffalo, by the Buffalo and New York city railroad.

2. With Niagara Falls, by the Conandaigua and Niagara Falls railroad.

3. With Cayuga Lake, from Oswego, by Cayuga and Susquehanna railroad.

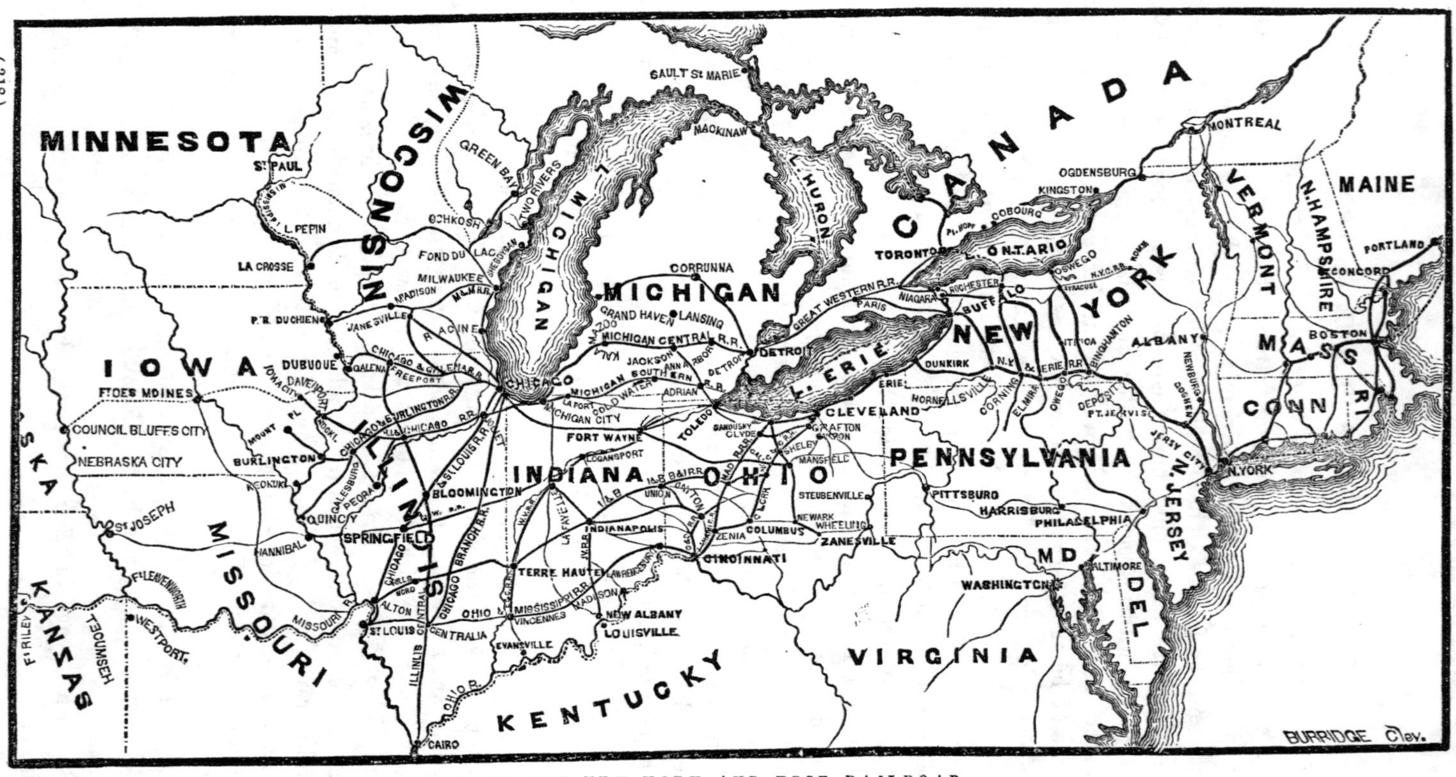

MAP OF THE NEW YORK AND ERIE RAILROAD

4. With Avon Springs and Rochester, from Corning, by Corning and Rochester railroad.

5. With Syracuse and Binghampton, by Binghampton and Syracuse railroad.

6. With Scranton, at Great Bend, by Delaware and Lachawana railroad.

7. With Philadelphia and Elmira, by Williamsport and Elmira railroad.

8. With Newburgh, at Middleton, by Newburgh branch railroad.

Among many other inducements for travellers to take the New York and Erie railroad, we may mention the circumstance that they will have one less change than they would have by any other route; and, besides, in travelling to New York city by this railroad, there is a saving of distance in comparison with the Albany route, as follows:—

27 miles saved in distance to and from Dunkirk to New York.
22 " " " " Buffalo "
17 " " " " Niagara Falls "

Persons leaving Cincinnati at 6 o'clock, A. M. daily, and Cleveland at twenty minutes past 3, P. M., arrive at New York city on the following day at thirty-six minutes past 12 o'clock, M. Those who leave Niagara Falls or Buffalo in the morning trains, arrive in New York city on the same day. Those leaving the same places in the evening rain, arrive at New York early on the following morning. See the map of this railroad on the opposite page.

In concluding our notice of the New York and Erie railroad, we are compelled by a sense of justice to speak of the efficient means which have been used on this road to insure the safety of passengers. With this great object in view, the prevalent error in the construction of railway tracks has been corrected by adopting a guage six feet wide—one foot and a quarter wider than that of the New York Central Railroad. This is an improvement in railroad building which must strike every judicious observer as one of the obvious necessities of railroad travel in the United States, although the narrow tracks, notwithstanding their manifest dangers and disadvantages, are still in general use. Owing to the unusual width of the track, the cars on this road afford very superior accommodations to the traveller, being more spacious than railroad cars generally are. As a security against those accidents to which travellers by railroad are commonly exposed, the New York and Erie company have established a telegraph line along the route, by which notices of delays, &c., may be transmitted, with the speed of lightning, from one extremity to the other; collisions on this road are therefore impossible. We can conscientiously recommend this line as the safest, cheapest, quickest, and in all respects, the best railroad route between the East and the West. The President of this company is Homer Ramsdale; General Superintendent, D. C. McCallum; General Western Agent, B. F. Smith.

THE EARTHQUAKE OF 1811.

This earthquake was the most remarkable phenomenon that ever occurred on the American continent within the memory of man. The shocks were repeated with more or less violence, for the space of three months, and were felt along the course of the Mississippi from Cairo to New Orleans. The central point of the convulsions appears to have been about seventy miles below the former place. The scenes which presented themselves during the earthquake, or succession of earthquakes, to speak more properly, were terrible beyond all powers of description. The first shock was felt on the night of December 16th, 1811; it made a great commotion in the waters of the river, and greatly alarmed the boatmen. The steamer Orleans, the first steamboat built in the west, was on her passage to New Orleans, and was tossed about as it were by a violent tempest. Just below New Madrid, a flat boat belonging to Richard Stump was swamped, andsix men were drowned. During the various shocks, the banks of the Mississippi caved in by whole acres at a time. Large trees disappeared under the ground or were cast with frightful violence into the river. At times, the waters of the Mississippi were seen to rise up like a wall in the middle of the stream, and then suddenly rolling back would beat against either bank with terrific force. Boats of considerable size were often cast "high and dry" upon the shores of the river. Frequently a loud roaring and hissing were heard, like the escape of steam from a boiler. The water of the river was much agitated. Whole islands disappeared. On the shores, the earth opened in wide fissures, and closing again threw the water, sand and mud, in jets higher than the trees. A dense fog or mist pervaded the atmosphere. The air was impregnated with a sulphurous effluvium, and a taste of sulphur was observed in the water of the river and the neighboring springs.

Each shock of the earthquake was accompanied by what seemed to be the reports of heavy artillery. A man who was on the river in a boat at the time of one of the shocks, declares that he saw the mighty

Mississippi *cut in twain*, while the waters poured down a vast chasm into the bowels of the earth. A moment more, and the chasm was filled, but the boat which contained this witness was crushed in the tumultuous efforts of the flood to regain its former level. The town of NewMadrid, Missouri, was almost entirely destroyed by these convulsions of nature. This town, which formerly stood on a bluff bank, fifteen or twenty feet above the summer floods, sunk so low that the next rise of the water covered it to the depth of five feet. Many of the inhabitants were drowned, and the buildings generally were destroyed.

One of the lakes formed by this earthquake is nearly sixty miles long and several miles wide. The legislature of Missouri, in 1851, made an appropriation for the purpose of reclaiming the sunken lands. A more terrible calamity of this kind has rarely been recorded in the history of the world. Fortunately, it occurred at a time when that part of the country was but thinly inhabited.

BURNING OF THREE STEAMERS.

Between the hours of 12 and 1 o'clock, on Monday morning, December 3d, 1855, a fire broke out on board of the steam packet George Collier, Captain Burdett, lying at the lower landing, Memphis, Tenn. The steamer had just arrived, and had not been made fast, when the mate discovered the fire in a small closet under a flight of steps in the forward part of the boat. From this small beginning, the flames spread to every part of the steamer, in less than five minutes. All efforts to arrest their progress proving ineffectual.

Captain Burdett, perceiving that the total destruction of the boat was inevitable, gave the alarm to the passengers in the cabin. His first efforts were directed to the preservation of the ladies, and in this, by almost superhuman exertions, he succeeded. The male passengers and some of the officers and crew were compelled to save themselves by jumping off, some into the river and some on the lower deck of the wharf boat, which lay near the Collier. This fine wharf boat, called the Mary Hunt, together with the steamer May Flower, which lay on the other side, was soon involved in the fate of the George Collier, and the three burning vessels are said to have presented one of the most magnificent and terrible spectacles ever witnessed in that locality. A flood of light, even at that dreary midnight hour, made every object distinctly visible for a great distance around the conflagration. Crowds of people rushed to the wharves, all in the most intense excitement and anxiety for the fate of the many people who were known to be on board the blazing steamer. There were more than forty passengers on the George Collier, who together with the officers and crew made a total of sixty-five or seventy people, all of whom, for a time, appeared to be doomed to an agonizing death. The register of the passengers names was destroyed with the boat. It is impossible, therefore, to state, with any degree of precision, how many lives were lost, but twelve persons, at least, are known to have perished.

The George Collier had just completed her trip from New Orleans to Memphis, with a valuable cargo, all of which was destroyed. None of the passengers had landed.

KILLED.—Arthur Dignan, of Philadelphia, assistant bar-keeper of the Mayflower; R. S. Candon, of Louisville, engineer of the Gaines' Landing Railroad; another gentleman attached to the same Railroad, name not mentioned; James Banks, cook of the Collier, and Sidney, a cabin boy of the same boat; several of the cabin passengers and three or four colored people, names unknown.

The George Collier was valued at $35,000; the Mayflower at $100,000, and the wharf boat at $15,000. The whole loss by this conflagration is estimated at $250,000.

THE MARTHA WASHINGTON.

The loss of the steamer Martha Washington, with its attendant circumstances, is one of the most extraordinary events in the records of marine disasters, a cloud of mystery hanging over the whole subject, which will probably never be cleared away. This steamer, Captain Cummins, commander, was on her way from Cincinnati to New Orleans, when she took fire on the Mississippi river, near Island No. 65, at about half-past one o'clock, on the morning of January 14, 1852. The boat was entirely consumed. Several passengers lost their lives, but all the officers and crew, except the carpenter, were saved. The work of destruction was completed within three minutes. A whole family, consisting of a man, his wife and two children, perished in the flames. Two or three other persons were either burned to death or drowned while attempting to escape from the fire. The books and papers were all lost.

The burning of this boat has given occasion for several law-suits and criminal prosecutions. A charge of conspiring to burn the boat has been made by Sidney C. Burton, of Cleveland, Ohio, against Wm.

Kissane, L. L. Filley, the brothers Chapin, Lyman Cole, Alfred Nicholson, the clerk of the Martha Washington, and several others. It was alleged that a heavy insurance on the cargo was obtained from several

BURNING OF THE MARTHA WASHINGTON.

offices, and that the boat had been fraudulently laden with boxes containing nothing more valuable than bricks, stones, and rubbish. It is said that in the summer of 1852, L. L. Filley, of Cincinnati, one of the persons implicated in this imputed crime, confessed on his deathbed that there had been no merchandize shipped on the Martha Washington, and that the boat had been designedly set on fire to defraud the Insurance Companies. Sidney C. Burton states that he shipped on this boat a quantity of leather valued at $1,500, and that he was unable to obtain the insurance money, because the insurance officers protested that the boat had been fraudulently set on fire. At the suit of Mr. Burton, the persons named above were arrested on the charge of conspiring to burn the boat, which involved the charge of murdering the passengers who were lost. Kissane was tried at Lebanon, Ohio, and afterwards at Cincinnati, and was convicted; he obtained a new trial, and was acquitted. All the persons implicated were afterwards tried at Columbus, Ohio, for conspiracy, forgery, &c., but the jury brought in a verdict of "not guilty." Burton then obtained a requisition from the Governor of Arkansas on the authorities of Ohio, and had all the accused parties arrested by officer Bruen, at the Walnut street house, Cincinnati, in 1854. They were hurried into an omnibus heavily ironed and ill-treated, and conveyed down to one of the wharves below Cincinnati, placed on a boat, and carried away to Jeffersonville, Ind., and from thence to Helena, Ark., to be tried for murder, arson, &c., where they were confined in a miserable jail three months.

They were again acquitted in the Court of Arkansas. But the determined prosecutor again returned to the charge. Kissane, one of the defenders, in order to raise money to defray the expenses of his legal defence, committed a forgery on the Chemical Bank of New York, in the summer of 1854. Some of his friends or advocates assert that he committed this deed in mere desperation, having been driven to the last extremity by the prosecutions or persecutions of Burton. Kissane was arrested for this forgery, but while in the custody of an officer, he contrived to make his escape from the railroad car by creeping through an aperture in the water closet. After concealing himself for some time, he was retaken, tried, and sentenced to the State's prison, at Sing Sing, two and a half years; but in December of 1855, he was pardoned by Governor Clark, of New York. In the same month and year, the Grand Jury of Hamilton county, Ohio, found a true bill against Burton, the prosecutor of Kissane, &c., and another person, named Coons, for perjury. Coons acknowledged that Burton had paid him for giving in false evidence at the trial of the persons charged with burning the Martha Washington.

Such being the facts of the case, there are many conflicting opinions in relation to the guilt or innocence of the parties charged with the horrid crime of setting fire to the steamer and sacrificing the lives of several passengers, for the purpose of obtaining a sum of money from the insurance offices. Several other incidents of a mysterious and romantic character are related in connection with this narrative. Sidney C. Burton, the prosecutor of Kissane, &c., lately died (December 11th, 1855,) at Cleveland, Ohio, in circumstances which give a color of probability to a prevailing suspicion that he was poisoned. It is mentioned also that an attempt was before made to poison him at a hotel in Columbus, Ohio. The whole affair presents a tangled web which it would require a good deal of ingenuity to unravel.

EXPLOSION OF THE LEXINGTON.

This disaster occurred at six o'clock, A. M., on the first day of July, 1855, about ninety miles below Louisville, on the Ohio river. Every person on board, except those of the crew who had been appointed to keep the night watch, were in their berths. Three boilers exploded at the same moment, demolishing the whole of the upper works forward of the wheel house, and hurling many of the sleeping crew and passengers into the water, without any premonition of danger. The steamer was under way at the time of the accident, and the engine had been working steadily without intermission, for two hours. There were about fifty cabin passengers, exclusive of eight ladies, one child, and a nurse, who, together with the officers, crew and deck passengers made a sum total of one hundred and thirty persons.

The explosion produced a deafening report and the wreck immediately took fire. "Then," says an eye-witness, "was presented a dreadful harrowing scene, such as no pen can describe, no imagination conceive. Many persons were blown into the river, a few of whom

EXPLOSION OF THE LEXINGTON.

swam ashore; many fell on the boat, and were mingled in awful confusion with the fragments of the wreck; all was lit up by the blazing timber, which, in that dead hour of the night, cast an unearthly gleam on the hideous spectacle. To the spectator, to whose harrowed sight were visible the blackened bodies of the dead and the expiring agonies of those who struggled in the water, and on whose ears rung the groans of those who were expiring on the wreck, the scene was one of the most terrific and heart-rending description."

The second mate, Peter Edds, ordered the anchor to be thrown overboard as soon as possible, and the steamer dragged for two miles down the stream. The scene of the disaster was near some wood-choppers' cabins, on the Kentucky shore. These people, as soon as they discovered the misfortune which had befallen the Lexington, came in their skiffs, and took off the surviving passengers. The ladies generally were saved. The males, with very few exceptions, were more or less injured.

KILLED.—W. C. Larkins, Madison, Ind.; Mr. Phillips, Liberty, Mo.; Henry Lewis; John Taylor, colored porter; Thomas Baldwin, and William Harrison, colored; James Miller, second clerk, Nashville; M. R. Fairchild, bar keeper; P. Willis, second engineer, Smithfield; M. Bernard, pilot; Samuel Lowery, colored; two brothers, names unknown; Mr. Haines, carpenter; a German deck hand; a colored fireman, and eleven others, names unknown, making a total of about thirty five.

WOUNDED.—Capt. Throop, Col. Bales and Thomas Payne, Louisville; Thomas Gibson, first mate; E. G. Davidson, first clerk, Paducah, Ky.; Sneed Strang, pilot, J. B Johnston and M. Twigg, Nashville; S. W. Anderson, assistant engineer; D. Harris, Cincinnati; Henry, colored boy; J. Gardner, King's Landing, Ky.; P. Flynn, Auburn, N. Y.; J. Johnson and A. Badger, pilot, St. Louis; W. P. Johnston, Madison; T. Ryan, St. Louis; Capt. Thomas White, Louisville; Mr. McElroy, Lebanon, Ky; J. Hall, Liberty, Mo.; Charles Squire, and others, names not mentioned.

The boat turned bottom upward, and sunk near Stephensport. The steamer D. A. Given took charge of those passengers who had been carried to the Kentucky shore by the wood choppers. It is remarked as a singular circumstance that few persons were scalded by this explosion. Most of the wounded were badly bruised or had their limbs broken. Many were drowned, of whom no account will ever be given, as the books and papers, and all the baggage, except that in the ladies' cabin, were destroyed.

Capt. J. V. Throop, the commander of the Lexington, has been engaged on the river for twenty-five years. He is a prudent and experienced officer, and this is the first accident that ever befel a boat under his command.

THE END.

www.ingramcontent.com/pod-product-compliance
Lightning Source LLC
LaVergne TN
LVHW020215110826
845151LV00003B/720

* 9 7 8 1 4 2 5 5 3 3 3 2 8 *